MODERN AUSTRIAN PROSE

VOLUME II

Studies in Austrian Literature, Culture, and Thought

General Editors:

Jorun B. Johns
Richard H. Lawson

Modern Austrian Prose
Interpretations and Insights
Volume II

Edited and Introduced
by
Paul F. Dvorak

ARIADNE PRESS
Riverside, California

Library of Congress Cataloging-in-Publication Data

Modern Austrian Prose ; interpretations and insights / edited and introduced by Paul F. Dvorak.
    p.   cm. -- (Studies in Austrian literature, culture, and thought)
Includes bibliographical references and index.
ISBN 978-1-57241-161-6
1. Austrian prose literature--20th century--History and criticism. I. Dvorak, Paul F. II. Series.

PT3822.M64 2001
838'.91408099436--dc21

                                   2001022780

Cover:
Art Director: George McGinnis

Copyright ©2012
by Ariadne Press
270 Goins Court
Riverside, CA 92507

All rights reserved.
No part of this publication may be reproduced or transmitted in any form or by any means without formal permission.
Printed in the United States of America.
ISBN 978-1-57241-161-6 (paperback original)

Contents

Preface v

Introduction 1
Paul F. Dvorak

Elisabeth Reichart's *Februarschatten*: The
Mühlviertler Hasenjagd and the Language
of Repression and Denial 10
Felix Tweraser

The Bestiality of Decency: Communal Cruelty in
Erich Hackl's *Abschied von Sidonie* 29
Geoffrey Howes

Victims and Perpetrators: Questions of Identity in
Norbert Gstrein's *Das Register* 56
Cynthia Klima

Memory and Identity in Doron Rabinovici's
Suche nach M 79
Francis Michael Sharp

Anna Mitgutsch, *Haus der Kindheit:* Mourning, Remembrance,
and Restitution 97
Maria-Regina Kecht

Julian Schutting's *Am Morgen vor der Reise*: A Playfully
Serious Postmodern EXCURSION through Childhood in Post-
War Austria 118
Angela Gulielmetti

Balancing Opposites: "Geometric" and "Regional" Aspects of
Gert Jonke's *Geometrischer Heimatroman* 148
Vincent Kling

Contextualizing and Decontextualizing Barbara Frischmuth's
Novel *Das Verschwinden des
Schattens in der Sonne* 180
Pamela Saur

From Habsburg Princess to Queen of Brazil: Gloria Kaiser's
Historical Novel *Dona Leopoldina* 203
Donald Daviau

For Whom the Turtle Weeps: Paulus
Hochgatterer's *Caretta Caretta* 229
Todd Hanlin

The Picaresque in Lilian Faschinger's
Wiener Passion 249
Joseph Moser

Kathrin Röggla's *wir schlafen nicht*:
Reality Fiction and the New Economy 266
Rebecca Thomas

Strange Bedfellows: Daniel Kehlmann's
Die Vermessung der Welt 283
Ronald Horwege

Communism, Immigration and the Necessity
of Faith: Dimitré Dinev's *Engelszungen* 306
Helga Schreckenberger

The Feminist Anti-Quest in Marlene
Streeruwitz's *Entfernung* 331
Raymond Burt

Contributors..352

Index..358

Preface

The fifteen articles collected in this anthology are intended to complement those contained in *Modern Austrian Literature. Interpretations and Insights* (Edited and Introduced by Paul F. Dvorak. Riverside: Ariadne Press, 2001). Drawing on the wealth of creativity in contemporary Austrian letters, Volume II attempts to bring to the forefront a characteristic work by each of the authors represented, none of whom were included in the first volume. The format and intent of the current volume remain essentially the same as in the first: to present readers with interpretations of significant works of modern Austrian prose within the broader field of German-language literature. Written in English with German reference material appended in order to appeal to the widest possible audience, the articles collected here cover major works by fifteen contemporary writers.

Counted among the well-established authors who could not be included in the first volume are such notable writers as Norbert Gstrein, Julian Schutting, Elisabeth Reichart, Erich Hackl, Barbara Frischmuth, and Gert Jonke. This group is complemented by a cohort of more recent authors who have established themselves within Austria and beyond within the last twenty years. They include Doron Rabinovici, Lilian Faschinger, Gloria Kaiser, Anna Mitgutsch, Paulus Hochgatterer, Marlene Streeruwitz, Kathrin Röggla, Dimitre Dinev, and Daniel Kehlmann. All of these authors are linked by language, history, and culture that ties them to a distinctly "Austrian" perspective. Reflecting the strong presence of the female voice within contemporary Austrian letters, almost half of the authors represented are female, a significant expansion over the number of female writers discussed in the first volume.

Contributors to the volume are highly respected scholars within the fields of Austrian and German studies both in the United States and abroad. With the exception of the works by Dinev and Streeruwitz, all of the works discussed are presently available in English translation. In sum, the authors, works, and contributors' commentary on them reflect the richness and diversity of the Austrian tradition. Although this volume in conjunction with the first fills in many gaps in presenting a comprehensive overview of the contributions of Austrian authors to contemporary prose writing, many other established and emerging authors have yet to be treated in either volume. As these authors and their works become more widely accessible through the availability of English translations, subsequent anthologies of this sort will likely be in demand.

Introduction

In his treatment of Elisabeth Reichart's *Februarschatten* (*February Shadows*), Felix Tweraser refers to the "complex relationship between personal experience, socialization, and physical location" as critical components in understanding a work focused on the memory of and the coming to terms with Nazism, World War II, and its aftermath. Indeed, this relationship in its myriad forms stands as a valid paradigm for interpreting all of the prose works under discussion in Volume II, including those that reach far beyond the immediate context of the historical setting of the post-war period. Following the format of the first volume of *Modern Austrian Prose: Interpretations and Insights*, Volume II presents a new series of authors whose works have been grouped into three general categories arranged broadly along thematic and stylistic lines rather than in strict chronological order of their year of publication.

Indeed, the first group of authors confronts directly Austria's relationship to the events surrounding World War II and of coming to terms with them (*Vergangenheitsbewältigung*). The second group comprises a loosely connected series of novels by writers less closely tied to the former, even though the works of two of the authors precede those of the earliest of the former group and several, indirectly at least still raise issues related to the first group. Lastly, the final four contributions to the anthology comprise works from the first decade of the twenty-first century and are clearly reflective of contemporary authors no longer preoccupied with the past but rather with an analysis of present-day Austrian and Western society. Despite this arbitrary arrangement of articles, the careful reader will undoubtedly discover a vast matrix of interconnections across the boundaries of these three somewhat arbitrary groupings.

The initial articles include works by Elisabeth Reichart, Erich Hackl, Norbert Gstrein, Doron Rabinovici, and Anna Mitgutsch that span the years 1984-2000.

Felix Tweraser's analysis of Reichart's *Februarschatten* (*February Shadows*) of 1984 presents the novel as an early example of Austria's long-delayed coming to terms with its past. Reichart attempts to puncture the "umbrella of silence" that virtually overshadowed Austrian society, politics, and culture up to the Waldheim affair of the mid-1980s. Reichart's novel "recounts the grisly murders of hundreds of Soviet prisoners of war at the hands of the local populace after they had escaped from Mauthausen concentration camp." The event of February 1945 became known as the "Mühlviertler Rabbit Hunt" (*Mühlviertler Hasenjagd*). The novel "documents the idiosyncratic memories of its central character, Hilde," as years later her daughter prods her to break the long-held silence about the event that saw Hilde witness the murders and the betrayal of her own brother, Hannes. Reichart's probing work drives a powerful wedge into the represssed confines of Austria's collective memory.

Geoffrey Howes' contribution tackles the topic of communal cruelty in his analysis of Erich Hackl's *Abschied von Sidonie* (*Farewell Sidonia*) from 1989, which "chronicles in fictional form the life of Sidonia Adlersburg, a Romani ("Gypsy") foster child who lived in Letten near the Upper Austrian town of Steyr and who was deported to Auschwitz, where she died in 1943." According to Howes, Hackl's method of fictionalizing history serves "to engage the reader in the fates of individuals who are caught up amid great historical forces." Upon the backdrop of Austrofascism, National Socialism, and the *Anschluss*, Howes analyzes how Hackl's work brings to the fore the issue of collective guilt and responsibility. Howes relies on the works of Götz Aly and Arno Gruen to set the theoretical framework for discussing the relationship between individual and society and the forces that created an "accommodating dictatorship" (*Gefälligkeitsdiktatur*) by which the self-interests of citizen's (economic, societal, religious) became aligned with National Socialist policies.

Cynthia Klima discusses Norbert Gstrein's *Das Register* (*The Register*) of 1992. The brothers, Vinzenz and Moritz, are the offspring of the older generation who experienced National Socialism and the war directly. These two main characters come to represent the identity split of Austria as first victim of Nazi aggression and as complicit collaborator in its worldview. The brothers essentially find themselves adrift in their identity crises as they attempt to come to terms with their father's and grandfather's generations. An analogy is drawn to the father-son conflicts of Kafka's work as Vinzenz and Moritz's struggle with what being Austrian means in the postwar context of the end of the twentieth century.

Francis Michael Sharp's study of "Memory and Identity in Doron Rabinovici's *The Search for M*" (*Suche nach M*, 1997) follows. Sharp frames Rabinovici's overall work in its historical context and as representative of the second generation of Holocaust survivors and also as a second generation of migrants. Born in Israel but growing up and educated in Vienna, Rabinovici considers himself Austrian. Since the Waldheim Affair of the mid-1980s, he has been a political activist infusing his creative work with central themes related to identity and memory. Sharp analyzes the complexities of these themes in the novel's two main characters, Arieh Arthur Bein and Dani Morgenthau and explicates "a densely packed entanglement of human stories forming a kind of a character landscape."

Completing the first group of articles is Regina Kecht's analysis of Anna Mitgutsch's *Haus der Kindheit* (*House of Childhood*) from 2000. Kecht frames the themes of mourning, remembrance, and restitution on the backdrop of the political events of 2000 that resulted in the establishment of the Austrian Fund for Reconciliation, Peace, and Cooperation, through which victims of aryanization and their descendants received compensation. Kecht thus views publication of Mitgutsch's novel in the same year as timely, and as unique in its treatment of the topic of aryanization and restitution in Austrian literature. Mitgutsch's career as a writer focuses here and in her other work on questions of Austrian complicity in the barbarities of National Socialism. Kecht analyzes the novel as a "literary adaptation of Jewish remembrance practices" (*Yizker Bikher*) and as "a very consciously Jewish inscription into contemporary Austrian literature. Accordingly, this novel is "a book of mourning for the vanished Jewish community as well as a gesture of respect offered to all the Jewish dead who have no final resting place and have, to add insult to injury, been erased and obliterated from collective memory through a veil of silence (*Totschweigen*)."

The second group of articles includes interpretations of works by Julian Schutting, Gert Jonke, Barbara Frischmuth, Gloria Kaiser, Paulus Hochgatterer, and Lilian Faschinger. The original publication of these works spans three decades from 1969 to 1999.

Indeed, Schutting's *Am Morgen vor der Reise* (*The Morning before the Journey*) bridges the gap between the first and second group of articles. Angela Gulielmetti discusses how the novel breaks new ground stylistically as it continues to treat recurring Austrian themes. The characters, Stephan and Judith, "approach the world playfully and without guile and their childlike observations proffer a satirical portrait of many aspects of contemporary Austrian society, including generational issues of authority and power, the role of the Church, the country's enduring silence about its Nazi past and lingering anti-Semitism in contemporary Austrian society." Furthermore, "Geographic and historical references to Austria and its past abound and firmly anchor the children's experience within a specifically Austrian framework. The children's rejection of adulthood should, therefore, be read as an exploration of the dark side of contemporary, post-World War II Austrian society." The remainder of this essay addresses the postmodern reflections in Schutting's insistence on the innate political nature of writing, his conception of textual *author*ity and the role of the reader, his questioning of Enlightenment sensibilities of individual subjectivity and, finally, a palpable skepticism toward authority figures.

INTRODUCTION

Vincent Kling examines how Gert Jonke typifies a generation of writers who "set a direction for literary critics, who stressed the radical, the revolutionary, and the avant-garde aspects of their art." Kling skillfully explicates Jonke's experimental novel, *Geometrischer Heimatroman* (*Geometrical Regional Novel*) by reconciling the seemingly incongruent descriptors "geometic" and "regional" and by exploring the novel's ties to the tradition of the Austrian regional novel (*Heimatroman*) and the anti-regional (*Antiheimatroman*), a genre popularized in Austria from the mid-1960s to approximately 1980. He explores how *Geometrical Regional Novel* aptly fits the category of the pastoral as he analyzes Jonke's unique stylistic elements. Writing at the height of the Cold War, Jonke exemplifies what Alfred Kolleritsch referred to as the "experimental" attitude of the late 1960s and declared that "today a concrete poem is just as clear a declaration of taking up arms against the establishment as is a…button with a picture of Mao."

Barbara Frischmuth's *Das Verschwinden des Schattens in der Sonne* (*The Shadow Disappears in the Sun*) is the topic of Pamela Saur's contribution. Frischmuth has long been a champion of women's rights set against the climate of contemporary political, cultural, and social issues. Saur investigates the personal cross-cultural conflicts the novel's Western-born female main character experiences as she attempts to navigate the Mideastern world. Originally published in 1973, the novel was reissued in hardback in 1996 because of its continuing relevance in attempting to bridge the gap between Mideastern culture, religion, and society and the West. Saur's interpretation expands the contextualized view of the novel to point out its decontextualized elements as well as a novel about the young protagonist's coming of age (*Bildungsroman*).

Donald Daviau's study of *Dona Leopoldina*, Gloria Kaiser's historical novel from 1994, completes the second grouping of articles. Daviau outlines Kaiser's evolving career as a writer – one that has kept her willingly out of the public spotlight in contrast to her activist contemporaries such as

Frischmuth, Elfriede Jelinek, and Robert Menasse. He describes the development of her connection to Brazil, which is critical to understanding this particular historical novel about the Empress of Brazil. After outlining the familial historical connections between the Habsburg Monarchy and Brazil, Daviau examines the author's style and techniques and draws the comparison between her and Stefan Zweig, whose historical biographies constitute his major claim to fame.

Leopoldina's marriage to Pedro I for political purposes followed the Austrian adage: *Bella gerant alii, tu felix Austria nube* ("While others wage war, Austria marries"). Kaiser's novel skillfully describes Leopoldina's difficult marriage and the stresses placed upon her by her husband, but despite her early death the triumph of her intellectual curiosity and her overwhelming sense of duty and responsibility. As Daviau assesses, the most compelling quality of the novel is the author's ability to portray Leopoldina in such a "gripping, intensely personal way." Finally, Daviau concludes that each of the author's biographical novels "presents an imposing historical personage, whose contributions to society and courageous approach to life serve as a universal model."

Daviau's article is followed by two authors whose works bridge the gap between the second and third categories: Paulus Hochgatterer's 1999 novel *Caretta Caretta* and Lilian Faschinger's novel of the same year, *Wiener Passion* (*Viennese Passion*).

Todd Hanlin frames Hochgatterer's work in the tradition of adolescent literature, both German and world-wide. Representing one of Austria's younger authors whose interest lies in modern-day societal issues far removed from the formerly predominant issue of *Vergangenheitsbewältigung*, Hochgatterer confronts issues facing today's youth from affluent middle-class society. The destructive and captivating aspects of modern-day capitalism, consumerism, permissiveness, egocentricity, and self-absorption all play into the plot involving the main character, Dominik. The use of predominantly first-person narration gives an immediacy to the text, though the veracity of Dominik's pronouncements is often in doubt. The author, himself a psychiatrist with a keen eye for realistic detail, captures the mindset and character of many of today's troubled youth.

Joseph Moser discusses Faschinger's *Wiener Passion* in its relationship to the *picaresque* tradition and in contrast to the tradition of the novel of education (*Bildungsroman*). Faschinger expands the traditional picaresque genre by replacing the male *pícaro* with a female *pícara* as she did in her prior novel, *Magdalena Sünderin* (1995; *Magdalena the Sinner* [1997]). Painting a picture of Viennese society at the end of the nineteenth and the twentieth centuries, Faschinger recounts the story of Magnolia Brown, an African-American woman of Austrian descent who travels to Vienna in the 1990s. The main plot revolves around Magnolia's great-grandmother, Rosa Havelka, who moved to Vienna in the 1880s as a Czech migrant worker and was hanged in 1900 for murdering her husband. In drawing a picture of Vienna's multi-ethnic makeup, Faschinger thematizes the city's conflicted attitude toward its ethnic heritage and the role that women have played within it. Roman Catholicism and its role as a politically authoritarian and oppressive force in Austria becomes a central theme. Right-wing racism, prejudice, and violence of the prior century continue to be played out in contemporary society. As Moser writes, "Contrasting Vienna at the end of the nineteenth and twentieth centuries, the novel shows that despite the tragic events of the twentieth century, xenophobia remains high."

The third grouping concludes with the works of Katrin Röggla, Daniel Kehlmann, Dimitré Dinev, and Marlene Streeruwitz that were first published between 2004 and 2006.

Rebecca Thomas's discussion of reality fiction in the digital age of the New Economy in Röggla's *wir schlafen nicht* (*we never sleep*) from 2004 provides a current example of a theme and setting removed from questioning the past. Thomas describes Röggla as a member of the "post-post-Waldheim generation," whose "fictional worlds represent the postmodern shift away from rootedness in national historical meta-narratives and towards the fragmentation and rootlessness of a post-historical, post-national, global present." Set at a trade fair, the novel deals with the dehumanizing elements of capitalism and consumerism as illustrated in the lives of upwardly moving workers consumed by their jobs. Having little to live and to hope for other than the next promotion, these workaholics can only communicate in a language filled with business jargon. They are in fact the producers of the name-brand products that Dominik and his friends in Hochgatterer's work so proudly wear and own. For both groups the future bodes ominously. Röggla's "narrative montage" creatively blurs the distinction between reality and fiction and results in what Thomas labels a hybridized "docunovel."

Ronald Horwege presents the strange bedfellows, Alexander von Humboldt and Carl Friedrich Gauss, in Daniel Kehlmann's enormously successful 2005 best-seller, *Die Vermessung der Welt* (*Measuring the World*). In this historical novel with a humorous, fictional twist Kehlmann deals with the "fictitious and quite humorous and entertaining recounting" of the personal lives and the human weaknesses of the giants of the early nineteenth century: Alexander von Humboldt, the noted explorer of South America and Carl Friedrich Gauss, the great mathematician and astronomer. According to Horwege, "Kehlmann chose these two interesting men as his main characters and brought them to life with their great attributes and their accomplishments but also with their human weaknesses." Horwege outlines how Kehlmann raises themes related to the essence of Germanness, aging, and ambition and achievement through the characters. Their predictions of the future add an often ironical twist for the contemporary reader looking back at these two individuals who eschewed political realities and the fine arts.

Helga Schreckenberger presents Dimitré Dinev's yet to be translated *Engelszungen* ("Angels' Tongues") from 2005. The novel challenges the concept of national literature by transcending literary and cultural boundaries, since German is not the native language of this émigré author from Bulgaria. His novel relates the story of three generations of two Bulgarian families whose destiny is closely connected to that of their country's history before, during, and after its communist regime. It delves deeply into the themes of migration and politics, language and identity, and alienation and memory. As Schreckenberger comments, the novel "explores the damaging impact of two extreme political situations – dictatorship and migration – on individual identity, on language and communication, on family, and on relationships. However, the novel also celebrates the survival of the human spirit and its ability to keep faith in a world that is neither predictable nor just and leaves individuals at the mercy of forces they cannot influence or even understand."

The anthology concludes with the second work not yet published in English, Marlene Streeruwitz's *Entfernung*. ("Distance.") from 2006. Raymond Burt frames his study of this experimental novel within the context of the author's other prose and of the feminist anti-quest. Abandoning the development of plot and action, Streeruwitz promotes "a radically different writing style – one which can express the experiences and perspectives of women." Burt comments: "Like Brecht, Streeruwitz wants her work to manifest the views of the author, but to do so by having the reader come to the same conclusions, not by argument or lecture, but by making evident the inherent, but generally invisible, injustices of the capitalist/patriarchal system." The period becomes the preferred form of punctuation because: "With a period the complete sentence can be prevented. The period ends the attempt. Sentences should not be formed." The author's fragmented style is reflective of the fragmented nature of the experience of her female protagonist. Burt adds: "Her fragments are like mosaic stones, individually meaningless, but together, with skillful placement, they form meaning."

Elisabeth Reichart's *Februarschatten*: The *Mühlviertler Hasenjagd* and the Language of Repression and Denial

Felix W. Tweraser

February Shadows, translated by Donna Hoffmeister, Ariadne Press, 1989.

Elisabeth Reichart (1953-), a trained historian before becoming a writer of fiction, is attentive to the complex relationship between personal experience, socialization, and physical location. In the post-war Austrian context, much of the effort to reconstruct the social fabric occurred without overt reference to the Nazi past, and it was the corresponding incentive to forget this past – in the interest of building a functioning society and polity – that has threatened to undermine the creation of a democratic political culture. Reichart's early fiction represents an attempt to puncture this umbrella of silence, depicting characters struggling to move beyond the received wisdom – that one must forget in order to build anew – about the Third Reich in Austria. As Donna Hoffmeister contrastingly puts it in her introduction to Reichart's early work, "the only way to a new beginning after the genocide sanctioned in Hitler's fascism is through an examination of that past"[1] and Reichart indeed explores the fractured relationship between lived experience and memory, pointing towards the positive effects of expiation and honesty with regard to a shared, repressed past. Reichart's major works from the 1980s, *Februarschatten* (1984), available in Hoffmeister's translation as *February Shadows* (1989), and *Komm über den See* (1988), reflect in many ways the author's upbringing – education, religion, family life – in the province of Upper Austria during the 1950s and 60s. Born in Steyregg, a suburb across the Danube from Linz and not far from the notorious Mauthausen concentration camp, Reichart grew up in a region and time that had a particularly fraught relationship with the legacy of Nazism in Austria because of proximity to some of its worst excesses, including the vigilante murders of February 1-2, 1945, that are described in *Februarschatten*. In fact, Reichart only learned the full scope of the local circumstances from her grandmother when she was a young adult; such organized circumspection awakened her personal and academic interest not just in the history of the events themselves, but more keenly in the shared imperative to forget their legacy that seemed to suffuse all aspects of daily life, most significantly how such a tacit agreement to forget the past worked at the level of everyday linguistic practice.

Februarschatten recounts the grisly murders of hundreds of Soviet prisoners of war at the hands of the local populace after they had escaped from Mauthausen concentration camp on the night of February 1, 1945, an event that has come to be known as the *Mühlviertler Hasenjagd*, or "Mühlviertler Rabbit Hunt." In the novel's crucial artistic turn, this history is revealed through the prism of one individual's thoughts and words, forty years later; only then does the protagonist begin to confront this past and her role in it. The novel documents the idiosyncratic memories of its central character, Hilde, someone who, as a young woman, not only witnessed the murders and did nothing to stop them, but betrayed her brother Hannes, who was hiding one of the escapees; still, Hilde's was a fairly typical attitude in the war's aftermath and such a generally held desire to evade responsibility has had unhealthy consequences for Austrian society and its political culture. Hilde's account itself is associative, non-linear, and impressionistic, and requires prompting from her daughter Erika, who is writing about her. By doing so, Reichart's compositional technique breaks with mimetic narrative conventions to reflect the fragmentary nature of such memories. In allowing the account to range freely back and forth across time and place, Reichart's work achieves a kind of "associative realism" characteristic of human consciousness, showing the reader what blocks self-reflection, what catalyzes it, and what defense mechanisms the mind develops to avoid its most painful truths.

In these two early novels Reichart emphasizes many of the concerns that animated her dissertation research at the University of Salzburg, which explored resistance to Nazi rule in Upper Austria, particularly among women. In an interview with the author conducted by Linda DeMeritt, Reichart groups these two novels together as an act of personal creative liberation, one tied to the long-suppressed memory of the victims of Nazi terror and those who actively resisted it:

> My development is actually one of liberation. Perhaps that sounds strange, because the war has always been there. But with *Februarschatten* and *Komm über den See* I still had the feeling that I needed to do right by someone. In *Februarschatten* it was the murdered escapees, and in *Komm über den See* it was the women resistance fighters. That was quite a burden while I was writing, because I felt like I not only could write what I wanted to, but that I also had to be careful to do honor to these people. (DeMeritt and Ensberg, 16-17).[2]

Februarschatten specifically reads in some ways like the transcript of an unedited oral history of the Nazi era. Hilde's reflections show the effects of the conflict between the need to forget that was sown by all the adults during her childhood and the desire to know herself and confront the actual guilt she feels. The defense mechanisms of denial, self-pity, and repression that have characterized her adult life come progressively unglued under Erika's questioning, and what results is in fact a new beginning, expressed metaphorically at the novel's conclusion when Hilde, at the wheel of her car, steps on the gas and accelerates into uncharted territory.

In the following discussion, I will briefly sketch out the historical context surrounding the appearance of Reichart's 1980s novels, which coincided with newly increased public interest in examining Austria's Nazi past, but also a strong backlash against such interest (one that unintentionally demonstrated the pernicious effects of the imperative to forget that prevailed in the immediate post-war generations). I will then discuss how Reichart examines Hilde's worldview from the inside out in *Februarschatten*, not without empathy, but equally unwavering in its depiction of the broader social effects of willfully forgetting the past.

The appearance of *Februarschatten* anticipated the gradual loosening of the self-serving mythology crucial to the founding and, indeed, success of Austria's second republic. The broad consensus that prevailed in Austrian political culture, at least until 1986, the year of the Waldheim affair and Jörg Haider's assumption of power in the Freedom party (*FPÖ*), had been reinforced by certain foundational historical narratives that bound various constituencies across party lines. One such dominant narrative was official Austria's assertion of victim status during the period of Nazi rule 1938-1945 – incidentally a policy officially promoted by the allied occupation powers in the Moscow Declaration of November 1943 – and correspondingly the less-than-forthright official and private confrontation with shared responsibility for the Nazi period, reinforced by the subsequent rapid reintegration into the Western sphere of influence during the Cold War. As new generations of opinion leaders who did not experience the war directly have assumed positions of power and influence, these foundational myths have had less and less force. The re-examination of such mythology was an unintended consequence of Kurt Waldheim's presidential campaign in 1986 and the changing geopolitical situation opened up previously unexplored avenues for dialogue with regard to the past, ranging from access to archival resources in the former Soviet bloc to the waning importance of the Cold War as ideological cover. The political and social realignments that have taken place in Austria since the Waldheim affair, while amply described and reflected upon in print media, also have come to have symbolic and visual analogs in public space: more ephemeral actions such as demonstrations, temporary art exhibitions, and performances have played an increased role in the last several decades; and the more permanent changes in the physical commemorative landscape, which provide opportunities for introspection, reflection, and expiation. This movement towards an honest engagement with the past is fundamental to the narrative in *Februarschatten*, which depicts such engagement as necessarily fragmentary and non-linear, subject to the interference of the mind's defenses, but nevertheless offering hope for a more honest assessment of personal responsibility in the face of terror.

As eyewitness accounts to the Holocaust fade, the visual and physical commemorative analogs in public space become more and more important to access historical memory. The rhetoric of commemoration as currently practiced does not necessarily support the preservation of such historical memory – and is subject to instrumentalization for various political ends – but the interrogation of property rights and the changes in the physical landscape may promote it in qualitatively different and more permanent ways.[3]

Why such memory work skipped two generations in Austria has been the subject of numerous theoretical reflections coming from the cultural critics of postwar Austria. Robert Menasse glosses this process with the term the *sozialpartnerschaftliche Ästhetik*, or aesthetics of the social partnership, the Austrian post-war government's emphasis on consensus and preemptive conflict resolution. Menasse's argument that cultural production was subordinated to the goal of building broad, even undemocratic, political consensus, was complemented theoretically by Joseph Haslinger's assertion of a uniquely Austrian *Politik der Gefühle*, or "politics of emotion," in which public pronouncements about coming to terms with the past (*Vergangenheitsbewältigung*) did not match the more powerful private and unofficial versions of this same historical narrative.[4] Such privately held opinions did not become the subject of public scrutiny until the Waldheim affair, the reactions to the commemorative practice of the *Bedenkjahr* 1988, and the crumbling of the Iron Curtain and the ideological cover it had provided. Menasse identifies correctly the anti-democratic aspects of the *Sozialpartnerschaft* and other extra-parliamentary conflict-resolution practices, and indeed a broad constituency emerged that began to tire of such behind-the-scenes patronage; it was to this constituency that Haider spoke, offering relatively facile solutions to complex problems, but also hitting a broad vein of resentment towards such corporatist arrangements. Haider also spoke the coded language of the privately held versions of the past, a political ideology promoted most potently by the daily *Kronen Zeitung* and unofficial, more local organizational forms. The force of these private opinions with respect to public institutional practice is personified in *Februarschatten* by numerous tangential figures who continue this practice even forty years after the war, for instance, the innkeeper in the town where Hilde grew up who, upon her return, is immediately suspicious about her intentions, or the local Socialist party functionary who recruits her and summarily banishes all references to the past.

How are such aspects of political ideology mapped onto the physical world around us? Heidemarie Uhl argues persuasively that the official policy towards the commissioning of public *Wehrmacht* veterans' memorials in the 1950s and 60s – be this at the federal, state, or local level – perpetuated a kind of historical amnesia that has only slowly eroded. While such memorials are common in Austria – here a confluence of local patriotism and Cold War ideology can be seen – there were hardly any monuments, even up until the most recent years, that honored the victims of Nazi persecution in any but vague terms. Uhl, like Haslinger, argues that a certain type of double-speak evolved, in which public declarations of solidarity with the Nazis' victims were kept vague, when uttered at all, while a private language and commemorative practices emerged that could emphasize continuity with the Nazi past without getting into specifics.[5] In *Februarschatten* the reader finds a condensed version of such topsy-turvy commemorative practice: Hilde's brother Hannes, the one person during her childhood who articulated an ethical imperative to resist Nazism and acted accordingly – by hiding one of the escapees from Mauthausen – pays for his convictions with his life and is hanged by the locals from a tree. Yet Hannes's courage is still seen almost forty years later by the vigilantes' descendants as betrayal when Hilde returns with her daughter to her home village. Nevertheless, more recently in Austria, there has been an increase in local initiative to correct such omissions in historical memory, witness the numerous new memorials to the victims of Nazism and the renovation and re-opening of the synagogue in Graz, as a majority of Austrians seems to be initiating a re-evaluation of commemorative practice at a local level. The public discussion of *Vergangenheitsbewältigung* has itself become more messy and pluralistic in Austria, but is arguably merely a reflection of the increasing public – and now private, as well – honesty with regard to this past; a different type of consensus has emerged, one in which a more open, democratic society breaks certain taboos that prevailed for many generations. Reichart's work was and is an important part of this process, as Hilde's story links personal history with collective memory in a landscape most resonant with allusive locations.

    To illustrate this movement towards more nuanced commemorative practice, one may compare the composition of two public monuments in central Vienna: Alfred Hrdlicka's monument to the victims of Fascism on the Albertinaplatz, unveiled in 1988; and Rachael Whiteread's monument to the Jews of Austria who perished at the hands of the Nazis, unveiled in 2000. Hrdlicka's is an ensemble of marble and bronze sculptures on mostly a grand scale; it gives specific form to many of the foundational myths of the post-war era in Austria. Victims of aggression associated with war and fascism are leveled: the allied bombing raids take a prominent place in the ensemble, while the miniature bronze figure of the kneeling Jew – an image taken from the time immediately after the *Anschluss*, when Jews were forced to clean off the painted slogans from the preempted referendum on Austrian independence – in its scale relative to the ensemble's other pieces and its depiction of abject victimization, actually perpetuates the prevailing attitudes. By contrast, the more abstract artistic vocabulary of Whiteread's composition is able to express the void of this history in compelling ways. Whiteread's concrete is sparse in its references: a rectangular structure depicts an inverted library, the books' bindings are hidden and that they face outward implies a void within the interior space of the monument. Whiteread engraves the monument with the names of the concentration and extermination camps where 65,000 Austrian Jews perished. The void at the center of the monument is an apt, indeed profound, symbolic rendition of the void left by the annihilation of this part of Austria's past; the monument invites the viewer's reflection on the ultimate implications of such empty space. (How was this empty space filled in the immediate post-war years? Not with honest confrontation, expiation, symbolic expressions of solidarity, or even the commission of a commemorative monument, in fact, quite the opposite.) Whiteread's monument speaks eloquently to both the actual void left and its implications for subsequent generations. The enigmatic composition is open-ended, allowing the viewer to imagine how the cityscape might be different if the library were not inverted, if the void were not so ever-present. The monument has become a place of private expiation and mourning in public space.

A concrete example of such a void in commemorative practice is evident in the way the *Mühlviertler Hasenjagd* of February 1945 resonates in the public consciousness. The historical record shows that on the night of February 1, approximately 500 inmates, mostly Soviet officers, broke out of the Mauthausen concentration camp; local authorities quickly convened militias from the surrounding villages to hunt down the inmates and all but a few dozen were shot on sight. After the war, in the context of denazification and the peoples' courts, only six defendants from among this local population were convicted of any crime, and a conspiracy of silence – one lived by

Reichart as a child – formed around these events. To the degree that the rabbit hunt was remembered at all, it was in the context of the Cold-War imperative to defend Austria from Communism, in which case the murderers could be stylized after-the-fact as early defenders of a free Austria. According to Peter Eigelsberger, "One suspects that particularly in the rural communities the mayors, community organizers, and *Volkssturm* commanders were all subsequently protected by the local population."[6] No monuments to the victims of the rabbit hunt exist beyond those at Mauthausen, and the effects of such willful repression of unsavory aspects of the past still manifest themselves in modern Austria. Hilde experiences this constellation up close: the Nazi ideologue Pesendorfer, who organizes the local search brigades; her own father, who arrests no one and is retrospectively treated well by the Soviet occupiers; and most importantly her brother Hannes, whose resistance to the murderous call to arms is itself punished by murder. Hannes's dictum haunts Hilde's memories and more generally Austria's: "Everyone...who doesn't do something against this manhunt makes himself GUILTY. Are you listening. Everyone. Even you!"(128)[7] His admonition to Hilde is part of the secret that Hilde has carried with her for many years, and once this secret is articulated under her daughter's questioning, it prompts wider-ranging reflection on her past. Klaus Zeyringer has delineated the importance of women as catalysts to a more nuanced engagement with the past, arguing that Reichart's novel is exemplary in this regard.[8] Hilde's move from fetishizing her own status as victim to re-assessing her role as historical actor and acknowledging her personal responsibility has greater global implications for Austrians in general, and anticipates the last twenty years' attempts to establish a more open dialogue with the past.

Februarschatten chronicles the events of the *Mühlviertler Hasenjagd* through the memories of Hilde, who has been prompted to relive them by her daughter Erika, a historian writing a book about her mother. Hilde, a young woman in February 1945, looks back on these years only after the death of her husband Anton, an academic with whom Hilde moved away from her childhood village located near the Mauthausen camp. Reichart constructs the novel in a spare, allusive form, one that mirrors the associative flights across time and space that characterize Hilde's reflections. Hilde's burden of guilt is specific, as are the consequences – her betrayal of her brother Hannes and the escaped concentration-camp prisoner whom he was hiding results in their murders by the local populace – yet it is instructive that any insight into her deeds' nature is achieved indirectly in an idiom that does not allow the past to be uncovered directly. The novel is self-reflexive in the sense that it lingers on the medium of its expression, the oral history that Erika writes about her mother, and the estrangement of its subject from the finished product – Hilde does not recognize herself, in fact, she denies that it is she portrayed in the manuscript's pages – injects a tone of ironic distance from what is described. At the same time, the novel evokes the historian's difficulties in compiling an accurate record: Erika's insistence that her mother come clean about the past does not prepare her for the psychic shock of her mother's actual revelations. Thus the dialogue that characterizes much of the narration is multi-directed; sometimes aimed specifically at daughter or deceased husband (here second person predominates), sometimes indirectly at herself (here third person is used, particularly in moments when the memory becomes too painful), but always at a silent partner, the reader, who is confronted with the messy, associative nature of memory and the intersection between ordinary life, racist ideology, and how these are reconciled in the war's aftermath.

Reichart builds associative links between Hilde's inconsistent and idiosyncratic memories by italicizing certain oft-repeated words, such as *übersehen* (to ignore), *vergiss!* (forget!), and *Wärme* (warmth); these words are associated in Hilde's mind with a certain feeling, which, in turn, provides access to increasingly specific memories. Each of these key terms stands in for something crucial to Hilde's relationship to the past: *über-

sehen suggests the importance to Hilde of her own insignificance with respect to historical events, one reinforced by her relationships to parents, siblings, husband, and daughter (the one exception here, interestingly, is her brother Hannes, who challenged Hilde to engage in ethical action); *vergiss!* in its imperative form becomes Hilde's mantra – told to herself and others, including Hannes – to deal with the trauma of witnessing the rabbit hunt; and *Wärme* describes the compensatory longing for domestic peace that Hilde feels for the abstract notion of "Germany" propagated by the Nazis, a warmth to be experienced by doing one's duty to the fatherland even if that goes against one's own family.

The verb *übersehen*, for example, becomes multivalent: Hilde uses it to characterize the relationship with her parents, whom she accuses of neglecting her in favor of more needy siblings, and with her husband Anton, particularly when he is discussing the past with Erika, who, at least initially, only seemed interested in her father's recollections. Hilde opens up to her daughter only after Erika uses the term *übersehen* when she admits that she has not appreciated her mother's experiences enough. The use of the term prompts Hilde to finally unburden herself, but also to recognize the investment in her own invisibility. When Hilde finally asks Erika point blank why she is writing about her, Erika replies: "Because I've neglected you for too long" (96) ("Weil ich dich zu lange übersehen habe" [81]). Hilde's response betrays how much she has invested in her victim status:

> I must keep control of myself. She must not notice anything. Why does she have to say this sentence. I didn't want to hear this sentence. I do not want to talk about it. We can talk about everything. But not about that. I must forget this sentence. Quickly. I want to be able to continue complaining. About my life, which was NEGLECTED (96).

Hilde's carefully constructed victimhood depends upon a version of her life that removed it from the actual historical events surrounding her childhood, but now, under Erika's questioning and prompting, this version becomes less and less binding. Indeed, the resentment that has accompanied Hilde's subsequent life with Anton has been projected onto her daughter, whose status as only child and whose ability to follow her professional calling Hilde begrudges. The estrangement between mother and daughter colors the narrative, and Hilde rejects Erika's attempts to bridge the gap: "Her hands on my back. Her head on my shoulder. All that just to win my favor" (97) ("Ihre Hände auf meinem Rücken. Ihr Kopf auf meiner Schulter. Alles nur Anbiederung" [82]). Nevertheless, Hilde opens up to Erika about the most traumatic aspects of her past, and though the mother-daughter relationship necessarily remains fraught and wary, the novel closes on a note of new beginnings based on the associative bridges of memory.

Such associative bridges between generations are suggested cogently in the third chapter, which is about cats. Taking in a stray cat becomes a marker across generations: Hilde's childhood cat is killed by her father; Hilde must take away Erika's cat because of the neighbor's complaints; and her own recently adopted cat, while comforting her after the loss of her husband, serves as the catalyst for unblocking access to the past. Hilde's initial focus on the cats highlights varying aspects of social and familial dysfunction: as example of the relationship to her father, who beat her and provided no ethical guidance, even though he was not a supporter of the party, thus making Hilde fertile territory for the Nazi ideology that leads to the betrayal of her brother; as an example of the passive-aggressive quality of post-war culture that shunned conflict but clung to the attitudes – though redirected to stress privacy and domestic tranquility – that flourished under Nazism; and finally as the catalyst itself to a more honest engagement with the past.

Reichart subtly underscores other examples of structural continuity between the Nazi and post-war eras, from the politically charged suggestion of similarities between the community politics under Nazism and those under the dominant post-war Socialist party (*SPÖ*) to Hilde's status as second-class citizen because of her childhood home, a communal arrangement between several families at society's margins. Once again, Hilde's connections between eras are allusive, elusive and idiosyncratic, but it is just such logical jumps that make an impression on Erika as recorder of her memories and, by extension, on the reader. Hilde recounts group meetings at her house growing up, meetings presided over by the resident Nazi ideologue, Pesendorfer, whom Hilde recalls lapsing into a voice similar to that of Hitler's on the radio. These meetings range from the vaguely comic, when Pesendorfer organizes a séance and medium through which the residents will see the future, to the most sinister, when Pesendorfer organizes the house's residents to do their duty in the rabbit-hunt, that is, to kill the escaped prisoners on sight, something that Hilde witnesses in the adjoining barn. The ideological organization of everyday life under Nazism depended on a network of organizers and a fearful and pliant population, and these are evoked in an understated manner by Reichart through the prism of Hilde's memories. "Germany" (*Deutschland*), the shorthand invoked by Pesendorfer to dictate correct behavior and ensure compliance with even the most horrific deeds, is expressed as a palpable emotional connection in Hilde, one that fills the vacuum of parental inattention and violence: "Hilde felt a strange WARMTH in her, when she heard that Germany NEEDED her tonight" (122) ("In Hilde wurde es *wärmer* als sie hörte, dass Deutschland sie in dieser Nacht *brauchte*" [100]). In this harrowing sequence, Hilde recreates the interior language that allowed her to betray her brother Hannes, finding in the abstract notion of "Germany" a destructive power growing out of a lack of ethical guidance in her environment.

      Hilde experiences a dim echo of such organization of everyday life after reluctantly agreeing to attend an evening of dancing that has been organized by the local Socialist Party. After assiduously preparing for the event, Hilde becomes more and more uncomfortable and eventually leaves the gathering early. Her remarks betray an overwhelming ambivalence about such gatherings, and the reader is able to connect this discomfort with her primal experience of community organization in the service of a racist ideology.

Hilde associates the survival strategy and safety of forgetting with shadows, and this is the metaphorical register that inhabits Reichart's text. It is these shadows that have allowed her to rebuild her life, but the veil they cast is becoming less powerful as she remembers the details of February 1945. In an early passage Hilde's remarks make the connection between shadows and guilt: "All the GUILT has been in me for a long time. Has been in the shadows. Which now make the darkness distinguishable. Tree-shadows, people-shadows, sound-shadows" (8) ("Alle Schuld ist schon lange in mir. Ist in den Schatten. Die nun die Dunkelheit unterscheidbar machen. Baumschatten, Menschenschatten, Geräuschschatten" [7]). Once again, the use of shadows is multivalent, evoking the memory of loved ones such as Hannes and the innocent victims of the rabbit hunt who haunt the area, while more generally giving a physical aspect to the processes of repression and denial upon which Hilde has consistently depended. The transfer of responsibility to the murderers' victims across generations is aptly rendered in the description of Erika's final appearance in the text: she has suddenly acquired "shadow eyes" (*Schattenaugen*). At the same time, Hilde, in unburdening her guilt to Erika, becomes more assertive, notably in the novel's final scene, in which she takes the wheel of the car and pushes down on the gas pedal, while a stunned Erika slides down into the passenger seat.

The trip that Hilde and Erika take to the village encompasses the final third of the novel. They wander a landscape where certain places are most resonant with historical significance: the house, where Hilde grew up, functioned as a kind of micro-community apart from the village, and its dwellers' second-class status was symbolized in its close proximity to the camp at Mauthausen. In Hilde's memories Mauthausen is rendered as "there" (*dort*), a place where, according to the adults, there is nothing to see, and Reichart is careful to underscore the linguistic turn of renaming the place in a more neutral manner to reflect the inability of the mind to grasp the true horrors of its grounds. The house's adjoining barn is the site where Hilde witnessed Pesendorfer's murder of three escaped inmates with a pitchfork. Finally, Hilde and Erika walk by the pear tree from which Hannes was hanged, noting that it does not bloom anymore. All these places of memory are haunted by the shadows of the victims in a way that cannot be approximated by official commemoration or memorial architecture.

Reichart's novel honors the victims of the *Mühlviertler Hasenjagd* by simultaneously evoking the events as experienced through the prism of Hilde's consciousness and the landscape and general attitudes cemented in the years following the war. By anchoring such memories in the physical landscape of her youth, and showing the power of place to evoke self-reflection, Reichart demonstrates the necessity of an honest confrontation with a shared heritage. Her novel represented the sound of a relatively lonely voice upon its publication in 1984, and its pathbreaking qualities may be lost in the multivocal and diffuse culture of memory that predominates today.

Endnotes

[1] Elisabeth Reichart, *February Shadows* (Riverside, CA: Ariadne Press, 1989) translated by Donna L. Hoffmeister, 155.
[2] "Meine Entwicklung ist eigentlich die einer Befreiung. Das klingt vielleicht komisch, weil der Krieg immer geblieben ist. Aber ich hatte bei *Februarschatten*, *Komm über den See* noch das Gefühl, dass ich jemandem gerecht werden muss. Bei *Februarschatten* waren es die getöteten Flüchtlinge und bei *Komm über den See* die Widerstandskämpferinnen im Salzkammergut. Das war eigentlich eine große Belastung beim Schreiben, weil ich das Gefühl hatte, dass ich nicht nur schreiben

kann, was ich schreiben will, sondern ich muss auch schauen, dass ich diesen Menschen gerecht werde." (DeMeritt and Ensberg, 16-17)

[3] See Heidemarie Uhl, "Zur Frage der Instrumentalisierung von 'Vergangenheitsbewältigung.'" In: Musner, Wunberg, Cescutti, eds. *Gestörte Identitäten? Eine Zwischenbilanz der Zweiten Republik* (Innsbruck: Studien Verlag, 2002): 10-26; the standard work for establishing historical memory through the investigation of property rights is Tina Walzer and Stefan Templ, *Unser Wien: Arisierung auf österreichisch* (Berlin: Aufbau, 2001).

[4] Robert Menasse, *Überbau und Underground: Die sozialpartnerschaftliche Ästhetik* (Vienna: Sonderzahl, 1996); Joseph Haslinger, *Politik der Gefühle* (Darmstadt: Luchterhand, 1987).

[5] "Das Argument der Verganheitsbewältigung bewegt sich heute in anderen Kontexten; es beschränkt sich nicht mehr allein auf den gesellschaftskritischen Diskurs, sondern ist vieldeutig und offen für unteschiedliche Instrumentalisierungen geworden. In der aktuellen österreichischen Situation lassen sich 'kritische' und 'affirmative' Verwendungszusammenhänge beobachten, die sich vor allem durch ihre Intentionen unterscheiden: Die Erinnerung an die dunklen Seiten der Vergangenheit kann sowohl den Appell an ein entscheidendes Vorgehen gegen Intoleranz, Fremdenfeindlichkeit und Antisemitismus intendieren als auch in image- und geschichtspolitische Strategien von Staat und Parteien integriert werden" (Uhl, 23).

[6] "Die Vermutung liegt nahe, dass besonders in den ländlichen Gemeinden die ehemaligen Bürgermeister, Ortsgruppenleiter oder Volkssturmkommandanten von der lokalen Bevölkerung gedeckt worden sind" (Eigelsberger, 214).

[7] "Jeder...der nichts gegen diese Menschenjagd tut, macht sich schuldig. Hörst du. Jeder! Auch du!" (104).

[8] "Als der Waldheim des Vergessens zum Staatsoberhaupt gewählt wurde und eine intensive Debatte über die republiktragende 'Opfer-Theorie' begann, traten die totalitären Ver-

gangenheiten auch vehementer in den literarischen Vordergrund. Dabei wurden die Schleusen der Erinnerung auffallend oft von Frauen geöffnet, von Autorinnen und weiblichen Figuren in den Texten. In Elisabeth Reicharts Roman *Februarschatten* von 1984 versuchen die Wörter der Tochter die Sprache des Verdrängens aufzubrechen. In stockendem Duktus ersteht die 'Mühlviertler Hasenjagd' – im Februar 1944 [1945! FWT] waren fast 500 Häftlinge aus dem KZ Mauthausen geflohen, fast alle wurden unter aktiver Mithilfe der Mühlviertler Bevölkerung ermordet" (Zeyringer, 62).

Works Consulted

DeMeritt, Linda. "The Art of Confronting Taboos," Afterword to her translation of Elisabeth Reichart, *La Valse* and *Foreign* (Albany, NY: SUNY Press, 2000): 137-47.
---. "The Possibilities and Limitations of Language: Elisabeth Reichart's *Fotze*, in Margarete Lamb-Faffelberger, *Out of the Shadows: Essays on Contemporary Austrian Women Writers and Filmmakers* (Riverside, CA: Ariadne Press, 1997): 128-42.
---. "Representations of History: The *Mühlviertler Hasenjagd* as Word and Image," *Modern Austrian Literature* 32.3 (1999): 134-45.
---. "The War between the Sexes: Gender Relations in the Works of Elisabeth Reichart," in Willy Riemer, *After Postmodernism: Austrian Literature and Film in Transition* (Riverside, CA: Ariadne Press, 2000): 283-97.
DeMeritt, Linda and Peter Ensberg, "'Für mich ist die Sprache eigentlich ein Schatz:' Interview mit Elisabeth Reichart," *Modern Austrian Literature* 29.1 (1996): 1-22.
Donaldson, Mara. "'She Kept on Fighting' 'A Discussion with Elisabeth Reichart about her Text *Sakkorausch*." *Glossen* 16 (2002).

Eigelsberger, Peter. "Mauthausen vor Gericht: Die österreichischen Prozesse wegen Tötungsdelikten im KZ Mauthausen und seinen Auslagern." In Thomas Albrich, Winfried R. Garscha, and Martin F. Polaschek. *Holocaust und Kriegsverbrechen vor Gericht: Der Fall Österreich* (Innsbruck: Studien Verlag, 2006): 198-228.

Haslinger, Josef. *Politik der Gefühle.* Darmstadt: Luchterhand, 1987.

Hoffmeister, Donna. "Introduction" to *February Shadows* (London: Women's Press, 1988): 1-8.

Kecht, Maria-Regina. "Faschistische Familienidyllen – Schatten der Vergangenheit in Henisch, Schwaiger und Reichart," in Donad G. Daviau, *Austrian Writers and the Anschluss: Understanding the Past, Overcoming the Past* (Riverside, CA: Ariadne Press, 1991): 313-37.

---. "Wo ist Mauthausen? – Weibliche Erinnerungsräume bei Elisabeth Reichart," *Modern Austrian Literature* 35.1/2 (2002): 63-86.

Menasse, Robert. *Erklär mir Österreich: Essays zur österreichischen Geschichte.* Frankfurt am Main: Suhrkamp, 2000.

---. *Das Land ohne Eigenschaften: Essay zur österreichischen Identität.* Frankfurt am Main: Suhrkamp, 1995.

---. *Überbau und Underground: Die sozialpartnerschaftliche Ästhetik.* Vienna: Sonderzahl, 1996.

Michaels, Jennifer E. "Breaking the Silence: Elisabeth Reichart's Protest against the Denial of the Nazi Past in Austria," *German Studies Review* 19.1 (Feb. 1996): 9-27.

Milchram, Gerhard, ed. *Judenplatz: Place of Remembrance.* Vienna: Jewish Museum of the City of Vienna, 2000.

Ovenden, Laura. "Body, Voice and Text in Elisabeth Reichart's Dramatic Monologue *Sakkorausch*, in Linda C. DeMeritt and Margarete Lamb-Faffelberger, *Postwar Austrian Theater: Text and Performance* (Riverside, CA: Ariadne Press, 2002): 236-56.

---. "Insanity, Inspiration and Insight: Considering 'weibliche Denkweisen' in Elisabeth Reichart's *Sakkorausch*, in Allyson Fiddler, *'Other' Austrians: Post-1945 Austrian Women's Writing* (Bern: Peter Lang, 1998): 25-33.
Preiferová, Dana. "Über die Tödlichkeit des Schweigens," *Script* 17 (1999): 44-49.
Reichart, Elisabeth. *Komm über den See*. Vienna: Franz Deuticke, 2001. All quotations from the Deuticke edition. The novel was originally published with S. Fischer in 1988.
---. *Februarschatten*. Vienna: Verlag der österreichischen Staatsdruckerei, 1984.
---. *February Shadows*. Trans. by Donna Hoffmeister. Riverside, CA: Ariadne, 1989.
Tweraser, Felix. "Elisabeth Reichart's *Komm über den See*: Upper Austria and the Excavation of its Past" in *Beyond Vienna*, ed. Todd Hanlin (Riverside, CA: Ariadne Press, 2008) 208-229.
Uhl, Heidemarie. "Zur Frage der Instrumentalisierung von 'Vergangenheitsbewältigung.'" In: Musner, Wunberg, Cescutti, eds. *Gestörte Identitäten? Eine Zwischenbilanz der Zweiten Republik*. Innsbruck: Studien Verlag, 2002.
Vansant, Jacqueline. *Against the Horizon: Feminism and Postwar Austrian Women Writers*. Westport, CT: Greenwood Press, 1988.
Walzer, Tina and Stefan Templ. *Unser Wien: Arisierung auf österreichisch*. Berlin: Aufbau, 2001.
Wiesenthal, Simon, ed. *Projekt: Judenplatz Wien*. Vienna: Zsolnay, 2000.
Zeyringer, Klaus. "Österreichische Literatur 1986-2001" in Lamb-Faffelberger and Saur, eds. *Visions and Visionaries in Contemporary Austrian Literature and Film*. New York: Peter Lang, 2004.

The Bestiality of Decency: Communal Cruelty in Erich Hackl's *Abschied von Sidonie*

Geoffrey C. Howes

Farewell Sidonia, translated by Edna McCown, Fromm International, 1992

Erich Hackl's (1954-) book-length story *Abschied von Sidonie* (1989) chronicles in fictional form the life of Sidonia Adlersburg, a Romani ("Gypsy") foster child who lived in Letten near the Upper Austrian town of Steyr and who was deported to Auschwitz, where she died in 1943. It is also an account of the Breirathers, the Austrian family who bravely took her in only to lose her to the National-Socialist genocide. The second of his works of historical fiction after *Auroras Anlass* of 1987 (also translated by Edna McCown as *Aurora's Motive*, 1989), this narrative exemplifies Hackl's approach of fictionalizing history in order to engage the reader in the fates of individuals who are caught up amid great historical forces.[1] He portrays these forces, however, not as impersonal tides beyond human control, but as the result in part of ethical decisions that individuals and groups make, whether consciously or unconsciously. Hackl's narrative depicts the fatal outcome of *Abschied von Sidonie* not so much as a single act of cruelty, but as the culmination of a series of seemingly harmless capitulations on the part of those in Sidonia's social environment. Capitulations to what? To common sense, to economics, to self-preservation, to a sense of belonging. In other words, few acts in the series are in themselves acts of cruelty, but in their tribalism, their self-interest, their expedience, and even their idealism, these choices incrementally sacrifice the interests of the girl, who is seen as an outsider, to the interests of the group to which she is not allowed to belong. The result is sanctioned murder.

This essay will trace the series of actions – or instances of inaction – that amounts to a collective agreement that the little Romani girl is expendable. Much of the literature on *Abschied von Sidonie* has, rightly, concentrated on the text as a document of the suffering of the Roma under National Socialism.[2] This theme, along with the principled resistance of the Breirather family, is certainly at the center of the narrative. But among Hackl's other accomplishments is his mostly dispassionate account of and accounting for the ways in which individual responsibility is blurred for the sake of maintaining integration into the community or, in the colloquial metaphor, to keep from rocking the boat.

One must bear in mind that one of the strengths of Hackl's text, as Karl Markus Gauss eloquently points out, is how he refrains from explaining and simply narrates events in clear, cool language.[3] Nonetheless, I will have to indulge in some explanation in order to isolate the thread of narrative that leads from one decision about the girl to the next and finally to her death. For this explanation, I will employ theoretical models offered by Arno Gruen in his account of the origins of "human destructiveness" in *The Insanity of Normality*, and by Götz Aly in his history of economic politics in the Third Reich, *Hitler's Beneficiaries*.

Distinguishing between schizophrenia and normality, Gruen states that "insane" people do whatever they can to maintain their inner emotional integrity, even at the cost of their social belonging, whereas "normal" people sacrifice that integrity precisely for the sake of integration into society. Eventually, the self-denial that such a split requires can build up emotional pressure and lead to violent self-assertion when this is possible without forfeiting one's social standing. This outburst of sanctioned destructiveness betrays the "insanity of normality." "Normal society" is fundamentally pathological because it is based on the "betrayal of the self" (to use another of Gruen's titles). Gruen writes:

> For those who slip into the disguise of "normal" behavior because they cannot tolerate the ten-

sion caused by the contradiction between the reality imposed on them and their inner world, real feelings soon cease to exist. Instead, these people operate with *ideas* about feelings, not with *experiences* of them. They display as their own those feelings that have been imposed on them and renounce their true feelings.[4]

This is what Gruen calls "the denial of reality in the name of realism." It involves denying the "contradictions and the fear" of reality not by diminishing oneself (as those do who suffer from the recognized insanity of schizophrenia), but by diminishing what lies outside oneself. Such a consciousness "does not reflect the integration of individual being and outer reality but the need to conquer this reality" (16). We mistake for feelings "what are actually only notions of what we think we *should* feel" (16). And this kind of thought, in its drive to suppress actual feelings, "is merely a quasi-logical disguise for vengeful and destructive feelings" (16). Gruen writes that National-Socialist theories about "lives unfit for life" are "an extreme example" of the rationalization of repressed violent emotions (16). As will be seen, in *Abschied von Sidonie* the Breirathers represent a healthy integration of inner feelings and outer world, a "realistic realism," as it were, whereas many of the people in Sidonia's community engage in a denial of reality in the name of realism, that is, the insanity of normality.

Götz Aly's historical study *Hitlers Volksstaat* (*Hitler's Beneficiaries*) posits that popular support for Hitler's state was based in part on its nature as a *Gefälligkeitsdiktatur*, a so-called "accommodating dictatorship,"[5] or in an alternative translation, a "complaisance dictatorship." That is, by aligning citizens' self-interest, especially material interests, with the interests of the state, the National Socialists were able to gain popular cooperation with or at least forbearance toward their policies. Aly writes:

> It [the Nazi Party] drew in left-leaning blue-collar workers, artisans, and office workers who hoped their children would enjoy upward social

> mobility. They were joined by those who had already profited from the educational reforms of the Weimar Republic and wanted to continue their rise in status. These groups sought not a new class dictatorship but rather the sort of meritocracy we take for granted today: a society in which the circumstances of one's birth have relatively little influence on one's eventual career and social standing (30).

In other words, National-Socialist politics attracted political support from the working class and petite bourgeoisie – the class identities of most of the actors in *Sidonie* – by appealing not so much to their ideologically based wish to be part of a "master race," but to their need for material stability – understandable after the economic traumas of inflation and the international economic crisis of the 1920s – and social mobility. Aly argues implicitly against Daniel Goldhagen's thesis in *Hitler's Willing Executioners* of a specifically German exterminist anti-Semitism and xenophobia, and places the origins of the Holocaust not in the years before World War I, when this virulent hatred supposedly became entrenched, but in the years after, when the expansive mood of the *Gründerjahre* (the boom years after the 1871 German unification) collapsed. Aly counters the idea of "Hitler's willing executioners" with the idea of "Hitler's beneficiaries," participants in a *Gefälligkeitsdiktatur*, a dictatorship that goes out of its way to appease the populace. The Nazi leadership tried constantly to gain popularity, or at least indifference, from as large a base as possible. This involved awakening the sense among the simple people that resources were being distributed fairly and generously (36).

    I do not intend to take sides in this historical debate, and indeed I do not see Goldhagen's and Aly's models as mutually exclusive. But Aly asks us to explore the complexity of the National Socialists' political methods, which involved not only encouraging racialist nationalism, but also a variety of other tactics for assuring public support. To understand the collective cruelty of the community in *Abschied von Sidonie*, we must also take into account the fundamental economic disruptions and social insecurity of the times, which motivated people to place their parochial interests above broader principles, and to justify this through a psychological mechanism like Gruen's "denial of reality in the name of realism." The actions portrayed in the story certainly exhibit xenophobia and racism, but they also show how much the competition for resources and the wish to belong played a role in the racist exclusion of Sidonia. It was precisely this competition, and this wish to belong, that the Nazi state knew how to manipulate to its advantage.

Gruen supplies a sociological and psychological framework, and Aly supplies a political and economic framework that complement each other to help us understand the motivations of everyday people who, often without conscious guile, enabled the fascist system to pursue its purpose of homogenizing the body politic of Germany and its eventual appendage, Austria, along supposedly racial lines. In *Abschied von Sidonie*, this increased identification with the regime takes the form of a gradual verging of conscience and duty. In the behavior of the Breirathers (and of some others), we see the prevalence of conscience (an inner motivation) over duty (an outward motivation). In some characters we can see a temporary victory of conscience over duty, but in the overall trajectory of the narrative the workings of the "accommodating dictatorship" allow the actors to bring their conscience into line with the duty they see being imposed upon them, relieving them of the tension between their inner integrity and outward integration. This allows them to find "realistic" reasons for treating others – Sidonia in particular – inhumanely, as less than human. The "insanity of normality" covers the cruelty and destructiveness of their ethical actions by making these deeds seem like either rational choices, or not choices at all, but obligations.

Historically, *Abschied von Sidonie* covers the last months of the first Austrian Republic in 1933 and 1934, the Austrofascist *Ständestaat* (corporate state) from 1934 to 1938, the *Anschluss* – the German annexation of Austria – in 1938, and the Second World War. The Breirathers are staunch Social Democrats, which means that their political standing in the community continues to erode during this period, as Austria becomes a conservative authoritarian state and then a territory of the Third Reich. Hackl intertwines two parallel and connected stories, the increasing political isolation of the Breirathers and the increasing discrimination against their foster daughter Sidonia. Indeed, the same sort of "denial of reality in the name of realism" and sacrifice of conscience for the sake of duty that affects attitudes toward Sidonia impinges on the Social Democrats, and more and more of those around the Breirathers go over first to the Christian-Socialist and then to the National-Socialist side. By presenting the parallel between political choices and personal behavior, Hackl is able to use fiction to show how people appropriate abstract ideals to rationalize the pursuit of material and social advantage while understanding and portraying their actions as being motivated by those ideals.

The plot can be summarized succinctly. In August of 1933 a Romani foundling is discovered on the doorstep of the state hospital in Steyr with a note that says "My name is Sidonia Adlersburg and I was born on the road to Altheim. I need parents" (1) ("Ich heiße Sidonie Adlersburg und bin geboren auf der Straße nach Altheim. Bitte um Eltern" [7]).[6] After a first foster stay is unsuccessful, Josepha Breirather, who has hoped for a second child in addition to her son Manfred, takes Sidonia in. Facing economic hardship, Josepha also can benefit from the state-supplied child-support money. Sidonia's early years with Josepha and her husband Hans are marked by both the unconditional love of her foster parents and the political and social unrest of the end of the first Austrian republic, and then the authoritarian Austrofascist state that displaced it. Hans is imprisoned for his activities on behalf of the outlawed Social Democratic Party and its militia, the Defense Corps. The state does not abandon its attempts to find Sidonia's natural mother so that it might be relieved of the burden of paying child support for a non-Austrian child. During the Austrofascist regime, a more ideological motivation is added to the search for Sidonia's progenitors: the official struggle against "gypsy terror" (52). By 1939, when Sidonia starts school, she has a new foster sister and fast friend in Hilda, who is nearly the same age. Now Austria is part of the Third Reich, and although much of the time the teacher and the other children accept Sidonia as just another school child, her "racial" difference becomes more and more salient, providing her teacher with an explanation for her weak performance in school, and then providing the authorities with a reason for removing her from the household where she has thrived so well. When officials who are rounding up Romani for deportation finally locate Sidonia's natural parents, they create the possibility of uniting her with her own kind. The local authorities ignore the Breirathers' pleas and bring about the reuniting of the Romani family. First Sidonia is taken to a concentration camp in Tirol, and then she is deported with her family to Auschwitz, where, as her foster family finds out after the war, she dies. The official cause of death is typhus, but her brother tells the "chronicler" that she died of grief (127-29).

Sidonia's first foster mother is Amalia Derflinger of Steyr, who returns the child to the hospital after two days. At first she mumbles something about lack of space, and that she underestimated how much work raising the child would be, but in her shame she reveals that her husband has "chased her and the 'black bastard' out of the house" (9) ("sie samt dem schwarzen Bankert aus dem Haus gejagt habe" [14]). "He had screamed at her, you want everyone making fun of us, even my apprentices. No one wants anything to do with gypsies, and you bring the plague into the house!" (9) ("er [hatte] sie angeschrien, willst dass uns alle auslachen, sogar die eigenen Lehrbuben. Jeder ist froh, wenn er mit Zigeunern nichts zu tun hat, und du bringst mir die Plag noch heim!" [14]). The power of the collective is reflected both in the fear of ridicule and in the statement about no one wanting anything to do with gypsies. In the original German, the phrase is actually "everyone is glad when he doesn't have anything to do with Gypsies." The positive "everyone" is even more inclusive than the negative "no one," and at the same time exclusive; "everyone" cannot include the Gypsies themselves, and so they are linguistically cast out beyond the realm of common sense and shared mores.

An economic motive for returning the child is added when Amalia Derflinger takes refuge with her parents, who in turn tell her that this cannot be permanent, that she has to return to her husband. Their reasons: a woman belongs at her husband's side; he is moreover "a respectable tradesman, his own master, and trade is a sure thing even in these times" (9) ("ein anständiger Gewerbetreibender...sein eigener Herr und Meister, und Handwerk hat goldenen Boden, selbst in diesen Zeiten" [14-15]). Amalia's parents anticipate any humanitarian objections on the grounds of the child's helplessness by maintaining that Gypsies don't need anyone's help: "There were more than enough gypsies, they were springing up everywhere, ill weeds grow apace" (9) ("Zigeuner gibt es mehr als genug und schlängeln sie sich auch überall durch, Unkraut verdirbt nicht" [15]). The German phrasing implies not only that the Gypsies are springing up, but also that they are able to get by, and this along with the maneuvering implied by the verb *durchschlängeln* (to sidle, to move furtively, from *Schlange*, "snake") lets on that unlike an upstanding German-Austrian craftsman, a Gypsy can rely on her inborn dishonesty and indecency to survive. One needn't have any pity for her. Weeds are hard to kill, and Gypsies are human weeds. This hard-headed rationalization is a prime example of "denying reality for the sake of realism." One of the realities that the husband and parents deny is Amalia's emotional need for and attachment to the child.

And so Amalia returns Sidonia to the care of the hospital, not because it is better for the baby, and not because Amalia wants to do it, but because the Derflinger family is unwilling to extend the mantle of decency and respectability beyond the socially accepted range of these attributes. Dignity – a person's worth – is not an inborn trait, but a grace conferred on the individual by a collective decision, and in this case it is the purpose of community to preserve not human dignity as such, but only the relative dignity of those who are marked as belonging.

Torn between her wish to nurture the child and her need for integration into her social environment, Amalia ultimately opts for the latter. This is a betrayal of herself in Gruen's terms, a rending of her inner emotional integrity. Her capitulation is a loss of humanity for the sake of economic expediency, which is further justified by racial exclusion. There is nothing immediately violent about her act, for Sidonia is not harmed physically, but the possibility of the child's healing is postponed and sacrificed on the basis of racist rhetoric to the perceived economic and social needs of the would-be foster family.

The loss of her first foster family turns out to be Sidonia's gain, because it makes her available to the more-welcoming Breirathers. But the short tale of Amalia Derflinger sets up the terms of what is to come, and shows why the Nazis' "accommodating dictatorship" found fertile ground when it moved into economically and racially insecure Austria in 1938. Ultimately, the society at large would take on the role of the Derflinger family, making "realistic" excuses as to why the Breirathers would have to give up Sidonia.

Even though she has been released from the hospital to the Breirathers, Sidonia is far from well. Economic necessity – the financial straits of the state hospital at Steyr – has required finding her a cheaper accommodation even if she still needs medical care. The continued efforts of the authorities to locate this child's parents imply that it is particularly undesirable for such an outsider to be a ward of the state. And although Sidonia is now within a caring family, racial prejudice emerges again when they take her to the doctor for treatment of her infections and bone ailments.

While waiting an hour to see the doctor, Josepha hears gossip about a local crime: a woman murdered her abusive husband and buried the body in her garden. At first blush, this seems to have no bearing on the larger story, but in fact it does. The husband is an exemplar of the "insanity of normality." He was a "big talker" who bragged about making his fortune in Brazil. "The country lads were amused by all this, while at the same time fascinated by the talk of huge herds of cattle and prosperous estates" and "a rich life with hammocks hanging in the shade of palm trees and naked Negresses who would fan him" (24) ("Die Bauernburschen hörten ihn amüsiert und gebannt zugleich an, wenn er von riesigen Viehherden schwärmte und fruchtbaren Ländereien...ein Leben im Überfluß, mit Hängematte im Schatten einer Palme und nackten Negerinnen, die ihm Kühle zufächelten" [28]). Unable to live up to his macho fantasies, he beats his wife – a brutal outlet for his pent-up "denial of reality in the name of reality" – and she finally murders him. Found out, the woman claims she killed him because he had made threats against his employer, but at the same time she admits she had stopped loving him and "so she had killed him, along with her desire for him" (25) ("und so hatte sie mit ihm ihre ganze Sehnsucht abgetötet" [29]). The first explanation – a socially acceptable but improbable plea for lenience on grounds of exigency and altruism – is less convincing than the second explanation that the woman was reacting against the continued forced denial of her emotional integrity. Hence this is what I have elsewhere called a "therapeutic murder," murder not as the culmination of madness, but as an attempt to stave off the madness of accepting her husband's world view.[7]

The subtext to this tale, like the story of Sidonia's first foster mother Amalia Derflinger, is one of barely suppressed disdain for women and people of color, masked by humor and what passes for common sense. It is prefaced by a remark when Josepha appears with Sidonia: "Who have you been fooling around with? someone asked, and pointed to Sidonia" (23) ("mit wem hast du dich denn eingelassen, fragte einer und deutete auf Sidonie" [27]). The lurid, racist remark, the "fascinating" racist and imperialist sexual fantasy of the murdered man, and the common-sense dismissal of the case as premeditated murder all reflect the "insane normality" of Josepha's and Sidonia's social environment, a seemingly ordinary discourse as a "quasi-logical disguise for vengeful and destructive feelings" (Gruen 16). The possibility of viewing the murder as an act of self-defense against this destructive normality is not even available to these people, although Hackl implies this possibility simply by including this lengthy interlude.

This dose of normality, the communal acceptance of cruelty, is thus the context for Sidonia's visit to the doctor, who in spite of his reputation for treating the uninsured at no charge gives Sidonia the brush-off: "When Josepha entered the examining room with Sidonia in her arms, the doctor scarcely looked at her. What shall I prescribe and who is going to pay for it?" (25) ("Als Josepha mit Sidonie im Arm ins Behandlungszimmer trat, schaute der Arzt kaum hin. Was soll ich verschreiben, wer zahlt denn das" [29]). It is significant that this takes place after May 1933, when the first steps toward establishing the Austrofascist state had been taken: the Republican Defense Corps (of which Hans Breirather was a member) had been outlawed, elections had been suspended, and opposition parties had been dissolved. The patriotic corporate state, with its equation of Austrianness and Catholicism, created a mood in which differences, whether political, religious, or racial, no longer had to be tolerated. Despite Josepha's assurances of payment, the doctor continues: "Doesn't matter. But why bring this dark one to me? She doesn't belong here" (27-28) ("Und überhaupt. Wieso kommen Sie mit der Schwarzen zu mir. Gehört ja gar nicht her" [29-30]).

This is another step on the path to Sidonia's ultimate exclusion. The first excuse is a "practical" one, the fear of nonpayment. But this is quickly shown to be a cover-up for the real reason for rejection: the girl does not belong. The incident in the doctor's office portends later, more brutal treatment, yet it remains relatively harmless, since it seems like a personal choice on the doctor's part. Still, as we will see below, it paves the way in the narrative for the later interpretation of "not belonging" as a positive excuse for persecuting the girl: everyone should be where he belongs, and it is in Sidonia's best interest to be with her people.

Furthermore, because Josepha is unable to identify with this kind of belonging, she and Sidonia are pushed even further out of the mainstream: she seeks out an herbalist who is able to cure the little girl's ailments with traditional medicine. At this point the Breirathers have been marginalized politically, economically, racially, and medically by those who, as they see it, are only seeking a better life. Yet the price of this better life – as shown when the doctor looks in on Sidonia because of his "bad conscience" (26) ("schlechtem Gewissen" [30]) – is the exchange of conscience for duty, of humanity for belonging. By contrast, clinging to her conscience, Josepha shows her willingness, for Sidonia's sake, to trade belonging for humanity.

The triumph of duty over conscience continues when the narrative chronicles events in February 1934, the brief Austrian Civil War in which the *Heimwehr* – the nationalistic "Home Guard" that fought for the authoritarian government of Chancellor Engelbert Dollfuss – put down the outlawed Social-Democratic Defense Corps. The *Heimwehr* raids the Breirathers' residence, smashing furniture and slitting mattresses. One of them, a certain Atzmüller, sees Josepha throw a list of hidden weapons in the fire and raises his pistol at her, but then begins to beat her with a nightstick. He stops when his companions return from the next room: "He was embarrassed that they had witnessed his sudden rage" (35) ("ihm war es peinlich, Zeugen zu haben für seinen Jähzorn" [38]). Here we see a flaring up of the insanity of normality, rage at the need to suppress one's actual feelings for the sake of an assumed reality in which the price of belonging is a loss of one's conscience. In Austrofascism, this normality countenances and even encourages violence. The dictatorial state rewards loyalty to itself – patriotic belonging – with the opportunity to release repressed, violent emotions.[8]

That Atzmüller still has a shred of conscience, that he is embarrassed in front of his colleagues, is a result of the strong sense of local belonging that has not quite been fully replaced by the patriotic Austrofascist ideology. Hackl invents an exchange between Josepha Breirather and the *Heimwehr* members that reveals how the sense of the community is torn apart by ideological differences, the same ideological differences that increasingly emphasize Sidonia's racial difference. Josepha boldly stands between the men and the kitchen credenza: "Well, look at that, she said. Max Schopf among the plunderers. What will your father have to say to this?" ("Da schau her, sagte sie. Der Schopf Max ist unter die Plünderer gegangen. Was wird denn dein Vater dazu sagen" [38]). Josepha taunts him with an appeal to tradition, to his family ties, and to their familiarity with each other. (*"Der Schopf Max"* is a very casual and familiar form of reference.) Schopf replies by denying he knows this Socialist, with a probable allusion to Peter's denial of Christ in the Gospel of Matthew: "I don't know this woman, Schopf said, attempting a crooked smile" (36) ("Ich kenn die Frau ja gar nicht, sagte Schopf und versuchte ein schiefes Lächeln" [38]).[9] Josepha points out that they were schoolmates, and even asks him if he is still so bad at arithmetic. This small personal victory on the side of conscience and community (however sarcastic) is immediately pushed aside by duty and obedience when the police officer in attendance (who represents the now-official status of the *Heimwehr*) states: "Leave the man in peace. This is an official visit" (36) ("Lassen Sie den Mann in Ruhe. Das hier ist eine Amtshandlung" [39]). Schopf denies the reality of his community connections in the name of the supposed realism that is being imposed by the new political order. This denial receives official sanction when the police officer's announcement that this is an official action excludes any role for nonofficial social relationships.

The conflation of church and state – of moral conscience and politics – in Austrofascism is brought home as well when Hans and Josepha, under duress, join the Catholic Church and undergo a church wedding so that their son Manfred will not be persecuted and disadvantaged. Hans, who is in prison for his Defense-Corps activities, is released temporarily, and Josepha is summoned to meet him, in the presence of a priest, at the prison. The chance to see Hans more than once every two weeks is an enticement, but more compelling is the implicit threat to Manfred, "who, polite and smart as he was, was earning poor marks due to the fact that he was a heathen" (41) ("der anständig sei und gescheit, aber schlechte Noten bekomme, weil er ein Heide sei" [43]). Hans tells Josepha that he has to rejoin the Church. "You don't have to do anything of the kind, Josepha cried. That's our decision alone" (42) ("Es gibt kein Muß, rief Josepha. Das geht nur uns etwas an" [44]). Josepha adheres to this liberal orientation toward individual conscience and human rights until Hans's principles are broken down by the priest's admonition that it is his fault if Manfred is disadvantaged. The priest Arthofer presents this extortion (as Josepha calls it) in Christian terms, as an invitation to enjoy the Church's forgiveness, mercy, and charity, in spite of Hans's criminal history (45), a litany whose hypocrisy he betrays when he makes explicit the Church's political co-optation: "let's bury the hatchet, and the whole world shall hear our vow today: Everything for the Fatherland!" (43) ("alter Zwist sei begraben, und alle Welt soll unsern Schwur heut' hören: Dem Vaterland gilt unser ganzes Streben!" [45]). The family can enjoy its human dignity as long as it is on the terms dictated by the authoritarian government and its constituent estate, the Catholic Church.

The prison guard, moved by the "remarkable, almost festive mood of the occasion" (44) ("der merkwürdigen, beinahe festlichen Stimmung" [46]), furtively gives Hans a packet of provisions from neighbors and workmates, but this only throws into starker relief the rigid, conformist context in which this act of conscience occurs, for he was "usually indifferent and unmoved by any request – he followed prison rules strictly" (44) ("Abgestumpft sonst und ungerührt allen Bitten gegenüber, nur der Gefängnisordnung verpflichtet" [46]). The German word *abgestumpft* ("indifferent," "jaded," "numbed") indicates that his being so duty-bound is not simply a character trait, but the result of a loss of conscience over time. When the exercise of conscience has become a violation of duty, the "insanity of normality" is entrenched.

We have now seen several examples of how political and religious ideologies conspire to replace the values of family and cooperation, which are grounded in mutual reliance within a community. An image emerges of pathological and expedient normality, masked by a superimposed sense of duty that only pretends to be communally based. This consciousness of duty, to invoke Arno Gruen, "does not reflect the integration of individual being and outer reality but the need to conquer this reality" (16). It mistakes for feelings "what are actually only notions of what we think we *should* feel" (16). As has been described, Josepha is increasingly isolated under these conditions, and the same happens to Hans, who is released from prison into unemployment. Community and conscience are not completely absent, for a Christian-Socialist colleague of Hans's, "who respected him in spite of their political differences" (46) ("der ihn trotz politischer Gegnerschaft schätzte" [48]) puts in a good word for him and he is rehired at the Steyr Works. But nonetheless, he is an outsider: "Breirather was lonely" (46) ("Breirather vereinsamte" [48]). The ranks of the Social Democrats have thinned. The workers in his town either participate in pro-government demonstrations "in exchange for raspberry schnapps and a few sausages" (46) ("[g]egen Himbeerwasser und ein paar Würstl" [48]) or join the National Socialists, illegal under the Austrofascist regime, but growing in popularity. Götz Aly explains that left-wing workers migrated to the right wing in hopes of a rise in status (30). Hackl emphasizes material inducements on the one hand, and the sense of belonging on the other, as motivations for giving up class consciousness. The Nazis meet illegally but openly in a pub and rail against the Social Democrats and Austrofascist Christian Democrats alike.[10] Theirs is the only pub that lacks a portrait of the late Chancellor Dollfuss, assassinated by the Nazis, decorated in mourning with black crape, "in the corner reserved for the crucifix" (47) ("neben dem Herrgottswinkel"

[49]), a detail with which Hackl once again underscores the alignment of church and authoritarian state.

This, then, is the background as Hackl finishes his tale of what happened to Sidonia under Austrofascism and National Socialism. The other children have only partly absorbed their parents' political predilections and prejudices. But the language of exclusion is available and put to use:

> To the children of the neighborhood, Sidonia was just one more playmate, even if she was conspicuous with her dark skin and shiny blue-black hair. Only when they fought, during a game of cops and robbers, say – I've got you, no you don't, yes I do – or a game of ball – you didn't touch me – it was easy to for the others to insult her with: Gypsy, you're a little gypsy. You're nothing but a gypsy. Or when the boys wanted to get rid of her: Go take a bath, blackie (49).[11]

Paradoxically, the children even want to protect Sidonia from the "Gypsies," who they imagine want to kidnap her, and they call to Josepha to hide Sidonia when the Roma appear. The ancient popular belief that "Gypsies" steal non-Roma children is given a twist here: the gypsies are suspected of wanting to *steal their own children back*. When this fear is invoked by children to protect one of their number, it is not yet virulent, but can be attributed to the children's wanting to guard their own world of shared community. Their loyalty to one another is still stronger than their allegiance to the prejudices of the adult world. But the social worker assigned to Sidonia shares this fear, and when she brings it up, she lays bare the tension between conscience and duty: "Right from the beginning, at her first official visit, the social worker had warned Josepha: Watch out! There are often gypsies in the area. You know how they are. They might steal the child at some point. They'll see at first glance that Sidonia is one of them" (49) ("Das war ganz am Anfang gewesen, bei ihrem ersten Pflegebesuch, daß die Fürsorgerin Josepha gewarnt hatte: Aufpassen! In dieser Gegend treiben sich oft Zigeuner herum. Man weiß ja, wie die sind. Ob die nicht einmal das Kind schnappen. Die sehen auf den ersten Blick, daß Sidonie eine von ihnen ist" [51]).[12] There is obviously a contradiction between the social worker's professional duty to protect the child because she is a client, a duty that is still in line with conscience, and the grotesque duty imposed by the strict racial categories of Austrofascism (and later Nazism) to protect the child from people *just like her*. I emphasize *just like her* because, given her upbringing, the only way they are "just like her" is their complexion, a racial category.

Ironically, and without the Breirathers' knowledge, the state is continuing its efforts to find Sidonia's parents. In other words, the Austrian government itself is setting up the possibility of doing what the "Gypsies" are suspected of: "stealing" Sidonia and returning her to her people. No matter that her people have abandoned her: the racial category has become more important than the reality of a caring family that is officially and duly acknowledged in reports to the District Youth Welfare Office: "*Child healthy, growth normal, well looked after and cared for*" (50) ("*Kind gesund, normales Gedeihen, sehr gut u. ordentlich gehalten und betreut*" [52]). Or: "*Meticulously looked after and cared for*" (50) ("*Tadellos gehalten und betreut*" [50]) (italics in original text). In Vienna, an "International Center to Combat Gypsy Terror" is established with the purpose of collecting fingerprints so that the "Gypsies" can no longer "deny their identity or change it at whim" (52) ("ihre Person abzuleugnen oder je nach Bedarf zu wechseln" [53]). This bureau does indeed locate the person it believes to be Sidonia's biological mother.

At the local level, no one yet knows about this, and the social worker assures the Breirathers that there is little chance of finding the actual mother. On the other hand, in a painful Catch-22, adoption proceedings – which the family wants to undertake in spite of the penalty of losing the child support given to foster families – cannot be started until the parents are found. Meanwhile Sidonia has invented a myth of her own origins, that she is the biological child of the only parents she has known. The conditions that will ultimately separate Sidonia from her de facto parents are thus established in the last months of Austrofascism: the primacy of duty to a race-based fascist state as opposed to conscientious commitment to the integrity of family relationships. After the *Anschluss*, things change even more in the town of Letten in the direction of the "insanity of normality" and the "accommodating dictatorship." The old munitions factory is reopened. A forced-labor camp is built. The first Polish prisoners, officers and weapons makers, are impressive and exotic, but soon they blend into the growing population of ragged "forced laborers from countries that no longer existed" (58) ("Zwangsarbeiter aus Ländern, die es jetzt nicht mehr gab" [58]). German nationals from the Sudetenland move into the Breirathers' apartment building, and these strangers, as reliable Nazis, have a higher status than some longtime residents. Meeting the house residents, a newcomer cries, "And what is that?...that black thing?...Heinz, I think we've fallen among Negroes" (59) ("Und was ist das da...dieses schwarze Ding ...Heinz, ich glaub, wir sind unter die Neger gefallen" [59]). Several adults laugh at the remark, signaling social approval of this attitude. This is one more step toward sacrificing Sidonia's interests to the group, the group that is increasingly defined not by community, but by racial and political criteria.

The chronicler states succinctly: "Red Letten had turned into Brown Letten" (59) ("Aus dem roten Letten war das braune Letten geworden" [59]). Immediately after the *Anschluss*, most of the remaining Social Democrats had joined the SA *en masse* (59), and Hans is almost completely isolated, except for a few younger comrades who are rounded up but do not betray him (64). Community members who under the accommodating dictatorship can now think "We're somebody now, after all" (65) ("Wir sind doch jetzt wer" [64]), spy on each other and report each other for supposed anti-regime sentiments. Josepha is called in for questioning, but someone must have put in a good word for her, so she escapes punishment. Still, the general sense of duty – feelings that are "actually only notions of what we think we *should* feel" (Gruen 16) – is making such acts of conscience ever more rare – and dangerous.

There follow "years without gypsies" (69) ("Jahre ohne Zigeuner" [68]) in the Letten area:

> The villagers took their absence to be a law of nature, or a sign of the rapid spread of civilization. It pleased them in the same way that the rapid decline in fires pleased them – earlier, not a month had gone by without some farmhouse burning to the ground; since old debts had been settled, the farmhouses and the barns remained standing (69).[13]

Here we see the confluence of the "accommodating dictatorship" and the "insanity of normality": people are doing better economically, and life has become more secure in general. If this includes the unexplained absence of an entire ethnic group, so be it: duty has replaced conscience because it demonstrably leads to better times. The danger of being turned in for treason is a concern only to those who have something to hide. The danger of disappearing altogether concerns only those who are politically suspect (like Hans's Socialist comrades) or who have the misfortune of belonging to the wrong group. Hence the absence of "Gypsies" doesn't matter to most of the people of Letten: "Only Hans and Josepha were worried" (70) ("Nur Hans und Josefa waren beunruhigt" [68]).

In the meantime, Sidonia and Hilde have started school, and here Sidonia's outward dissimilarity from her classmates has more menacing implications than it did among her younger playmates. After she reads a report about her family, a boy says: "That's not right, what Sidonia wrote about her parents. Because they aren't her real parents" (75) ("Das stimmt nicht, was Sidonie von ihren Eltern geschrieben hat. Weil das nämlich nicht ihre richtigen Eltern seien" [75]). When Sidonia protests that they are too her parents, she looks to the teacher for support. But "the woman, perplexed, looked back at the class" (74) ("die Frau sah ratlos in die Klasse" [74]). At this moment, the teacher could have spoken up in favor of a family based on community. Her silence shows her caught between conscience and duty. Given the atmosphere that has developed in Letten, she does not have the strength to correct the boy's remark. After school as well, she does not reassure Sidonia, who has stayed after to try to wash her dark skin light. Like the doctor's rejection, like the Sudeten woman's remark, this is relatively harmless when compared to eventual deportation and death, but it is a step in that direction.

The lack of civil courage that these instances embody takes on its most deadly form when the central authority for combating the "Gypsy plague" finally identifies Sidonia's biological mother and demands they be reunited. The run-up to this starts in the fall of 1942, when a policeman knocks at the Breirather home, asking if they have received an official communication from Steyr or Linz. When Josepha says no and asks what this is about, the policeman (who has adjusted to the times and changed his Czech name Lebeda to the German Lindner) demurs, putting his duty ahead of his conscience, a conscience that is only slightly apparent when he says he does not wish to alarm her, that they should not lose their heads. Of course, Josepha is already alarmed – she assumes it has something to do with Hans's illegal resistance activities. But no letter has yet arrived when Cecilia Grimm, a social worker, comes to the Breirathers' door on Epiphany of 1943.[14] While Grimm says she is there for a routine inquiry into how Sidonia is doing, she steers the conversation "to the girl's mediocre performance at school and to her tendency to flatter her foster parents with demonstrations of love" (84) ("auf den mangelnden Schulerfolg des Mädchens und deren Neigung, den Pflegeeltern durch Liebesbeweise zu schmeicheln" [83]). Josepha recalls this shift in interest when, in March 1943, she finally does receive the letter, from the Youth Welfare Office, which has been instructed to bring the girl immediately to her biological mother (84).

The truth comes out later, however: in fact the decision whether Sidonia should stay in her foster family or be brought to her Roma parents has been left up to the local authorities in the Youth Welfare Office (90). The social worker Grimm and her superior Korn, nonplussed and irritated at such a responsibility, tell the Breirathers that their hands are tied, when in fact they have decided to reinterpret the facts of the case negatively so that they have a justification for removing Sidonia from her family, which will be a way to remove what could be a continual problem for them. This accounts for Grimm's assessment that Sidonia's poor school work and her excessive dependence are somehow a symptom of the girl's not being where she "belongs." In spite of the Breirathers' desperate attempts to keep Sidonia, including forfeiting child support payments and even having her sterilized (91), Grimm and Korn continue to gather negative information, even asking for a direct report from the school principal Frick on Sidonia's behavior and character, "good or bad" (93) ("sei es in gutem oder schlechtem Sinne" [92]). The chronicler, who is starting to intervene in his story with more and more direct judgment, writes: "It is difficult to believe that Frick, one of the senior teachers, did not know what was at stake. He had a spine, but it was as malleable as the bamboo cane he used when teaching the children spelling" (93) ("Schwer zu glauben, daß Oberlehrer Frick nicht wußte, was auf dem Spiel stand. Ein Rückgrat hatte er, biegsam wie sein Rohrstock, mit dem er den Kindern die Rechtschreibung einbleute" [92]). He reports that the child is anxious, sensitive, and sometimes boisterous. *"The girl is in good hands with her foster parents, who supervise her learning, but more discipline is called for"* (94) (*"Das Mädel ist bei den Pflegeeltern in guter Pflege u. Lernbeaufsichtigung, doch wäre mehr Strenge nötig"* [92]) (italics in original, indicating an actual documentary source). Katie Korn also convinces the mayor, whom the Breirathers had approached for help, to write, even if the Breirathers are "decent people" (93) ("anständige Leute" [93]): "I find it proper that the child be with her mother, and will continue to recommend this" ("Ich finde es ganz in Ordnung, wenn das Kind zu seiner Mutter kommt, und befürworte dies auch jederzeit" [93]). The chief inspector of the county also concurs, saying that Sidonia will always be a gypsy, and if she is returned to her mother she will be "among her own kind, she won't stand out and will adapt quickly enough...And what about when she finishes school, gypsy children are not allowed to become apprentices" (95) ("da ist sie unter ihren Artgenossen, merkt keine Unterschiede und lebt sich schnell ein...Und was, wenn sie mit der Schule fertig ist, eine Lehre darf sie als Zigeunerkind ja auch nicht machen" [93]).

At this point, the chronicler inserts a terse remark, a sentence fragment: "The bestiality of decency" (95) ("Bestialität des Anstands" [93]).[15] Invoking the child's best interests, which are threatened not by the parents themselves, but by the racially exclusionary social system that has been constructed by the "accommodating dictatorship," could be termed cynical and hypocritical, but those concepts do not quite go to the core of what is happening here. "The bestiality of decency" is not contempt for values (cynicism), nor is it a professing of beliefs that one does not possess (hypocrisy). It is mistaking for feelings notions of what one only *thinks* one should feel, that is, it is Gruen's insanity of normality. It is denial of reality (the girl is best off with the Breirathers) in the name of realism (since she is "only a Gypsy," she will do best among Gypsies). And especially in Grimm's and Korn's thoughts and actions, it "is merely a quasi-logical disguise for vengeful and destructive feelings" (Gruen 16), feelings that arise when one abandons conscience for duty. This pseudo-logic on supposed humanitarian principles leads in Sidonia's case to her being removed, interned, and sent to her death at Auschwitz.

Sidonia's fate is the result of a general agreement, partly inculcated from above by accommodating dictatorships, and partly negotiated within the community, that Sidonia would be better off among "her people," even if there was a general awareness that these people were at best being interned and at worst being murdered. Hackl's narrative carefully shows this agreement as the collective result of a series of individual decisions in which the actor is choosing between inner emotional integrity – an intact conscience – and outward social integration – duty. That it does not have to work this way, that this is not some Utopia of unrealistic ethical expectations, is shown by Hackl's brief account in the closing paragraph of a similar historical case in Styria in which the community, collectively, meets the threatened deportation of a girl like Sidonia with indignation, turning away "from the aims of the movement and from the leader of the great historic period" (134) ("von den Zielen der Bewegung und vom Führer der großen Zeiten" [128]). Why did Hackl not write inspirationally about this instance with a happy ending, rather than critically about Sidonia?[16] One can only speculate why, but the story of the saved girl would be about a "miracle" (134) ("Wunder" [128]), not about normality, and it is the bestiality of decent, normal behavior that we need to understand.

Endnotes

[1] Jörg Thunecke, in his article "'Ein liebenswerter Untermensch?': Erich Hackls Erzählung *Abschied von Sidonie*," *Visions and Visionaries in Contemporary Austrian Literature and Film*, eds. Margarete Lamb-Faffelberger and Pamela S. Saur (New York: Peter Lang, 2004) 225, criticizes this approach in Hackl and others as a loss of literary creativity, since the tale is driven by its plot and not by its linguistic composition (226). It is hoped that my contribution will show that Hackl made careful choices in arranging information, imaginatively recreating dialogue, and precisely portraying what I call "communal cruelty."
[2] See, for example: Marlene Kadar, "The Devouring: Traces of Roma in the Holocaust: No Tattoo, Sterilized Body, Gypsy Girl," *Tracing the Autobiographical*, eds. Marlene Kadar, Linda Warley, Jeanne Perrealut, and Susanna Egan (Waterloo, Ontario: Wilfrid Laurier UP, 2005) 223-46; Klaus-Michael Bogdal, "Eliminatorische Normalisierungen: Lebensläufe von 'Zigeunern' in narrativen Texten," *Jahrbuch der ungarischen Germanistik*

(JUG) (2000) 39-50; and Erika Thurner, "Roma und Sinti: Der geleugnete und vergessen Holocaust," *Abschied von Sidonie von Erich Hackl: Materialien zu einem Buch und seiner Geschichte*, ed. Ursula Baumhauer (Zürich: Diogenes, 2000) 289-313.
[3] Karl-Markus Gauß, "Über Geduld und Ungeduld, Erzählen und Erklären, Stil und Moral. Anmerkungen zu Erich Hackl," *Abschied von Sidonie von Erich Hackl: Materialien zu einem Buch und seiner Geschichte*, ed. Ursula Baumhauer (Zürich: Diogenes, 2000) 267.
[4] Arno Gruen, *The Insanity of Normality: Realism As Sickness: Toward Understanding Human Destructiveness*, trans. Hildegarde and Hunter Hannum (New York: Grove Weidenfeld, 1992) 14-15.
[5] Götz Aly, *Hitler's Beneficiaries: Plunder, Race War, and the Nazi Welfare State*, trans. Jefferson Chase (New York: Metropolitan, 2006) 36.
[6] All German quotations are taken from Erich Hackl, *Abschied von Sidonie* (Zürich: Diogenes, 1989). English renderings of quotations are cited with page numbers in the body of the text from Erich Hackl, *Farewell Sidonia*, trans. Edna McCown (New York: Fromm International, 1991).
[7] Geoffrey C. Howes, "Therapeutic Murder in Elfriede Czurda and Lilian Faschinger," *Modern Austrian Literature* 32:2 (1999) 79-93.
[8] "Patriotic" has a particular historical and technical sense in the context of Austrofascism, for the Dollfuss state called its conservative union party the *Vaterländische Front*: the "Patriotic" or "Fatherland Front."
[9] The phrase in Luther's New Testament translation is "*Ich kenne den Menschen nicht*" (Matthäus 26:72). The King James Bible (Matthew 26:72) has "I do not know the man." Peter's choice between inward conscience and outward obedience is the same one that Max Schopf makes here.
[10] Edna McCown translates "*Hahnenschwänzler*" (48) as "Mussolini's troops in the south" (47), but the term, which is

also spelled "*Hahnenschwanzler*" to reflect dialect pronunciation, refers to the members of the Austrofascist Heimwehr. The "*Hahnenschwanz*," the cock's tail, alludes to the decorative tuft of gamecock's feathers they wore on their hats.

[11] "Für die Kinder aus der Nachbarschaft war Sidonie, auch wenn sie mit ihrer dunklen Hautfarbe und den blau-schwarz schimmernden Haaren hervorstach, eine Spielkameradin mehr. Nur wenn sie aneinandergerieten, als Räuber und Gedarm, ich hab dich, nein hast mich nicht, hab dich schon, oder beim Spiel mit einem Fetzenball, abgeschossen, nicht berührt, taten sich die anderen leicht, ein Schimpfwort zu finden: Zigeunerin. Zigeunerkind. Bist ja eh nur eine Zigeunerin. Oder wenn die Buben sie weghaben wollten: Putz dich, Schwarze." (50)

[12] The German verb "*sich herumtreiben*" used by the social worker to describe the Roma is more pejorative than the translation "There are often gypsies in the area." It implies "hanging around," "loitering," or "roaming the streets."

[13] "Die Dorfbewohner nahmen ihr Ausbleiben als Naturgesetz hin, oder als stürmisches Vorwärtsdrängen der Zivilisation, es befriedigte sie wie die rapide Abnahme von Feuersbrünsten, früher war kein Monat vergangen, in dem nicht ein Bauernhaus eingeäschert worden war; seit alte Schulden getilt waren, blieben Hof und Scheune stehen." [68]

[14] Hackl identifies the day by its place in the Catholic calendar, not only because this is how such a day would be remembered, but to underline that the charity central to the belief and practice of Christianity is about to be violated in a country where that is the official religion.

[15] Thunecke (see note 1) criticizes Hackl (and cites others who have criticized him) for breaking the apparently factual course of the narrative to insert such judgments from the author (232). Thunecke seems to fault Hackl both for relying too much on the facts (225) and for interrupting the narration with non-factual interjections. The occurrence of these interjections alone does not violate the aesthetics of Hackl's self-imposed rules, it

changes the rules: the apparently cool, objective narrative is not one after all. It has been counterposing sets of values all along. [16]Thunecke asserts that Hackl's consideration of the possiblity of a less terrible ending is somewhat naïve, since it seems to work against the supposed purpose of the narrative: telling once again how terrible people in the Third Reich were (231). But Hackl does not tell the story with the happier ending, he only mentions it. He tells Sidonia's story. And this objection loses its traction if we assume that Hackl's purpose was not simply to tell historically how evil people were in the past, but to examine literarily how evil comes about even if none of the perpetrators is particularly evil.

Works Cited

Aly, Götz. *Hitler's Beneficiaries: Plunder, Race War, and the Nazi Welfare State.* Trans. Jefferson Chase. New York: Metropolitan, 2006.

Bogdal, Klaus-Michael. "Eliminatorische Normalisierungen: Lebensläufe von 'Zigeunern' in narrativen Texten." *Jahrbuch der ungarischen Germanistik* (JUG) (2000) 39-50.

Gauß, Karl-Markus. "Über Geduld und Ungeduld, Erzählen und Erklären, Stil und Moral. Anmerkungen zu Erich Hackl." *Abschied von Sidonie von Erich Hackl: Materialien zu einem Buch und seiner Geschichte.* Ed. Ursula Baumhauer. Zürich: Diogenes, 2000. 267-76.

Gruen, Arno. *The Insanity of Normality: Realism As Sickness: Toward Understanding Human Destructiveness.* Trans. Hildegarde and Hunter Hannum. New York: Grove Weidenfeld, 1992.

Hackl, Erich. *Abschied von Sidonie.* Zürich: Diogenes, 1989.

Hackl, Erich. *Farewell Sidonia.* Trans. Edna McCown. New York: Fromm International, 1991.

Howes, Geoffrey C. "Therapeutic Murder in Elfriede Czurda and Lilian Faschinger." *Modern Austrian Literature* 32:2 (1999) 79-93.

Kadar, Marlene. "The Devouring: Traces of Roman in the Holocaust: No Tattoo, Sterilized Body, Gypsy Girl." *Tracing the Autobiographical*. Ed. Marlene Kadar, Linda Warley, Jeanne Perrealut, and Susanna Egan. Waterloo, Ontario: Wilfrid Laurier UP, 2005. 223-46.

Thunecke, Jörg. "'Ein liebenswerter Untermensch?': Erich Hackls Erzählung *Abschied von Sidonie*." *Visions and Visionaries in Contemporary Austrian Literature and Film*. Ed. Margarete Lamb-Faffelberger and Pamela S. Saur. New York: Peter Lang, 2004. 223-35.

Thurner, Erika. "Roma und Sinti: Der geleugnete und vergessen Holocaust." *Abschied von Sidonie von Erich Hackl: Materialien zu einem Buch und seiner Geschichte*. Ed. Ursula Baumhauer. Zürich: Diogenes, 2000. 289-313.

Victims and Perpetrators: Questions of Identity in Norbert Gstrein's *Das Register*

Cynthia A. Klima

The Register, translated by Lowell A. Bangerter, Ariadne Press, 1995

It probably can't be anything else with Kreszenz's stale concepts of morality. We only know that we will tell her nothing, as always. Or we'll be as general as possible, as unrevealing as possible – and memory, memory: Magda's wedding is tomorrow.[1]

  Das Register (1992) can be interpreted as a novel that tackles complicated issues of identity, both personal (psychological) and historical (political). The author Norbert Gestrein (1961-) belongs to a generation of Austrian writers who, in the aftermath of World War II, began to question Austria, its identity as a nation, its role in that war, and where the country and its citizens fit into this historical context. Such questions as, "What role did Austria play in the war?" "What defines 'Austrian' and 'Austrian characteristics?'" and "How is 'Austrian' distinct from 'German?'" begin to emerge as one reads this novel of two brothers, one a professor and the other a champion skier. Their identities are inseparable, yet their lives have taken vastly different paths. Elements of the novel appear to be somewhat autobiographical, as Gstrein himself became a professor and writer while his own brother followed a successful skiing career, even representing Austria in the Olympic Games in Calgary in 1988.

  In addition to Gstrein, contemporary Austrian authors, such as Elfreide Jelinek, Thomas Bernhard, Peter Handke, and Peter Turrini, have addressed similar questions and criticized Austria's inability to come to grips with its history. Ruth Klüger's autobiography *Still Alive: A Holocaust Girlhood Remembered* (1995) reactivated the memory of Austria's past as well and brought the question of guilt for its role in the war to the forefront. Such literature has invoked inquiry into Austria's role during the Holocaust and questions why Austria has identified itself as "victim" and not "perpetrator." Gstrein, too, illustrates these questions and their need for answers by drawing characters that not only question their own identities and their experiences during childhood, but also follows up with answers to these queries using the characters' own life experiences to express a possible solution to the problems that Austria faces as a country with an identity that is not only overshadowed by Germany and its past, but also inseparable from the term "German."

With the fall of the Berlin Wall, the opening of secret archives, and the growing tome of information about varying incidents during the war, Gstrein's psychological probings and narrative style tie into possible answers and indicate the need for more investigation. His technique consists of back and forth recollections of incidences from childhood as well as adulthood, all of which intertwine with the present-day dilemma that has separated the brothers and caused a rift in the family, a rift that the brothers have long ignored. In so doing, they have unwittingly left open wounds caused by their family's past and their own deeds. This technique continues throughout the novel, at times shifting from the near past to the distant past, the latter represented in italicized sections that relate childhood memories and are labeled as *Regieanweisungen* (stage directions).

Ignorance of one's past is exactly what Gstrein is dealing with in this work, and he uses the brothers to represent the current questions concerning Austria's neglected residual wounds from its own Nazi past. Indeed, the *Anschluss* brought Austria into the arms of the Third Reich, which embraced it as just another appendage of the Nazi regime. Were Austrians willing participants? Innocent victims? Were they indifferent to the entire affair? Egon Schwarz stated that "it seems strange that a bitter controversy has broken out in the Austrian public sphere" and he calls the act of forgetting "Austria's favorite pastime."[2]

Such issues are certainly worth exploring, and Gstrein's generation, a generation too young to remember the war directly or to suffer guilt in its aftermath, has been at the forefront of inquiry as to what part Austria played and what it means to be Austrian.[3] *The Register* raises questions in an attempt to tackle the themes of individual identity and the role of guilt as attributes of an identity crisis. Understanding this crisis suffered by the two brothers Moritz and Vinzenz is tantamount to comprehending the complexity of identity, how it ties into guilt, and furthermore, how it all relates to Austrians whose own identity is questioned by this new generation of Austrian writers.[4]

Unraveling the complexities of identity can prove to be a daunting task when individuals are reluctantly forced to assume specific roles in life. Gstrein's novels set the individual(s) up against the hidden pitfalls of identity concerns and the constantly changing world. One sees this conflict reflected in his earlier novel *Die englischen Jahre* (1999) (*The English Years* [2002]), when the writer Max Hirschfelder first began to question his Jewish identity during the war by calling himself Smith.

Certainly an inability to "fit in" or "cope" can be associated with an identity crisis and can put an individual into harm's way, as Bernd Simon has noted. Identity influences how people interact socially, and an inability to come to terms with their past can lead to problems similar to those seen in the personal interactions in *The Register*. Simon states: "[I]t is difficult to imagine how loyalty, solidarity or social cooperation could be achieved and maintained without a sense of shared identity."[5] Estrangement from family, feelings of guilt, and an inability to come to grips with memory, both near and distant past, are all seen as characteristics of a deep-seated family crisis that is evidenced at the beginning of *The Register*.

The identity crisis reveals itself at the beginning of the novel when the two brothers, who have been estranged for years, appear for the wedding of a former mutual girlfriend. Old memories and past rivalries are dredged up and pour forth as the brothers come into contact with their sister Kreszenz, who eventually becomes a unifying force between them. Distrust and tension are major factors that the reader immediately perceives in the brothers' relationship not only to one another, but also to other family members. Moritz and Vinzenz possess similar personality traits but differ immensely in the paths they have taken to adulthood. They are both at a loss as to who they are as individuals. Moritz, the math whiz, has become a professor and represents the intellectual side of the Austrian, while Vinzenz, a champion skier, symbolizes the athletic Tyrolean Austrian.

Moritz's pursuance of an academic career is reflective of the great intellectual influence that shaped Austria in the late 19th to early 20th centuries. Yet, by leaving his village, obtaining a college education and going abroad, he has broken away from the traditional Austrian ties of family and home. Conversely, Vinzenz remains the provincial Austrian attached to the out-of-doors and the familial village. But neither brother has discovered his own personal niche or purpose in life. They remain disconnected from one another, and instead of dealing with their differences and seeking common bonds, they ignore discussion of their problems. It is not until their encounter at home that they are forced to come to terms with their shared past and their guilt.

Significantly, the brothers cannot define who their father was and do not seem to have had any emotional attachment to him when he died. The experiences each had with his father is the central problem in the brothers' relationship to one another: they avoid discussion of their distance from him. The rift between them has grown ever wider and reconciliation becomes even more difficult. Memories of the past, as seen in the stage directions, and unresolved problems all rush forth alongside guilt for past transgressions. An entire kaleidoscope of psychological features opens up as Gstrein weaves the origins of these dilemmas together via the use of his narrative technique, which I term "narrative switch." It purposefully confounds and further illustrates the characters' lack of differentiation, which is the root cause of their difficulties with one another. The narrator at the beginning of the novel is the observer, the one whose objective is "to release the author from any accountability for the 'facts' of fictional narrative."[6] Thus Gstrein, in line with Richard Walsh's thinking, is removed from the brothers' narration and serves to tie their stories together.

Through the narrator's and the brothers' narration, the reader is able to develop a clearer picture of their unwillingness or incapacity to share the trials and tribulations of their lives. The omniscient narrator recounts their initial moments at seeing one another for the first time in years, thereby introducing the predicament. When they meet at the train station, "He [Moritz] simply regards Vinzenz like an apparition, and sees how alike they are" (7) ("[er] schaut ihn nur an wie eine Erscheinung und sieht, wie ähnlich sie sich sind"[14]).

The narrator then relates his observation of Vinzenz's reaction at seeing Moritz in a similar fashion: "he simply looks at him and sees, sees again – and again defenselessly – how alike they are – or at least that is what people say about them when they don't know what else to say" (10).[7] The word "defenseless" (*wehrlos*) already implies an inability to cope and a lack of strength to solve an issue. Certainly neither brother possesses the ability alone to face the past; each requires assistance from Kreszenz, in order to identify and solve long-rooted issues. At moments when the brothers' different perspectives on their lives (or common perspectives as "we") have been presented, the narrator returns to add yet another aspect to their narration which ties together their pasts and propels the novel forward to an eventual realization that reconciliation must occur.

Gstrein's narrative switch segues well into the question of identity, for Moritz and Vinzenz are not only indivisible as first-person narrators, they are indivisible as characters. Who is at fault is not revealed by use of this technique, and when faced with issues of who is guilty of past transgressions a generation ago, Gstrein seems to leave it to the reader to judge whether this past really matters. When past history reemerges, the deeds already are irrevocable anyway. However, each narrator serving as a character in the novel has to come to terms not only with himself, but with the other narrators as well.

Gstrein makes identification of the narrator purposely difficult, but he provides the reader with the knowledge that the identity crisis is one of a complex and difficult nature with which the two brothers must come to terms if they are to reconcile and begin atoning for their past behavior. In addition, Moritz and Vinzenz must come to terms with their lives in order to start living. Their sister Kreszenz becomes mediator between them, a task she has taken on despite her own dissatisfaction with her childhood and current life. Conspicuous by her absence and lack of connection to them, the brothers' mother plays little role in the novel. Kreszenz has assumed the role of a mother-figure in the brothers' lives, and they themselves even regard her as the conduit for reconnecting themselves to one another. Kreszenz is "the only connecting link…like one of the constellations of our childhood, where one of us has always lined up with her against the other" (11).[8]

She has never left their village, but has remained behind with what is termed a "normal" life – she has married and had children – and seems reconciled to her lot in life and the childhood she experienced. But she is not content with the lack of communication between her brothers, and her own attempt to find contentment in life is undermined by their lack of connection. She continues to slash herself out of frustration with her family and its inability to communicate and bond. "In her worst attacks, she slashed the backs of her hand with a razor blade" (21) ("In ihren schlimmsten Anfällen zerschnitt sie sich mit einer Rasierklinge die Handrücken" [29)]). The significance of this action cannot be denied: Moritz's and Vinzenz's inability to bring the family back together drains her mentally. She is the only mediator who cares about reconciling the brothers, and her own patience with them is wearing thin:

> They'll come in a few hours, Vinzenz and Moritz. And again, defenseless as always, as

usual I'll think how similar, or dissimilar they are. They're exactly alike. And at the same moment, I'll think that my thinking is wearing out in recognition, in repetition, in a dull *aha*! (22)[9]

A nervous tick affects her body language as she rocks back and forth (189) [221], as if in deep meditation or concentration as she attempts to reconcile the brothers. She wonders whether they were aware of Magda's "double-dipping" (*Doppelspiel*) with them, or of her attempted suicide: "What do you know about Magda's – it's an ominous word – 'attempted suicide?'"(150) ("Was wisst ihr über Magdas – es ist ein ominöses Wort, 'Selbstmordversuch?'"[177]).

It occurs to the brothers that they do not know much about their former mutual girlfriend. In fact, neither one of them has had much success with women since. Moritz sleeps with his young female students and then fails them in his classes; Vinzenz, as a café owner after his career as a champion skier is finished, hires and fires waitresses on whims. Even as adults, their memories of their childhood prevent them from developing interpersonal relationships, especially those with women.

Moritz's desire to break out of his predictable routine as a professor leads him to visiting prostitutes to add more excitement to his life. Again, he is involved with people who cannot provide him intimacy, friendship, or family. He does not know how to live any differently:

> In reality, in words that had already been used who knows how many times, it meant, there would be so much, so much to do if only one had a life, any life at all, and another, and again, again, and again another, and after each one, still one more, with a guaranteed right of exchange and return (187).[10]

His career as a professor of mathematics is a commentary on his life, as he repeatedly uses the same notes and has no desire to change lesson plans or routines, such as his usual coffeehouse fare or card games with other bored professors. Occasionally he publishes an article and that provides the only highpoint in his otherwise dreary existence.

His is a life of predictability and of regularity. It is a life away from his family and the issues of his own past. Silence in his family life has led to an empty life as an adult. His life has been preordained, much like the stage directions that describe his childhood in such a matter-of-fact manner. *"Father locked us in the refrigeration plant of our uncle's hotel, sat down in front of it, and watched to see that nobody let us out early* (72)." *("[Vater] sperrte uns im Hotel des Onkels in die Kühlanlage, setzte sich davor hin und sah zu, dass uns niemand vorzeitig herausließ"* [88]).[11] Even math, his chosen discipline, is a science of prediction, a supreme science; for Moritz: "mathematicians were heroes" (100) ("In Moritz' Vorstellung waren Mathematiker von vornherein Heroen" [121]), a reference to the fact that his father is not the leading figure in life.

Vinzenz, once a champion skier who knows nothing else but skiing and is a failure as a café owner, has lost his fan support since his retirement. His identity remains tied to his prowess as an athlete. As a world-famous skier, he played a part for the public and participated in heavy drinking and superficial behavior with fans who "loved" him (167) [196]. As a member of the ski team, he was taught etiquette and was manufactured into an athletic star. However, he gained very little in terms of interpersonal skills. Whereas his body and image were refined, his inner self remained superficial, and he never mastered the techniques necessary to form lasting bonds with friends or even his family. His sponsors covered his racing suit in advertisements and he became a virtual walking billboard: "Not one spot on his body was free anymore" (135) ("und an seinem ganzen Körper war kein Fleck mehr frei" [160]). He was more a tool to attract money rather than a human being. Upon retirement he is a burned out has-been.

With hopes of creating a new life outside of skiing, Vinzenz buys a café. He temporarily experiences "the café's days of glory" (202) ("die Sternstunden des Cafés" [236]) that mirror the illustrious career of his youth. But much like his career, in which he was only identified as a ski hero or hero of the nation and not as Vinzenz the person, the café soon begins a downward slide: "Vinzenz's restaurant actually seemed indistinguishable from others" (202) ("Sonst war es ein unscheinbares Lokal, wie es sie zu Dutzenden gab" [237]). As with his own existence, both pre- and post-skiing, the café becomes a mundane entity. Vinzenz is friendless, out of touch with Moritz, and eventually, fatherless. The café is treated like his past relationships: untended and finally abandoned.

The root causes of this dilemma, which can be analyzed from past occurrences in the brothers' lives, should be considered. The psychological pressures to conform to modern society and family expectations are factors that come to mind. Certainly individuals seek to succeed and conform to established societal norms in order to "fit in." But to be satisfied with mere conformity robs one of one's self and one's individuality. In this case, it is helpful to look at the brothers' childhood, their history together, and the father who molded both boys' personalities and futures.

It is helpful to note the stage directions, (30-35) [41-47], with which the past is brought forth via a slide show of memories of a seemingly normal childhood. Life is not a preordained script over which the characters have no control, a reference to the possibility that the boys' are not at fault for their childhood problems. But more than that, the stage directions provide a background that embodies the essential essence of the novel. They capture the pictures and scenes from memory, and though incomplete, they provide bits of information that are key to the identity problems facing the brothers. As children, however, Moritz and Vinzenz cannot be held accountable for the actions they took at that time, a reference to the modern-day children of Austria who cannot be held responsible for World War II. Here Father is introduced as the type who laughs at them (33) [44] and encourages rivalry between them. They vie for his approval (35) [46] and readily give the respect he demands. But

Father has a secret: he lives with the constantly looming legend of his own overbearing and larger-than-life father. Here one sees the political identity crisis unfold when the boys admit "We hadn't known our grandfathers" (40) ("Wir hatten keinen gekannt" [52]).

Interestingly, one grandfather is described by the we-narrator as a Nazi-sympathizer who names his daughter Adolphine, "a monstrous name" (45) ("ein scheußlicher Name" [58]), while the other as apolitical, a "so-called opponent of Hitler" (45) ("zu einem Gegner Hitlers" [58]). Indeed, the fact such observations are related by the we-narrator is significant, for these are singular points that the two boys can agree upon. It can be surmised that "Adolphine" is the boys' mother, the only parental name made known to the reader.

By not naming Father, Gstrein empasizes his lack of individuality and inability to cope with his own father's legendary status, however fabricated it may be. Political confusion is apparent in the family, with one side sympathetic to the Nazi cause and the other in opposition to it. This confusion is also evident in Austria's own past. Whether Austria was an innocent victim of the Third Reich standing in opposition to Hitler or a willing participant in the perpetuation of Nazi ideology remains an argument to this day. The comparison of the two families is an ingenious representation of this "Austrian Question."[12]

Father's father [Grandfather] represents order, power and organization. He is a mythical and historical figure about whom the boys hear tales and around whom life appears to be centered. Indeed, the identity the boys have chosen is one that revolves around legend and not reality, a presence that is not their memory but rather a patchwork of their father's imagination and the whispers of the townsfolk. Grandfather is described as "a pigheaded man, a cunning, contrary man" (46) ("ein Dickschädel, ein bauernschlauer Querkopf" [59]) and a representative of the past, often spoken of by their father as "the days before proud Tyrolean people degenerated into a hoard of bootlickers and toadies, and the holy country into a rental brothel"

(46) ("bevor das stolze Tiroler Volk zu einer Horde von Speichelleckern und Arschkriechern verkam, das heilige Land zu einem Zinsbordelle" [59]).

Even more, Grandfather represents Austria's past in its relations with Germany when he states, "We should let the German into the country, clean them out thoroughly, and kick them out again stark naked?" (46) ("man solle die Deutschen hereinlassen ins Land, aus- und aussäckeln und splitternackt wieder hinausschicken, mit einem Tritt?" [59]). As seen here, Austria's identity is wrapped up in Germany's presence, a fact that certainly affects the troubles of the individual within not only one's family, but within one's social circles and society in general.

When Grandfather's construction of his hotel and other property is sabotaged, "It fit his [Father's] self image well to be the son of a persecuted man" (46) ("es passte zu gut in sein Selbstbild, Sohn eines Verfolgten zu sein" [60]), again alluding to an identity as "victim" instead of "perpetrator." What is more, Moritz even identifies Grandfather with the American Dream (47) [60] and these lofty, grandiose illusions contrast starkly with Father's own personal failure (49) [62] at realizing his own dreams and place in society. Grandfather's cleverness (41) [53] and noble background (42) [54] make for an attractive identity to which to adhere.

His status is built up on a supposed encounter with Hemingway on the Tyrolean slopes (43-44) [56-57], which lends more credence to his status. Father begins to identify with Hemingway's greatness and imagines himself to be a writer of a talent ascribed to world-class authors but is ultimately a failure. He cannot possibly live up to Hemingway's literary standards and most certainly cannot compete with the famous author's adventurous spirit. This passage shows how Father's memory became so mixed with absolute fantasy that he was unable to distinguish his own reality from legend. In essence, he was leading a life built upon falsehoods.

In social circles, Father's desire to impress visitors (51) [65] with expensive delicacies adds to his pretentiousness and he appears to be that which he is not: his own father and a wealthy intellectual. He becomes a ridiculous, humiliated figure as "the mocking in their [the villagers] voices kept increasing" (53) ("aber mit Fortdauer des Abends, nahm in ihren Stimmen der Spott immer mehr zu"[67]). His sons are not the only ones to see the preposterous situation, but his fellow townspeople are now laughing behind his back. Suffering the humiliation of such a defeated father, the boys begin to distance themselves from him and direct their attention toward the "legendary" Grandfather, whom they never knew. "We weren't the children of a teacher, we were the grandchildren of a hotel owner" (82) ("wir waren keine Lehrerkinder, wir waren Enkel eines Hoteliers"[100]). In essence, their identification with Grandfather is much more truthful than Father's – Grandfather was admired by the village and was indeed wealthy, whereas Father lives on a dream that he is still rich and powerful. Thus, the influence of legend becomes stronger than Father, who is submissive, weak, and unable to garner success (48) [61-62].[13]

The boys call their contact with Father "collisions" (73) ("Zusammenstöße" [89]) and vow to pay him back "with interest and interest on the interest" (73) ("Mit Zinsen und Zinseszinsen" [89]). Father even creates a "register" (67) ("Register" [82]) of expenses he incurred while raising them, expecting them both to return the favor in his twilight years. Instead of emotionally attaching himself to his sons, he alienates them: "We avoided Father more and more (80) ("Wir gingen Vater immer mehr aus dem Weg" [97]).

In their frustration at having to deal with their lack of connection to their father, the boys take in a pregnant stray cat and immediately commit acts of sheer brutality upon the animal in order to establish control over something in their lives. When the cat gives birth, they are elated, stating "We were fathers" (88) ("Wir waren Väter" [107]). They are so desperate to identify themselves with any living being, even if it is just a cat. But they indirectly pay back Father for his treatment of them – the cat becomes a replacement for his absence and the boys torture the cat to death in a symbolic act of revenge: "And nothing remained, or only a blurred consciousness of their guilt."(90) ("Und es war nichts, was blieb, oder ein verschwommenes Bewußtsein ihrer Schuld" [109]).

One can note paternal similarities in Gstrein's work to Kafka's, most notably, *The Judgment* (*Das Urteil*) and *A Letter to Father* (*Ein Brief an den Vater*). Both authors deal with issues of fatherly power and identity with the power figures in a family. However, Gstrein's illustrations offer a more cautiously optimistic future than Kafka's, signaled only toward the end of *The Register* as the brothers attempt to reconcile. The boys have already identified a powerful father-figure in Grandfather, who is no longer alive to reject them, making him a very safe choice. They have someone to whom they can aspire; however, one sees a similar father-son conflict in *The Judgment*.

This work is an example how Vinzenz's and Moritz's own father was treated by his father, leaving their own father a weakened, ineffective parent. Although the father in *The Judgment* is sickly and near death, he retains control over his son George by revealing that George never had a friend in Russia, that the friend was always loyal to George's father. He berates his son for being oblivious to this fact by stating:

> For he knows everything, you stupid boy, he already knows everything! I've been writing to him, because you forgot to take my writing things away from me. That's why he hasn't come for years. He knows everything a hundred times better than you do yourself. He crumples up your letters unread in his left hand, while in his right hand he holds my letters up to read.[14]

Thus the male role-model that Moritz and Vincenz had as an actual example of how to conduct their lives cannot cope with his own failure as a son. In his interpretation of the father-son relationship in the Afterword to his translation of *The Regis-*

ter, Lowell Bangerter compares Gstrein's father-son relationship to the one seen in Kafka's *A Letter to Father*. In fact, *A Letter to Father* is indeed the story of the brothers' own father at the mercy of Grandfather. At the heart of Kafka's work is the reconciliation sought by the son with his overly-dominating father. A major factor in the tension between Kafka and his father was the older man's perception that his son's literary activities had no practical value. By portraying the father in his novel as a weakened individual who writes a worthless book before his eventual death, Gstrein actually reverses Kafka's pattern for his particular generation of sons.[15]

So the role-model they choose to identify themselves with – Grandfather – is one that does not exist, one that is fabricated and no longer available to them as an actual standard. He approximates George's father in the way he wielded power over their own father. Vinzenz's and Moritz's decision to identify with power and wealth will prove to be a choice that ignores the reality of life and will lead them on a path of failure. They end up having no living role-model and as a result, their own identities remain underdeveloped. Neither Father nor the brothers can extract themselves from a past created for them by a more powerful figure. George resolved his situation by committing suicide, and Vinzenz and Moritz's father dies, yet his death does not provide any resolution for them.

Such is the case with Austria's own identity problems. Austria's past is inextricable tied to Germany as a result of the *Anschluss*, even though "Austrians were the cultured victims," a myth perpetrated by the Second Republic.[16] Moritz's close working relationship with a taskmaster German professor is indicative of Austria's inability to extract itself from its past: "And really, what better reputation could he have than to be a taskmaster, a slave driver, and to want to do away with Austrian slovenliness, Austrian congeniality, Austrianness in general?" (101).[17] Moritz, whose father has abandoned him in favor of his brother Vinzenz and Vinzenz's skiing career, "placed in him, in the professor, his entire confidence and clung to him...And he followed him" (102) (So setzte er in ihn, in den Professor, sein ganzes Vertrauen und hielt an ihm fest...und er lief hinter ihm her [123]). This fact contrasts to what Vinzenz has become, for "he was impudent, lazy and a liar" (103) ("dass er frech, faul und verlogen war"[124]). His relationship with Father is described as a "comradeship" (103) ("Kameradshaft" [124]). What's more, Father never corrects him and never disciplines him because Vinzenz is "getting ready to accomplish something great" (103) ("sich anschickt, etwas Grosses zu leisten"[125]). He identifies his life with money and luxury (104) [125], and Father sees his own chance to be a success like Grandfather. It is indeed here in his relationship with Father that Vinzenz plays his role as victim successfully, as if to say, "I cannot help it. I am representing Austria." Thus, in his effort to be a success, Vinzenz is in reality playing out the role of victim, and victims are rarely questioned about their behavior since someone else was responsible for forming it in the first place.[18]

But when Vinzenz fails, Father wants nothing to do with him (117) [141]. As Vinzenz begins to realize his power over Father, he begins to mock him and his writing (118) [142], all the while growing more arrogant and taking more risks. Despite this, he is a "Model Austrian" (127) ("Vorführösterreicher" [151]) but it is a life that he hates because it is not a life that is his own. It is a life modeled for him by Father, sponsors, and money. All in all, he leads an artificially created life, a scripted identity, much like the artificially created innocence of the Austrian nation. "People can acquire mastery of the present only when they are able to master their past, rather than being mastered by it."[19] Vinzenz has never dealt with his relationship with his brother, and his relationship with his father remains superficially based upon skiing. When Father dies, the issues clearly remain unresolved.

By comparison, Moritz, lacking a father-son relationship, deepens his ties to the German professor, and in their cooperative work on glaciers, he comes to the realization that he is also investigating history. When the professor speaks about ice ages, interglacial periods, and deep bores in the ice (112) [135], he is speaking of his own mental state. And the professor considers giving false and inaccurate measurements to be fully in order, if the work gets to be too much for him, even though he is a paid professional in his field (114) [136]. It is evident from this act that the inaccuracies the professor presents are simply accepted, no one questions the calculations and yet, both he and Moritz reap the fruits of their labor by being paid well and gaining respect for the "contributions" they are making to an inaccurate body of science. They are producing what they perceive to be an acceptable assemblage of false information and moving on as if such inaccuracies did not matter.

Even Tyrol plays an important part in establishing, or rather, re-establishing identity in this novel. As a geographical region split between Italy and Austria, it retains a dual personality. The Olympics are mentioned as being a part of the Tyrolean landscape, a time to have the world's eyes on the people of the Tyrol, but there is actual confusion as to what "Tyrolean" means here in the "so-called state capital" (94) ("der sogenannten Landeshauptstadt" [113]). The description of activities relates the artifice present during the games and the townsfolk engage in this charade alongside the tourists and out-of-towners. The sparkle is meant for the rest of the world and covers up the reality for the "Men and Women of Tyrol" (94) ("Tiroler und Tirolerinnen" [114]) and "they knew what was concealed behind it" (95) ("was sich dahinter verbarg"[114]).

Everyone is involved in this artificial representation of Tyrolean life. Brand name products that exude the name "Tyrolese" or "Tyrolean" (96) [115] are on display, but there is no real joy in partaking in celebrations that are not really celebrating anything but commercialism. There is no cultural reality attached to the Olympic Games, the visitors have no idea what a Tyrolean is (nor do they care) and busy themselves with the fanfare, while real Tyroleans are visiting a brothel away from the sports center in order to escape the charade: "You were momentarily elsewhere" (98) ("man war augenblicklich an einem anderen

Ort"[118]). Moritz's eventual departure for the U.S. is a further attempt to escape the confinement of Austrian life and artifice to find himself elsewhere, if not totally reinvent himself as a new and different person. This is indeed a defining point in the novel, for the following utterance releases a flood of pent-up feelings Moritz has been holding onto for years:

> *I don't want to be one anymore* – a front-yard Vorarlberger, a rucksack Tyrolean, a Salzburg semolina dumpling, an Upper or Lower Austrian cider head, an SS Carinthian, a boring or stony Styrian, a bootlicking Viennese, a Burgenland-joke Burgenlander – *I don't want to be Austrian anymore!* (153)[20]

It is in America that Moritz finds that he cannot be anything other than what he is. He will never speak English without an accent, he will forever be a tourist in this land, a "greasy Austrian, an Austro-Hungarian subject" (157-58) ("ein schmieriger österreichischer, österreichisch-ungarischer Untertan" [185]). He will always be "Other." He begins to realize his connection to Austria the longer he stays away, and when he returns, he becomes very fastidious with a standard style of speaking standard German. He is made fun of for his accent in shops and it is then and only then, upon this return from America and his attempt to return to an Austrian lifestyle, that memories of his past come flooding back to him (166) [195].

Vinzenz attempts to rekindle a skiing career in the U.S. after his retirement in Austria and he has hopes of becoming a film star. But he is confined to bit roles cast as an Austrian, and his scenes end up on the cutting-room floor of an editor's office. His American Dream has failed him, much as Moritz's did. This is the breaking point for both brothers, for not only is Father dead, but Grandfather, who had represented the American Dream for them both, has died a second death. In effect, they realize that they have been raised by no one and that the guiding beacon they had followed was not only unrealistic but had never existed at all.

The failure of their American Dream is not the only common link the brothers have. Their relationship with Magda, an outsider with red hair, an "Other," is also a bond that they share and the reason for their return home. She does not seem to fit in with anyone except Moritz and Vinzenz. They trusted her – but they both lose her. And they begin to forget her. This common bond is the one that will reunite the brothers as they try to recall her in their memory: "What you forgot was not just forgotten. It is as if it had never been. It was dead." (193) ("Was man vergaß, war nicht nur vergessen, es war, als ob es nie gewesen wäre, tot" [225]). Her failed attempt at suicide and her inability to hold a job also befit her role as an outsider, as one who has also made little attempt to connect herself to Austrian society. However, she makes a valiant attempt by entering into marriage, which will not only unite her and bond her to someone, but will give her a place in society. She will have a chance to reconcile herself with Austrian life, just as Kreszenz has done.

And reconciliation does take place. It must take place if the past is to be overcome and understood. This is the hopefulness present in the novel, in true opposition to Kafka's pessimistic view of man's fate. Gstrein's use of the narrative switch becomes a potent force in the Epilogue and it is impossible to determine whether the narrator is Moritz or Vinzenz. In effect, the inability to determine the narrator is evidence of a possible attempt at reconciliation. The narrative dialogue becomes more rapid as the narrator begins to describe those present at the wedding celebration and to pan the entire wedding party as if he were a camera. All in all, what is being recorded is basic human activity that could be taking place almost anywhere, not just in the Tyrol. But in the Epilogue, the first vestiges of reconciliation are taking place, though the reader does not yet know if it will succeed.

The most interesting aspect of the Epilogue is that people are talking, especially two older gentlemen with pig-like faces "who converse so pretentiously" (248) ("sich so prätentiös unterhalten" [289]). They begin to discuss suicide within earshot of Moritz/Vinzenz, suggesting that it would be all right to kill themselves at any moment (251) [295], but they act as if they have said nothing of the sort when Moritz/Vinzenz turns to confront their gaze. The gentlemen's megalomania melts away and they are exposed for the gossips they are. As the narration begins to focus on the details of the wedding, the reader can no longer distinguish between Moritz and Vinzenz. There is joy at the wedding, there is revelry, and there is hope. One can indeed see a parallel in this activity, as Egon Schwarz states, "A new generation of Austrians has grown up and among them every returnee can find human solidarity and charity, which had been horribly lacking" (191). It is thus with the last lines, "We're still alive! Hurrah! We're alive! Hurrah! Hurrah! We're still alive! (258) ("Wir leben noch, hurra, wir leben, hurra, hurra, wir leben noch!" [300]), that the final resolution to reconcile with one's past, identity, and guilt must occur. Questions do remain, however. Will the brothers be successful in coming to terms with their past? Or are they doomed to resume ignoring their dilemma? Gstrein leaves the ending open, and the reader is left wondering what path Austria itself will follow.[21]

Endnotes

[1] Norbert Gstrein, *The Register*, trans. Lowell A. Bangerter. (Riverside CA: Ariadne Press, 1995) 29. All English translations are from this edition. German quotes from Norbert Gstrein, *Das Register*. Frankfurt am Main: Suhrkamp Verlag, 1992.
"es geht wohl nicht anders, mit Kreszenz' vertrockneten Moralvorstellungen; wir wissen nur, wir werden nichts, wie immer nichts erzählen, oder möglichst allgemein, möglichst nichtssagend – und Erinnerung, Erinnerung: Magdas Hochzeit ist morgen" (39).

[2] Egon Schwarz, "Austria, Quite a Normal Nation," *New German Critique*, No. 93 (Autumn 2004) 181. Schwarz continues with an interesting commentary on the past and dredging it up; these are arguments that have recently come to the forefront regarding Austria's past. He states: "Some of the principal arguments entail that there is no point sermonizing to a new, completely uninvolved generation about events that have faded into the same oblivion as the conquest of Carthage. Further along those lines, they [those who do not see benefit in bringing up the past] claimed that it is not meaningful to stir up the past for educational purposes and their purported intent of avoiding relapses. People simply do not learn from the past" (181).

[3] The problem of identity can further be seen in the German-language media, which is standard in Austria. German culture, German books, and German newspapers are all drunk in by Austrians, whereas Austrian literature and newspapers are not widely read by Germans. "Thus, much of Austria's voice occurs abroad. An Austrian who really wants to be heard, read, seen, or otherwise perceived and received has to articulate some of her/his talents with things German in some way sooner or later...Austrians simply have very few exit options from the German dominance of virtually every aspect of their cultural scene." Andrei Markovits, "Austrian-German Relations in the New Europe: Predicaments of Political and National Identity Formation, *German Studies Review*, vol. 19, No. 1 (February 1996), 94. Markovits continues with "...it was Austria's neutrality which formed the most important pillar of constructing a viable identity of "Austrianness." The latter had to develop in some opposition to – or at least a clear separation from – the political entity of Germany" (106).

[4] The discomfort many Austrians feel concerning their historical background can be seen in this novel when Kreszenz wonders how many Austrians would like to have Jews or even gypsies as neighbors (149) [175]. This is, of course, central to the silence that is pervasive in Austria today. Egon Schwarz contends that

"[s]cholars of literature attest that an 'uncomfortable silence' dominated Austrian literary scholarship until the 1970s...Jews did not exist at all" (184). Gstrein and his contemporaries are among the first modern Austrian writers to work with the silenced past.

[5] Bernd Simon, *Identity in Modern Society: A Social-Psychological Perspective*. Malden, MA: Blackwell Publishers, 2004: 1. Bernd further states that "the general popularity of (the notion of) identity suggests that most people, irrespective of their hope or fears, are fascinated by identity and what it does to and for themselves and others" (1).

[6] Richard Walsh, "Who is the Narrator?" *Poetics Today*, vol. 18, no. 4 (Winter 1997) 500. Another source for narrative explanation can be found in Elinor Ochs' and Lisa Capps' article "Narrating the Self," *Annual Review of Anthropology*, vol. 25 (1996), p. 19-43. Especially engaging are commentary on narrative by Milan Kundera, Michel Foucalt and Mikhail Bakhtin.

[7] "schaute ihn nur an and sieht, sieht wieder, und wieder wehrlos, wie ähnlich sie sich sind – oder wenigstens ist es das, was man von ihnen sagt, wenn man nicht weiss, was sagen" [17].

[8] "als einziges Bindeglied...war es wie eine der Konstellationen unserer Kindheit, wo stets einer von uns mit ihr gegen den anderen angetreten war" [18].

[9] "In ein paar Stunden werden sie kommen, Vinzenz and Moritz, und wieder, und wieder wehrlos, wie immer werd' ich denken, wie ähnlich, oder nicht ähnlich – genau gleich sind sie, und im selben Augenblick, daß sich mein Denken im Wiedererkennen, im Wiederholen erschöpft, einem stumpfen Aha" [31].

[10] "In Wirklichkeit, in wer weiß wie oft schon erprobten Worten hieß es, so viel, so vieles gäbe es zu tun, wenn man nur im Leben, irgendeines und ein anderes und wieder, immer wieder ein anderes und nach jedem noch eines hätte, mit guarantiertem Eintausch- und Rückgaberecht" [219].

[11] See pages (30-35, 71-73, 106-108) [41-47, 87-89, 128-130].

[12] In the Moscow Declaration of 1943, the Second Austrian Republic was essentially given a clean historical slate as "victim" rather than "collaborator." This essentially let Austrian reestablish itself free from war crimes and to use money invested by the Nazis to improve itself economically. This is termed *Geschichtslüge* or *Lebenslüge*, "how the foundation lie...of modern Austria came about." Steven Beller and Frank Trommler, "Austrian Writers Confront the Past, 1945-2000: An Introduction." *New German Critique*, No. 93 (Autumn 2004) 15.
[13] See also (53) [66-67].
[14] English version from: Franz Kafka, *The Judgment*. Translated by Ian Johnston. Published as e-text: http://records.viu.ca/~johnstoi/kafka/judgment.htm
"Er weiß doch alles, dummer Junge, er weiß doch alles! Ich schrieb ihm doch, weil du vergessen hast, mir das Schreibzeug wegzunehmen. Darum kommt er schon seit Jahren nicht, er weiß ja alles hundertmal besser als du selbst, deine Briefe zerknüllt er ungelesen in der linken Hand, während er in der Rechten meine Briefe zum Lesen sich vorhält." Franz Kakfa, *Das Urteil*. Leipzig: Kurt Wolff Verlag, 1916. Published as e-text no. 21593: http://www.gutenberg.org/etext/21593.
[15] Lowell A. Bangerter's *Afterword* in *The Register*, 262.
[16] Schwarz 184.
[17] "in welch besserem Ansehen konnte er stehen, als ein Schinder zu sein, ein Sklaventreiber, und mit dem österreichischen Schlendrian, mit der österreichischen Gemütlichkeit, mit dem Österreichischen überhaupt aufräumen zu wollen" [121].
[18] Moishe Postone indicates that Austrian development has been formed by its National Socialist past. See Moise Postone, "After the Holocaust: History and Identity in West Germany." *Coping with the Past*, ed. by Kathy Harms, Lutz R. Reuter and Volker Dürr. Madison, WI: University of Wisconsin Press, 1990: 233. Although Postone's essay has to do with West Germany, in his notes he states that one can assume that the same vestiges of guilt and ignored attention to the past are evident in Austria,

though as a nation, it perceives itself in the "other" category, i.e., as victim, not as perpetrator.

[19]Ibid. 233.

[20]"ich will keiner mehr sein – Vorhofvorarlberger, Rucksacktyroler, Salzburger Nockerl, Mostschädelober – oder – niederösterreicher, SS-Kärtner, Stockfisch- oder Steinsteirer, Schleimscheißwiener, Bürgenländerwitzbürgenländer – , ich will kein Österreicher mehr sein" [179].

[21]"We shall remember, though, that literature does not represent the sterile realities of life. Rather, literature begins where reality breaks down, where the facts crack and leave a gap. This gap becomes the space for fiction. Literature is an intriguing blend of reality and invention, of fact and fiction. Hence, it is the Other – aesthetically dispensed; the Other, that serves as a looking glass through which we may rediscover the world and see new and different possibilities and prospects." Margarete Lamb-Faffelberger, "Beyond the Sound of Music: The Quest for Cultural Identity in Modern Austria." *The German Quarterly*, vol. 76, No. 3 (Summer 2003): 295.

Memory and Identity in Doron Rabinovici's *Suche nach M*

Francis Michael Sharp

The Search for M, translated by Francis M. Sharp, Ariadne Press, 2000

Doron Rabinovici (1961-) belongs to a large number of contemporary world writers whose lives have been radically altered by a modern-day diaspora and whose identities are multiply hyphenated. He writes "outside the nation" of his birth (Seyhan) as well as those of his parental roots, but through naturalization, education, and assimilation, he is Austrian. By birth Rabinovici belongs to the second generation of Holocaust survivors and by early childhood experience to a second generation of migrants. His parental heritage is marked, like so many others of his generation, by the mass displacement of Eastern and Western Europeans in the wake of the Holocaust. The son of Eastern European Jews who had found refuge from Hitler in Palestine during the war, he moved with his family to Vienna in the sixties when he was three. It was here in his adopted country that he was educated and has chosen to make his home, although he maintains both Austrian and Israeli citizenship. Rabinovici made his literary debut in 1994 with a collection of short stories, *Papirnik*, published by Suhrkamp. His first novel, *Suche nach M.: Roman in zwölf Episoden*, appeared three years later, a work translated into English in 2000 as *The Search for M*. Rabinovici's second novel, *Ohnehin*, appeared in 2004.

Few contemporary Austrian writers draw from such varied personal and professional background as Rabinovici. A historian by education and writer by inclination, this promoter of a politically 'New Austria' has also been a critical commentator on national politics since the Waldheim affair.[1] Until the mid-eighties, Rabinovici's political focus had been on the Middle East but shifted with Waldheim's emergence onto the domestic Austrian scene. He has bluntly declared: "One could say that Waldheim is the reason that I became an Austrian" (Bair). The successes of the Freedom Party (FPÖ) in Austria of the nineties was a particularly strong catalyst for his political activism. His essays and commentaries on the contemporary political scene have appeared regularly since then in the Viennese daily, *Der Standard*. After co-organizing the mass political demonstration in Vienna on November 12th, 1999, he was actively involved in the civil protests against the populist successes of the Freedom Party and its leader, Jörg Haider. His co-edited volume of essays by writers and intellectuals who had taken part in the November demonstration appeared two months later. In the preface to this collection, he and his co-editor proclaim "the emergence of civil society" (*Aufbruch der Zivilgesellschaft*) in Austria (Misik 9-14). Beyond his continuing commitment to political activism, journalism as well as historical research, Rabinovici told an interviewer in 2003 that literature had become increasingly attractive and more personally satisfying and that he wanted to invest a larger share of his intellectual effort in writing fiction ("Sie sollten").

In an anthology entitled *Contemporary Jewish Writing in Austria*, Dagmar Lorenz describes the development of the Austrian Jewish minority in terms of its relationship to the majority in the postwar period. The initial historical circumstance that determined the shape of this relationship was the view given currency by the Allies in the Moscow Declaration of 1943 and then cultivated during the postwar years by the Austrians themselves. This Declaration not only absolved Austria of complicity in Nazi aggression but named the state its first victim (Bischof 18). In the immediate postwar years the government issued no call to Jewish exiles to return and demanded silence and assimilation of those Jews who did finally settle in Austria. Then in the mid-eighties as the myth of Austria's victim status became increasingly untenable in the aftermath of the Waldheim affair – as Lorenz puts it – "silence and assimilation ceased to be options for children of Holocaust survivors and exiles" (xiii). It is at this point that there began to develop what she terms a Jewish "minor or subculture" (xx) with a distinctive voice increasingly resistant to co-optation by the majority culture. According to Lorenz, Jewish writers have carved out their own niche in the larger cultural scene in which "their sense of difference is the force that drives their writings" (xx). For Matti Bunzl, the youngest contributor to the volume and son of an Austrian Jewish father and Israeli mother, the anti-Semitism that the Waldheim affair unleashed in Austria came as a surprise. Born in 1971, he had spent his childhood secure in his identity of an Austrian-Jewish symbiosis. This symbiosis, however, undermined by re-emerging anti-Semitic sentiment, had mutated into an identity of ethnic otherness, a sense of apartness and difference (349-358).

Doron Rabinovici also traces his own minority self-awareness – in a tension-filled juxtaposition to a majority belatedly reconciling itself to its past – to recent political developments in Austria. Several years prior to Haider's rise to prominence on the national political scene, a journalist asked him if he would immigrate in the event that Haider became *Bundespräsident*. He recalls his reaction to the question in the essay "Literature and the Republic or all of Baden is Reading the *Krone*." ("Literatur und Republik oder ganz Baden liest die Krone") For some, he responded, this would clearly be the rational and prudent course of action, and he reminds the reader how many young Jews had considered leaving Austria for Israel during the Waldheim affair in 1986. For him personally, however, emigration was not a choice. Even in the face of the alienation (*Fremdheit* 129) that enveloped Austrian Jews, he rejected the role of victim that such a forced desertion of his adopted homeland would entail. In answer to the journalist's question, Rabinovici foreshadowed the activist political stance that he has long held: "Emigration is not a political category.

Instead, one ought to put all one's efforts into stopping an extremist rightwing chief of state" (127).[2]

Rabinovici's awareness of a minority status, his refusal to play the role of Jewish victim, his determination to exercise his civic responsibility toward his residence of choice while still retaining Israeli citizenship – all these factors make for a very complex and unsettled sense of identity. He claims ties of tradition to Judaism rather than those of religion, once claiming kinship with David Ben Gurion as an "orthodox atheist" (*orthodoxer Atheist*), and calls himself a "tradition-conscious Jew without God" (*traditionsbewußter Jude ohne Gott*) ("Laßt die Synagoge"). In an essay entitled "Der nationale Doppler" (The national Double) that appeared in *Der Standard* in 1999, Rabinovici explored what he called his "schizoid situation" (*schizoide Situation*). The twin souls he accommodates in his breast are those of Austrian as insider and Israeli as outsider. He points to the national elections at the time as an irritant to the constant agitation and disquiet that already existed between these two. As an Austrian by choice, on the one hand, he declares himself free to elect his own choice of candidate, but asserts the right of the Israeli to have diplomatic relations with whomever he wants. He reminds himself as insider at one point that Haider's anti-foreigner sentiments were not, after all, directed at Austrian Jews, but at "foreigners" (*Ausländer*). Sobered by the naiveté of this assertion, the Israeli counters by raising the spectre of history and the associations that the campaign of the Freedom Party called up in the minds of "every halfway educated human being" (*jedem halbwegs gebildeten Menschen*). While less refined and attuned to local detail, this outsider Israeli perspective has the advantage of the larger view, both geographically and historically. It reasons that if official Austria had not defended Haider, it would not have run the risk of being confused with him and his policies. Moreover, it points out that, while few Austrians would have equated Haider with Hitler, the eyes of the world are much less attuned to Austrian political nuance.

While questions of identity are central to Rabinovici's personal and political life, they are central to his fiction as well. It is populated with second generation, post-Holocaust Austrian Jews, simultaneously at home and alien on the streets and squares of Vienna that form the unnamed backdrop of his stories and novels. These figures search for and find their identity not only in formative interaction with the broader social environment, but with the generations of their parents and grandparents as well. Amos Getreider, the seventeen-year-old main character in Rabinovici's short narrative "Der richtige Riecher" ("The Right Nose") in his first collection of fiction, *Papirnik*, is such a character. The climax of the story comes when Amos belatedly responds to an admonition his mother had given him years earlier. When her son was still in elementary school, she had encouraged him to retaliate physically against a classmate who had taunted him with an anti-Semitic remark. At the time he had rejected her violent method because his faith in the moderating power of language and discussion still held sway over his inclinations. Only years later does Amos strike out violently – against a youth who had been his close friend – and, by this act, become the family hero at the story's end.

This change in Amos's response – his mother's words dormant for years in his inner ear – is the goal at which the narrative events of "The Right Nose" culminate. Earlier in the day when the story takes place, Amos had been walking in the inner city past small groups of people in agitated discussions about a political demonstration that had just ended. Gradually it becomes clear that these discussions had a focal point in the "crimes of the past": "The majority considered the crimes of the past the decisive issue, a small minority, however, focused on the timelessness of the crimes" (126).[3] Although he does not explicitly situate the story in relation to historical events, Rabinovici evokes a public mood during a time of transition from a conspiratorial but tranquil silence to a time of troubled and troubling dialogue. Joined by his friend Peter Bach, Amos parries increasingly anti-Semitic remarks of the crowd with his usual composure and linguistic dexterity. He seems to enjoy the spectacle of a populace turning itself into knots with evasions and equivocations. After an old lady makes a particularly nasty remark about Polish Jews, he laughs at her embarrassed guilt when he reveals that his mother comes from Poland.

Yet later when Peter points to a group of orthodox Jews and expresses understanding of local resentment against them because of their apartness in dress and customs, Amos ends their friendship by punching him in the nose. His action is not only a response to his mother's admonition, but an affirmation of the part of his identity that he has inherited. Several weeks later, he announces his intention of living in Israel after his graduation from high school.

Amos's change of tactics in "The Right Nose" demonstrates in fictional terms a turn to a more direct and aggressive confrontation with Austrian attitudes toward Jews that Rabinovici as well as others viewed at the times as stale and sanctimonious. One of the old men involved in the open discussions on the street suggests a reversal of roles: we don't hate the Jews, he asserts, they hate us. A short while later, another man pleads for "a little more tolerance" (132) ("Ein bißchen mehr Toleranz" [69]) for what had been a blatantly anti-Semitic remark. A dialogue that has become convoluted to this degree demands radical realignment with historical reality. The Viennese born Holocaust survivor Ruth Klüger has advised Jewish writers: "Become quarrelsome, look for an argument" ("Werdet streitsüchtig, sucht die Auseinandersetzung"), while the German-Jewish writer Rafael Seligmann has demanded that the "German-Jewish archaic structures" ("deutsch-jüdischen Verkrüstungen") be destroyed with the "hammer of feuding" ("Hammer des Streits") (cited in Weidauer 280).

Rabinovici's novel *The Search for M* mirrors this confrontational attitude particularly in the attitudes and actions of Arieh, one of its two main characters. Both Arieh and Dani, the other key figure in the plot, are the offspring of Holocaust survivors. In response to his father Jakob's steadfast silence about his own past and experiences as a Polish Jew during the Holocaust, Arieh seeks out and finds indirect connections to his paternal heritage in a youth group of second-generation Jews. Matthias Beilein has pointed out that the Austrian Jewish youth coming of age in the second half of the twentieth century found themselves not only confronted by "the silence of the perpetrators" but by "the silence of the victims" as well (250). One evening the conversation of Arieh and his companions turns to the brutal assault of a local gang on a minority group of young people, an attack accompanied by a racist slur hurled at one of the victims. Arieh is aware that such an assault on his own group is an ever present danger in a state whose courts and police regularly turn a blind, and at times even sympathetic, eye, toward such xenophobic outbursts. After all, he reasons with postwar history as his witness, it is the same system that had repeatedly failed to bring war criminals to justice:

> War criminals were not brought to court and everything recalling the crimes once committed as well as actions provoking persecution and mass murder was deliberately ignored rather than prosecuted. Guilty parties were just not to be found in a country that claimed to be without blemish (29).[4]

While his father's generation in the postwar era had passively suffered at the affront of Austrian silence and forgetfulness, Arieh decides to force the system of justice into action. His plan is to find a key member of the gang and trick him into committing a crime against an established business that the authorities will have to investigate and prosecute. Exploiting a supersensory power he had felt even at school that brought about in him "a change resembling an allergic reaction" (32) when he came near someone who had wronged him, Arieh successfully tracks his prey.[5] With an uncanny ability to assume and act out a forged sense of identity, he seems literally to absorb the xenophobic hatred of the man he is seeking (33). By adjusting his persona so as not to arouse the suspicions of the man he is stalking, he ingratiates himself and works his way into his confidence. But in his attempt to set up and enact the crime that will implicate the thug as well as his friends while forcing the authorities to act, he accidentally kills him. Arieh's botched individual effort to counter the passivity of his father's generation and to adjust the scales of justice brings only a more intense suspicion down upon the Jewish community in its wake. Arieh himself takes immediate flight to Israel where he is soon recruited and his talents as a human "bloodhound" exploited by the Israeli secret service (42) ("Spürhund" [66]).

Dani Morgenthau, the novel's other main character of the younger generation, also has an uncanny aptitude to discern guilt. Unlike Arieh's ability, however, Dani's sensitivity over the course of the novel increasingly dominates any other sense of self that he has inherited, finally to the point of self-eradication. Even as a child Dani's inner moral compass had demonstrated a preternatural capacity to register the vibrations of wrongdoing or potential wrongdoing originating in the minds and souls of others. As an adult, his inner being has become so malleable and unsettled that he not only senses a criminal's innermost secrets but undergoes a kind of metamorphosis in which he takes on the subjectivity of the real culprit.

Dani's ability had begun apparently in harmless fashion during his childhood when he amused adults by taking responsibility for infractions he had obviously not committed and astounded playmates by knowing in advance what mischief they had in mind. Rabinovici figuratively uses this hypersensitivity to the sins of others to express the legacy of survivor guilt that had been passed from his parent's generation to their offspring. It is guilt grounded in the simple fact that they had survived the Nazis' extermination policies while friends and family members had perished. Austria shares the blame for the survival of this legacy into the second generation of Jewish survivors by having failed to promote healing national discussions in the immediate postwar period. Such discussions, however, would have necessitated breaking the state's silence about its role in Holocaust

atrocities and forced it and its citizenry into a policy of redress toward the victims. But such an official attitude and policy came into being only many years later. In the decades following the war:
> No one here had called back those who had been driven away. No political party had fought for compensation for those who had been robbed. No government had put up a fight to convict the murderers (55).[6]

Dani's father had attempted to gain official recognition as a victim and to confirm that crimes had been committed against his family in order to give Dani concrete evidence of their innocence. But he had run up against bureaucratic intransigence, and Dani, out of guilt for their renewed suffering, had disappeared at this point from their lives. Only years later do they see him again and learn of the new identity he had assumed after his disappearance.

After he leaves home, Dani's obsession with uncovering, pursuing, and claiming guilt brings him into contact with the most hardened of rapists, serial murderers and other criminals whose deeds grab the headlines of the local newspapers. His allergic reaction to their guilt, the sores and pustules that form on his body, intensify on this larger arena to the point that he must wrap himself completely in bandages. As the mysterious figure called Mullemann he comes into the national spotlight when a newspaper publishes the letters in which he confesses to a series of murders and gives detailed knowledge of the crimes. Wrapped in a disguise of bandages like a living mummy, he lurks in the shadows of Vienna stirring the fears of everyone who has something to hide:

> Who – numerous grandfathers asked with quavering index finger – in this city and this country was free of guilt? How many crimes, squabbles, and animosities had been painstakingly swept under the carpet and how many bodies buried under ground? Should all the

efforts of their generation have been in vain? Hadn't they covered over all the tracks during reconstruction, blotted out all the memories with their determined silence? Who knows, the old men wondered, which ghosts from the past were lurking beneath the layers of material covering this man? (125).[7]

While Arieh tracks down and flushes out enemies of the Jewish state in Israel into the open so that they can be killed by an assassin, Dani as Mullemann stirs up ghosts from the past in the citizens of a country that had forgotten it.

Both Arieh's role as executioner's helper and Mullemann's obsessive lamentations of *mea culpa* are the products of identity processes gone awry, processes perverted by the silence that surrounds them, the traumatized silence of their fathers and the self-protective silence of their countrymen. The figure of Mullemann serves a central symbolic function in Rabinovici's novel. Through his metamorphosis into a living mummy Dani has physically repeated the psychic mistakes of his father. Similar to the Holocaust survivors of his parents' generation he mummifies the guilt-ridden past, smothers and silences it beneath his bandages and tries to cut it off from the context of present and future. Writing to Dani from Tel Aviv at the end of the novel, Arieh tells him that he has shed "the masquerades and disguises" (180) ("die Maskeraden und die Tarnung" [259]) that played a key role in his work for the Israeli secret service. He then passes on the central insight of the novel that his father's friend Leon Fischer had given him earlier.[8] Fischer had told Arieh that the only escape for his generation from a legacy of guilt was a return to the past through memory. He encourages Dani as Mullemann:

> [n]ot to be tied down by the shackles of time like a mummy, to reject all the techniques of preservation, to shed the layers, undo the knots, to go after the knotting together, to feel for the

lumps, to unlace and remove the straps: this is
the work of memory (180-181).[9]
Arieh continues in his letter: "Sometimes all I see around me is
M. Even myself. Mullemania everywhere" (181).[10] Mullemann
is a kind of Austrian everyman with a stored inner reservoir of
guilt locked in by outer protective bandages, removed from the
effects of time's passage, and nourishing the festering wound of
identity. For the minority Jewish community in Austria – and
implicitly for all Austrians – the key to unlocking these bandages
is revisiting this past, airing it in the changed atmosphere of the
here, and now and using it to mold an identity for the future.

Arieh's and Dani's stories are embedded in a narrative
structure that vividly reflects Austrian history during the latter
two-thirds of the twentieth century. Their ficitional lives are,
however, only the central strands of a densely packed entangle-
ment of human stories forming a kind of a character landscape, a
landscape of intertwined fates described by one reviewer as "an
almost ludicrous network of relationships" (Buckl, "ein fast
schon irrwitziges Beziehungsgeflecht"). The first two of the
novel's twelve episodes play out mainly among members of the
first generation Jewish community in Austria of the sixties while
the following two advance the narrative by twenty years which
place both Dani and Arieh at turning points in their lives. Yet it
is not only the Jewish characters who live and function in the
shadows of more remote times. The shady figure of Rudi Kreuz,
for example, serves as a historical conduit from the Nazi to the
post Cold War era. In the first of his several appearances on the
opening page of the novel he makes vague – and initially for the
reader – unintelligible remarks to Jakob. Only gradually in the
further course of the plot do these remarks and the significance
of Kreuz's complicated life story of shifting identities and poli-
tical intrigue assume clarity and a place in the larger narrative.
As the turbulent times demanded, he took on and shed multiple
allegiances, always identifying with the political power in ascen-
sion at the moment. Ironically, this amoral master of chameleon-
like transformations finally falls victim to the assassin he had

himself hired to murder a former adversary. In a further twist of irony, he dies because he has – in yet another case of mistaken identity – given the assassin's earned wages to the bandaged Mullemann whose self recriminations he had believed to be those of the assassin.

The stories of Dani and Arieh form the core of this novel filled with mistaken identities, with characters known by multi ple names at various times in their lives and with individuals searching and seeking for others as well as for themselves. The sole direction of their efforts at the novel's end, however, is in a retreat to a past time. Based on Jewish tradition and family urging, they move toward repair of aberrations of past identity development. Arieh decides to quit the secret service and make a pilgrimage to Cracow – the city of his father's roots and academic success and where he later survived the pogrom because he was mistaken for another internee – after he realizes that he has become an enigma to his daughter just as his father had been to him. He is destined to break the silence between the generations of post-*Shoah* Jewish families. Dani is at the novel's end released from his work as an interrogator for the Austrian criminal investigator Karl Siebert. Following the determination of Dani's innocence in the eyes of the law – despite his constant confessions – his uncannily precise knowledge of a criminal's mind and his ability to coerce confessions from the most hardened malefactor had proven to be an invaluable investigative tool. But Arieh, writing from Israel and convinced that his own path into a personal past will help clarify who he really is, advises Dani to return to a voyage of self-discovery that had already begun at one point in the novel but which had been interrupted. Arieh urges him to return to the woman Sina Mohn, who had fallen in love with him earlier and in whose arms the healing process had once begun. The efficacy of the novel's proposed retro-cure for Dani remains an open question at the novel's close, the question whether Rabinovici's version of the *das Ewig-Weibliche* (the eternal feminine) will be able to undo the acquired compulsion to absorb guilt and reverse the momentum of the identity process toward a rediscovered innocence.[11]

For these main actors in Rabinovici's first novel, the goal of what has been called a hybrid identity, one that evolves from interaction with and influence by members of other minority groups seems remote.[12] This malleable and constantly changing sense of self characteristic of some multicultural societies – a repudiation of all essentialist theories of identity formation – may be more appropriately expected of the third generation of Holocaust survivors in Austria; that is, to the children of an Arieh, of a Dani. As Beilein points out, however, the feeling of solidarity with a minority figure does play a role in both characters' "path to their identity as Jew" (254) ("der Weg zu ihrer Identität als Jude"). For Arieh it is with the black man slandered with the racist epitaph "nigger bastard" (28) during the gang attack who is the spur to his ensuing actions. At a key point in his development into Mullemann, Dani finds solidarity with the Turk Yilmaz, a man on trial for murdering another Turk who has insulted his wife. Serving as a member of the trial jury, Dani recognizes in Yilmaz a reflection of his own combination of innocence and the compulsion to claim the guilt of others (Beilein 255). A further evocation of solidarity at the end of the novel – one with greater implications for the Middle East than for Austria – ties Arthur Bein (Arieh) to the Palestinian agent (Sayid) he has been tracking to set up for assassination. Coming initially by chance into contact with Sayid's wife and daughter and later by planned encounter with Sayid himself, Arieh develops an empathic identification with his wouldbe victim, recognizing in him a reflection of his own roles as husband and father.

But the solidarity perceived and displayed between ethnic groups in the Vienna of Rabinovici's first novel is slight, the distances unbridged by mutual interaction. The judge at Yilmaz's trial, for example, a representative of native Austrian attitudes, fixes with his remarks both the Turkish identities of the accused and Dani's Jewishness along widely held stereotypical lines. Rabinovici alludes in his novel to a Viennese multicultural society of various minority groups living side by side, but with few bonds of empathy and understanding between them. And while the central two figures in *The Search for M* are oriented backwards in time toward essentialist constructs of identity, Rabinovici's second novel, *Ohnehin*, features an ethnoscape within Vienna itself that is much richer in ethnic texture and fraught with possibilities of hybridity. It is a step perceptibly closer to the celebration of ethnic and cultural intermingling in the postmodern, postcolonial world of Salman Rushdie's *The Satanic Verses*.[13]

Endnotes

[1] He founded "Club New Austria" (*Club Neues Österreich*) as a rallying point for politically reformist young Austrians.
[2] "Auswandern sei keine politische Kategorie. Vielmehr müßte mit aller Kraft versucht werden, einen rechtsextremen Regierungschef zu verhindern."
[3] "Das Vergehen der Vergangenheit war den meisten, die Unvergänglichkeit der Vergehen einigen wenigen das entschiedene Anliegen" (*Papirnik* 61).
[4] "Kriegsverbrecher wurden nicht vor Gericht gestellt, und alles, was sich auf die Untaten, die hier einst begangen worden waren, berief, zu Hatz und Massenmord aufforderte, wurde nicht verfolgt, sondern geflissentlich übersehen. Schuldige durften nicht zu finden sein in einem Land, das allgemeine Unbeflecktheit beanspruchte" (47).
[5] "Bereits in der Schule war er von einer solchen Veränderung befallen worden, die einer Allergie gegen jene Person glich, die er finden wollte" (51).
[6] "Niemand hatte hier die Vertriebenen zurückgerufen, keine Partei für eine Entschädigung der Beraubten, keine Regierung für die Verurteilung der Mörder gefochten" (84).

[7]"Wer, so fragten einzelne Großväter mit zitterndem Zeigefinger, wäre in der Stadt und in diesem Land denn frei von Schuld? Wie viele Delikte, Streitigkeiten und Feindschaften seien doch bloß mit Mühe unter den Teppich gekehrt, wie viele Leichen unter der Erde verscharrt worden? Sollten all die Anstrengungen ihrer Generation vergeblich gewesen sein? Hatten sie nicht alle Spuren im Wiederaufbau verwischt, alle Erinnerungen mit verbissenem Schweigen ausgelöscht? Wer wisse, so die Alten, welche Gespenster der Vergangenheit unter den Stofflagen dieses Mannes steckten..." (182-183).

[8]"It may be that you've been forced to live with the legacy of our burden of guilt, but if you want to set yourselves free from it, you have to look at history's register. The only way out of the past into your own future goes through memory" (129-130). ("mag sein, daß ihr mit den Hypotheken unseres Erbes leben müßt, aber wenn ihr euch davon befreien wollt, müßt ihr in das Grundbuch der Geschichte schauen. Der einzige Weg aus der Vergangenheit in die eigene Zukunft führt über die Erinnerung" [188]).

[9]"Nicht in den Banden der Zeit eingelegt zu sein wie eine Mumie, allen Techniken der Konservierung eine Absage erteilen, die Schichten abstreifen, die Knoten aufdröseln, ihrer Verknüpfung nachgehen, die Knubbel ertasten, die Riemen umschnüren und ablösen, das ist Erinnerung" (259).

[10]"Zuweilen sehe ich um mich herum bloß Mullemann. Auch ich. Mullemania überall" (259).

[11]Where Goethe's Faust famously found salvation at the end of *Faust II*.

[12]In his essay "Vom Ethnozentrismus zur Multikultur...," Paul Michael Lützeler has written that "characteristic of the transition from the modern to the postmodern constellation are changes in identity from the static to fluid, from unambiguity to ambivalence." (Bezeichnend für den Übergang von der modernen zur postmodernen Konstellation sind die Veränderungen der

Identitäten vom Statischen zum Flüssigen, von der Eindeutigkeit zur Ambivalenz 95).

[13]Compare Sharp, "Doron Rabinovici's *Ohnehin*: Selective Memory and Multiple Pasts." Rushdie himself described the fluid concept of identity of his novel in the following words: "*The Satanic Verses* celebrates hybridity, impurity, inter-mingling, the transformation that comes of new and unexpected combinations of human beings, cultures, ideas, politics, movies, songs. It rejoices in mongrelisation and fears the absolutism of the Pure. Melange, hotchpotch, a bit of this and that is *how newness enters the world*. It is the great possibility that mass migration gives the world. And I have tried to embrace it" (A Pen 482).

Works Cited

Bair, Ethan, Anne Royer, and Jacob Teter. "Doron Rabinovici: 2002 Max Kade Writer-in-residence." *Oberlin online: Department of German Language and Literatures*. 1 p.1 Mar. 2008 <http://www.oberlin.edu/german/InsidePages/Writer/rabinovici.htm>

Beilein, Matthias. "Unter falschem Namen. Schweigen und Schuld in Doron Rabinovicis Suche nach M." *Monatshefte* 97 (2005): 250-269.

Bischof, Günter. "Victims? Perpetrators? 'Punching Bags' of European Historical Memory? The Austrians and Their World War II Legacies." *German Studies Review* 27 (2004): 17-32.

Buckl, Walter. "Verheddert in den Bandagen." Rev. of *Suche nach M.*, by Doron Rabinovici. *Tages-Anzeiger* 24 Mar. 1997.

Lorenz, Dagmar C. G. *Contemporary Jewish Writing in Austria: An Anthology*. Lincoln: University of Nebraska Press, 1999.

Lützeler, Paul Michael. "Vom Ethnozentrismus zur Multikultur: Europäische Identität heute." Multikulturalität: Tendenzen,

Probleme, Perspektiven im europäischen und internationalen Horizont. Eds. Michael Kessler and Jürgen Wertheimer. Tübingen: Stauffenberg, 1995. 91-105.
Misik, Robert, and Doron Rabinovici, eds. *Republik der Courage: wider die Verhaiderung*. Berlin: Aufbau, 2000.
Rabinovici, Doron. "Laßt die Synagoge im Dorf!" *Der Standard*. 10 Oct. 1997. 18 May 1999 <http://derstandard.at/arc/19971010/110.htm>
Rabinovici, Doron. "Literatur und Republik oder ganz Baden liest die Krone." *Was wird das Ausland dazu sagen?: Literatur und Politik in Österreich nach 1945*. Ed. Gerald Leitner. Wien: Picus, 1995. 127-139.
Rabinovici, Doron. "Der nationale Doppler." *Der Standard*. 18 October 1999. 5 Nov. 1999 <http://derstandard.at/arc/19991018/155.htm>
Rabinovici, Doron. *Ohnehin*. Frankfurt: Suhrkamp, 2004.
Rabinovici, Doron. *Papirnik. Stories*. Frankfurt: Suhrkamp, 1994.
Rabinovici, Doron. "The Right Nose." Trans. Dagmar C. G. Lorenz. *Nothing Makes You Free: Writings by Descendants of Jewish Holocaust Survivors*. Ed. Melvin Jules Bukiet. New York: W.W. Norton, 2002. 125-135.
Rabinovici, Doron. *The Search for M*. Trans. and Afterword Francis Michael Sharp. Riverside, Ca.: Ariadne, 2000.
Rabinovici, Doron. "Sie sollten es merken." Interview mit Franziska Werners und Markus Gick. *Hagalil.com* 16 Aug. 2003. 4 Mar. 2008 <http://www.hagalil.com/archiv/2003/10/rabinovici.htm>
Rabinovici, Doron. *Suche nach M.: Roman in zwölf Episoden*. Frankfurt: Suhrkamp, 1997.
Rushdie, Salman. "A Pen Against the Sword." *One World, Many Cultures*. Comp. Stuart Hirschberg. New York: Macmillan, 1992. 480-492.
Rushdie, Salman. *The Satanic Verses*. New York: Viking, 1989.

Seyhan, Azade. *Writing Outside the Nation*. Princeton: Princeton UP, 2001.

Sharp, Francis Michael. "Doron Rabinovici's *Ohnehin*: Selective Memory and Multiple Pasts." *Trans: Internet-Zeitschrift für Kulturwissenschaften* 16 (2006). 4 Mar. 2008 <http://www.inst.at/trans/16Nr/05_2/sharp16.htm>

Weidauer, Friedmann J. "'Fighting for Defeat': Jewish Identity in Postwar German and Austria" *seminar* 34:3 (1998): 280-299.

Anna Mitgutsch, *Haus der Kindheit:* Mourning, Remembrance, and Restitution

Maria-Regina Kecht

House of Childhood, translated by David Dollenmayer, New York: Other Press, 2006

In the historical process of Austrian collective remembrance of National Socialism, the year 2000 was a significant one. It was not an anniversary, but the Nazi past still had to be confronted. The formation of a center-right coalition government of the ÖVP (Austrian People's Party) and FPÖ (Austrian Freedom Party) resulted in international condemnation, EU sanctions, and the challenge for the Austrian leadership to present internationally acceptable political positions on the country's Nazi past. "It is time," so Chancellor Wolfgang Schüssel in his Statement of Government Policy of February 2000, "that we prove to all skeptical observers in Austria and abroad that we will find the right words and do the right deeds in our political decision-making."[1]

Even extremely critical observers of the political scene were stunned by the swift pace of action that the Schüssel government immediately demonstrated regarding the controversial issue of restitution. The decision to invite the representatives of the victims to the table definitely contributed to the solid basis for constructive negotiations focusing on the Slave and Forced Labor question as well as the "gaps and deficiencies" in previous restitution measures concerning aryanized property.[2] The leading Austrian negotiators, Ambassador Dr. Ernst Sucharipa (former Director of the Austrian Diplomatic Academy) and Dr. Maria Schaumayer (former President of the Austrian Federal Bank), whose integrity and good will earned international praise, took every opportunity to stress Austria's moral responsibility to compensate victims for the crimes of the Nazi years. Both made it quite clear that admission of guilt and complicity was a *sine qua non* and that any compensatory payments could not be more than a symbolic gesture – given their lateness and their inadequacy. What had been taken from the victims could not really be restituted, neither in material nor in emotional or psychological terms. The key negotiators on the Austrian side insisted that recognizing the victims' claims and offering compensation were overdue. They considered their task an obligation to make restitution (*Bringschuld*) and thus reverse the long-standing, previous practice of expecting the victims to fight for and demand their rights (*Holschuld*). Within a few months an agreement was reached; the decisions were approved and written into law by parliament; and the Fund for Reconciliation, Peace, and Cooperation generated the promised payments to the victims and their descendants. This outcome helped create a new image of Austria that contradicted the popular national myth of the victim (*Opferthese*) and, instead, adopted the more complex concept of Austria as a country of victims *and* perpetrators.[3]

Haus der Kindheit, the sixth novel by Anna Mitgutsch (1948-) could not have been more *au courant* in 2000 because on the level of plot, it deals with the aryanization of Jewish family property, the expulsion, deportation, and destruction of its owners, and with the enormous efforts of the descendants to get back what was stolen from them. No other Austrian novel specifically treats the topic of aryanization and restitution.

Readers may recall that already at the beginning of Mitgutsch's career as a writer, she attributed special significance to the question of how Austria could have become complicit in the barbarities of National Socialism. "My shame about it," Mitgutsch stated in an interview in 1989, "is actually the fundamental issue of my life; of my writing, too…I have to take up this topic almost compulsively: in every novel, and always anew, because fascism has, as we know, many faces."[4] This sociopolitical dimension was not foregrounded in her early works – from *Die Züchtigung* (1985), *Das andere Gesicht* (1986), *Ausgrenzung* (1989), to *In fremden Städten* (1992) – but became quite relevant in *Abschied von Jerusalem* (1995) and is of great importance in *Haus der Kindheit*.

Haus der Kindheit, for which Mitgutsch was awarded the *Solothurner Literaturpreis* (2001), is thematically a kind of historical documentation: the story draws upon external political reality and reflects the "gaps and deficiencies" of Austrian laws as well as the constantly deferred restitution measures in the decades following WWII; it also illustrates the conflict-ridden coexistence of Jewish and non-Jewish Austrians, who are unable to share their memories of the *Ostmark*. The novel itself – in print before Chancellor Schüssel constituted the two Austrian Commissions for the "Reconciliation Fund" and the "General Settlement Fund" – is a gesture of restitution.

Mitgutsch chooses a specifically Jewish narrative genre as her template, or *Vorlage* in the sense of pre- (rather than inter-) text, to realize her notion of genuine remembrance that would restore respect and mourning for the Jewish dead. *Haus der Kindheit* is a literary adaptation of Jewish remembrance practices and thus represents a very consciously Jewish inscription into contemporary Austrian literature.

Mitgutsch's literary exploration of modes of remembrance and their inherent power to construct identity tries to prove at all levels of her composition – thematically, structurally, and in terms of her poetics – that commemoration (*Eingedenken*) is essential for a reflective human existence. And it seems as if the author wanted to offer the Jewish memorial culture as one possible path towards such a goal.[5] Through *Haus der Kindheit* Mitgutsch makes the absence of Austrian Jews visible; she constructs a memorial to the dead and the survivors of the Shoah in the fictional provincial capital H. (but probably also in her real hometown Linz). It is a form of recognition of the contributions Jewish citizens have made to their town; and it is a book of mourning for the vanished Jewish community as well as a gesture of respect offered to all the Jewish dead who have no final resting place and have, to add insult to injury, been erased and obliterated from collective memory through a veil of silence (*Totschweigen*).

I read *Haus der Kindheit* as an adaptation of so-called *Yizker Bikher* and see Mitgutsch utilize the intent and the formal elements of this genre.[6] The Yiddish term *Yizker Bikher* refers to the remembrance texts composed predominantly by Eastern European survivors of the Shoah about their destroyed hometowns in an effort to transmit the memory of the dead to the next generations – as the Torah text from Deuteronomy exhorts them to do.

The word "yizker" comes from the Hebrew and is the first word in the phrase "yizkor elohim" ("May God remember"), which introduces memorial prayers for the dead. The supplicant appeal inscribed in these prayers is transferred to the purpose of the remembrance books in order to pay tribute to the dead of a specific community. In the late forties, *Yizker Bikher* were mostly written in Yiddish, in the following decades in Hebrew, and in the last couple of decades many have been translated into English to assure access by a wider audience.

Some scholars believe that *Yizker Bikher* as a documentation – in their depiction of Jewish life in specific towns and regions – represent the most important memorial act on the part of Shoah survivors. Often they were initiated in camps for displaced persons and continued in exile either in Israel or the United States. These remembrance books – of which there are several hundred – follow a particular compositional pattern across several sections. The content is not necessarily arranged in historical chronology but rather follows the associative stream of memory. Inevitably there is an historical account of the particular Jewish community with a focus on the time period between pre-WWI and the Shoah. Personal memories of events before WWII – often corroborated by photographs – are as much part of the *Yizker Bikher* genre as are eyewitness testimonials about the situation during Nazi occupation (from ghetto life to deportation and extermination). Furthermore, the book usually also contains a list of the deceased, which in connection with the customary cover design emphasizes the symbolic significance of *Yizker*

Bikher as paper tombs or paper burial sites. According to the Jewish Studies scholars Kugelmass and Boyarin, "Such memorials did not supersede local efforts at commemoration; they bound communities together, recreating on paper the community of the past."[7] Thus *Yizker Bikher* helped Shoah survivors at their places of exile to recall and make present their lost homeland (*Heimat*) and their community.

Experts explain the large number of *Yizker Bikher* by referring to several traditions: the Jewish texts of mourning (e.g., the biblical jeremiads), memorial books paying tribute to religious figures and community leaders (going back to the Middle Ages), and the practice of *pinkas*, a form of town chronicle which recorded special events and honorable achievements of community members. This indebtedness to a variety of different models underscores the conscious interconnectedness that *Yizker Bikher* sought to establish between the past, the present, and the future, in order to counteract the Nazis' efforts even to extinguish the memory of the crimes against the Jews. "Jews have always looked to their history for confirmation of the belief that in time all enemies are vanquished. The unequal struggle between Nazis and Jews was a struggle between those attempting to obliterate memory and those holding on to it as a guarantee of eternity...The memorial books are the fruit of the impulse to write a testament for future generations. They constitute an unprecedented, truly popular labor to record in writing as much as possible of a destroyed world."[8] *Yizkher Bikher* allowed the Shoah survivors to archive the communicative memory and in this way preserve it for posterity.

The books were intended to be more than archives, however. They also were to function as memory triggers. Leafing through them, readers were inspired to release their own memories and narrate their own stories, adding to what has been recorded. They can disrupt silences and promote dialogue. Given the increasing number of translations of *Yizker Bikher*, we can assume that there is growing interest in them among the young. Access to this sort of written legacy gives the survivors' descendants a better understanding of their own background, "providing a format for members of the post-war generation to re-explore the history and lives of lost Jewish communities, whilst simultaneously allowing them to explore their own identity in relation to that time and place."[9] The strength of identity one can draw from sharing the memory of the community's past combines the look back with one's own glance ahead, which is indispensable for any personal perspective on life.

In *Yizker Bikher* the site of origin is critical for their format of reconstructing the lost *Heimat*. Apart from photographs, there usually are also maps, sketches, etc. included so that readers gain a vivid image of life in the hometown. The graphic and visual illustrations are particularly painful in their emblematic representation of everything that has disappeared. After all, many East-European towns with Jewish communities were totally destroyed by the Nazis. "In writing [a memorial book]," the scholars Kugelmass and Boyarin comment, "a town's survivors gave it back its Jewish and human name along with the most fitting burial they could think of for an annihilated community. They erected a stone and on it they wrote all they could remember about a time and place that now exist only in memory. In so doing, they and others fulfilled an ancient and solemn obligation."[10]

Readers will recognize many of the features described above in Mitgutsch's memorial book *Haus der Kindheit*. The novel links the life story of Max Berman, an American and Austrian-Jewish emigrant, to his family's history, which again is indissolubly connected to the collective history of the town H. in Upper Austria. We can observe the family's development and fate over three generations in the course of about a hundred years – exactly the time span encompassed by communicative memory. Through Max Berman we gain access to the narratives so typical of *Yizker Bikher*: we learn about the history of the Jewish community, its suffering during the Nazi takeover, its decimation due to expulsion and extinction, and its cautious efforts of reconstruction since 1945. The novel's four sections follow the chronology of Max's life, even though by contrast, subjective time and complex temporal levels characterize each section. Each section promises a new beginning and always turns into another parting, another loss – not only because of the death of others but also because of Max's advancing age. His visits to H.– of which there are not more than three – give Max, who left the town at age five, the opportunity to pursue the goal of reclaiming the aryanized "Haus der Kindheit" and ultimately restoring the restituted property. The depiction of these stays in H. allows Mitgutsch to include in her narrative various sorts of documents: lists of household items, letters, financial contracts, bank documents, statements from political and juridical authorities, etc. Of particular significance in her memorial text is the intratext of a town chronicle that Max Berman decides to compose in order to learn more about the history of H. and its conflict-ridden relationship to the Jews, and to situate his family and himself in this context (to locate his identity). A good number of photographs – not visually but only verbally presented – become sites of memory as well as memory triggers. The town maps or graphic sketches of topography so typical of the genre of *Yizker Bikher* resurface in Mitgutsch's novel as excursions to various parts of the town as well as in the form of historical "tours" that illuminate the evolution of the town and its architecture. In this way information about Jewish communal buildings and property owned or inhabited by Jews is imparted.

An overview of the major narrative compcnents of Mitgutsch's *Haus der Kindheit* will illustrate in how many ways this is a literary "book of the dead" (*Totenbuch*) and a "memorial book" (*Gedenkbuch*).

The narrative perspective diverges from the customary stance of a Shoah survivor in the *Yizker Bikher*. Neither Mitgutsch nor her protagonist Max Berman, author of the intratext of the "chronicle," is witness to the Nazi crimes. Both, however, are inheritors of the historical trauma and its consequences. Their sense of being Jewish or rather their decision to embrace a Jewish identity – through conversion for Mitgutsch and as a result of his visits to H. for Berman – also brings with it a strong sense of following the commandment of "zakhor," (remembrance) exemplified in their texts. And their perspective is marked by "postmemory," a term coined by the literary critic Marianne Hirsch, which implies that not personally experienced but transmitted memories with strong affective impact are recalled and retained. "Postmemory characterizes the experience of those who grow up dominated by narratives that preceded their birth, whose own belated stories are evacuated by the stories of the previous generation shaped by traumatic events that can be neither understood nor recreated."[11] The "post" in Hirsch's term refers to the generational distance that separates "postmemory" from memory. She stresses that the concept applies to all secondary carriers of the memory of collective and culturally traumatic experiences. The profound and long-term impact of the transmission of such memory is the critical element which transforms the older generation's stream of images and stories about their past into quasi-autogenic memories that become an integral part of the descendant's identity.

Mitgutsch's central character, Max Berman, occupies the position of "postmemory": He considers himself American but is focused on Europe (and the past) particularly because of the extraordinary vividness of his mother's memories, her images of loss, mourning, and painful yearning transmitted to Max in countless ways. There, so he speculates, he will arrive some day; there he will belong and be at home. The images, however, no matter how colorful they are in Max's mind, do not capture reality, since there is no way the past can be retrieved and "made" present. Reluctantly Max is forced to accept that the image archive accumulated and preserved in his "postmemory" will not offer the key to the restituted house of his childhood and will not show him the way back to his hometown. Instead, it is the friction between reality and "postmemory" that motivates Max to find his very own approach towards the sites of memory in the hope that he will experience a sense of belonging. Renovating the family property, which was inhabited by strangers for almost fifty years, and composing a chronicle about the ignored history of the Jewish community of H., Max succeeds in gaining knowledge and experiences in H. that offer him his very own memories. It does not matter that this fulfillment comes late in life, but it is important that the mental substitution of images leads to a liberating recontextualization of the inherited memories and to Max's desire to transmit *his* story of the Jews in H. to the next generation.

Haus der Kindheit presents communities drawing their group identity from their shared repertory of memories: at the personal level there is the extraordinarily tight bond of memory that conjoins Max Berman and his mother Mira, whose colorful and nostalgic tales about her life in H. have profoundly shaped Max and imposed on him the goal of restitution almost as a kind of teleology. Already as a child he envisions himself as the trusted protector of his mother's dreams, which he is intent on transforming into tangible reality:

> He would be a grown-up and would send money to her in Europe. She would live in the house with the high-ceilinged sunlit rooms, sit in a wicker chair on the white terrace and eat breakfast, look out over the river and into the distance, and think of him to whom she owed it all. (16)[12]

The mother's self-destructive melancholy about her loss and her naïve desire for a happy return to their house in H. create in Max an overwhelming, a symbiotic sense of emotional connectedness to her world and thus to the Austrian *Heimat*. Her recurrent exhortation not ever to let go of memories – because "memories were the one thing you couldn't lose" (3) ("dass die Erinnerungen das einzige waren, was einem nicht verloren gehen konnte" [7]) – becomes an absolute mandate for Max governing his choices, his decisions, and shaping his identity. The memorial community that Mitgutsch creates here in the family circle is quite typical of the transgenerational experience of exile. The loss of "the world of yesterday" and the refusal, as in Mira's case, to adjust to the alien, new environment burden the immediate family members – even if they are still children – with the onerous task of contributing to the construction of a retrospective mirage and create an alternative reality that allows to ignore the present circumstances.

This biographical model of a memorial community that exerts great influence on its members and gives them strength is supplemented in Mitgutsch's novel by a depiction of a larger (and historical) collective confronted with loss and painful memories. The small Jewish community of H. – consisting primarily of Shoah survivors – has to maintain its practice of remembrance in a social setting that constantly provokes counter-memory. Their rituals, celebrations, and shared historical experiences support their sense of identity, despite or because of their marginal position:

> They all had similar life stories and no relatives except for the immediate families they themselves had founded forty, forty-five years ago, most of them here in this town, in a camp for DPs, in transit. They had ended up staying. Their recollections of earlier times had to leap over a longer and longer span of time. The life they told stories about lay far in the past (158).[13]

Life in H. means life in a diaspora for the Jewish citizens because neither their German nor their local dialect can turn them into native local citizens (*Einheimische*); they remain a minority whose collective experience is not integrated into the social and cultural memory of H. Their relationship to H. characterizes the town as *Gedenkort* (memorial place). In contrast, the predominantly non-Jewish community of H., who makes claims to the town as *Generationenort* (generational place), shares a completely different set of memories that do not include even traces of a Jewish presence. As is the case in *Yizker Bikher*, Mitgutsch's novel offers the contradictory communities without any intention of balance. The focus rests on the Jewish population and their life, whereas the non-Jewish inhabitants of H. are presented only in their relation to their Jewish fellow citizens – a relationship filled with distrust and prejudice.

The town of H. presents itself as an emotionally laden site of memory as much as it also embodies an urban space that has renewed itself repeatedly through eradication of past architectural layers. It offers a topography of remembrance as well as forgetting – depending on one's point of view. Most inhabitants consider H. their property-like *Generationenort*, which the cultural historian Aleida Assmann defines as a place "to which families or groups have a long-term bond. From this a close relationship between people and place develops. The place shapes the peoples' modes of life and their experiences as much as the people affect the place with their traditions and their history."[14] This sort of mutual influence of place and people generates a sense of belonging and affinity for one's home (*Heimatgefühl*), which are based on normative cultural memories.

If continuity characterizes the nature of a *Generationenort*, it is discontinuity – the radical difference between the past and the present – that is typical of a *Gedenkort*. However, the relics of this ruptured historical flow are present, even if no connection is established between them and their current surroundings, even if they are overlooked and ignored. Thanks to Max's own curiosity and his friend's, Arthur Spitzer's, insistence on remembrance, or in the Austrian context perhaps countermemory, these relics of the local Jewish history spanning centuries are re-contextualized and transform H. into a "memorial landscape" (*Memoriallandschaft*) just as if a map had been overlaid by the parameters of memory-referencing similar to the use of global positioning so crucial in today's reconstruction of historical cityscapes. We accompany the two fictional characters on their strolls through H. and learn which stores on the main street used to belong to Jewish families, which property was never returned to their owners after theft and murder, which houses were erected on Jewish cemeteries, which prayer halls were razed, on which façades one can still discern Hebrew inscriptions, and how a close look at Jewish gravestones reveals the suppressed history of the Jews of H. Even though these discoveries serve as impulses for shared communicative memory within the narrative, they are of no consequence to the majority's awareness of the past. Only within the circle of those sharing the historical discontinuity do the urban lacunae become visible as traces of destruction.

We can certainly also consider Max's childhood home as a *Gedenkort,* a space and site marked by historical discontinuity. Almost fifty years of illegal ownership disrupted the connection of the families Berman and Kalisch to their own property that had provided the setting for social bonding and family traditions before emigration, deportation, and death intervened. Like the town of H, the house accommodates multiple historical sediments that depend on people's memory in order to emerge and become visible or legible. The process of aryanization takes Max's family property out of the purely personal realm and places it into public, collective history – thus giving the process of restitution and the ensuing restoration of the house symbolic significance. This is also how we have to interpret Max's strenuous renovation efforts that go far beyond the mere physical project. He is intent on removing all traces of memory the illegal residents have left behind so that the restored dwelling might reconnect with the past or at least with his mental images of that past. This sort of emotional restitution is intricately linked to Max's construction of his very own memory space – even if he has to realize that what has been lost cannot be retrieved, cannot be restored or restituted: "The house of his childhood could not be regained. The more progress his restoration was making, the more faded the old images became: "But the house of his childhood was not retrievable. The further his renovations progressed, the more the old images faded (209)."[15] The fading of these emotionally so powerful images of his childhood in this house give way to a mature approach that allows Max to create social connections and fill his house with a community spirit, which promotes – at least ephemerally and as a *mémoire involuntaire* – an experience conjuring up transgenerational continuity and a sense of belonging. Occasionally then, his house transforms itself from a mere *lieu de mémoire* into a *milieu de mémoire*.[16]

As I have mentioned earlier, the genre of *Yizker Bikher* always includes photographic documents of the (vanished) Jewish community and a sort of chronology of events that occurred in this community. Both types of historical accounts and reconstruction give rise to memory at the individual and collective levels. Both media of materialized remembrance – pictures and writing – offer a *memento mori* and draw the dead closer to the living. Mitgutsch adopts these memorial practices in her composition of *Haus der Kindheit* and effects in her protagonists an emotional connection to the past. We readers can, in turn, surmise the impact of an affective relationship to history.

The purely textually presented pictures of the house and the family serve as memory trigger as well as memory archive, and at the same time exemplify the significance attributed to photography *per se*, namely their intrinsic gesture of mourning and loss for what once was and no longer is. Theories of photography – from Kracauer and Benjamin to Barthes and Sontag or Bourdieu – agree, as we know, on the notion that the photographic medium is filled with an aura of death because photos always represent a particular point in time. They are "uncanny tomb[s] of our memory,"[17] from which the dead rise. In that sense death is the *eidos* of photography. Through detailed description of the photographs in *Haus der Kindheit* Mitgutsch determines perspective and interpretation. We cannot "see" anything else than that which she verbally presents. The narrative voice directs our own view and understanding, no matter whether we are presented with family portraits, photos in books or exhibits, or documentary visuals. Various kinds of photos are included throughout the narrative, but their number and importance is greatest at the beginning and the end of the novel. Thematically we follow a panorama that starts with the prominent representation of the family's house, then leads to portraits of the family and to snapshots of family members, moves on to a series of photographs with artistic claims, and concludes – after our leafing through a photo album of a Polish-Jewish family – with pictures of abandoned and forgotten Jewish cemeteries in Eastern Europe. Thus, even in content, we never leave the circle of death, even if the central observer of these photos, Max Berman, is only gradually capable of perceiving his own mortality reflected in the pictures.

The sequence of pictures that Mitgutsch assembles for her readers corresponds in theme and metaphorical significance to the function of *Yizker Bikher*. The photos illustrate the life of a lost community, they represent the vanished "world of yesterday," and they evoke the memory of those who are deceased. The pictures are substitutes for non-existing gravesites and for collective mourning rituals that could never take place. They tell a history – "a history of ghosts and shadows."[18] Inscribed in text and pictures of *Haus der Kindheit* is Mitgutsch's desire to let the reality of the life of the forgotten Jews arise from the "history of ghosts and shadows" so that it would continue at least in our memory.

The last essential element of Mitgutsch's literary version of *Yizker Bikher* to be mentioned here is the fascinating intratext of Max's own chronicle of the history of the Jews in the town of H. The chronicle allows readers to embed the specific history of Max's family in the communal experience of Jews settling in H. since the Middle Ages. This correlation between the individual and the collective is most influential in Max's acceptance of his Jewish identity. Only through his archival research in H. does he gain an understanding of the local Jewish history, which allows him to place his family's fate in a century-long chain of discrimination and persecution. Max is challenged to take a stance and confirm his place inside the Jewish community. This admission of a specific identity position is an unexpected outcome of Max's undertaking. His motivation stems from his irritation about the complete absence of the historical presence of Jews in the official accounts of the history of H. Writing a counter-history in German, in his mother-tongue, becomes a monumentally important responsibility for Max – and instead of imitating abstract historiography, he is intent on composing a vivid, authentic account of Jewish life in H.: "Actually, I've come up with a special kind of historiography for myself...life stories, the fates of individuals that are illuminated for a mere moment when measured in historical time, sometimes only at the moment of their death" (238).[19]

This undertaking turns Max into the sort of historian that the British social scientist Peter Burke postulates, someone who is a "remembrancer" – and he refers to the term in its earlier euphemistic use for a civil servant who was assigned to collect debts, who would go and remind others of that which they preferred to forget – a debt-collector (*Schuldeneintreiber*).[20] As Max wants to supplement the missing history about the Jews in H. and thus archive the victims' memory in writing, he compels the Christian inhabitants of H. to remember their guilt (*Schuld*). Preserving the victims' memory in writing allows the extension of communicative, generational memory; the record may enter cultural memory and contribute to its evolution.

This intellectual-analytical approach towards H. and its history, which Max decides upon quite spontaneously only during his last and longest sojourn in Austria, is a counterpoint to his previous, emotionally laden "postmemory" relationship to H. His thorough archival research and the serious commitment that Max brings to this project transform ideas propelled by personal curiosity into a compelling assignment benefiting others. He works on the chronicle "for the Jews who will live here in twenty or fifty years. Just so people know that there were Jews here from the beginning. So they can't forget it anymore" (239).[21] Through the chronicle Max also fulfills the commandment of "zakhor" – transmitting the history of the Jews to the succeeding generations. Through this chronicle that Max calls his "appointed task of my final years" (245) ("Lebensaufgabe [s]einer letzten Jahre" [266]), he succeeds in endowing his stay in H. with a meaning and a mission far exceeding the original purpose of restoring and inhabiting his family's house.

In a way we can also consider Max's chronicle a form of restitution: his narrative of counter-memory transforms barely legible traces into a well-documented illustration of the existence of a Jewish community. The writing process permits Max to establish connections to this community and consciously adopt his Jewish identity that he had ignored for a long time. Only his written legacy for the collective, in fact, makes Max's return to the home of his childhood possible – as a restitution of his belonging to the world of his Jewish ancestors. Mitgutsch assigns her protagonist the responsibility of a chronicler, who has preserved the Jewish tradition of *pinkas* (keeping a town chronicle), which she, as the author, incorporates as a quasi-separate text genre and supplement to her literary version of *Yizker Bikher*.

Haus der Kindheit is a multilayered memorial text, where individual, collective, and cultural memories are expressed. Aesthetically Mitgutsch devises associative streams of memory that transcend time and space, that bring the past to the fore, and conjoin the present moment with a long forgotten past – even though there is a chronology underlying the narrative course of events.

Documented history – the rule of the Nazis and their practice of aryanization as well as the restoration of the Austrian Republic after 1945 and its prolonged and procrastinated legal process of restitution – provides the core material for the literary work of remembrance, which Mitgutsch proposes as a medium for greater insight and understanding. The aesthetic shaping of remembrance is intended to offer truth that cannot be found in factual reality. Only when the authenticity of memory emerges from the literary language, Mitgutsch stated in her Graz lectures on poetics, only when this memory is "generally valid and understandable as something that the reader can accept as her very own truth [allgemeingültig und nachvollziehbar als etwas, das sich der Leser als seine eigene Wahrheit aneignen kann],"[22] has the author's creative intention been realized.

Mitgutsch places her novel in the context of the Jewish tradition of "zakhor" and borrows from the specifically Jewish genre of *Yizker Bikher* in order to inscribe the history of Austrian Jews in contemporary Austrian literature and to position herself as a writer with Jewish remembrance practices. In her literary recognition of Jewish memorial traditions, Mitgutsch creates a space for the Jewish victims of National Socialism – perhaps not just in the canon of contemporary Austrian literature but also in the national memory – so that these victims would not be forgotten again, and commemoration (*Eingedenken*) would indeed be restituted.

The text emphasizes remembrance as a moral responsibility, without which we could not possibly define our own identity. If we develop a reflective approach towards history and recognize the validity of the memory victims have preserved, we ought to be capable of creating a genuine dialogue across generations and ideological differences. In this way new *Erinerungsgemeinschaften* – communities with a repertory of shared memories – could be formed, and suppression, silence, and denials overcome.

Endnotes

[1] "Es ist Zeit, die Skeptiker im In- und Ausland durch eine Politik der richtigen Taten und der richtigen Worte zu überzeugen." One can download the statement as a pdf document from the website http://www.demokratiezentrum.org/media/pdf/regierungserklaeung.pdf

[2] See Gunther Bischof, "'Watschenmann der europäischen Erinnerung'? Internationales Image und Vergangenheitspolitik der Schüssel/Riess-Passer – ÖVP/FPÖ – Koalitionsregierung," in Michael Gehler et al., eds. *Österreich in der Europäischen Union. Bilanz seiner Mitgliedschaft* (Wien, Köln, Weimar: Böhlau, 2003) 445-478: "Die vormaligen Opfer als ehrenwerte und gleichwertige Verhandlungspartner zu akzeptieren erlaubt

ihre 'moralische Restauration' und macht die Versöhnung erst möglich. Zudem wird ihnen ein ebenbürtiger Platz im nationalen Geschichtsnarrativ zugestanden" (461).

[3] Bischof 470.

[4] "Die Scham darüber ist eigentlich das Grundthema meines ganzen Lebens. Auch meines Schreibens...Dieses Thema muß ich immer fast zwanghaft angehen. In jedem Roman immer aufs neue. Denn der Faschismus hat ja viele Gesichter." In Andrea Kunne, "Im Gespräch mit Anna Mitgutsch," *Deutsche Bücher* 19.1 (1989): 18.

[5] The significance of remembrance derives from the Bible, particularly from the Book of Deuteronomy, which describes the Covenant between God and Israel. The mandate to remember, which God imposes on the Jewish people – so that they would never forget His divine interventions in their history or fate – is an absolute one. This mandate is to be preserved by means of rituals and traditions. No other people have a religious law prescribing remembrance. The cultural historian Jan Assmann observes, "Im Deuteronomium erscheint das Gesetz als eine zeitlose, für immer gültige, eine für allemal erlassene Ordnung, die von Ewigkeit zu Ewigkeit besteht, aber in einem bestimmten geschichtlichen Augenblick dem erwählten Volk ‚gegeben', das heißt offenbart wurde...Das Deuteronomium nennt nicht weniger als sieben verschiedene Verfahren kulturell geformter Erinnerung." See his „Erinnern, um dazuzugehören. Kulturelles Gedächtnis, Zugehörigkeitsstruktur und normative Vergangenheit" in Kristin Platt und Mihram Dabag, eds. *Generation und Gedächtnis: Erinnerungen und kollektive Identitäten* (Opladen: Leske und Budrich, 1995) 51-75, here 69.

[6] In the existing scholarly responses to *Haus der Kindheit*, the topic of memory and remembrance is addressed in a more or less thorough fashion. No critic has made a connection between Mitgutsch's novel and Jewish memorial practices. For different, topically relevant readings of *Haus der Kindheit*, see Kristin Teuchtmann, "Zur Darstellbarkeit der Zeit: Erinnerung und Er-

findung in Anna Mitgutschs *Die Züchtigung* und *Das Haus der Kindheit"* in *Modern Austrian Literature* 35.1//2 (2002): 43-61; Monika Shafi, "'Enteignung' und 'Behaustheit': Zu Anna Mitgutschs Roman *Haus der Kindheit"* in *Modern Austrian Literature* 36.1/2 (2003): 33-51; Günther Höfler, "Memories are made of this: Ein Buch des Erinnerns. Nachbemerkungen zu Anna Mitgutsch; *Haus der Kindheit"* in *Informationen zur Deutschdidaktik (IDE)* 27.1 (2003): 97-100; Julia Neissl, "'Manchmal ist das Thema mit einem Roman noch lange nicht erschöpft.' Autobiographische Erfahrungen und kollektive Erinnerungsspur in Texten von Anna Mitgutsch," in Hildegard Kernmayer und Petra Ganglbauer, Eds. *Schreibweisen. Poetologien. Die Postmoderne in der österreichischen Literatur von Frauen* (Wien: Milena, 2003) 379-396; und Christa Gürtler, "Abschied von einem fremden Haus" in *Die Rampe* (2004): 73-76.

[7] Jack Kugelmass and Jonathan Boyarin, ed. *From a Ruined Garden. The Memorial Books of Polish Jewry* (Bloomington, IN: Indiana UP, 1998) 10.

[8] *From a Ruined Garden*, 17.

[9] Katharina Hall, "Jewish Memory in Exile: The Relation of W.G. Sebald's *Die Ausgewanderten* to the Tradition of the Yizkor Books," in Pól Ó Dochartaigh, ed. *Jews in German Literature since 1945: German-Jewish Literature?* (Amsterdam: Rodopi, 2000) 153-164, here 153.

[10] *From a Ruined Garden*, 43.

[11] Marianne Hirsch, *Family Frames: Photography, Narrative, and Postmemory* (Cambridge, Massachusetts: Harvard UP, 1997) 22.

[12] "Er würde erwachsen sein und ihr Geld nach Europa schicken, sie würde in dem Haus mit seinen hohen hellen Räumen wohnen, morgens auf der weißen Terrasse in einem Korbstuhl frühstücken und über den Fluss in die Ferne blicken und an ihn denken, dem sie dies alles verdankte." Anna Mitgutsch, *Haus der Kindheit* (München: DTV, 2002) 22.

[13] "Sie alle hatten Geschichten, die sich ähnelten, und keine Angehörigen außer der Familie, die sie selber vor vierzig, fündundvierzig Jahren gegründet hatten, meist hier, in dieser Stadt, in einem DP-Lager, auf der Durchreise. Dann waren sie geblieben. Ihre Erinnerungen an früher mussten immer größere Zeiträume überspringen, das Leben, von dem sie erzählten, lag weit in der Vergangenheit" (175).

[14] "[Die Bedeutung eines solchen Generationenortes entsteht] mit einer langfristigen Bindung von Familien oder Gruppen an einen bestimmten Ort. Dabei entsteht ein enges Verhältnis zwischen Menschen und geographischem Ort: Dieser bestimmt die Lebens- und Erfahrungsformen der Menschen ebenso, wie diese den Ort mit ihrer Tradition und Geschichte imprägnieren." Aleida Assmann, *Der lange Schatten der Vergangenheit: Erinnerungskultur und Geschichtspolitik* (München: Beck, 2006) 309.

[15] "Das Haus seiner Kindheit ließ sich nicht zurückgewinnen. Je weiter die Restaurierungsarbeiten voranschritten, desto mehr verblassten die alten Bilder" (227).

[16] This well-known distinction was made by Pierre Nora in his book *Zwischen Geschichte und Gedächtnis*. Transl. Wolfgang Kaiser (Berlin: Wagenbach, 1990). Nora is convinced that we have reached the end of an authentic memorial culture because we have lost our inner connection to the past. Instead, we establish a multitude of ways that may give us access to the past. According to Nora, there are so many memorial sites and memorial events exactly because there is no continuous relationship to remembrance as an authentic experience. Previously existing *milieux de mémoire* have become mere *lieux de mémoire*.

[17] Eduardo Cadava, "Words of Light: Theses on the Photography of History," *Diacritics*, 22. 3/4 (1992): 84-114. Here 92.

[18] Cadava 90.

[19] "Eigentlich stelle ich mir eine besondere Form von Geschichtsschreibung vor...Lebensläufe, Einzelschicksale, die nur

für Augenblicke, in historischer Zeit gemessen, ans Licht getreten sind, manchmal nur im Augenblick ihres Todes" (259).
[20]Peter Burke, "Geschichte als soziales Gedächtnis," in Aleida Assmann und Dietrich Harth, eds. *Mnemosyne: Formen und Funktionen der kulturellen Erinnerung* (Frankfurt: Fischer 1991) 289-304, here 302.
[21]"Für die Juden, die in zwanzig oder fünfzig Jahren hier leben werden. Einfach damit man weiß, daß es hier Juden gegeben hat, seit es diese Stadt gibt. Damit man es nicht mehr vergessen kann" (259).
[22]Anna Mitgutsch. *Erinnern und Erfinden. Grazer Poetik Vorlesungen* (Graz: Droschl, 1999) 11.

Julian Schutting's *Am Morgen vor der Reise*:
A Playfully Serious Postmodern EXCURSION through
Childhood in Post-War Austria

Angela Gulielmetti

The Morning before the Journey, translated by Barbara Zeisl
Schoenberg, Ariadne Press, 1999

Neither a newcomer to, nor an expert in, Julian Schutting's (1937-)[1] works would be surprised that the author titled his two volumes of lectures on poetics, *Zuhörerbehellingungen* (1990, "Inspiring My Listeners") and *Leserbelästigungen* (1993, "Bothering My Readers").[2] An initial glance at Schutting's work – from the non-traditional layout of paragraphs to a distinctive abrogation of standard rules of punctuation to linguistic complexity at phonemic, morphemic, lexemic, semantic, and syntactical levels – reveals a literature that (self-)consciously makes great demands on the reader to engage personally *with* the text and to actively participate in the construction *of* the text.

In *Zuhörerbelligungen* Schutting contests the traditional conception of a poem as a rarified, static, literary artifact or accomplishment of an individual and poses it instead as the starting point for an infinite number of artistic expressions. A poem represents a mere "plaything" (*Spielmaterial*) that readers can reformulate, reinterpret, and reconstitute for themselves. A former teacher, Schutting proffers future prospects in his audience at the University of Graz "a little help with befriending *Gymnasium* students with poems" ("eine kleine Hilfe, wie Gymnasiasten mit Gedichten zu befreunden wären"). Schutting's choice of the words "plaything" and "befriend" offers insight into not only his avowed aesthetics of poetry, but also into his "preference for childlike theorizing" ("Vorliebe für kindisches Theoretisieren") (ZB5). In *Leserbelästigungen* he credits his development as a writer *not* to his formal education in history and *Germanistik*, but rather to "childhood moments" (*Kindheitsaugenblicke*). He encourages his readers to take mental leave of their education and instead "discover" anew for themselves the philosophy and psychology of language, as well as aesthetics and logic. Innate childlike curiosity ("Sinn für das Kuriose") (*LB*5), rather than the prescriptive structures of academe should guide their interaction with and interpretation of literature – poetry and prose alike.

Precisely this call for a highly self-conscious *rejuvenation* of aesthetic experience and moral consciousness underlies *The Morning before the Journey* (1978).[3] In the foreword Schutting describes the work as "a kind of love story between two grownups, who, no matter how much they still love each other as adults, have difficulty accepting the fact that they never knew each other as children – thus the story of their imaginations, how they might have experienced the kinds of things together as children which they only recently have found out about each other...if only..."[4]

This shared act of imagining allows the adult lovers to explore together the world through the lens of a child, marvel in its wonders and idiosyncrasies, and ponder its contradictions, cruelties, and seemingly inexplicable complexities, without the taint of socially mandated forms of observation and categories of probation. More like protagonists in a picaresque novel than a German *Bildungs-* or *Entwicklungsroman*,[5] the siblings, Stephan and Judith,[6] approach the world playfully and without guile, and their childlike observations proffer a satirical portrait of many aspects of contemporary Austrian society, including generational issues of authority and power, the role of the Church, the country's enduring silence about its Nazi past, and lingering anti-Semitism. Like Oscar Matzerath in Günter Grass's *The Tin Drum* (*Die Blechtrommel*, 1959), the two observe the adult world from a critical distance and make the conscious decision to delay the journey into adulthood. The book thus ends with a discussion of Judith's dream in which she visualized their peaceful sleep on the beach threatened by oncoming cold – a cold which would force them to leave the safe world of childhood and enter into adulthood.

The protagonists challenge and ultimately reject not merely adulthood, but specifically adulthood in Austria. Geographic and historical references to Austria and its past abound and firmly anchor the children's experience within a specifically Austrian framework. Therefore, the children's rejection of adulthood should be read as an exploration of the dark side of contemporary, post-World War II Austrian society. Surprisingly, many critics have argued that the tone of the work is politically and morally neutral, if not innocuous. Harriet Murphy, for example, finds the work "indifferent to evil, to corruption, to the dark side of life." Murphy asserts further that the "story's exploration of anything resembling corruption is perfunctory. An awareness of the possible complexity of socio-political issues seems to be lacking" especially in comparison with Schutting's early poetry.[7] Although Murphy recognizes the power struggle between the main characters and adult figures of authority and correctly locates in the children's resistance to entering adulthood a subversive challenge to "authority outside the self" and a source of "power, strength and happiness within and between other like-minded selves,"[8] she overlooks the very highly-charged nature of Schutting's criticism of Austria's long-maintained silence about its role in the Nazi era or his related challenge to parental, societal, an church authority. She does not see their act of subversion as a real political or social challenge to the norms of Austrian society. Murphy thus incorrectly terms the work an expression of Schutting's "deeply felt conservatism," which is "not fashionable at the present time." Such conservatism, she contends, robs Schutting of the "international endorsement" given to contemporary Austrian writers such as Anna Mitgutsch, Brigitte Schwaiger, and Peter Turrini whose "predictable 'radical critiques' of contemporary or near-contemporary life rely so heavily on aggressive ideas about victims and aggressors, in roughly the same way that they are aggressively opposed to the very idea of the kind of self-conscious literary language pursued by Schutting."[9] In a later blistering essay detailing and, indeed, condemning what she perceives as Schutting's descent into an "actively anti-clerical writer" in later works dealing with the Church and issues of faith, Murphy draws a radically different conclusion about Schutting's prose and compares him more closely to Gerhard Roth, whom she dismisses as a "Viennese intellectual who continues to create a position for himself within Austrian culture as 'Conscience of the Nation" whose "glib and dismissive postures" against the Church she finds sensationalist and irresponsible.[10] Given that Roth represents one of the first Austrian authors to address critically the issue of Austria's enduring silence about its role in Nazi atrocities, it becomes clear that Murphy is disturbed by Schutting's determination to challenge the silence of the Church about its complacency during the Nazi era.[11] Notably, Murphy no longer praises Schutting's "self-conscious literary language" but charges him with offsetting the "practice of religion" with the "religion of letters."[12] The numerous anti-Catholic polemics in his work represent a form of "heresy,"[13] "arid nihilism,"[14] and merely a private, self-serving agenda to display his virtuoso literary talents in order to "ride roughshod over tradition, truth and meaning."[15] She concludes her analysis with an emphatic denouncement: "Schutting's contribution to the debate about the value and function of Catholicism is sterile and bankrupt because of his own prior commitment to literature and to literary posterity."[16]

Remarkably, however, Murphy reaffirms her assessment of the work as non-polemical, terming it Schutting's most "sympathetic and least controversial treatment of Catholicism," a work in which the children's sentimental imagining of Church sacraments and figures represents but innocent child-play rather than blasphemy and the Austrian Church represents a "source of imaginative delights." This work, Murphy maintains, continues to stand in stark contrast to his more recent work which is "postmodernist...often with an anarchic effect and purpose."[17] In fact, Schutting's "self-conscious literary language" in *The Morning before the Journey* does not reveal a conservative, sentimental embrace of contemporary Austria and, in particular, the Church, but on the contrary, represents a playful, yet no less critical, postmodern challenge to the pillars of Austrian society and wages what Hermann Herzmann describes in Schutting's prose and political poems as a "war on the danger of amnesia" about Austria's past.[18]

That Murphy does not recognize the postmodern elements is not surprising. As Hanns-Josef Ortheil, Ingeborg Hoesterey, and Paul Michael Lützeler[19] all note, academic interest in or, indeed, recognition of postmodernism came late to German-speaking countries and its early reception proved anything but laudatory. Ortheil references Joachim Fest's well-known disparagement of the offerings of the *Buchmesse* in 1981, "Bücher, Bücher, aber nichts zu lesen" as representative of the vehement rejection of works with postmodern elements. Despite more than 50,000 new publications in 1981 and accolades by numerous literary critics of new releases, Fest asserts the inferior nature of such literature by paraphrasing Karl Kraus's well-known, but certainly tongue-in-cheek, lament about the "unmistakable" disparity between the quality of literary criticism and that of literature itself.[20] The "crisis" of contemporary literature expresses itself in part in the rejection of literary traditions, the narcissistic tone of works full of painfully personal excursions into strained generational relationships, a tedious exploration of the mundane and, ultimately, the authors' inability to tell "poetically" and "artistically" a good story.[21]

Ortheil recognizes in Fest's vociferous condemnation a rejection of increasingly postmodern elements in contemporary German literature, which Ortheil traces back to movement away from "traditional" narrative in the post-war years and, in particular, to the student movement of the late 1960s. Authors such as Peter Handke and Rolf Dieter Brinkmann sought to give societal protest an equally critical, literary voice.[22] Drawing inspiration from the experimental *nouveau roman* and modern theories of language and linguistics, Handke, among others, embraced what Ortheil terms the provocative effect of exposure (*Entlarvungs-*

effekt) of deconstructive literary techniques through which he demasked the ritualized "language games" through which societies defined themselves.[23] Ortheil recognizes in the movements of post-historicism, post-modernism, and post-colonialism, a further "branching out" (*Verästelungen*) of literary discourses which challenged long-standing beliefs about society, subjectivity, reason, history, and progress, i.e. what Jean-François Lyotard terms the "grand narratives" or "master narratives" of a society.[24] The very difficulty scholars have in defining postmodern literature – Hoesterey deems it a "hydra-headed monster"[25] – bespeaks the complexity and plurality of discourse that expresses itself through the breaking of traditional literary and linguistic boundaries and the embrace of multiple possibilities of meaning, which Lützeler terms "openly admitted uncertainty."[26] Published in 1978, a scant three years before Fest's famous lament, *The Morning before the Journey* proves fraught with such "openly admitted uncertainty" and represents linguistically, structurally, and thematically one of the earliest works of postmodern Austrian literature to participate in that which Lützeler views as central to postmodern literature: a playful "a dialogue with history."[27] The remainder of this essay addresses the postmodern reflections in Schutting's insistence on the innate political nature of writing, his conception of textual *author*ity and the role of the reader, his questioning of Enlightenment sensibilities of individual subjectivity and, finally, a palpable skepticism toward authority figures.

Schutting reveals as his ultimate goal the provocation of the listener/reader to a raised consciousness of the world and proclaims unequivocally the impossibility of apolitical or nonpolitical works. He expresses his wish to inspire in his listeners a new consciousness of their world (*ZB*5) and insists that a work of art cannot separate itself completely from "reality" (*Wirklichkeit*). Art's goal is to make political the "apolitical," to offer alternative rules of engagement and to discern – and make known – the essence of a reality that can be measured *only* by artistic sensibilities.[28] Schutting also stresses the responsibility of the artist to explore critically the past and to reveal the abiding presence of past sensibilities in the present day and, ultimately, to prevent the repeat of past atrocities. The artist must, therefore, be skeptical of the "appearance of reality," minutely examine the mundane and seemingly harmless – Schutting often refers to his writing as a form of "vivisection" – and seek to uncover both private and collective fears of individuals and societies. In particular, one must be alert to the fact that the crimes of the past may not only return, but may already be present. Schutting's insistent call for a political, historical consciousness clearly corresponds to what Linda Hutcheon considers basic tenets of postmodernism, namely its "fundamentally contradictory, resolutely historical, and inescapable political" nature and its resolute recognition of the enduring "presence of the past."[29]

Schutting makes evident the presence of the past not only thematically but also in the complex language constructions he creates, which often lack an indicative verb form that specifies time. Bartsch writes of the "language irritations" that abound in Schutting's work and, in particular, points out his generous use of parentheses, and a plethora of convoluted hypotactic, as well as participial and infinitive constructions. The overt "agrammaticality" (*Agrammakalität*) of his sentences produces an "indefinite, yet very palpable sense of uneasiness."[30] Bartsch argues that what he terms Schutting's "spiritual instinct for play" (*vergeistigter Spieltrieb*) represents not an empty-gestured virtuoso play with language for its own sake, but rather a means of intensifying the reader's experience and, therefore, forcing him/her to engage directly with the text. Thus, Schutting explores and exploits the relationship between word and reality (*Wort und Wirklichkeit*) on every possible level, be it syntactic, semantic or pragmatic.[31]

Citing Schutting's own representation of his language as a form of "more or less senseless playing about," Waltraud Maierhofer offers an analysis and register of Schutting's various forms of word play that includes the conscious elimination of particular parts of speech at varying junctures in a sentence, repetitions, and play with visual images and sounds to force the reader to engage intensely and personally with the text in order to endow it with meaning.[32] The seemingly disjointed, non-grammatical array of images is especially apparent in STREETS (STRAßEN), which offers the reader a wealth of richly visual words with no clearly elucidated relationship to one another. Thus, one of the children poses a rapid-fire series of questions more evocative of free association than linear storytelling:

> how does the Venetian mouth of the canal get so
> close to the arm of the Danube? What business
> does that dog have in Tiger Street, and where's
> the tiger after which it's named – did it come
> from Circus street and then creep into Blood
> Street? (17)[33]

The reference to body parts (mouth/arm), geographical disorientation (Venice, Danube), species confusion (dog/tiger) and association of "Circus" with "Blood" does not further a story line, but instead challenges the reader to search his/her own experience with these words and attempt to establish for himself or herself a relationship between the words themselves and what they represent.

As noted above, Schutting desires to expose the hidden collective fear of a society and bring to light the lingering of the past in the present. Grammatically, he creates what Mike Rogers terms an "eternal simultaneity" (*ewige Gleichzeitigkeit*) [34] through an associative method such as that seen in STREETS predominantly in the present tense and in which no one action need precede another in a linear time frame.[35] Schutting further creates this experience of timelessness, as Sigrid Schmid notes, through his extensive use of the "modal field" (*Modalfeld*) including the subjunctive, modal verbs, modal adverbs, and 'as-if' sentences.[36] Lützeler has noted the preference of postmodernism for such "as-if" structures for their liberating effects: authors can play and conjecture without the burden of proffering "truth" to their assertions or ponderings.[37] Schutting reveals that he believes that this "as-if" condition represents the very core of the creative process: "The laws of art are different from the laws of life. The basic situation of the poet is the 'as if' condition. In these 'as if' moments, reality is transformed into art."[38] Herzmann notes that as the "mode of potentiality," the subjunctive represents a "fusion (contamination) of different levels of time." Heightening this experience of timelessness or, at the very least, indistinct time, is, as Sigrid Schmid notes, the extensive use of the present tense or participial and infinitive constructions, void of tense markers.[39] Such conditional "as-if" and other subjunctive constructions abound as well, from the preface in which Schutting introduces the lovers' imaginative exploration of their childhood *as if* they had been brother and sister to the very last scene in which Stephan exclaims it were "as if" seagulls had awakened him so that he might hear Judith's desire that they remain children just a bit longer.

The very title of Schutting's work on poetics, *Leserbelästigungen* ("Bothering My Readers") already reveals insights into his view of textual authority. The "bothering or irritation of the reader" to which Schutting refers inheres in the very active participation required of the reader to constitute his or her own text from the array of possible meanings offered by the author. Rogers explains that Schutting conceives of literature "as the communal and democratic creation, by the reading public and the writing author, of a multiplicity of associative meanings on the basis of a linguistic work of art."[40] Schutting expresses his utmost respect for and confidence in the reader's ability to discern the meaning of the text without the author having to follow rules of grammar that demand, for instance, the inclusion of a subject and predicate.[41]

In reference to Schutting's poetry, Bushell discusses the complexity of the language and recognizes that the reader requires "considerable tenacity...to break into the poem's own internal cycle of justification," (13) a sentiment echoed by many literary scholars of Schutting's poetry[42] and clearly recognized by Schutting, who urges his readers to read aloud what he terms the "slalom course" of his texts (*ZB* 108)[43] until they find the proper rhythm that aids in their interpretation. Of *The Morning before the Journey*, Murphy notes the extreme demands the work makes on "a reader's ability to concentrate and create order out of chaos."[44] One of the most challenging aspects of the text is discerning who is speaking at any particular point. It often becomes clear only at the very end of the utterance and at other times the speaker/subject is never revealed. Margarete Lamb-Faffelberger notes the author's tendency toward a "linguistic" blurring of the identity of subject (*Entsubjektivierung*) through an abundant use of the gender-free pronoun "they" as opposed to "he" or "she," as well as the pronouns "I" and "you," and the essential interchangeability of Judith and Stephan.[45] Entire passages omit the children's names and in the dialogue it is impossible to discern who is uttering which lines. Indeed, it is often unclear if both the children are speaking at all. In DREAM-ING UP EXCUSES (ENTSCHULDIGUNGEN AUSDENKEN), for instance, "I" represents the only subject pronoun used and no linguistic or textual clues indicate if one or both children is/are speaking making it impossible for the reader to attribute the feelings and experienced expressed to either child. This uncertainty leaves the reader with the sense that the characters are interchangeable or at least involved in a dynamic process of identity formation that renders moot the question of who is speaking. Enlightenment conceptions of the sovereign individual and knowable subjectivity thus give way to a postmodern dissolution of the hero.[46] The absolute instability of individual identity is nowhere more evident in the passage HAVING THOUGHT IT OVER (NACHGEDACHTHABEN):

> just imagined what I discovered today: I'm me!
> that can't be right – you're you!
> how can I be you? You are the one who's you!
> me? I'm not you – after all, I always say "you" to you!
> You can't really believe that I'm you, then you'd have to be me! (15)[47]

Particularly striking in this exchange between "brother" and "sister" is the fluidity of gender identity between the two protagonists. Although the dialogic nature of the above passage demands the use of the non-gendered pronouns "I," "you," and "me," Schutting pointedly refrains from including the gendered pronouns "he/she" or "him/her" throughout the text when referring to Judith and Stephan and, in so doing, refuses to assign to either character a clearly defined, socially recognized and sanctioned gendered identity. Shortly following his official change of gender and accompanying name change from Jutta to Julian in 1989, Schutting discussed in interviews in the Austrian press how his own transsexuality influenced his writings. His experience as a hermaphrodite[48] in a predominantly conservative, Catholic society that demands the clear demarcation of the sexes prompted him, to "flee" into the world of art, since art itself is "gender-free."[49] One might, therefore, conclude that Schutting consciously spares his protagonists the anguish of having to conform to rigid constraints of gender identity that he himself experienced in what Lamb-Faffelberger refers to as his "life-long identity crisis.[50]"

    Accompanying this fluidity of identity is a fluidity of narrative structure. Lützeler notes as a hallmark of postmodern literature the rejection of traditional structures of linear-storytelling and the preference for more amorphous or organic forms of storytelling more closely resembling the labyrinth or the rhizome.[51] Since postmodern literature is no longer concerned with a mimetic representation of "reality," a postmodern work can begin anywhere and be purely episodic with no sense of "verifiable" plot. Schutting's work eschews plot and epic structures in favor of a non-linear series of episodes that do not support any chronological framework, and as Anthony Phelan notes is "characterized by the disruption of continuity and textual expansion which generally typifies narrative.[52] *The Morning before the Journey* is written in an "essentially additive process" of a series of short "textual units" that Phelan terms "short prose" (*Kurzprosa*). "Each textual unit," Phelan explains, "functions as a closed moment, held and examined for the duration of its syntax. The practice of naming the textual units of any given text demonstrates their relative independence from the remainder of the work of which they are, in some sense, a "part."[53] The sheer number could also be seen as overwhelming as there are 149(!) such "individual sketches" or short texts. A brief glance at the titles of the first five "short texts" reveals the lack of an overt cohesive narrative structure: BAPTISM, TRAIN RIDE, GAME OF FORGETFULNESS, TOMBSTONE, CHILDREN'S TEA PARTY. (TAUFE, BAHNFAHRT, VERGESSLICHKEITS-SPIEL, GEDENKSTEIN, KINDERJAUSE). Without regard to linearity or transition, the action described in these texts appears as unconnected to one another as their titles would indicate and only after multiple readings may a relationship between at least some of the texts become recognizable. It should be noted that the very act of capitalizing each letter of the "title," as well as an index at the back of the book, appears to further endow each short text with an autonomy of its own.

As noted above, Lyotard defines *postmodern* as "incredulity toward metanarratives," i.e., those grand discourses, narratives, or shared truisms upon which a society constitutes and continually seeks to legitimate its identity. Schutting squares off with a number of such metanarratives including patriarchal, generational authority, specifically parental authority, and, in particular Church authority. Schutting's challenge to authority figures proves unrelenting; he addresses the issue of generational authority so widely explored in the German *Väterliteratur* of the 1970s and 1980s in which authors who came of age in the postwar period aggressively raised the previously taboo topic of their parents' conduct during the Nazi era. A clear questioning of paternal authority finds expression in the text WHERE ARE WE? (WO SIND WIR?) which begins with the exclamation "Paul's poor grandfather!" Although Paul's grandfather has lived with Paul's parents for ten years, presumably the ravages of Alzheimer's Disease or dementia have robbed him of his senses and memory and prompt him to ask "with a scared or amazed expression" (24) ("mit einem erschrockenen oder erstaunten Gesicht") "Paul, where are we actually?" ("Paul, wo sind wir denn eigentlich?" [36]). His obvious relief, upon being reassured that he is at home, remains fleeting, however, for he poses this query numerous times throughout the day – every day. Herzmann has noted that Schutting's political texts often thematize "the process of remembering" and that the "conscious effort of remembering" represents the prerequisite for retrieving past events, forgotten or repressed. [54] In this respect, the grandfather's inability to remember could be seen as the result of an unconscious desire to forget the past. In COAT RACK (KLEIDERSTÄNDER), an old woman expresses similar existential fears and takes refuge in the coat rack holding onto the hem of a coat thinking perhaps of security once offered by her mother's apron or the divine intervention of the "caped Madonna" (Schutzmantelmadonna). The text's first line echoes that of WHERE ARE WE? as it begins with the lament "oh, the poor old woman! Last night she called for help, her daughter then found her, kneeling and holding onto one of the coats, in the dark hallway, sometimes she wakes up so disoriented from her sleep" (41) ("ach, die arme alte Frau! Heute nacht hat sie um Hilfe gerufen, ihre Tochter fand sie dann, kniend an einem der Mäntel geklammert, im finsteren Vorzimmer, so verwirrt schreckt sie manchmal aus dem Schlaf" [59]). In both passages, the old person has lost not only a personal sense of security, but also generational authority as each continually turns to children or grandchildren for answers to the most basic questions: who and where am I?

Given Schutting's highly self-reflective nature, it is not surprising that two of the passages that challenge the strictures of parental or familial authority deal with the issue of writing: WRITING LETTERS (BRIEFESCHREIBEN) and STATIONERY (BRIEFPAPIER). WRITING LETTERS begins tumultuously with "have you finally written auntie? one of the children's mothers says threateningly" (15) ("'hast du jetzt endlich der Tante geschrieben'?, mahnt die Mutter eines der Kinder" [15]).

Clearly, the admonishing tone of the question undermines the chance of dialogue between the two and serves instead as a warning, rather than a mere query. The mother proceeds to interrogate the child about the content of the letter and is disturbed to learn that, while the child's letter was full of heartfelt thanks for the time spent with various animals with which he/she romped, it made no mention of the child's gratitude toward the adults and therefore fell short of the conventional niceties that bind "fine" society. In this passage Schutting stresses the disconnect between children's perspectives and value systems and the priorities of adult society which values formulaic, empty expressions of gratitude over genuine expressions of joy. Similarly, in STATIONERY Judith bemoans the obligation that a gift of stationery from her aunt on her birthday has imposed upon her. Now, she is compelled to write to the aunt and has no reasonable excuse for not doing so. The letter that Stephan dictates to Judith in a loving attempt to save her birthday from being spoiled by this intrusive present represents an agile attempt to rob the letter of any true meaning and, thereby, rob the aunt of a "true" expression of thanks. Judith proclaims:

> I thank you for our apartment on the fourth floor of building fourteen because if we didn't live at the address where you wrote me, your present wouldn't have arrived. And finally I thank you for all the experiences worthy of reporting which I am going to write about for as long as the stationery lasts, and especially for your living so far from us (19).[55]

The circular language of the letter of thanks becomes acrobatic and the irony palpable as Judith cleverly rejects both her aunt and a gift she finds constrictive and manipulative, since it forces her to participate in a dialogue not of her choosing.

Further challenges to parental authority evidence themselves in a most chilling fashion in two scenes that appear to express a death wish for the parents. In COMPETITION

(WETTLAUF), following a short familial hike, the children decide to run directly home and see if they can beat their parents' return with the car. While still anxious to "maintain their lead," they wonder that their parents have not yet overtaken them and they conjecture about various scenarios including misplaced keys, the cold motor reluctant to start, a ticket from a policeman for illegal parking, and, lastly, the risk of an accident. One thus poses the possibility, "And maybe they'll have a little accident, it's so icy at the bridge – but look, nothing happened. Here they are! What a shame!" (8) ("und vielleicht haben sie jetzt einen kleinen Unfall, an der Brücke ist es so eisig, aber schau – nichts ist gewesen, sie kommen schon! wie schade!" [14]). It is unclear if their lament refers to their parents' safe homecoming or simply the fact that they have lost their quest to arrive home first. In MOUNTAIN CABLE CAR ACCIDENT (SEILBAHNUN-GLÜCK) the children read in the newspaper details of a horrific accident in which a ten-year-old boy lost his parents and sister. The last to arrive at an overcrowded gondola, the boy signals to his parents that he will await the next one and "waved goodbye to them." His family's gondola proceeds to crash, killing all on board, and Judith and Stephan contemplate both the boy's salvation and his role in his family's tragedy. Thus, they conjecture both about the presence of a guardian angel who, at the last minute, held him back and, more disturbingly, about his possible culpability in the death of his family members:

> And in case his relatives missed an earlier gondola on his account, he might have forgotten all that due to the shock, for otherwise he might always ask himself over and over again, whether his parents and his sister were dead because in his greed he didn't want to wait another ten more minutes to have a ham sandwich (39).[56]

Both COMPETITION and MOUNTAIN CABLE CAR ACCIDENT reveal an underlying tension in the familial constellations and, in particular, an overt challenge to parental authority that may or may not result in the parents' demise.

Stephan and Judith are witness to what might arguably be considered the most disturbing display of familial dynamics in the book in FINGER SUCKING. (FINGERLUTSCHEN). On a bus they observe a "massive young man, next to him a woman with a sleepy, shiny gnomelike face" (34) ("ein massiver jüngerer Mann, neben him eine Frau mit einem verschlafen blinzelnden Zwergengesicht" [57]) and a little girl. The man, whom they assume to be the girl's father, proceeds to make a bizarre series of hand gestures directed toward the little girl. He finally sticks his finger in his mouth and while "looking dreamily at the child" ("noch immer den Blick, am ehesten forschend, auf das Mädchen gerichtet" [58]) begins to suck on it in a lewd manner that meets the silent disapproval of both the woman with the "gnome-like face" and the passengers who shake their head, but nonetheless say nothing. When finished with his crude display, he "wipes off the finger on his pants, as if it were a pocket knife, kisses it laughing and smacking his lips, and stands up at the same time as the little girl, looking at her again, his finger on his mouth, as if he wants to say to her, 'please, don't tell anybody.'" (40)[57] Stephan and Judith anxiously steal glances at the little girl to see her reaction to this obscene display of sexuality. As they do so, they marvel at the contrast between this beautiful, well-dressed child and her unkempt, drunken parents, and they are heartened to see her disavow them by walking ahead of them and ignoring them completely, deaf to her father's moaning pleas: "stay here, come here, hey, don't be like that, wait for me!" (40-41) ("da bleibst, komm her, geh sei ned so, wart auf mich!" [59]). The scene not only reveals the precocious child's rejection of her parents' perverse behavior, and by extension, their authority, but also appears to condemn the silence of the passengers who failed to intercede on the child's behalf.

Schutting directly addresses the issue of silence in STREETCAR TROUBLE (STRAßENBAHNSTÖRUNG) in which Judith and Stephan are disturbed by the inexplicable silence and seemingly freeze-framed appearance of their fellow passengers. When someone breaks this odd spell by asking what is the matter and people begin to move and complain again, Judith expresses her relief that they have not fallen into an eternal silence, a "sleeping-beauty kind of sleep" ("Dornröschenschlaf" [100]) until some brave individual "would be able to take hold of himself and yell his protest against torpidity into the silence, and be the first one to cross the room and show us the way to salvation" (71).[58]

The children can least expect "salvation from silence" through the Church, a powerful entity that Schutting represents ironically throughout the text. The book opens with a parody of a baptismal scene; Judith carries a gladiola, enveloped in white cloth, to the baptismal font, and Stephan, attired in a "rain poncho-chasuble" baptizes the flower with three drops of water. Given Schutting's affinity for Latin,[59] the choice of a gladiola, a flower whose name stems from Latin *gladius* or "sword" and that is commonly known as the "sword lily" is significant. Welcomed into the community of the Church through the cleansing sacrament of baptism is, therefore, not a symbol of peace, but rather a symbol of war and violence, a tool of bloodletting and domination. Schutting thus appears to undermine the role of the Church as one of peacekeeper and protector of Christian morality. Furthermore, Stephan's donning of a "waterproof" chasuble seems to indicate that this baptismal water poses some sort of danger or threat from which he must protect himself. Schutting's refashioning of a liturgical garment into water-impermeable attire clearly seeks to undermine the authority that the wearing of such vestments might imply. Though Schutting offers numerous parodies throughout the work whereby the children expose superficial adult rules of propriety,[60] this parody of a baptism functions in a particularly subversive manner. Just as the first sacrament represents an initial welcoming into the Catholic faith, so the scene Schutting creates welcomes the reader into his work and immediately confronts him/her with a familiar, yet disorienting scene from lives of predominantly Catholic Austria. The theme of violence and the Church is also evident in ASYLUM GARDEN AND PARK (ANSTALTGARTEN UND PARK) in which a young nun attends to mentally handicapped children in a garden. Schutting describes a deceptively pastoral scene of gentle nature and playing children and the "nun in a white dress" who quietly stands up and as if immersed in holy thoughts...stepped over the small wall between the ponds and then just as engrossed in thought through a meadow and over to a little girl who stood there all by herself and who was pulling her bathing cap over her ears, stopped in front of her, gave her a slap, and then went back exactly as she had come, smiling, she stopped at the edge of the wall, pushed one of the larger boys into the water and then sat down again on her bench (62).[61]

The incongruity between the peacefulness of the scene, the apparent serenity of the nun, and the brutality of her assault on a mentally handicapped child brings Judith/Stephan: "I had never thought that anyone could entertain giving someone a really good spanking with so much gentleness, and yet the head of the little girl had been turned around a bit by the force of the blow" (62).[62] In ANASTASIA OF SIRMIUM (ANASTASIA VON SIRMIUM) the children impute yet another form of violence to the Church: that of censorship and thereby, the support of the silence they so fear. In this passage they ponder the odd symbols of Saint Anastasia of Sirmium, martyred under Diocletian, whose symbol is a pair of scissors and who is considered the patron saint of censorship. One child explains: "scissors are a symbol for a certain St. Anastasia, who cut out so many magazines, until only something edifying like the Church newspaper was left over, she's the patron saint of censorship!" The second child replies, "then I know several countries who are really devoted to her!" (38).[63]

Vienna's iconic St. Stephen's Cathedral also plays a role in the text not only as representative of Catholicism in Austria but also of the centuries-long symbiotic relationship between

Church and State in its very roof, which bears the double-headed eagle of the Habsburg Empire as well as the coats of arms of the City of Vienna and the Austrian Republic. Visiting Vienna, Stephan is anxious to see the cathedral after whose patron saint he was named and the image of which he knows so well from the wrappers of *Mannerschnitten* wafers. Short of time, his harried aunt, however, passes off a local parish church as St. Stephen's. Horribly disappointed by the structure's ordinariness, Stephan refuses to eat his wafers, vows to visit Vienna never again, and more importantly, comes to the belief that one cannot trust what one is told.[64] The Church thus serves for him as a symbol of deception and dashed expectations.

Perhaps the harshest indictment of the Church appears in TIROLEAN WALKS in which children wonder at the inscription above a crucifix. Instead of the usual INRI they see: "Rabies Quarantine Area/dogs and cats not on a leash/will be shot!" (102) ("TOLLWUTSPERRGEBIET Freilaufende Hunde und Katzen werden ERSCHOSSEN!" [143]). The children finally conclude:

> of course the state authorities must take caution that rabies not be brought in by run-away dogs and cats from an infested area, it's better to have a preventative killing than many virulent deaths, but what should Jesus have brought into the area, Tirol has been Catholic for a long time and immune to the kind of Christianity that is taken too much at its word! (102-103)[65]

Ironically, the savior is now the carrier of disease, the rabid being whose teachings of mildness and love will fall on deaf ears in a community so long steeped in a perverted Catholic tradition that it has become immune to such messages of kindness.

This immunity to kindness and embrace of violence evidences itself most clearly in Austria's Nazi history and its legacy of violence for following generations. The specter of the war and the Holocaust looms large in the work. In CHILDREN'S BOOK (KINDERBUCH) Stephan and Judith discover a book from the Nazi era in the attic that extols the virtue of housewives' frugality in preparing supper through the portrayal of a brightly-colored sausage which hops in and out of a soup pot to improve the taste of the cabbage soup, but "despite its roasted skin...survives being eaten for lunch" ("daß trotz seiner geröteten Haut das Mittagessen überlebt"). While simultaneously bemoaning the pain endured by the sausage and celebrating its ultimate survival, the children are disturbed by such extreme admonitions to thrift until they remember "that back then, when the book was being written, there was war and hunger and frugality" (18) ("Ihre Ratlosigkeit findet sich mit der Erklärung ab, daß damals, als das Buch entsanden ist, Krieg und Hunger und Sparsamkeit gewesen sei" [27]). In DOORS (TÜREN), the children express their gratitude toward open doors but express, however, their sorrow for those innocent people transported to prison camps to whom open doors were forever denied. NUMBERS (ZAHLEN) explores the question of blind acceptance of authority as the children ponder what they consider the inherent violence of mathematical calculations using the vocabulary of war to describe the various processes of division, multiplication, subtraction, and addition. Torn with guilt for the pain they are inflicting upon numbers, they console themselves, however, with the thought that they bear no moral responsibility for the consequences of their actions, but were merely following orders: "if another one dies from all your maneuvers, well then it's stamped out, and anyway, that's not a problem, you're only doing what the teacher told you to do" (14) ("und wenn eine andere von deinen Operationen restlos stirbt, so ist sie ausgerottet und das macht nichts, du tust ja nur, was dir die Lehrerin befohlen hat!" [22]).

In ROSENAU CASTLE (SCHLOß ROSENAU), Stephan tells of a school excursion to an exhibit entitled "Freemasons in Austria." The former Freemason lodge housed Georg Ritter von Schönerer, founder of the Pan-German Party in Austria, whose virulent anti-Semitic diatribes influenced Hitler. Stephan laments the incongruity between the reason and tolerance of the Freemasons with the hate-filled invectives of the "Knight of Rosenau": "in the rooms of this castle, where so many learned conversations had taken place, the Knight of Rosenau lived and wrote, whose evil writings Adolf Hitler was soon to, you know – isn't that sad? (94) "(in den Räumen dieses Schloßes, in denen so viele gelehrte Gespräche geführt worden waren, lebte und schrieb dann der Ritter von Schönerer, dessen böse Schriften bald Adolf Hitler, du weißt schon – ist das nicht traurig?" [132]). Judith likewise regrets that the "evil knight" remained untouched by the spirit of the "gentlemen who believed in reason, humanity and tolerance" and continued to pen his "evil hate songs" (94) in this bastion of enlightenment.[66] In DEFILING GRAVES (GRÄBERSCHÄNDUNG), the children directly address a contemporary instance of anti-Semitism and conjecture upon their own generation's collective guilt for the crimes against Jews of both the past and the present. Someone has smeared the word "Jew" on gravestones and the more disturbing phrase "*Juda verrecke*" on the cemetery wall. The force of this imperative resonates within the children and makes them feel like accomplices of the Jew-haters.

This fear of an inherited intolerance expresses itself forcefully in BILLBOARD (PLAKATWAND) in which the children observe a well-dressed child kicking the face of a bound, chained man portrayed on a billboard supporting the mission of Amnesty International. Remembering Judith's reaction to a *Max and Moritz* story in which she attempted to "undo" the protagonists' attack on their old schoolmaster by gluing the book's pages together, they first consider the possibility that the child's aggression could be seen as a denunciation of any acts of torture. Ultimately, however, they conclude that the child consciously has chosen to inflict pain on an innocent person, comparing the figure on the billboard to Jesus, whose crucifix must be hung high or guarded in a chapel to protect him from attack.[67] That the boy's violence represents an endemic passion for violence in society can be inferred from Stephan's plea in GUILELESS (ARGLOS) to his aunt, a teacher, that she assign vocabulary words that appeal to a higher morality, reason, and tolerance. Thus, she should assign words like "guileless, charming, provident, impertinent, timorous, circumspect, and well-brought-up" so that like, "endangered species" in a wild animal preserve, these words might "ultimately...find their way into normal everyday speech.!"[68] His aunt's quick reply serves as a resounding condemnation of contemporary society: "that wouldn't make any sense...because your favorite words would demand the kind of character traits that nobody can use nowadays!" (60) ("das hätte keinen Sinn...denn deine Lieblingswörter würden solche Charakterzüge fördern, die heute keiner brauchen kann!" [85]).

Herzmann has argued that Schutting's political poems reveal that there is "no escape into a safe past" from the "simultaneity of terror and coziness" of the contemporary world.[69] In corresponding prose form, *The Morning before the Journey* similarly depicts Austria as a society haunted by the specter of violence. The language of war infiltrates the children's games, and dark themes of suicide, murder, hypocrisy, abuse, and betrayal course throughout the work. In a particular gruesome passage entitled "HACKED-UP CORPSE WITH PIERCED INDEX FINGER" (ZERSTÜCKTE LEICHE MIT ZERSTOCHENEM ZEIGEFINGER), they seek news of "authentic criminal findings in the old capital and imperial city of Vienna" (107) ("authentischen Kriminaltatsachen in der alten Haupt- und Residenzstadt Wien" [150]) only to come upon the gruesome details of a young girl whose mutilated body was found in several pieces throughout the city. At first unable to imagine such an atrocity, one of the children admits to an even greater fear: the possibility of forgetting such unimaginable cruelty. He/she proclaims: "I fear that one day I may forget the horror that happened to her, maybe not her head found in a trench on account of ground birds, but never her index finger" (110) ("ich fürchte, ich werde das Furchtbare, das ihr zugestoßen ist, einmal vergessen haben, den Kopf in einer Ackerfurche nur wegen der Erdzeiseln vielleicht nicht, nie aber ihren Zeigefinger" [153]). Memory, thus, becomes a moral imperative. Memory is, however, inevitably laden with the consciousness of pain and guilt, as well as fear. Not surprisingly, faced with such harsh realities and having witnessed how forays into adulthood have turned their "trust in their happiness" ("Vertrauen zu ihrer Heiterkeit") to "frightful dreams" (111) ("Traumerschrecken"), the children seek to postpone this passage and remain "children of honor" (110) ("Ehrenkinder" [155] for just a bit longer.

Endnotes

[1] Born Jutta Schutting in 1937, the author changed his name legally to Julian Schutting in 1989.
[2] Titles translated by Anthony Bushell in "Implying or Denying the Reader," in Harriet Murphy (ed.) *Critical Essays on Julian Schutting* (Riverside: Ariadne, 2000) 6. Julian Schutting, *Zuhörerbehelligungen* (Graz: Droschl, 1990) and *Leserbelästigungen* (Graz: Droschl, 1993.) All citations will be cited as "ZB" and "LB," respectively.
[3] *The Morning before the Journey,* translated and with an afterword by Barbara Zeisl Schoenberg (Riverside: Ariadne, 1999). Schutting's original, *Am Morgen vor der Reise: die Geschichte zweier Kinder,* first appeared under the author's birth-name Jutta Schutting (Salzburg: Residenz, 1978).
[4] "so ist dieses Buch auch die indirekte Liebesgeschichte zweier Erwachsener, die, sosehr sie sich auch als Erwachsene lieben, sich nicht damit abfinden wollen, daß sie sich nicht schon als Kinder gekannt haben – somit die Geschichte ihrer Imaginationen, wie sie dies und das, was sie jetzt erst entdecken, als Kinder miteinander erlebt hätten…wenn…" (5).
[5] For a discussion of the work against the backdrop of German literary history and, specifically, German children's literature, see Harriet Murphy, "Schutting's Transformation of Childhood

in *Am Morgen vor der Reise*," in Harriet Murphy (ed.), *Critical Essays on Julian Schutting* (Riverside: Ariadne, 2000), 45-63.

[6] In her afterword to *The Morning before the Journey*, the translator Zeisl-Schoenberg notes that Stephan and Judith are modeled after the brother and sister in Adalbert Stifter's *Bergkristall*, 118. For more on Schutting and Stifter, see "Julian Schutting's Aesthetic of Reading and Writing," in Arthur Williams (ed.) *Contemporary German Writers, Their Aesthetics and Their Language* (Bern: Peter Lang, 1996), 204, and Kurt Bartsch, "Wie in einem Laboratorium: Beobachtungen zur Kurzprosa von Julian Schutting" in Herbert Herzmann. (ed.) *Literaturkritik und erzählerische Praxis: deutschsprachige Erzähler der Gegenwart. Tagungsakten des internationalen Symposiums* (Tübingen: Stauffenberg, 1995), 604.

[7] Murphy, "Transfiguration" 51. See Herbert Herzmann's article, "Exercises in Remembering: Julian Schutting's Political Poems" in Harriet Murphy (ed.) *Critical Essays on Julian Schutting* (Riverside: Ariadne, 2000), 26-44.

[8] Murphy, "Transfiguration" 53.

[9] Murphy, "Transfiguration" 59.

[10] Murphy, "'Ich habe die schönen Hochämter am liebsten aus dem Bett angehört'" Anti-Catholic Polemic and the Religion of Art in the Work of Schutting," in Harriet Murphy (ed.), *Critical Essays on Julian Schutting* (Riverside: Ariadne, 2000), 199.

[11] Although Roth problematizes the issue of Austrian silence about its own fascist past in many of his works, he addresses the question most forcibly in his cycle, *Archive des Schweigens*.

[12] Murphy, "Anti-Catholic "200.

[13] Murphy, "Anti-Catholic" 196.

[14] Murphy, "Anti-Catholic" 200.

[15] Murphy, "Anti-Catholic" 194.

[16] Murphy, "Anti-Catholic" 201.

[17] Murphy, "Anti-Catholic" 183.

[18] Herzmann 41.

[19] See Hanns Josef Ortheil, "Zum Profil der neuen und jüngsten deutschen Literatur." *Spätmoderne und Post-moderne: Beiträge zur deutschsprachigen Gegenwarts-literatur* (Frankfurt: Fischer, 1991), 36-51; Ingeborg Hoesterey, "Ästhetische Postmoderne and deutschsprachige Literatur," in Robert Weninger and Brigitte Rossbacher (eds.) *Wendezeiten, Zeitenwenden; Positionsbestimmungen zur deutschsprachigen Literatur, 1945-1995* (Tübingen: Stauffenberg, 1997), 99-11; Paul Michael Lützeler, "The Discussions of Narration in the Postmodern Context," in Gisela Firnau and Karin MacHardy (eds.) *Fact and Fiction: German History and Literature 1848-1924* (Tübingen: Francke, 1990), 57-67; as well as Paul Michael Lützeler, "Die Präsenz der Geschichte: Postmoderne Konstellationen in der Erzählliteratur der Gegenwart," *Neue Rundschau* 104 (1993), 91-108.

[20] "In Abwandlung eines Wortes von Karl Kraus ließe sich sagen, das Niveau der Kritik steige unablässig, nur steht die Literatur selber nicht mehr darauf." Joachim Fest, "Bücher, Bücher, aber nichts zu lesen," in Volker Hage (ed.) *Deutsche Literatur 1981. Ein Jahresüberblick* (Stuttgart: Reclam, 1981), 223-224.

[21] Fest 224.

[22] Ortheil 42.

[23] Ortheil 42.

[24] Jean-François Lyotard. *The Postmodern Condition: A Report on Knowledge.* Trans. Geoff Bennington and Brian Massumi. (Minneapolis: U of Minnesota, 1989.)

[25] Hoesterey 99.

[26] Lützeler, "Discussion" 58.

[27] Lützeler, "Discussion" 58.

[28] "selbst ein Kunstwerk, das sich ganz in sich zurückzieht, kann sich nicht ganz von der Wirklichkeit lösen: die Welt sollte anders sein, sagt es, andere Spielregeln sollten sie lenken, und so muß Apolitisches politisch werden./ daß die Kunst das Wesenhafte aus den Dingen herauslecke, das heißt nicht nur, daß die Kunst Unsichtbares sichtbar mache, das enthält auch den Glauben, daß

künstlerische Sensibilität als ein Meßinstrument funktioniert, wofür es kein Meßinstrument gibt." (*ZB* 76).
[29] Linda Hutcheon, *A Poetics of Postmodernism* (New York: Routledge, 1988) 4.
[30] Bartsch 163.
[31] Bartsch 170.
[32] Waltraud Maierhofer, "Vetter Grüne. Goetherezeption in Julian Schuttings 'Zuhörerbehelligungen' und 'Leserbelästigungen,'" *Zeitschrift für deutsche Philologie*. 116 (1997): 611-612.
[33] "wie kommt die Venediger Au an die Nähe der Wiener Donau? was hat dieser Hund in der Tigergasse verloren, was ist mit dem Tiger, nach welchem sie heißt? ist er aus der Zirkusgasse gekommen und dann in die Blutgasse geschlichen?" (25)
[34] Mike Rogers, "Zuhörerbehelligungenbehelligungen," in Herbert Herzmann (ed.) *Literaturkritik und erzählerische Praxis: Deutschsprachige Erzähler der Gegenwart* (Tübingen: Stauffenburg, 1995), 175.
[35] See Margarete Lamb-Faffelberger's interview with Schutting for a discussion of the simultaneous, rather than successive nature of his writing, the result of which is long sentences through which the reader must intellectually and psychologically negotiate. Margarete Lamb-Faffelberger, "Ein Gespräch mit Julian Schutting." *Literaturkritik und erzählerische Praxis: deutschsprachige Erzähler der Gegenwart. Tagungsakten des internationalen Symposiums*, in Herbert Herzmann (ed.) (Tübingen: Stauffenberg, 1995) 156.
[36] Sigrid Schmid, "Moglichkeiten: Zur Prosa von Jutta Schutting," in Gerlinde Weiss (ed.) *Festschrift für Adalbert Schmidt zum 70. Geburtstag* (Stuttgart: Heinz, 1976) 417.
[37] Lützeler 61.
[38] Beth Bjorklund, "Architectonic 'As if'": Interview with Jutta Schutting. *The Literary Review*. 25.2. (1982), 277.
[39] Schmid 417.
[40] Mike Rogers, "Julian Schutting's Aesthetic of Reading and Writing," in Arthur Williams (ed.) *Contemporary German*

Writers, Their Aesthetics and Their Language (Bern: Peter Lang, 1996) 201. See Lützeler, "Präsenz" for a discussion of postmodernism and the democratization of textual interpretation.

[41]"in meinem frühesten Prosatexten sehen Sie diese Hochachtung vor dem Leser so weit getrieben, daß in vielen Sätzen das Subjekt oder Prädikat fehlt, nämlich überall dort, wo es leicht zu ergänzen ist, sich von selbst versteht..." (*ZB* 107). See Bushell for an overview of critics' primarily negative assessment of Schutting's language complexities and abrogation of grammatical rules, as well as an excellent discussion of the role of the reader in Schutting's works.

[42]Bushell 13.

[43]Schutting concedes that for many his texts are more accessible when read aloud and in this respect compares himself to Karl Kraus: "ich weiß das von Lesern, die mich einmal lesen hören haben und von da an wußten, wie ich zu lesen bin; so gesehen ist meine Prosa vielleicht eine zum Vorlesen oder Lautlesen wie die von Karl Kraus." (*ZB* 109).

[44]Murphy "Transfiguration" 56.

[45]Margarete Lamb-Faffelberger, "Die Kunst ist geschlechtsfrei: Zur 'Sein/Schein'-Ästhetik als seelisch-geistige Haltung in Julian Schuttings Werk," *Literaturkritik und erzählerische Praxis: deutschsprachige Erzähler der Gegenwart. Tagungsakten des internationalen Symposiums*, in Herbert Herzmann (ed.) (Tübingen: Stauffenberg, 1995) 149.

[46]See Lützeler, "Präsenz" 98 for discussion of the postmodern dissolution of the hero.

[47]"stell dir vor, worauf ich heute gekommen bin: ich bin ich! das kann nicht stimmen-du bist doch du! wie kann ich denn du sein? das bist doch du! du kannst doch nicht glauben, daß ich du bin, dann müßtest du ja ich sein! Das sag ich dir ja: ich bin ich, und da ich ich bin, bist du nicht ich, sondern bist du and bleibst du du!" (23).

⁴⁸In an interview with Lamb-Faffelberger, Schutting describes his existence as a "Zwitterwesen ... gespannt zwischen zwei Pole." Lamb-Faffelberg, "die Kunst" 147.
⁴⁹"Transsexualität...]ür mich bedeutet ..., daß ich transozeanisch unterwegs bin, als ein Fisch von einem Gewässer in ein anderes hinüberschwimme, ... wohin mich eine starke Strömung schon immer gezogen hat, weil es das meine ist." Cited by Lamb-Faffelberger, "die Kunst" 147. On this page Lamb-Faffelberger also cites his assertions that "Die Triebkraft zur Kunst ... etwas Pathologisches [ist]" and "Ich flüchtete in die Kunst, denn die ist geschlechtslos."
⁵⁰Lamb-Faffelberger, "die Kunst" 147.
⁵¹Lützeler, "Präsenz" 96.
⁵²Anthony Phelan, "The Occasions of Writing and the Aesthetics of Kurzprosa (Half Adalbert Stifter, Half René Margritte" in Harriet Murphy (ed.) *Critical Essays on Julian* Schutting (Riverside: Ariadne, 2000) 163.
⁵³Phelan 171.
⁵⁴Herzmann 26-27.
⁵⁵"danke ich dir für unsere Wohnung im dritten Stock des Vierzehnerhauses, denn wenn wir nicht dort wohnten, wohin du mir geschrieben hast, wäre dein Geschenk nicht angekommen. und zuletzt danke ich dir für alles an Berichtenswerten, das ich solange das Briefpapier reicht erleben werden, und vor allem dafür, daß du weit weg von uns wohnst" (29).
⁵⁶"und falls seine Angehörigen seinetwegen in der Gaststube der Bergstation eine frühere Gondel versäumt haben, möge er das in seinem Schock vergessen haben, denn sonst wird er sich immer wieder fragen, ob Eltern und Schwester tot sind, weil er aus lauter Gier nicht zehn Minuten länger auf ein Wurstbrot warten wollte!"(56-57).
⁵⁷"als ihm die Gnomin bedeutet, daß es Zeit zum Aussteigen sei, wischt er den nassen Finger wie ein Taschenmesser an der Hose ab, küßt ihn lachend und schmatzend und steht zugleich mit der Kleinen auf, legt dabei, sie wieder anschauend, den Finger auf

den Mund, als ob er ihr 'bitte nichts weitersagen!' sagen wollte" (58-9).

[58]"irgendeiner wird sich schon überwinden, in die Stille hinein seinen Widerstand gegen die Erstarrung zu rufen, als erster den Saal zu überqueren und uns so einen Weg in die Rettung zu weisen" (100).

[59]See *Zuhörerbehelligungen* 104.

[60] See PRACTICING BEING AROUND ADULTS (UMGANG MIT ERWACHSENEN ÜBEN) and DREAMING UP EXCUSES (ENTSCHULDIGUNGEN AUSDENKEN).

[61]"einmal stand sie langsam auf, zupfte an ihrem Kleid und ging dann wie in heilige Gedanken versunken über das schmale Mäuerchen zwischen den Bassis und dann genauso bedächtig durch die Wiese auf ein Mädchen zu, das dort ganz allein stand und sich eben die Badehaube über die Ohren zog, blieb vor ihm stehen, gab ihm eine Ohrfeige und ging dann genauso gemächlich zurück, auf dem Mauerrand blieb sie lächelnd stehen, schubste einen der größeren Buben ins Wasser und setzte sich dann wieder auf ihre Bank" (88).

[62]"ich hätte nie gedacht, daß so sanft an die Vollstreckung einer richtigen Ohrfeige herangegangen werden kann, und doch war der Kleinen von dem Schlag der Kopf ein Stück weggedreht worden, sie stand so verdattert da, als wäre eben aufgegangen, was ein Blitz aus heiterem Himmel " (88).

[63]"die Schere ist das Symbol einer heiligen Anastasia, die für ihre Gemeinde Zeitschriften wohl so zusammengestutzt hat, bis etwas Erbauliches wie die Kirchenzeitung übriggeblieben ist, sie ist die Patronin der Zensoren! Dann weiß ich einige Länder, in welchen sie eifrig verehrt wird!" (56).

[64] Stephan also experiences this sense of familial betrayal and broken trust In THE BLUE STAMP (DIE BLAUE MAURITIUS) in which his Uncle Fritz boastfully offers him a stamp of great rarity. Stephan's joy is dashed, however, when his parents inform him that Uncle Fritz had merely played a joke upon him. His disappointment and, more significantly, sense of

betrayal are evident in his lament: "I knew that the worst thing about my blue Mauritius was: that uncle hadn't only disappointed and made me ashamed, but he also had lied to me." (23) "wußte ich, was das Schlimmste an meiner Blaeuen Mauritius war: daß der Onkel mir nicht nur die Enttäuschung und Blamage, sondern auch diese Lüge angetan hatte" (34).

[65]"natürlich muß die Landesbehörde achtgeben, daß nicht durch aus einem verseuchten Gebiet zugelaufene Hunde und Katzen die Tollwut eingeschleppt wird, besser eine vorbeugende Tötung als viele gestorbene Tote, aber was sollte Jesus denn einschleppen können, Tirol ist doch längst katholisch und gegen allzu wörtlich genommenes Christentum seit langem immun!" (144).

[66] "keiner der Herren, die an die Vernunft, Humanität und Toleranz geglaubt haben, ist dem bösen Ritter erschienen, als er dort schrieb und schlief, wo sie ihre großen Ideen entwickelt und gelebt haben, ungestört von ihren Gedanken hat er gleichsam in ihrer Mitte seine bösen Haßlieder niedergeschrieben!" (133).

[67]"he would have done the same to our crucified Savior, but crucifixes are hung so high that feet and fists are unreachable, or if not, then they are kept in small chapels behind a protective barrier" (48) "er würde auch mit dem Gekreuzigten so verfahren, aber Gekreuzigte hängen ja so hoch oben, daß sie Füßen und Fäusten unerreichbar bleiben, und wenn nicht, dann werden sie in kleinen Kapellen hinter einem sie schützenden Gitter gehalten" (69).

[68] "ach bitte ... laß deine Schulkinder Wörter wie 'arglos' 'sorgsam' 'ungehörig' 'zaghaft' 'behutsam' und 'wohlerzogen', nur mehr der Großvater gebraucht sie, recht oft in Übungssätzen verwenden, vielleicht sterben sie dann doch nicht aus: deine Schulkinder werden sie anderen Kindern und ihren Kindern weiterschenken, und dann werden diese Wörter wie vom Aussterben bedrohte und deshalb eine Zeit lang in einer Reservation gehaltene wilde Tiere auch in freier Rede wieder leben! (85)
[69]Herzmann 38, 35.

Balancing Opposites:
"Geometric" and "Regional" Aspects
of Gert Jonke's *Geometrischer Heimatroman*

Vincent Kling

Geometric Regional Novel, translated by Johannes W. Vazulik,
Dalkey Archive Press, 1999

> Convention may become invention,
> thus creating reality anew (Poggioli 36)

Gert Jonke's *Geometric Regional Novel* (*Geometrischer Heimatroman*) (1969)[1] shows its governing formal process right in its title, which announces a constant negotiation of the apparent dichotomy its two adjectives announce. Those adjectives point with equal emphasis in seemingly opposite directions, to the long-standing conventions of regional writing on one hand and the individual inventions of "geometric" processes on the other. "Regional" is charged with emotive, idyllic means of apprehending and encompassing space as a landscape that mediates between the outer world and the observer's feelings, while "geometric" implies an impersonal, emotionless method of calculating and measuring that same space, a detached grounding in the rigor of logic and mathematics.

While Jonke (1946-2009) brings this balancing act to a successful conclusion – unlike one of his possible doubles in the novel, the tightrope walker (17-27; 18-30) – by structuring a coherent unity from start to finish through his dynamic balance of tradition or convention and innovation or invention, critics are almost unanimous in their disproportionate emphasis on one side of the polarity. Jonke's emergence in the second half of the 1960s came at a time of cultural and political wars being fought more quietly but perhaps even more fiercely in Austria than elsewhere. Living at the easternmost edge of the Iron Curtain and bordered in several directions by Soviet-bloc states, many Austrian writers judged every question of language, form, or style as a Cold War issue, so much so that a cadre of aesthetically hide-bound writers connected with the P.E.N. Club in Vienna rejected even mild literary experiment as proof of Communist infiltration and imminent cultural anarchy (Schramm 125-32), which response caused their adversaries to present themselves in turn as much more experimental, much more sharply at odds with tradition than they were. The poet and editor Alfred Kolleritsch succinctly characterized the "experimental" attitude in 1969 when he wrote that "today a concrete poem is just as clear a declaration of taking up arms against the establishment as is a....button with a picture of Mao" (Kaukoreit and Pfoser 138).

Such radical statements by these writers of Jonke's generation set a direction for literary critics, who stressed the radical, the revolutionary, and the avant-garde aspects of their art. Remaining consistently detached from all overt polemics, for which his nature is too playful and ironic, Jonke indeed exhibits characteristics of experimentalism and avant-gardism in every genre in which he has worked, from lyric poetry through novellas and novels through stage plays to film scripts, and these features have been widely analyzed since he came to notice with his first novel, *Geometrischer Heimatroman*, in 1969 and secured renown as the first winner of the Ingeborg Bachmann Prize in 1977. The essays by Bartsch (289-300), Düsing (87-105), and Kunne (201-32) are especially clear in their presentation of Jonke's invention as against his adherence to convention.

Johannes W. Vazulik, whose translation and commentary have been indispensable in presenting Jonke to readers with limited German, follows that standard line of analysis in his critical work. He has written two lucid introductory analyses of Jonke's narrative fiction (Vazulik, Daviau 293-311; Vazulik, *Dictionary of Literary Biography*), and his translation of Jonke's *Geometrischer Heimatroman* appends an afterword (Vazulik,

Afterword) essential for situating Jonke and his work. Jonke found his first important literary support in the *Forum Stadtpark* in Graz, "that enclave of the avant-garde in Austria named for their meeting place in a park" (Vazulik, Afterword 119), after he had begun in 1962, at age sixteen, under the spell of Georg Trakl and the Italian "Hermeticists," to publish poems in a journal of new writing (Kling, Gert Jonke 8-10). So when Vazulik assigns Jonke a place as one of the new "progressive literary and artistic talents linked by their impatience with conventional themes and techniques and their aim to illustrate the complexity of reality by antitraditional and experimental means" (Afterword 119), he is being true, as far as he goes, both to Jonke's art and to the direction other critics were following. His estimate accurately characterizes Jonke's novel, but it insists somewhat too strongly on its "geometric" processes, for these balance against "regional" approaches that endorse uncritical, undetached acceptance of the "conservative values," the "idealization of rural life in contrast to life in the alienating, hostile metropolis," and the patriarchal structures that accompany the "rootedness in the soil" common to standard regional literature (Vazulik, Afterword 121).[2] All of the lyricism, the narrative immediacy, the rhapsodic agrarianism, the pathos and exaltation of regional device form a tense, creative equilibrium with the deconstructing work of minute calculation, the recording of empirical data, the extreme attention to detail, and the deliberate defamiliarization arising from the geometric approach.

Almost all treatments of *Geometric Regional Novel* confine themselves to the category of regional and anti-regional literature, the latter a reaction against the mendacity of depicting rural life as harmonious and gentle. For about fifteen years, from roughly 1965 to 1980, Austrian writers of anti-regional novels (the so-called *Antiheimatroman* as opposed to the traditional *Heimatroman*) exposed in unforgettable detail the brutality, the cruelty, and the abuse built into agricultural and village life in Austria. Franz Innerhofer's *Schöne Tage* (1974) (*Beautiful Days*, 1977) and Josef Winkler's *Der Leibigene* (1979) (*The Serf*,

1997) are impeccably crafted examples combining documentation and art with great success. Anti-regional is too narrow a categorization for *Geometric Regional Novel*, though, too restricted a confinement to one particular time, whereas Jonke's work comes into its own only when seen in the context of a more encompassing category, that of pastoral. Through adapting pastoral traditions and approaches, *Geometric Regional Novel* ranges wider than the scope of Innerhofer and Winkler by revealing not just the outward structures of power – like Winkler's village built in the form of a cross, with all that shape implies – and the harrowing individual details of serfdom, but by entering into the deeper structures, the social presuppositions of power and authority and projecting them outward.

Regional writing, which arose mainly with the emergence of Realism in the nineteenth century, exists as a subset of pastoral, a conspicuously idyllic and bucolic approach consciously stylized away from Realism, since pastoral is, at least on the surface, a "dream" with "no other reality than that of imagination and art" (Poggioli 2), while the regional as such is a more realistically grounded, even Naturalistic variant of the pastoral "ideal landscape" (Curtius 183-202) codified by the ancient Greeks, perfected by Virgil in the *Eclogues* and *Georgics*, and prevalent as a positive or negative shaping force in descriptions of landscape throughout Western literature since. "Regional" writing attempts to renew the stylized and codified elements of landscape by modifying them away from the idyllic artifice to which the eighteenth century had subjected them and appropriating them to the Realism of the nineteenth and twentieth centuries, to settings that appear more like "real" landscapes actually encountered in nature.

By the very enthusiasm with which it embraces artifice, the wider category of pastoral ignores the restrictions of regional realism, but it thereby paradoxically has always provided a cover under which can be investigated precisely those political and social problems the artifice would seem to be barring. If the pastoral mode is indeed a "dream," as Poggioli contends (2), then it is a Freudian dream, enacting through the imagination a covert but searching confrontation with anxieties and problems not as apparent as they would be in the mode of realism.

Reading *Geometric Regional Novel* from the broader perspective of pastoral enables the reader to grasp the overarching form of the whole novel as a series of dialogues, so much so that it comes closer to drama than to conventional narrative. Pastoral always enacts a retreat from the noise and greed of the world and a striving for innocence and happiness restored in some ideal place of withdrawal (Poggioli 1-16), so it would seem to be completely unsuited for engagement with social and political problems. Yet the desired retreat is never undertaken in solitude. From the very first, pastoral in general and the eclogue in particular, which appears to be one main structural model for *Geometric Regional Novel*, have proceeded by dialogue. Even if the participants in the conversation are not physically present, they are so thoroughly imagined through direct address in absentia as to be dynamic presences in the interchange of thought and feeling. The Arcadian landscape so passionately invoked may be remote, but it is never solitary. From the time of Virgil on, pastoral poetry, however precious or idyllic in its rendering, always involves a social give and take. And because dialogue, essential to the structure of pastoral, is inherently social, pastoral unexpectedly lends itself to examination of social and political issues. One of the most significant discussions of the pastoral mode carries the subtitle "The Pastoral View of the Social Order" and argues the dynamically social character of the eclogue through dialogue, a consistent structure from Virgil through Rousseau to Mallarmé ("*L'après-midi d'un faune*") (Poggioli 194-219). Pastoral is, after all, a product of city breeding and did not exist until there were cities of significant size, as Poggioli notes (3-4). Accordingly, it is a fantasy construct of wish fulfillment onto which urban, political, social problems can be projected in stylized but unmistakable form.

In the dialogue between Tityrus and Meliboeus in Virgil's First Eclogue, as an example more explicit though not less characteristic than most, a pointed political and social criticism arises out of Meliboeus's expulsion from his land, which has been reassigned to a returning soldier: "*Impius haec tam culta novalia miles habebit*" ("Some barbarous soldier will enjoy it" [the order of the planted fields] [Virgil 8-9]). Meliboeus's fear of losing his livelihood by not finding new grazing for his flocks, his complete displacement through homelessness, his deep sense of grievance, his awareness of mortality, his shock at the abrupt reversal of fortune balances against the concluding scene of serenity, of hearth and home temporarily restored, of friendship with Tityrus, and of the rightness of nature's order beyond human injustice. Even in the more hermetic singing contests between shepherds or the ecstatic, prophetic invocation of a restored Golden Age in Eclogue Four, problems of power, ownership, social rank, and caprice by rulers are never absent.

As a protracted eclogue in what Vazulik (Afterword 124) calls "twenty-one essentially selfcontained text segments,"[3] *Geometric Regional Novel* by definition develops almost entirely through dialogue. Even extended description in passages of a kind usually associated with an omniscient narrator is addressed by one character to another, so there is never a detached voice reporting at a distance on the world being depicted. The participants in the dialogue appear to shift, but they almost begin with and emerge from the "I" and the "you" who discuss whether or not the village square is empty and whether or not to try to cross it in the face of what appears to be some unspecified danger. These two participants may not agree on even fundamental perceptions (71; 85), but they are always in dialogue, and there is almost no segment of the text that does not involve an active interchange of views.

As a modernist pastoral set in a pre-industrial society but written in a post-industrial age, *Geometric Regional Novel* enriches its tradition by approaching with irony and ambiguity the social and political problems typical of pastoral (Poggioli 33-4). Dialogue in most drama, and in the eclogue from Virgil to Miklós Radnóti,[4] enacts a movement from divergence toward consensus; at the end, conflicting views and realities have been reconciled. But in Jonke, as Vazulik observes that "narrative levels shift frequently" and the two eyewitnesses of the village's life, the "I" and the "you" who want to cross the square, are allowed to leave their contradictions of one another's statements unreconciled (Afterword 124). There can be no question of the kind of harmony Tityrus and Meliboeus achieve at the end of Virgil's First Eclogue, for example, where conflict gives way to peaceful participation in the common rituals of sacrifice to the gods before a shared evening meal.

But if there is an irony in the lack of resolution just where the communal form of dialogue seems to foster such resolution, there are additional aspects of creative irony in Jonke's method. Participants in a discussion may not achieve consensus, but there is a willing embrace of uncertainty, a moral rectitude, and an acceptance of communal involvement in their refusal ever to break off the conversation, no matter how inconclusive, and in their corresponding respect shown by making the search for reality a matter that involves others. Only when a single reporter trusts his unchecked individual perceptions does reality grow distorted and subject to manipulation. As long as it can be negotiated communally, reality may be indeterminate, but the effort to ascertain it is marked by ethical sensitivity. For example, one narrator who seems unusually alert to all the responsibilities attendant on fact-checking and eyewitness accounts in reporting events offers a report of the tightrope walker's performance (17-24; 18-26). This narrator appears not to have been present, since he makes repeated reference to what is "said to" have happened, so he calls on the memories of a person who was in the audience and can state definitely, at least up to a point, what actually took place. The direct witness to the performance includes such anchoring or verifiable "geometrical" details as exact sequences and descriptions, down to a captioned diagram of the acrobat's tent (19; 19), but he soon breaks down and begins reporting contradictory memories of the same detail, becoming vague and subjective, whereupon the narrator decides to call upon "the objective and factual report of the press" (24) ("wenn wir uns an den objektiven und wahrheitsgetreuen Bericht der Presse halten" [26]). But in an especially pointed irony, with devastating effect as media critique and analysis, the "objective" newspaper article (25-27; 27-30) turns out to be a tissue of inaccuracy, impressionistic self-indulgence, ineptly aestheticized language, smugness and pretension, abnegation of reportorial function, arbitrary judgment, and innuendo – of exactly the kind indulged by the P.E.N. authors – directed at purported leftists and liberals, a betrayal of open-ended truth by a single reporter irresponsible in his claim to judge reality for everyone else and an example of the pompous emotionalism and veiled politicizing that marks much regional writing.

Like so many segments of *Geometric Regional Novel* and so much of Jonke's work from the beginning, the newspaper report is an exuberant parody, outrageously lampooning the overblown language of arts pages. Behind what might appear a clownishly overdone parody, however, is Jonke's ceaseless questioning of inbred aesthetic concerns dwelt on by isolated individuals as a possible moral transgression. It is typical that the art critic praises the deft symmetry with which the acrobat breaks his back at its exact center without saying that the acrobat died! And if the critic's article is guilty of dehumanization, he is responding like the audience, which "responded with enthusiastic applause, and burst into frenetic demonstrations of approval" (26) ("bedankten sich mit enthusiastischem Applaus und brachen in frenetische Beifallskundgebungen aus" [29]). While creating a masterpiece of culpable journalistic obfuscation and toadying to mob psychology while pretending to superiority, the newspaper reporter abandons the proper caution and frank tentativeness of the earlier account, which had been marked by that social respect for consulting others, and the crowning irony is that the more careful and conscientious first narrator, influenced perhaps by a growing authoritarianism as the plot of *Geometric Regional Novel* develops, cedes authority to the distorted news report.

The language of Jonke's indictment, ironic like all modern pastoral, is so parodistic that it might at first appear self-indulgent or shapeless, but it goes to the heart of his method, using the inconclusiveness of the dialogues to engender a methodical critique of social and political problems in the village. Dialogue is messy, because it is a negotiation, unlike unilateral pronouncement, but the very struggle to agree on reality, while unsettling and unresolved, is ethically mature. Only when dialogue is forfeited and the newspaper reporter is given full credence in his unchecked manipulative pontifications does the atmosphere become stifling. The newspaper account is characteristic of Jonke's tendency, like that of many Austrian authors, to avoid direct commentary in favor of calling into question the ethics of language and artistic form rather than confront overt "issues." Schmidt-Dengler (362) assesses as a "careless reduction" the widespread judgment against Austrian authors as having "withdrawn from social and political reality" to dwell in a hermetic fixation on art, because that judgment fails to realize that this fixation is itself a politically critical stance.

Such a political stance arises in part out of Jonke's individual "antipathy to authoritarianism in any guise" (Vazulik, Afterword 124), but it is again an inherent component of pastoral, which always "condemns and denies...the temptations of profit and glory, of trade and war, of struggle and strife" (Poggioli 115). The pastoral mode fears even the signs of might and power, because they always entail cruelty and injustice (Poggioli 10).

If greed is the "worst crime" in pastoral (Poggioli 4), then *Geometric Regional Novel* is pastoral indeed, for the destructive power of greed underlies every aspect of conflict in the work that goes beyond the simple debate about crossing the village square. As Vazulik so well expresses it (Afterword 124), Jonke "makes visible the process by which bureaucracy and official regimentation insidiously pervade society." But bureaucracy and regimentation, at least to the extent to which they dehumanize the villagers in Jonke's novel, can only flourish where property ownership and the power needs of property owners require serfdom, stupefaction, conformity, obedience to authority, and complete lack of initiative. The villagers are reduced to automata as their lives come increasingly under the control of patriarchal authority figures like the priest, the schoolteacher, and the mayor, all mutually reinforcing the authority of the others. The teacher tells the children, for example, that the *"mayor is the top man in the village; eveything he does is for the good of the village; if he weren't there to enforce the prevailing law of the land the village would disintegrate in no time"* (43) (*"Der Bürgermeister ist der oberste Mann im Dorf, regelt alles zu unserem Wohle, ohne ihn würde das Dorf sofort verrottet sein, falls er nicht mehr unsere herrschende Landesordnung bewahrte"* [48]). The teacher's lists of rules typically grow longer and longer in each recurrence; his lists of prescriptions and prohibitions end up extending over several pages with rapid cascades of action verbs governing what the children may and may not perform (43-46; 48-53). The ten commandments have multiplied into the hundreds. Adults have it no better; posted regulations are practical and reasonable enough at first, like the warning about not standing under trees during storms or being careful when walking on snow and ice (9; 8), but they expand, proliferate, restrict action to the point of paralysis (29; 32). As regulation and regimentation grow ever tighter, surveillance by bureaucracy completely stifles the villagers. To use a current expression, every imaginable activity is micro-managed to the point of insanity; the extensive rules and regulations covering the operation of the bridge and the conduct of the operators, for example, are pedantic, fussy, madly detailed, and circumstantial with all their paraphrases, footnotes, and repetitions (34-39; 38-43). By the end of the novel, anyone wanting to take a walk in the woods must fill out a gigantic application form (98-103; 119-25) complete with fines and other punishments for the slightest lapse or infraction. Readers who lived through the bureaucratic horror of the Third Reich (setting aside its more infamous aspects) report, by the way, that this extremely fanciful application form exaggerates by only a very slight degree the crushing mountains of paperwork mandatory for every imaginable activity from 1933 to 1945. This is control gone maniacal, a triumph of Jonke's gift for comedy, especially since the application form is part of a statute calling itself "The New Law" (96-108; 116-31), a phrase often associated with the freedom and redemption of the Christian dispensation but ironically reversed here.

All this authoritarian control is motivated by profit. The village elders have long since bought up the surrounding tracts of woodland and are stripping the entire forest: "the intention is to cut down all forests, tree-lined roads, and, if necessary, fell trees standing alone in the countryside" (105) ("man will alle Wälder, Alleen und, falls nötig, auch einzelstehende Bäume in der Landschaft fällen" [128]), giving a list of numbered reasons, all for the supposed benefit of the villagers (105-06; 128), but actually to have all the lumber worked into a huge inventory (106-07; 129-30) of tools, household items, farm implements, handicrafts, and building materials made of wood, all of which they will then sell, so that "the whole land will probably very soon be decorated and paneled with wood" (107) ("das ganze Land werde bald darauf mit Holz austapeziert und vertäfelt" [130]). Need it be asked who owns the lumber mills? As outrageous as the devastation of the forest is, Jonke's art is keeping up with life here. After all, how far-fetched is it to show a whole forest being cut down, when at least once in history the vast tracts of the Vienna Woods, surrounding the city for miles, were stripped almost entirely bare (Pohanka 141-2)?

Fear is the powerful means whereby the elders have been able to gain so much destructive control. In classic demagogic style, they conjure up an invisible enemy whose existence is merely asserted: "For reasons of security it will henceforth be prohibited to walk through forests and along tree-lined roads in order to protect the population from the black men who hide so well in the shadows of the trees that they can hardly be distinguished from the darkness of the tree-lined roads" (97) ("Aus Sicherheitsgründen wird es hinkünftig verboten, durch Wälder und Alleen zu gehen, um die Bevölkerung vor den schwarzen Männern zu schützen, die sich in den Schatten der Bäume so gut verstecken, daß sie manchmal mit der Dunkelheit in den Alleen so gut wie identisch werden können" [117]).

Jonke's novel would appear, then, to be mainly a searching, pertinent condemnation of capitalist greed as it came fully of age in the last decades of the twentieth century. In the course of *Geometric Regional Novel*, workers and artistans, puppets of the profit motive, are hired and fired at authoritarian whim; the paternalistic structure of village life insures total regimentation and mind control; that structure in turn yields by logical stages to an all-engulfing totalitiarianism that has no need to use force; capitalism comes to be the sole motive of communal activity as totally unnecessary consumer goods made of wood are manufactured, incidentally destroying the entire surrounding ecosystem; the forests are leveled for profit and deals are made with charcoal burners, furniture factories, and paper mills, all in the name of keeping the black men from being able to hide in the trees.[5] The whole history of the village, moreover, as recorded in the chronicle (47-49; 54-57), shows that these deprivations of freedom have always been a latent possibility in the village's authority structure, but we watch them expand into dimensions never dreamed of as consumerism engulfs the environment. For that matter, the power-holders appear to have selectively rewritten or at least reinterpreted the history of the village so as to make their ascendency look like the final stage of an inevitable progression.

Yet the greed of the village elders is not an exclusively capitalist manifestation, for it inheres in pastoral itself, as the harm caused by property ownership and rights of occupation in Virgil's First Eclogue has shown. Shepherds are easily displaced, because they have no fixed place and move with their flocks.

From the beginning, eviction and violence have always been perpetrated by property owners or stakeholders. Abel was a "keeper of sheep," more innocent and more bucolic than his brother Cain, a "tiller of the soil," who is then bound to a fixed place and needs to exert control over the land he farms. The story (Genesis 4, 2-8) illustrates the power of ownership to violate bonds of kinship. "In the pastoral dispensation," as Poggioli expresses it (194), "the humble and the poor lead a life that is almost safe from internal disorder; yet their harmless happiness is all too often threatened by the encroachments of the proud and the powerful." And there is no limit or boundary to the greed of owners, who cannot rest until they have taken all the available property and assumed unlimited control (Poggioli 204-14). Their impulse is always totalitarian, with all the meanings that term could imply for an Austrian writer.

Of course, Poggioli is discussing Theocritus and Virgil, but he could equally be describing the plight of the villagers in *Geometric Regional Novel*. Not surprisingly, then, Jonke's novel shows the same configurations of power and encroachment presented in the pastoral scenes from Goethe's *Faust*. In "Offene Gegend" and "Palast" from *Faust II* (333-40) – the first two scenes of Act V – Faust gives the order to remove the peaceable, gentle old couple Philemon and Baucis from their modest cottage by force, because it angers him that their house impedes a totally untrammeled view of his surroundings. Behind his restlessness is his whole being, but behind his autocracy is Mephistopheles, who persuades Faust of the need to displace the harmless, loving old people. There is no indication that Jonke modeled the unbounded rapacity of the village elders in *Geometric Regional Novel* directly on *Faust*; instead, the configuration of greed in the pastoral mode itself forms a permanently accessible pattern of reflection and comment in European culture. For that matter, Mephistopheles in his turn harks back to the story of Naboth's vineyard, coveted by a restless, rapacious Ahab, from 1 Kings 21: "Auch hier geschieht, was längst geschah / Denn Naboths Weinberg war schon da"

("Here's an old story, ever the same – / Naboth's vineyard once again") (Goethe 340, ll. 11286-87). This is the same Mephistopholes whose political and economic philosophy contains, albeit in nautical imagery, the whole history of pastoral's misgivings about the linkage of property and power: "Man hat Gewalt, so hat man Recht. / Man fragt ums Was, und nicht ums Wie. / Ich müßte keine Schiffart kennen: / Krieg, Handel und Piraterie, / Dreieinig sind sie, nicht zu trennen" ("Since it's a fact that might is right – / not *how* but *what* will be the only question asked. / Unless I'm all at sea about maritime matters, / war, trade, and piracy together are / a trinity not to be severed") (Goethe 337, ll. 11184-88). That is why this essay is emphasizing the longer pastoral tradition over the more historically recent categories of regional and anti-regional writing; the rapacity and violence, the control and dehumanization, the exploitation and abuse of power that are at the heart of *Geometric Regional Novel* are far deeper-seated in human affairs than can be compassed by Marxist indictments of capitalism and consumerism alone, cogent as these are. The specifically late twentieth-century adaptation of the traditional pattern consists in Jonke's representing the villagers not as displaced persons being driven directly from their dwellings but as dehumanized puppets mindlessly conforming to an authoritarian structure based on consumerism that is in the process of destroying those dwellings and the surroundings in such a way that the inhabitants will soon be displaced in any case.

Even the trees in the village square have been cut down (60-62; 71-74; 87-89; 105-107), purportedly because they were damaging the buildings, but actually, the narrator suggests, to save the cost of paying the street sweeper and to sell the lumber. This narrator is droll, sometimes even zany, but his tone only underscores by contrast the elegiac atmosphere, the sense of lament that pervades the account of the woodcutters' work of destruction. Citing "*public health, beautification, improvement, upgrading of education, emergency relief, recreational activity, satisfaction, beautification, public health*" (91) ("*Volksgesund-*

heit, Bildungshebung, Notstandsbeseitigung, Freizeitgestaltung, Befriedigung, Verschönerung, Volksgesundheit" [109]), the town council votes unanimously to have benches installed after the uprooting of the tree stumps leaves the villagers with no place to sit, but the benches are then abruptly removed later, a central meeting place taken away. This destruction of the trees echoes a universal common practice by "developers," but it also echoes Jonke's requisition of classic pastoral landscape. Citing ancient and early medieval sources, especially Libanius, Curtius establishes (197) that the perfect idyllic landscape, the Arcadian *locus amœnus*, had long been codified to include at least three of the following items: springs, plantations, gardens, soft breezes, flowers, birds' voices. It could well be asked what else one *would* find in a landscape, but the notable feature of *Geometric Regional Novel* is Jonke's drawing on them all, making them the foundation on which the entire novel is built. Once again, it is not so much that Jonke is consciously following Curtius but that the descriptions of landscape in this novel are modeled on a continuous literary tradition strong enough to shape the setting through a common inventory of formal means.

Jonke's comic and ironic bent leads him to reverse all the items of this conventional beauty and show how their destruction or degradation produces harm culminating in natural disasters. Reversal of the pastoral, in fact, is one of the consistent techniques for producing "geometric" contrasts, for showing how the vitality of living things becomes mechanically rigidified, the supple and pliant elements of nature swerving out of control through human abuse and ending in the sterility of the surroundings and the paralysis of the villagers. Henri Bergson proposed in his renowned essay *Le rire* (76-79) that laughter arises when the fluid, adaptable quality of life triumphs over the inflexibility and the rigidity of mechanistic processes, thereby producing a comic incongruity. Jonke uses the items in the unspoiled, idealized landscapes of the *locus amœnus* to the diametrical opposite of their traditional effect, showing how Libanius's six main manifestations of life and fecundity have either been destroyed or have become destructive through human interference and have turned from vital to deadly. In a typical movement of greed, for example, three of the items – spring, plantations, and gardens – have been subordinated to the profit motive, rearranged and redirected to serve "General and Specific Economic Measures," to cite a chapter heading (83-85) ("Allgemeine und spezielle wirtschaftliche Maßnahmen" [100-02]). And that is the very best of it, because the three items at least are able to retain vestiges of their natural functions here, as opposed to the destructive reversals everywhere else. The very consistency of the reversal shows Jonke's indebtedness to the pastoral landscape, at the heart of which is always some variation of the inventory of items that make up the *locus amœnus* as categorized by Libanius and reported by Curtius (197). In fact, the brief inventory (116;143) of natural beauties and pleasures that the villagers hope they will be able to enjoy if they leave the benches outside after the last bird attack tallies closely enough with Curtius's list to suggest again that Jonke's items are derived from a common store of landscape description codified within the pastoral mode. (See the appendix for a survey of items of the *locus amœnus* and Jonke's consistent reversal of their harmony and beauty.)

It might seem that calling attention to passages in which a confident narrator assures his hearers that "careful planning and the incorporation of cybernetics will guarantee the economic boom in the land" (107) ("sorgfältige Planung und Einbeziehung der Kybernetik werden den wirtschaftlichen Aufschwung des Landes garantieren" [131]) would be the best way to focus on the specifically "geometric" elements of Jonke's novel. And indeed the geometry of the novel's form and viewpoint is rich with diagrams, technical language, blueprints, mathematical calculations, and similar devices: the tightrope walker's tent (19; 19), the dimensions of the bridge (32-36), and the irrigation system (84; 101) are presented as diagrams, for instance; banishing all pastoral picturesqueness, the contours of the mountains are described as "a sine curve, a cosine curve, and a sine and a cosine curve, each displaced by one and three-quarter phases" (9) ("eine Sinuskurve, eine Cosinuskurve und eine Sinus- und eine Cosinuskurve um je eindreiviertel Phasen verschoben" [8]); the rigorously mechanical and measurable are everywhere in evidence, even if they are describing structures and arrangements that eventually collapse in chaos. These are the manifestations of geometry in the most literal sense of the word, the measurement of the earth, the quantitative description and analysis of structures and forms.

Before examining that aspect further, however, the reader may observe that Jonke's work draws on musical development as its most fundamental and indeed all-encompassing geometric structural principle. Geometric because what strategies of form could ever demand a rigor greater than the discipline musical structure necessarily imposes, in which every aspect of the sound must logically have relation to every other aspect, where proportional relations must be made manifest, both horizontally and vertically, at every point, where random sounds are organized into an utterance that must cohere entirely if it is to be apprehended at all? In *Geometric Regional Novel*, the specific principle of musical structure is rondo-variation form, which alternates a relatively simple theme (A) with progressively more elaborate variations developing from that theme; the structure is $A - B - A - C - A - D - A - E$, and so on.[6] Jonke's theme, the A in *Geometric Regional Novel*, is represented by the chapters entitled "The Village Square," ("Der Dorfplatz"), which always begin with the same brief exchange between two people debating how to cross the empty village square without being observed. That theme creates a clearly discernible and literal point of departure for progressively more extended, complex, and wide-ranging variations, each of which moves geographically ever farther from the square to encompass more and more of the surroundings while incorporating more and more of the deeper history and wider organization of the village. The chapter that begins with the first reversion to the starting point – always the dialogue about crossing the square

(15-29; 16-32) – illustrates the process clearly, and it is even more clearly marked by musical structure in the most recent German edition, since Jonke slightly but significantly revised the text for a new printing in 2004, well after the English version appeared. The nine chapters each previously called simply "The Village Square" ("Der Dorfplatz") are now numbered 1 through 9, like the items in a numbers opera or a set of variations. In "Der Dorfplatz 2," there is a restatement of the rondo theme (16-17); a two-part "Intermezzo" designated as such, with Part A titled "Vorführung des Künstlers" (18-26) ("The Artist's Performance" [17-24]) and Part B "Bericht auf der Kulturseite der Zeitung" (27-30) ("Report in the Fine Arts Section of the Newspaper" [25-27]), and finally a "Fortsetzung Der Dorfplatz 2" (31-32), a continuation of the chapter explicitly labeled as such.[7]

Like many authors who emerged in Austria after 1945 – Thomas Bernhard, Ernst Jandl, Elfriede Jelinek, Hans Lebert, Gerhard Rühm, to name a handful – Jonke is a trained musician with more than passing competence. His mother was a pianist who, at her five-year-old's insistence, used to play him Ravel's *Jeux d'eau* every night; he reports that he would refuse to go to bed until she did. He had considerable conservatory training in piano himself and added university course work in musicology and music history, but he stopped preparing for a concert career upon deciding to become a writer (Kling, Gert Jonke 24).

Musical structure in *Geometrical Regional Novel* serves a thematic purpose in tandem with the underlying themes of pastoral by enacting the spread of tyranny as the increasing complexity of the variations models the growing encroachment of authoritarianism through greater control of seemingly harmless, traditional social arrangements meant to uphold good order. The vehicle for that structural movement is the simple theme, the verbal exchange at the start of alternate chapters, beginning with the first, in which readers can already detect a vague, pervasive apprehension or even muted fear of a paternalistic authority that eventually engulfs everything. Sets of rules and regulations grow constantly longer and more intrusive with each new development of the theme; history extends farther and farther back, but it is more subject to being distorted through legend-making by the village elders; all processes and procedures grow more elaborate and burdensome. This essay has already mentioned the culminating variation, the chapter called "The New Law" (96-108) ("Das neue Gesetz" [117-132]), but it might be worth pointing out here that this variation delineates the utmost control over the villagers, the most extreme infringement on their freedoms, the almost complete stifling of life, the most elaborate extension of the variations in keeping with rondo form, that is, only to be followed by a description of an apocalyptic battle with killer birds in the last of the "Village Square" chapters. The rondo-variation form may be the vehicle for depicting increasing elaboration in the refinement of tyranny, but that form is powerless in the political and social order to keep extremity of control from ultimately tipping over into a chaos caused by the very pursuit of control in the first place.

If pastoral tends to draw the reader into an ideal setting, to conceal at first the conflicts, fears, and losses it always depicts under the beguiling surface of an idealized beauty in nature, then the geometric aspects of Jonke's novel counterbalance that beguilement in the same way that some modern buildings achieve an unconventional beauty by placing systems like heating ducts, water pipes, and electrical cables on the outside. Rather than hiding the workings, the geometry, behind walls, these are now not only laid open to view, but they become as integral a part of the architectural effect as the traditional elements. In that sense, the geometric modification of the pastoral constantly follows the modernist process of disclosing how pastoral is working, forming a structural and formal commentary rooted in the incongruity whereby a work of art calls attention to itself as an artifact, a crafted object, a structure, making that procedure a part of the very theme. An inventory of these geometric effects will help show the added impact of *Geometric Regional Novel* as an invention within convention by noting the resulting irony, the way in which it simultaneously advances traditional devices and calls them into creative question.

Geometric Regional Novel forces readers to consider the truth of story line, for instance, by creating a well-nigh plotless plot about two people wanting to cross the village square unseen and then frustrating an expected explanation by never even addressing the question of why they want to be unobserved in the first place. Traditional "suspense" is built in and then ignored.

The novel's rondo-variation form challenges the linear progression that the successful crossing of the square achieves by embedding in that progression a potentially endless circular eternal return, cycling back to the same words at the start of each of the sections titled "The Village Square." The crossing is a single movement in a predictable direction, but that crossing is placed into a pattern of infinite possible regress and replication.

Jonke's novel breaks the illusion of a "real" world being left behind at the end, rupturing any illusion about the extreme artifact of pastoral by dissolving the colors and the objects of the whole countryside and by closing with a suggestion that the narrator, or even the reader, might want to wrap the village in paper and toss it away, so as to *"make a turn into another region"* (118) (*"um in eine andere Landschaft einzubiegen"* [146]), implying that artifice is the one reality of a literary work and that the whole process of crafting and inventing could begin again, like another variation in the rondo. That dissolving stands in opposition to the markedly idyllic ending of regional fiction, in which the setting would be made transcendent, apotheosed into a never-changing, harmonious "isle of the blessed," a place of mutual enrichment between humanity and nature as the conservative values underlying the social structure are elevated to sacredness.

As part of a larger strategy, *Geometric Regional Novel* disturbs the traditional, sacrosanct illusion of distance between author and narrator in a self-referential way by having a family named Jonke living in one of the houses around the village square in the diagram (41; 47). More broadly, it also subverts a related structural canon, that of the work as a sovereign closed world of the artist's making, by bringing the reader directly into its pages. The reader is permitted to take part in tossing away the village at the end, and, among the many divergent voices commenting in chorus-like fashion through this novel, thus opening it to communal participation rather than individual autonomy in form, there seems to be the active presence of the reader, to whom the warnings about the bull, for example (10-14; 9-13), or the elaborate instructions for crossing the bridge (30-39; 33-44) appear to be directed.

Geometric procedure questions the authority of narrative to mediate reality, its own included, by virtuosic displays, as in the section "Corrugated Iron and Door" (72-73) ("Wellblech und Tür" [86-88]), of how the simplest act of perceptual awareness relies not on solidly external, universally ascertainable objective structures, not on an incontrovertibly solid world "out there," but on fleeting, relative, and momentary physical phenomena that appear and vanish in a literal flash. Raising a window or opening a door can cause a whole vista to disappear instantly.

It suggests the illusory nature of free human agency by showing the simplest of movements, like shaking hands (8; 6), as if they were the programmed, awkwardly mechanized actions of robots. That radical questioning of freedom on the most basic level operates in contrast to a beloved major theme of standard regional fiction, according to which the individual gains greater freedom by submitting more and more deeply, with greater and greater humility, to a communal order that mirrors the eternal laws of nature and thus elevates the individual to dignity as part of a universal cycle. If pastoral equates freedom with a lack of exactly those constraints regional writing extols, as idealized in Adalbert Stifter's invocation of the "gentle law" governing all nature, then the geometrical side of Jonke's novel proposes that restrictions on freedom could well be intrinsic to the need for order in human existence.

Geometric Regional Novel demonstrates a feasible contrast to that indwelling restriction by advocating the utter freedom of the imagination. It is not only possible, but permissible (118) ("durchaus erlaubt" [146]) to set aside the artistic creation made and sustained throughout by the artist, with the reader's help, so that democratic cooperation and collaboration can take place in making and disposing of art. It is not an elitist pursuit. Though the villagers are regimented by repressive communal arrangements, the structure which examines them enacts open process by including many voices without feeling a need to reconcile the differences among them; no one view has to prevail. In this way, *Geometric Regional Novel* enacts in its use of collaborating voices an alternative to the repressive, paternalistic structures depicted within it. The rules, the prohibitions, the restrictions and restraints, the growing totalitarianism, do not apply in the world of art, though the exercise of art may be powerless to halt the tyranny in any direct way. The pen is mightier than the sword, but unfortunately in the long haul only.

The geometric adaptation of pastoral demonstrates that any theory of "natural law" as a justification for legislated order is a related illusion, a deceit grounded in massive projection of human categories onto nature. Just as "natural" human actions are described geometrically, so the pathetic fallacy ("weeping" skies, "gentle" hills, "harmonious" landscapes, "furious" winds) is shown, through depictions of the surroundings in geometric terms, in radically physical descriptions – as in physics, that is – stripped of all emotive connotations, to be a distortion of exclusively human origin. The ending also reveals that this village has no "real" existence outside the imagination. It was all the construct of an artist, a set to be struck, a drawing to be tossed away. That reminder of easy disposablility in turn removes works of art from any arrogant claim to be representing, let alone replacing, a higher truth and casts into doubt any artist's claims to be reforming society, while the chastening of lyric description through denotative geometrical terminology enacts an ethical warning that the freedom of the imagination may not be abused by the esthetic desire to be merely beautiful, to rhapsodize, to use "poetic license" and write just anything.

Geometric process challenges the privileged status of all orderly or "scientific" arrangement in turn, since order in itself is no guarantee of a truth congruent with something outside itself. The precise, minute processes of description, which include several diagrams that look like blueprints or engineers' drawings, would seem to endorse the tendency to examine phenomena and objects in great detail as a way of apprehending them in external reality. This is the procedure of the natural sciences and of humanistic scholarship founded on exhaustive primary documentation. What actually happens as often as not is that historical chronicles here wander off into speculation and uncertainty (47-49; 54-57), undermining the very sense of objectivity for which they are aiming, while the meticulous "scientific" description of objects and processes becomes so minute that the description itself is thwarted ("The House of the Blacksmith" (50-59) ("Das Haus des Schmiedes" [58-70]) or ends up shading off into paranoia not recognized as such because observation and documentation give it the look of objective fact, as in the "New Law" chapter (96-108) ("Das neue Gesetz" [116-132]). Out of the supposedly progressive, objective approach of science comes a rationale for totalitarian control, since careful enough recording of data in themselves can be put to any purpose, used to justify anything, as the flourishing of racial biology in the National Socialist world and the "scientific" genetic studies of Trofim Lysenko in the Soviet Union show. Totalitarianism of any stripe can put science to good use, provided it ignores the inherent limitations of science. Crudely put, *Geometric Regional Novel* dramatizes the popular expression that statistics can prove anything – as in totalitarian governments they indeed do.

Geometry further parodies naïve beliefs that comprehensive description of physical phenomena will capture the essential truth of their nature by taking methods of "objective" description so far into minutiae that all sense is lost of what is being described. That process, known as "defamiliarization," leads to an excruciating focus on minute detail in the chapter about the blacksmith's house, for instance (50-59; 58-70), such that it becomes impossible to follow the very sequence that all the detail is meant to clarify. The thread is drawn out so fine that no reader can follow it. Defamiliarization undermines the claims of both science and art to sovereign representation; science thinks it has found some truth when it describes phenomena in sequential, exhaustive detail, and it was always one of the cornerstone processes of regional literature to work in miniature, evoking and describing small objects in precious isolation.

Likewise, Jonke's geometric view further undermines any sense of logical or chronological plot development, any sense of expected proportion or pace by recording how such carefully garnered data spin madly out of control when they are over-organized, as if the very effort to gain control were the quickest way to trigger off chaos. That artistic process has direct political implications. Especially where anything suggestive of an imposed social order, anything in the realm of instructions or guidelines is concerned, whatever forward movement of the story line there was comes to a halt and a kind of unstoppable proliferation, a compulsion to enumerate, takes over, the manic quality of which exposes the insanity, the need for total control, of those trying to impose this order. Again, totalitarianism makes much deeper inroads by regulating through bureaucracy than through violence. Two main examples are the pages-long list of guidelines given to the schoolchildren (43-46; 48-53,) about what behaviors are allowed and prohibited, and the new law, mentioned several times already, that governs walks into the woods. (Nor should we forget that the woods are being plundered out of existence anyway; the paperwork grows as the raw material for filling it out dwindles.)

Overall, geometry challenges the unexamined assumption that language (and, by implication, fictional genres and structures, which take form in it) has within itself any necessary ability to create understanding or communication at all. Ludwig Wittgenstein minutely explored the conditions under which an utterance can have meaning that is not tautological, as Jonke pointed out (Kling, Casebook, "Circling the Village" 27), but

Jonke went on to say that his own thinking about language depends far less on Wittgenstein than on Fritz Mauthner's *Beiträge zu einer Kritik der Sprache* (*Contributions to a Critique of Language*) (1902) and *Philosophisches Wörterbuch* (*Dictionary of Philosophy*) (1910). Wittgenstein began with the axiomatic presupposition that language has meaning when reduced to its essence, Mauthner with the presupposition that it has not. According to Mauthner, summed up by Jonke, "Die Sprache ist kein Verständigungsmittel" – there is nothing within language itself that makes it inherently a vehicle of communication. Fundamentally, no two people, as Jonke reviews Mauthner, ever have exactly the same set of associations with any given word. Moreover, most verbal exchanges in social settings have less to do with communicating the lexical meanings of the words than to promote ritualized exchanges, the words mere tokens of meanings conveyed by the whole encounter but not by the words in themselves. Hence the mechanized nature of so many meetings between people in *Geometric Regional Novel*, beginning with the scene of people shaking hands on the village square (8; 6). In connection with Mauthner's ideas, Jonke mentioned further his experience as a young writer – he was twenty-three when he wrote *Geometric Regional Novel* – of how meanings emerge on their own, most surprisingly and quite independently of the writer's intent. He reports that many of his lists of words began as a purely neutral technical exercise, an attempt to find within a body of synonyms exactly the right connotation or shade of meaning, but that the lists themselves autonomously took on satirical and parodistic elements that he had no conscious thought of creating. Only when the list was there did its absurdity manifest itself. An additional part of the parody is his playful creation of compound nouns that go on for lines and lines, redolent of bureaucratic language in German at its most nightmarish–an effect it would be hard for a translator to capture, by the way, without turning inspired higher nonsense in one language into incomprehensible gibberish in the other.

Connection rescues language from incoherence: grammar, syntax, word order, perhaps even a purely alphabetical arrangement, as in a dictionary. The less randomness, the more meaning, and art coheres by providing the material of its articulation with form shaped by cultural history. In harmonizing a rigorous formal adherence to long-standing traditional structures and attitudes of Western literature with a counterbalancing radical modernist technique, Jonke has achieved in *Geometric Regional Novel* a coherent novel in itself and an example of Poggiolo's point (36) that invention is often at its most fertile when it adheres closely to convention.

Appendix
Elements of the *locus amœnus* as Defined by Curtius (197) and Jonke's Reversals

Element	Pages	Jonke's Reversal
Springs	67-71; 79-85. 94-5; 111-15. 113-14; 138-42. 30-39; 33-44. 83; 100.	Pleasant springs become destructive torrents deadly in their intensity; flooding everywhere; birds are fought with killing high-powered blasts from hoses; water engulfs the cosmos, as at the start of creation in Genesis; digging of canals to transport coal, since no wood is left for fuel; a bridge described in entirely functional geometric terms, as a technological artifact that displaces attention to the fluidity of the river below it.
Plantations	15-16; 16-17. 28-29; 31-32. 87-89; 105-07.	Complete uprooting and destroying of once-abundant trees from the center of the village outward; forest made virtually inaccessible through

	96-108; 116-32.	bureaucracy and eventually stripped bare.
Gardens	74; 89. 87-88; 105-07. 111-12; 136-38	Plants: hollow, lifeless trees arranged in baroque style, burning without being consumed, like a parody of Moses's calling in Exodus 3, 2-22; piles of dug-up trees artfully arranged. Animals: monstrously mutated destructive maggots, worms, and beetles living in and nourishing themselves from an ecosystem of concrete, mortar, limestone eaten by the birds who are wrecking the village.
Soft Breezes	110; 134. 113-14; 138-39.	Singing, shrieking, screaming air caused by the rush of birds hurtling to attack (aside from the birds' own noise); deafening noise and wind from the extreme pressure of the water hoses; hissing from water mains.
Flowers	107-08; 131.	Marsh marigolds emerging out of knotholes in worked wood; access to fruits, nuts, and berries–all later stages of blossoms–prohibited by posted notices to gatherers, who are chased away, even driven to death.
Bird-Voices	93-95; 109-116. 110-12; 135-40	Apocalyptic destructiveness of dive-bombing birds causes havoc, practically destroying the village; ominous caws and cries of the approaching swarms; deafening sound of screeching and squawking birds; crunching of beaks as the birds feed on the mutated insects.

Endnotes

---

[1] Two other editions have appeared since the first publication in 1989. Jonke subjected *Geometrischer Heimatroman*, along with his other extant novels, to considerable revision in 1980. Vazulik traces the process in his afterword to the English translation. Yet another revision, less extensive than the first, appeared in 2004. All references to both English and German texts of the novel will be cited in parentheses, with page numbers to the left side of a semicolon for the English and to the right for the German. This essay draws on the 2004 revision.
[2] Readers of American literature may find parallel views and values in the collection of essays entitled *I'll Take My Stand*, by "Twelve Southerners," an impassioned set of arguments for a Southern, agrarian, pre-industrial culture and its implied social and political values. See the Works Cited. This collection continues to resonate strongly; it seems never to have gone out of print since its initial publication in 1930. As Poggioli points out (26-31), pastoral tends toward conservatism and preservation of the status quo – wherever land and agrarian values are to the fore, there is a strong tendency toward resisting change, industrialism, modernity. This is the spirit in which *I'll Take My Stand* is best understood, as a document of pastoral ideals with no relativizing irony or concession to its time.
[3] This essay will offer a more specific analysis of the formal structure of the "text segments" later.
[4] Radnóti (1909-1944) responded to the violence of his times by composing a set of eclogues, in strict imitation of Virgil, dealing with the Spanish Civil War and World War II. Most of these remarkable poems can be found in his collection *Clouded Sky*; see the Works Cited.
[5] For discussions of consumerism as the third and most insidious wave of totalitarianism, following fascism and Soviet communism, see the introductory materials in Arato and Gebhardt as well

as the essays by Adorno, Benjamin, and Horkheimer in that collection, listed in the Works Cited.

[6] Among many possible instances, two great arias by Mozart are especially clear textbook examples of rondo-variation form, Fiordiligi's "Per pietà, ben mio perdono" from Act II of *Così fan tutte* and Vitellia's "Non più di fiori" from Act II of *La clemenza di Tito*.

[7] Previous editions in German lack this amount of structural-musical indication, as does Vazulik's translation, which follows the 1980 edition. The numbering of the overall "Village Square" chapter title and of all the subsections is not present in earlier editions, as is the genre designation "Intermezzo" that links the heading "The Artist's Performance" (Vazulik's translation 17-24) and "Report in the Fine Arts Section of the Newspaper" (25-27). Further, the lack of any indication that the next section, titled simply "The Village Square" in previous editions and in Vazulik's translation (27-29), is part of "Der Dorfplatz 2" makes it appear as if that part were a discrete chapter instead of the "Fortsetzung" or continuation Jonke titles it in the 2004 edition. Jonke's new headings bring out much more clearly than before the relation of the parts in the overall chapter "Der Dorfplatz 2" (16-32) as subsections of the second statement of the rondo theme and its development through contrasting intermezzo and *ritornello* as recurrence of the theme.

Works Cited

Amann, Klaus, ed. *Die Aufhebung der Schwerkraft: Zu Gert Jonkes Poesie*. Vienna: Sonderzahl, 1998.
Arato, Andrew and Eike Gebhardt, eds. *The Essential Frankfurt School Reader*. New York: Urizen, 1978.
Bartens, Daniela. "Die Zeitschrift ›manuskripte‹." Kaukoreit and Pfoser. 137-9.
Bartsch, Kurt. "Damals vor Graz: Die verspätete Aneignung von Moderne und Avantgarde in der Literatur aus dem Umkreis

von Forum Stadtpark Graz und der Zeitschrift *manuskripte.*" *Études germaniques* 50 (1995): 289-300.
Bergson, Henri. *Le rire: essai sur la signification du comique.* http://classiques.uqac.ca/classiques/bergson_henri/le_rire/le_rire.html. Published 1900. Accessed 15 Jan. 2008.
Curtius, Ernst Robert. *European Literature and the Latin Middle Ages.* Trans. Willard R. Trask. Bollingen Series 36. Princeton: Princeton UP, 1990 (1953).
Daviau, Donald G., ed. *Major Figures of Contemporary Austrian Literature.* New York: Lang, 1987.
Düsing, Wolfgang. "Avantgardistische Experimente mit einer konservativen Gattung: Gert Jonke 'Geometrischer Heimatroman.'" Polheim 87-105.
Esslin, Martin. "Ein neuer Manierismus? Randbemerkungen zu einigen Werken von Gert F. Jonke und Thomas Bernhard." *Modern Austrian Literature* 13.1 (1980): 111-128.
Goethe, Johann Wolfgang von. *Faust. Werke.* Hamburger Ausgabe. 14 vols. 5th ed. Ed. Erich Trunz. Vol. 3. Hamburg: Wegner, 1959.
Hillach, Ansgar. "Beheimatung im Medium: Gert Jonkes *Geometrischer Heimatroman.*" *Literatur und Provinz: Das Konzept 'Heimat' in der neueren Literatur.* Ed. Hans-Georg Pott. Paderborn: Schöningh, 1986. 131-151.
Innerhofer, Franz. *Schöne Tage.* Salzburg: Residenz, 1974.
Innerhofer. *Beautiful Days.* Trans. Anselm Hollo. New York: Urizen, 1976.
Jelinek, Elfriede. "Hier ist Dort. Ein paar Überlegungen zu Gert Jonke." Amann 17-19.
Jonke, Gert. *Geometric Regional Novel.* Trans. with an afterword by Johannes W. Vazulik. Normal, IL: Dalkey Archive Press, 2000 (1994).
Jonke, Gert. *Geometrischer Heimatroman.* Frankfurt/Main: dtv, 1971 (1969).
Jonke, Gert. *Geometrischer Heimatroman.* Salzburg and Vienna: Jung und Jung, 2004 (1980).

Kaukoreit, Volker and Kristina Pfoser. *Die österreichische Literatur seit 1945: Eine Annäherung in Bildern.* Stuttgart: Reclam, 2000.
Kling, Vincent, ed. A Casebook on Gert Jonke's *Geometric Regional Novel.* http://www.dalkeyarchive.com/casebooks/casebook_geo/introduction_geo.html. 15 Jan. 2008.
Kling, Vincent. "Gert Jonke." *Review of Contemporary Fiction,* 24.1 (Spring 2005), 1-57.
Kunne, Andrea. *Heimat im Roman: Last oder Lust?* Amsterdam: Rodopi, 1991.
Poggioli, Renato. *The Oaten Flute: Essays on Pastoral Poetry and the Pastoral Ideal.* Ed. A. Bartlett Giamatti. Cambridge, MA: Harvard UP, 1975.
Pohanka, Reinhard. *Das römische Wien.* Vol. 1. *Geschichte Wiens.* 6 vol. Vienna: Pichler, 1997.
Polheim, Karl Konrad. *Wesen und Wandel der Heimatliteratur: am Beispiel der österrecihischen Literatur seit 1945.* Ein Bonner Symposion. Bern: P. Lang, 1989.
Schmidt-Dengler, Wendelin. *Bruchlinien:Vorlesungen zur österreichischen Literatur 1945 bis 1990.* Vienna: Residenz, 1995.
Schramm, Ingrid. "Heimatersatz und Schauplatz des 'Kalten Krieges': Hilde Spiel und der P.E.N." *Hilde Spiel: Weltbürgerin der Literatur.* Ed. Hans A. Neunzig and Ingrid Schramm. *Profile.* Magazin des österreichischen Literaturarchivs, 2.3. Vienna: Zsolnay, 1999. 125-32.
Schrembs, Edigna. "Experimentelle Prosa der letzten Jahre und ihr Verhältnis zur gesellschaftlichen Wirklichkeit – am Beispiel Thomas Bernhard, Ror Wolf, Jürgen Becker, Gert Friedrich Jonke." *Der Deutschunterricht* 25 (1973): 68-82.
Twelve Southerners. *I'll Take My Stand: The South and the Agrarian Tradition.* Intro. Louis D. Rubin, Jr. Baton Rouge: Lousiana State UP, 1962 (rpt. 1983) (1930).
Vazulik, Johannes W. "An Introduction to the Prose Narratives of Gert Jonke." *Major Figures of Contemporary Austrian*

Literature. Ed. Donald G. Daviau. New York: Lang, 1987. 293-311.
Vazulik, Johannes W. "Gert F. Jonke." *Austrian Fiction Writers after 1914*. *Dictionary of Literary Biography*, vol. 85. Ed. Donald Daviau. 224-32.
Vazulik, Johannes W. Afterword. Jonke, *Geometric Regional Novel*. 119-131.
Welty, Eudora. "Place in Fiction." *The Eye of the Story: Selected Essays and Reviews*. New York: Random House, 1978. 116-133.
Winkler, Josef. *Der Leibeigene*. Frankfurt: Suhrkamp, 1979.
Winkler, Josef. *The Serf*. Trans. Mike Mitchell. Riverside, CA: Ariadne, 1996.

Contextualizing and Decontextualizing Barbara Frischmuth's Novel *Das Verschwinden des Schattens in der Sonne*

Pamela S. Saur

The Shadow Disappears in the Sun, translated by Nicholas J. Meyerhofer, Ariadne Press, 1998

The fiction and essays of contemporary Austrian writer, Barbara Frischmuth (1941-), have always demonstrated her involvement in current political and social issues. Her successful literary debut at age twenty-seven with *The Convent School* (*Die Klosterschule*, 1968) exposed the oppressiveness of Austrian boarding schools and became associated with the international student movement of late 1960s.[1] Her initial perceived public role as champion of the young, as reflected in later novels on mothers and children and in her own books for children, was later enhanced by a variety of thoughtful feminist messages in her fiction. Frischmuth authored several provocative stories and novels on women's issues in the 1970s and early 1980s that were not only relevant to the day but were ahead of their time as early documents of the feminist movement to come.[2] Likewise, her 1973 novel *Das Verschwinden des Schattens in der Sonne* (*The Shadow Disappears in the Sun*) represents an early exploration of the cultural concerns and studies, not to mention real-world conflicts that have developed in the ensuing decades. Were it not for an already long-standing tradition of travel literature,[3] the novel could be labeled prophetic as it preceded the enormously influential movements promoting multiculturalism and multicultural education, cultural literary criticism and cultural studies associated with language programs, and the still ongoing debates about Orientalism, exoticism, Eurocentricism, and globalization.

These developments have influenced and been influenced not only by literature and literary scholarship, but by political and social realities and educational goals at all levels.

In an interview Frischmuth herself pointed to the fact that this 1973 novel was "republished as a hardcover edition in 1996 because the problems it discussed have become very relevant to the present situation."[4] The novel as a cultural document is also important in the context of Frischmuth's own later writings, for in the ensuing decades she has authored numerous fictional works as well as essays and speeches that demonstrate her interest in cultural topics and her passionate commitment to promoting cultural understanding. Indeed, doing so is an integral part of her identity and mission as a writer. In 2004 Francis Michael Sharp commented on this mission, "While the Austrian writer Barbara Frischmuth has no illusions about the political effectiveness of literature in a postmodern world, she holds onto a belief in its social function." He quotes her 1998 comments on the subject, "It has become quite clear to us all that literature has passed the zenith of its political effectiveness. But that does not mean that it no longer plays any role at all in human interacttions; perhaps not directly, as we sometimes might wish, but in a roundabout way it still does have influence."[5] Sharp concludes, "The indirect social role which Frischmuth's own fiction often plays is the demonstration of cultural rapprochement that is possible in complex human interchange...Frischmuth creates a micro-world in which characters form close human bonds not only in spite of, but often because of cultural differences...The unknown and unfamiliar have been centrally attractive forces for the figures in Frischmuth's novels from her earliest to her most recent works" (1).

In the Afterword to his English translation of the novel, Nicholas Meyerhofer offers insightful comments on its relevance to events of recent years:

> *The Shadow Disappears in the Sun* remains popular and current...in large measure because of its thematization of the difficulty and com-

plexity of cross-cultural understanding. For Western societies that have frequently demonized the world of Islam as being fundamentalist and intolerant, the English translation of this literary exposure to the Islamic traditions and culture of Turkey should be as important and timely as when the original was first published in German nearly a quarter of a century ago (157).[6]

Unfortunately, his comments on Islamic fundamentalism and East/West conflict are even more relevant today than they were in 1998.

A number of critics have recognized the significance of the context of Frischmuth's voluminous oeuvre to *The Shadow Disappears in the Sun* and provided illuminating readings of the novel in light of Frischmuth's later writings and spoken comments on cultural issues. A typical view is found in Monika Strañáková's 2007 article about the homeland versus the foreign in Frischmuth's work where she states, "The first step in the direction of foreign cultures that the author dared to take was her interlude as a student in Turkey. She reworked these experiences in her first novel *The Shadow Disappears in the Sun*."[7] The identification of the novel and the experiences it was based on as a "first step" reveals the common tendency to interpret the book in light of works that have been published in later years as well as to view Frischmuth's own experiences as a student in terms of her own personal and creative development as an adult.

Less recognized is the need to read the novel in a more literal, indeed decontextualized way as well, to focus on the text in itself and not as a slice of autobiography, an introduction to Frischmuth's later thought and creation, a textbook on multiculturalism, or an allegory of clash between Western and Eastern culture. On this level, the book relates the experiences of an individual student embarking on a brief "study abroad" sojourn. The student experiences degrees of success and growth, as well as limitations, stress and failure, that one might expect from anyone in her circumstances. She also undergoes a "coming of age" experience that amounts to one significant but brief phase in a process of development or *Bildung* with an uncertain outcome, for the book is surprisingly open-ended. The protagonist is an adolescent, a foreign language learner, a traveler vulnerable to "culture shock," and a young student, with not only a student's limited wisdom and sophistication, but also a student's special interests and narrow purposes for travel. The goal of reading the novel in a "decontextualized" manner is not to deny the importance of its rich literary and cultural context, but to bring out aspects of the book that may easily be overlooked in more "contextualized" readings.

Jennifer Michaels places this novel in the context of Frischmuth's essays and her translations of Turkish texts, all writings that promote dialogue, understanding, and tolerance among cultural groups. Michaels states that Frischmuth "has sought to nurture 'a genuine interest and a readiness to become spiritually and emotionally involved with the other.'"[8] Michaels quotes Frischmuth's 1995 essay "Looking over the Fence" which reveals the author's early interest in other cultures, stimulated by meeting guests at her mother's hotel in rural Austria and by reading *A Thousand and One Nights*. Frischmuth studied Turkish and English at the University of Graz and spent nine months as a student in Turkey, a "study abroad" experience like that recounted in the novel. Michaels makes an important point regarding the parallel with Frischmuth's own life: "Like Frischmuth, the first-person narrator is a student living in Turkey who is researching the dervish order of the Bektashi for her dissertation. Although the novel contains many autobiographical references, Frischmuth stresses that this is not her story. Rather it deals with the narrator's attempts to adapt to and understand another culture and the difficulties involved in this process" (70-71).

Another commentator, Monika Shafi, prefaces her examination of the unnamed protagonist's cross-cultural experience with reflections on the difficulty of defining "success." She says that she is not attempting to measure the sojourner's "mastery in overcoming" "displacement" or "erasing" "alienness, for such an approach oversimplifies what is at stake in this rapprochement. Though one certainly can identify attitudes and strategies that help cope with alterity, by its very nature alterity will always maintain an elusive, unattainable quality." She adds: "Dietrich Krusche thus argues for approaching a foreign culture not with the goal of seeking to comprehend. Instead, he advocates the provisional suspension of understanding." She notes that Frischmuth's student does try to "understand the other culture on its own terms" and "from within," and adds that she "follows Krusche's suggestion of suspending comprehension in order not to preliminarily fit and fix the other into her own value system. To the extent possible, she is thus trying to completely mold her behavior according to the rules of her immediate environment and be like the people around her."[9] Shafi emphasizes that the student collects impressions and "deliberately withholds comparisons and conclusions" (248). Welcoming the "blurring of past and present, of dreams and reality, and the ensuing loss of self," the student avoids judging, categorizing or looking down on the new culture. Shafi concludes, "In this regard, the young woman's pursuit of another culture is very productive...her view is non-hegemonic, and she comes to know herself differently" (249).

A contrasting negative view of the novel and of its protagonist's cultural insights has been developed by Dagmar Lorenz, who asserts, "Frischmuth's narrator reproduces the traditional Orient, as a realm replete with magic, legendary creatures, and romance, fantastic and antimodern." She also cites touches of "exotic appeal," and "impression of foreignness," and "an air of lawlessness and despotism," and notes, "In the violent ending...the protagonist's exotic love interest is eliminated." Lorenz sums up:

> In conclusion, it can be established that as far as plot line, imagery, positionality within the narrative, and intellectual rigor are concerned, Frisch-

muth's representation of the Orient, i.e. Turkey, does not break new ground...Only superficial contacts between members of Eastern and Western cultures are discussed; no avenues of negotiating cultural discourses are explored.[10]

In the same vein, Petra Fachinger asserts that despite Frischmuth's "acute awareness of the pitfalls of Orientalism," Turkey in this novel is "a Eurocentric construct"; its depiction reinforces the stereotype that Turkey "remains both a place of sensuality and a place of violence."[11]

Turning toward a decontextualized reading of the story set apart from the context of Frischmuth's other works and larger cultural issues, I wish to contend that critics ought not inadvertently place too many demands on the young student at the heart of the debate or place unreasonably large expectations on her brief experience of study abroad. Although it is of course quite appropriate to critique Frischmuth's presentation of Turkey and cultural interactions in the novel, the varied opinions about the subject reveal that well-intended people may well differ on these complex issues, which have been viewed differently in different decades. I contend that an additional fruitful approach to the novel is to set such complex contextual issues aside and focus on the young woman and her story as presented in the book itself. Reading thus, on a literal and individualized level, let us attempt to assess the young student's international sojourn from the point of view of her parents, counselors, academic advisors, and teachers. These interested parties would not expect original insights into rapprochement between Eastern and Western cultures, nor would they expect an adolescent in 1973 to negotiate the fine points of cultural theories developed in the last quarter of the twentieth century and thereafter. Rather, they would be interested in pragmatic questions: the young woman's academic success, foreign language learning, personal adjustment, and ability to live in a foreign culture without suffering the worst symptoms of "culture shock,"[12] and perhaps also the suitability of the chosen host country as a safe and appropriate destination for future students.

The question of academic success is crucial, for the specific goal of the young woman's sojourn to Turkey to conduct research for her dissertation. The substance and accuracy of her findings would be a prime measure of her success in this realm. As Christoph Gellner points out, the actual content of the protagonist's research comprises a considerable portion of the novel's content. According to Gellner, "The book proceeds on two levels: On one, conducting *research* for the dissertation to be written, the first person narrator seeks *origins*, immerses herself in *Turkish-Islamic history, religion, and culture.*" Gellner identifies the "other level" of the book as the narrator's attempts at "*coming closer to the other, Muslim-Oriental culture* in the form of encounters and relationships."[13] One Moslem scholar who speaks highly of the book's insights into Turkish mysticism and its effects on history is Muhammed Abu Hattab Khaled. He asserts that the book is worthy of the attention of scholars, and offers this highly favorable conclusion: "A positive aspect of literary works with themes of this kind undoubtedly also lies in the fact that a broad public who ordinarily would rarely turn to specialized publications can be gained for largely unknown Oriental themes and issues."[14]

As Gerald Chapple has pointed out, not only did Frischmuth herself spend time in Turkey when she was twenty, but "[t]he heroine is carrying out research for a dissertation on exactly the same topic that Frischmuth chose for *her* dissertation." He adds that Frischmuth denies that the novel was autobiographical, "while admitting that *The Shadow Disappears* was what her 'unwritten dissertation' had ultimately turned into." Chapple goes on to say, "I would prefer to regard it as her *rewritten* dissertation, because the historical research material comes alive thanks to its being embedded in an extensive fictional narrative about a young Austrian student's first encounter with a Muslim country."[15] Readers of the novel frequently recall that Frischmuth herself did not finish the dissertation sketched in the book, but salvaged her time and efforts in Turkey in order to produce this successful novel incorporating many of her experiences as well as details of her research project into a fascinating poetic whole. The novel does not reveal whether the fictional student ever finishes her dissertation, nor in fact, any details about her life beyond the fact that she is preparing to return home when the book concludes. Fachinger comments that the novel "leaves it open whether or not the narrator is actually going to benefit in the long term from her experiences. Unlike the traditional *Bildungsroman,* this novel does not follow its protagonist back home to depict her reintegration into society" (243).

One often overlooked thematic thread in the novel involves the process of researching and writing a dissertation in the humanities. Awareness of the fact that Frischmuth herself did not finish her own dissertation may make the issue seem irrelevant; yet those who have gone through the process can attest to the accuracy of the depiction of the student's struggles. The protagonist is a fledgling researcher strongly interested in her research domain but struggling to identify the angle and scope of her projected study. The indeterminacy of her task creates in her alternating cycles of euphoria and enthusiasm, followed by disorientation and self-doubt; she also feels compelled to conceal her troubles and to give her hosts the impression that she is making good progress. She reveals some of the difficulties of her situation as a researcher:

> It was still difficult for me to read the old texts…Sometimes I asked myself in all seriousness why I had gotten involved in all of this in the first place…I forgot what I had learned and learned what I had forgotten…A string of sentences would occur to me, but as soon as I sat down to transcribe them, they struck me as so inconsequential that I didn't even dare to take them as my starting point (21-22).[16]

Several passages reveal the protagonist's lengthy struggle to find a topic. At one point, she says, "I had considered devoting my entire study to this Kaygusuz, but somehow his poems dissolved in my hands" (70).[17] Later on she writes, "I kept departing from my original topic and was finding it impossible to write a study about anything concrete. It was as if I had opened a door to have a look in a certain direction, but instead the entire wall came crashing down" (119-120).[18] Her lack of progress is emphasized by the fact that her professor, on one of the last pages of the book, gives her some advice suggesting that her project is still at a very early stage. He mentions the importance of coming up with a "new angle" ("einen neuen Aspekt" [116]) and advises her, "Just get started writing your study, he said then. After the first sentences everything will be easier. You'll write and write, you'll fill up reams of paper and wonder where you're getting it all from" (148).[19] Instead of beginning to write, however, the student takes the approach recommended by the professor's wife to memorize poetry. She announces that she has decided on a poet, and the older woman is pleased, "You've decided? She asked. For Pir Sultan Abdal? Yes, I said several times in a row in order to strengthen my resolve. I'm happy you're reading poetry again" (149).[20] However, the reader is not informed whether this decision refers to the choice of a dissertation topic. The reader is not told whether the narrator will give up her academic work, as author Frischmuth did, or use her research in Turkey to complete a dissertation in her homeland. There is plenty of reason for optimism on this score, for she has displayed considerable diligence and tenacity as a student, despite her failure to produce a written product. Her knowledge of the Turkish language also attests to her academic ability, and either her extensive research into Turkish history and culture or her appreciation of poetry seem likely to provide an appropriate topic that she will be able to develop in coherent fashion if she so chooses.

A secondary academic and personal goal of the student's sojourn is enhancing her spoken and written proficiency in the

Turkish language. In her often-quoted essay, "Looking over the Fence," Frischmuth reflects on her own study of Turkish:
> Turkish belongs to the family of agglutinative languages. I embraced this differently structured language without reservation, and it seemed to broaden the horizons of my soul. I was young enough that I could, at least in the beginning, abandon myself to this different manner of organizing reality. And when I wrote, I tried to remain as close as possible to my new way of experiencing the world...Once I felt comfortable in the Turkish language, it no longer seemed foreign to me.[21]

The novel provides a record of the typical cycles of progress and discouragement experienced by learners as they acquire and employ a second language. As all language teachers and learners know, acquisition does not proceed in a lock-step linear fashion. The narrator relates an encounter with two women in a mosque who treat her like a foreigner who cannot speak Turkish. She speaks to them "in a string of sentences," ("mit einer Reihe von Sätzen") but their attitude causes her to regress: "And all at once the words I was saying struck me as stupid, so that I began to join them in their sign language and gibberish." (10) ("Auch mir kamen die Worte, die ich sagte, mit einemmal so tölpelhaft vor, daß ich auf ihre Zeichen und das Kauderwelsch einging" [14]). She mentions another incidence of this regression: "I had difficulty constructing sentences and regressed to the phase of the first weeks, when I could only make myself understood with great effort despite the fact that I had already read entire books in the language"(12). [22] The narrator faces particular linguistic challenges understanding "Persian and Arabic loan words" in the old texts she is reading and new words or "neologisms" in people's everyday speech. She is daunted by the great difficulty the new terms pose:
> It became clear to me that I would never possess a precise feel for the status and usefulness of

> these words that were being created every day. It
> also didn't help much to write down the new
> words right after the old ones, since the conver-
> gence was never one hundred percent. (21)[23]

Despite these setbacks, it is apparent throughout the novel that the protagonist is proficient in Turkish: she not only carries on face-to-face conversations with various people but establishes relationships with them. Her ability to carry out research on a high level, using older as well as current texts, is evidence of a very high level of proficiency. As she prepares to leave, she imagines coming back in the future, thinking, "How many years would it be? I would tell myself that I really had to go back now if I didn't want to forget how to speak the language" (143).[24]

Despite frequent moments of self-doubt and disorientation, the narrator actually succeeds quite well in terms of cultural adjustment to her living environment. Like her language acquisition and use, her cultural adaptation does not progress in a straight linear fashion, but displays "ups and downs." In contrast to foreign students who dwell in enclaves of people from their own countries and interact little with their hosts, this sojourner lives with Turkish people, adapts to their daily routines, and forms a number of personal relationships with them. She makes conscious efforts to acculturate, saying:

> I tried to adapt, to live as though I was able to
> understand and accept the system of the sundry
> relationships in which I found myself. I wanted
> to commit as few mistakes as possible, but I
> knew I was destined to commit some blunders
> ...I attempted to observe the rules that dictated
> daily dealings. (11-12)[25]

As she goes through the process of coping with cultural difference, she is like many sojourners who experience "a roller coaster of highs and lows as they surmount barriers to communication and contact only to discover abysses of value and perceptual difference" (Lewis xix). Although in general she adapts well to the heat, the food, housing conditions, and transportation in her new environment, she does suffer somewhat from time to time. In a public bathroom, an attendant pours lemon water over her hands and gives her a fresh towel and a mirror. She is surprised at her own reaction: "And suddenly I was overcome by a longing for a certain type of comfort of the kind that I never thought I would miss" (62).[26] While most of her low points are psychological, she mentions one that involves abnormal behavior as well, when she seeks out a piece of ham as a symbol of her home culture. She recalls:

> But there were still days on which my having achieved "insider" status struck me as illusory, when I felt like I was standing naked among people who were all fully dressed...And then suddenly the smells were once again nauseaatingly strange, and I searched and searched until I found a Greek butcher who sold ham, only to then carry it around in my bag until it turned green, which soon happened in the heat. (12-13)[27]

After such low points, the student always perseveres, learning and internalizing not only enough of the language and cultural mores to meet her daily needs and carry out her research, but to interact and maintain relationships with a number of local people.

In addition to her status as a student, the protagonist is also a single woman of late adolescent or young adult age. During her sojourn she has casual sexual relationships, revealed in a matter-of-fact way, with two local men, the doctor Aksu and, later, Turgut, the teacher and political activist who lives with her and another woman. Her situation is contrasted with that of a pregnant married woman, her teacher's wife. As a parent might, she presses the younger woman, to her annoyance, about the future of her relationship with Aksu. She refuses to answer, saying, "I didn't let myself be drawn into this conversation," (58) ("Ich ging nicht darauf ein" [50]) and changes the subject. The older woman confides that she is pregnant and will lose her editorial position at the university and have to interrupt her studies. The narrator is embarrassed by her lack of knowledge about pregnancy: "I admitted I hadn't noticed a thing, but she said I simply didn't know what to look for yet...I felt ashamed and ignorant" (59).[28] Contrasting this young woman, at a stage of life when she holds men at bay because she is uninterested in commitment, marriage or children, one is again tempted to think of Frischmuth's own biography and the progression of themes in her oeuvre that to some extent trace the phases of her own life. In a brief article on Frischmuth in 1980, Ulrike Kindl summarizes the novel and immediately refers to Frischmuth's life in the phase after her international study:

> Barbara Frischmuth lives in Austria again, marries, becomes pregnant. Pregnancy becomes her central experience, that up to now – even in the figures of her female protagonists – always has been present under the surface, and now becomes the main theme of her writing: her identity as a woman.[29]

Turning to personal adjustment, we realize that any assessment of this domain must take into account both the protagonist's youth and the briefness of her sojourn. Donald Daviau has concluded that the student does mature and become wiser through her experiences in Turkey. He asserts that "the protagonist learns from her failure, and in this sense the work is a *Bildungsroman*."[30] According to Petra Rau, this genre ("novel of education" or "novel of development") "charts the protagonist's actual or metaphorical journey from youth to maturity. Initially the aim of this journey is reconciliation between the desire for individuation (self-fulfillment) and the demands of socialisation (adaptation to a given social reality)."[31] This novel, relating experiences of a single year, does not present a complete process of *Bildung*, but it does present one crucial phase.

Shortly before her departure from Turkey, the protagonist learns that her friend Turgut, who recently became her lover, was shot at a political demonstration. In addition to mourning his death, she is disoriented when she realizes that she had been ignoring not only his political activities but also the atmosphere of danger and unrest around her. Turgut's violent death is a salient, dramatic and frightening event; for the protagonist such a shocking loss at the end of her time in Turkey must surely entail a measure of the "loss of innocence" associated with "coming of age" stories in literature. The placement at the end of the novel, only one page before the last one, encourages the reader to regard it as conclusive and decisive, and an interpretation of its meaning is suggested by the narrator. She blames herself for her blindness to realities around her, and berates herself for concentrating too much on the past:

> I had imagined I would be able to discover the key to the present in the past, and I had hoped to overcome my foreignness by means of this, by the fact that I was searching for origins that were supposed to make me understand...I was ignoring my surroundings...making the present insignificant by comparing it with the past. (110-111)[32]

She reproaches herself for lack of persective, "My critical faculties had become secondary to my desire to adapt." (144), ("Ich hatte mein Kritikvermögen hinter die Anpassung gestellt" [113]). In moments dominated by negative thoughts she may be drawn to unreasonable conclusions, either that she could have foreseen or prevented Turgut's death, or that his loss had somehow erased all value from both her research and her life in Turkey. Yet, her reactions to her approaching departure also contain moments of affection for the Turkish people she has known: "And suddenly I was happy, happy about the fact that I knew Sevim and Turgut, and I knew that in some special sense we really loved each other" (141).[33] At another point, she realizes "I loved Aksu and I loved Turgut, I loved Sevim, Ayten and the Tartar women. I even loved Engin Bey." (144) ("Ich liebte Aksu und ich liebte Turgut, ich liebte Sevim Ayten und die Tartarin, ich liebte auch Engin Bey" [113]). As she anticipates her return to her home country and former life, about which the novel reveals little, the protagonist undoubtedly experiences a variety of bewildering emotions that she will need to sort out later.

    Although Turgut's shocking death seems to be the grim and pessimistic end of the novel, the ending in regard to the narrator's future is quite open. During the sojourn depicted she has demonstrated intelligence, insight, poetic sensitivity, self-reliance, and resilience; the reader is likely to assume that she will recover from the trauma and lead a productive life. However, it is unclear if she will be able to organize and direct the findings of her research in Turkey to produce the planned dissertation and thereafter pursue an academic career. Instead or later on she may also follow the model of the Tartar woman (and the author) by committing herself to becoming a wife and mother, permanently or temporarily setting her studies aside. In addition to the lack of information on her future, little has been revealed of the narrator's past life, personal identity, or relationship to her home culture; the ultimate integration of her sojourn will also be influenced by insights the experience gave her into her pre-sojourn self. Read either in a decontextualized way as the story of a year in the life of one student, or as a document presenting various multicultural issues and reflecting aspects of the author's life and thought, the book ends on a note of ambiguity and incompleteness. As Daviau writes, "The ambiguous ending... stresses life's possibilities or alternatives" (193). The protagonist is poised between East and West, student and adult roles, homeland and the wider world; she has learned a good deal, both academically and personally, including the grim knowledge of our inability to control events or prevent such terrible misfortune as the unexpected death of a young person. The book does not reveal the direction in which this growth, gained over one short year, might take her, if indeed it proves to have a lasting impact.

    In spite of its relevance to its author's life story and to multicultural debates of recent decades, the book is a work of fiction, a story, and an intriguing and moving record of believable human experience, thought, and emotion. Reasons for the decades-long popularity of this early book by Barbara Frischmuth are to be sought in its text, not its context or any particular messages it contains. *The Shadow Disappears in the Sun* is still read because readers appreciate its poetic merging of ancient poetry and wisdom, academic, cultural and personal struggles, beauty, novelty, and danger in an unfamiliar realm, all perceived by the sensitive eyes, ears, and heart of a young, developing person whose future is unknown but has wide and wonderful potential.

Endnotes

---

[1]"From the beginning, reviews and debates were stimulated by Barbara Frischmuth's first book, *The Convent School*, of 1968. It made the twenty-seven-year-old author famous almost overnight, and was received as a contribution to the student revolution of the time; coming from a rural Catholic corner, it was unexpected, but therefore all the more welcome." Waltraut Schwarz, "Barbara Frischmuth: Rebellion und Rückkehr." *Amsterdamer Beiträge zur Neueren Germanistik* 14 (1982): 229.
[2]See Pamela S. Saur, "A Feminist Reading of Barbara Frischmuth's Trilogy." *Modern Austrian Literature* 23.3/4 (1990): 167-179.
[3]See Pamela S. Saur, "Real and Imaginary Journeys in Barbara Frischmuth's Writings." *Germanic Notes and Reviews* 28.2 (Fall 1997): 97-109.
[4]Evelein, Johannes F., Ed. and Intro. "On Language, Writing, and Crossing Borders: An Interview with Barbara Frischmuth." *Barbara Frischmuth in Contemporary Context*. Ed. Renate S. Posthofen. Riverside: Ariadne, 1999: 131.
[5]My translation of: "Es ist uns wohl allen deutlich bewußt, daß die Literatur den Zenit ihrer politischen Wirksamkeit überschritten hat. Aber das heißt nicht, daß sie keinerlei Rolle mehr im Zusammenleben der Menschen spielt. Vielleicht keine so unmittelbare, wie wir es machmal gern hätten, aber auf Um-

wegen wird sie noch." Quoted in Francis Michael Sharp, "Barbara Frischmuth: The Theory and Practice of Mediating Cultures through Literature." *TRANS. Internet-Zeitschrift für Kulturwissenschaften* 15 (August 2004): 05.09 "Austrian Writers and the Unifying Aspects of Cultures." Ed. Donald G. Daviau.
[6]*The Shadow Disappears in the Sun.* Translated and with an Afterword by Nicholas J. Meyerhofer. Riverside: Ariadne Press, 1998. References to the German text are from *Das Verschwinden des Schattens in der Sonne.* Munich: Deutscher Taschenbuch Verlag, 1980.
[7]My translation of: "Den ersten Schritt in die Richtung fremder Kulturen wagt die Autorin mit einem Studienaufenthalt in der Türkei, dessen Erlebnisse sie in ihrem ersten Roman *Das Verschwinden des Schattens in der Sonne* verarbeitet." Monika Straňáková, "Heimat und Fremde im Werk Barbara Frischmuths." *Von Aussen Betrachtet: Österreich und die österreichische Literatur im Spiegel der Auslandsrezeption.* Ed. Anthony Bushell and Dagmar Košt'álová. Wechselwirkungen. Österreichische Literatur im internatlionalen Kontext, Vol. 13. Bern: Peter Lang, 2007, 63.
[8]Jennifer Michaels, "Multiculturalism in Barbara Frischmuth's Works: The Representation and Mediation of Turkish and Other Islamic Cultures in *Das Verschwinden des Schattens in der Sonne* and in Various Short Pieces" in *Barbara Frischmuth in Contemporary Context.* Ed. Renate S. Posthofen, Riverside, CA: Ariadne Press, 1999, 67.
[9]Monika Shafi, "Resident Aliens: Home and Displacement in Barbara Frischmuth's *Das Verschwinden des Schattens in der Sonne* and Waltraud Anna Mitgutsch's *In fremden Städten.*" In Posthofen, 244-245.
[10]Dagmar Lorenz, Dagmar, "Dismantling Islam: Orientalism and the Women's Perspective in Barbara Frischmuth's Novel *Das Verschwinden des Schattens in der Sonne.* In Posthofen, 276-278.

[11] Petra Fachinger, "Orientalism Reconsidered: Turkey in Barbara Frischmuth's *Das Verschwinden des Schattens in der Sonne* and Hannah Mede-Flock's *Im Schatten der Mondsichel*." *Studies in Twentieth-Century Literature* 23.2 (Summer 1999): 242.
[12] A term coined by anthropologist Kalervo Oberg in 1960, the year of Frischmuth's own sojourn to Turkey. Lewis, Tom J. and Robert E. Jungmann, Editors. "Introduction." *On Being Foreign: Culture Shock in Short Fiction. An International Anthology.* Yarmouth: Intercultural Press, Inc. 1986, xv.
[13] My translation of: "Das Buch verläuft auf zwei Ebenen: Auf der einen, der *Recherche* für die zu schreibende Dissertation, forscht die Ich-Erzählerin nach *Ursprüngen*, vertieft sich in *türkisch-islamische Geschichte, Religion und Kultur*. Christoph Gellner, "Grenzüberschreitungen zwischen Orient und Okzident: Literatur, Multikulturalität und Religionsdialog" in *Barbara Frischmuth: Fremdgänge: ein illustrierter Streifzug durch einen literarischen Kosmos*. Ed. Daniela Bartens and Ingrid Spork. Salzburg. Residenz, 2001: 222.
[14] My translation of: "Ein positiver Aspekt einer derartig thematisierten Literatur liegt sicherlich auch darin, daß ein breites Publikum, das sonst kaum zu fachwissenschaftlichen Publikationen greifen würde, für weitgehend unbekannte orientalische Themen und Fragestellungen gewonnen werden kann." Khaled, REFERENCE, 306.
[15] Chapple, Gerald. "Will the Real Barbara Frischmuth Please Stand Up? On Autobiography and Literary Creation." *The Fiction of the I: Contemporary Austrian Writers and Autobiography*. Ed. Nicholas J. Meyerhofer. Riverside: Ariadne, 1999: 20.
[16] "Es fiel mir immer noch schwer, die alten Texte zu lesen... Manchmal fragte ich mich allen Ernstes, wozu ich mich auf das alles eingelassen hatte...Ich vergaß, was ich gelernt hatte, und lernte, was ich vergessen hatte...Da fiel mir eine Reihe von Sätzen an, doch sobald ich mich hinsetzte, um sie niederzu-

schreiben, erschienen sie mir so unwesentlich, daß ich nicht wagte, auch nur davon auszugehen" (22-23).
[17]"Ich hatte schon daran gedacht, meine Arbeit ganz auf diesen Kaygusuz zu konzentrieren, aber irgendwie zerfielen mir seine Gedichte unter den Händen" (59).
[18]"Ich kam immer wieder vom ursprünglichen Thema ab und noch weiter von den Möglichkeiten, eine Arbeit über etwas Bestimmtes zu schreiben. So als öffnete ich eine Tür, um einen Blick in eine ganz bestimmte Richtung zu tun, aber statt dessen fiel die ganze Wand ein" (95).
[19]"Fangen Sie nur mit Ihrer Arbeit an, sagte er dann, nach den ersten Sätzen wird alles einfacher sein. Sie werden schreiben und schreiben, ganze Stöße von Papier werden Sie vollschreiben und Sie werden sich noch wundern, wo Sie das alles herhaben" (117).
[20]"Sie haben sich entschieden? fragte sie. Für Pir Sultan Abdal? Ja, sagte ich mehrmals hintereinander, um mich selber darin zu bestärken. Ich bin froh, daß Sie wieder Gedichte lesen" (117).
[21]Barbara Frischmuth, "Looking over the Fence." Trans. Lisabeth Hock. *World Literature Today: A Literary Quarterly of the University of Oklahoma*. 69.3 (June 1, 1995), 5.
[22]"Ich hatte Schwierigkeiten, Sätze zu bilden, und fiel in das Stadium der ersten Wochen zurück, in denen ich mich nur mühsam verständigen konnte, obwohl ich schon Bücher in der Sprache gelesen hatte" (16).
[23]"Mir wurde klar, daß ich nie ein präzises Gefühl für den Stellen- und Gebrauchswert dieser Wörter, die jeden Tag neu entstanden, haben würde. Es half auch nur wenig, wenn ich mir zu den neuen Wörtern die alten dazuschrieb, die Konvergenz war nie hundertprozentig" (22).
[24]"Wie viele Jahre würden es dann sein? Ich würde mir sagen, daß es absolut an der Zeit war, wenn ich das Sprechen der Sprache nicht verlernen würde" (113).
[25]"Ich versuchte mich anzupassen, so zu leben, als würde ich das Funktionieren des Systems der verschiedenen Beziehungen, in

denen ich stand, durchzuschauen und akzeptieren. Ich wollte so wenige Fehler wie möglich machen, obwohl ich wußte, dass ich immer wieder welche machen würde... versuchte die Regeln zu beachten, die den täglichen Umgang bestimmten" (15).

[26]"Und mich überkam eine unbegreifliche Sehnsucht nach einer bestimmten Art von Komfort, von der ich nie gedacht hatte, daß sie mir abgehen würde" (53).

[27] "Doch es gab immer wieder Tage, an denen ich mein Einbezogensein für Schein hielt und mir war, als würde ich nackt unter lauter Angezogenen stehen...Und plötzlich waren mir dann die Gerüche wieder auf ekelerregende Weise fremd, und ich suchte und suchte, bis ich einen griechischen Fleischhauer fand, bei dem ich Schinken kaufte, um ihn dann so lange in meiner Tasche herumzutragen, bis er grün geworden war, was bei der Hitze sehr bald geschah" (16).

[28]"Ich gab zu, daß ich es ihr keineswegs angesehen hatte, aber sie meinte nur, ich hätte einfach noch nicht den richtigen Blick dafür...Ich kam mir beschämt vor und unwissend" (51).

[29]My translation of: "Barbara Frischmuth lebt wieder in Österreich, heiratet, wird schwanger. Die Schwangerschaft wird zum zentralen Erlebnis, die Selbsterfahrung als Frau rückt das Problem in den Mittelpunkt, das bisher – schon in der Gestalt weiblicher Protagonistinnen – stets untergründig vorhanden war, jetzt aber zum Hauptthema ihres Schreibens wird: ihr Frau-Sein." Ulrike Kindl, "Zur Biographie: Barbara Frischmuth." In *Barbara Frischmuth, Jahre; Zeit Schechow zu lesen; Unzeit; Bleiben lassen: mit Materialen.* Ed. Gisela Ulrich. Stuttgart: Klett, 1983: 145.

[30]Donald Daviau, "Barbara Frischmuth." In *Major Figures of Contemporary Austrian Literature.* New York: Peter Lang, 1987: 191.

[31]Petra Rau, REFERENCE, 1

[32]"Ich hatte mir eingebildet, in der Vergangenheit den Schlüßel für die Gegenwart zu finden, und ich hatte das Fremdsein

dadurch überwinden wollen, daß ich nach Unsprüngen suchte, die mich verstehen machen sollten" (88).
[33]"Und plötzlich war ich glücklich, glücklich darüber, daß ich Sevim und Turgut kannte, und ich wußte, daß wir uns auf eine besondere Art wirklich liebten" (111).

Works Cited

Chapple, Gerald. "Will the Real Barbara Frischmuth Please Stand Up? On Autobiography and Literary Creation." *The Fiction of the I: Contemporary Austrian Writers and Autobiography.* Ed. Nicholas J. Meyerhofer. Riverside: Ariadne, 1999. 10-33.

Daviau, Donald G. "Barbara Frischmuth." *Major Figures of Contemporary Austrian Literature* New York: Peter Lang, 1987. 185-206.

Evelein, Johannes F., Ed. and Intro. "On Language, Writing, and Crossing Borders: An Interview with Barbara Frischmuth." *Barbara Frischmuth in Contemporary Context.* Ed. Renate S. Posthofen. Riverside: Ariadne, 1999. 126-133.

Fachinger, Petra. "Orientalism Reconsidered: Turkey in Barbara Frischmuth's *Das Verschwinden des Schattens in der Sonne* and Hannah Mede-Flock's *Im Schatten der Mondsichel.*" *Studies in Twentieth-Century Literature* 23.2 (Summer 1999): 239-253.

Frischmuth, Barbara. *The Convent School.* Trans. Gerald Chapple and James B. Lawson. Riverside: Ariadne, 1994.

—. *Die Klosterschule.* Frankfurt am Main: Suhrkamp, 1968.

—. "Looking over the Fence." Trans. Lisabeth Hock. *World Literature Today: A Literary Quarterly of the University of Oklahoma.* 69.3 (June 1, 1995). 5pp.

—. *The Shadow Disappears in the Sun.* Trans. and Afterword Nicholas J. Meyerhofer. Riverside: Ariadne Press, 1998.

—. *Das Verschwinden des Schattens in der Sonne.* Munich: Deutscher Taschenbuch Verlag, 1980.

Gellner, Christoph. "Grenzüberschreitungen zwischen Orient und Okzident: Literatur, Multikulturalität und Religionsdialog." *Barbara Frischmuth: Fremdgänge: ein illustrierter Streifzug durch einen literarischen Kosmos.* Ed. Daniela Bartens and Ingrid Spork. Salzburg. Residenz, 2001. 211-239.
Kindl, Ulrike. "Zur Biographie: Barbara Frischmuth." Barbara Frischmuth, *Jahre; Zeit Schechow zu lesen; Unzeit; Bleiben lassen: mit Materialen.* Ed. Gisela Ulrich. Stuttgart: Klett, 1983: 114-118.
Lewis, Tom J. and Robert E. Jungmann, Editors. "Introduction." *On Being Foreign: Culture Shock in Short Fiction. An International Anthology.* Yarmouth: Intercultural Press, Inc. 1986, xv-xxv.
Lorenz, Dagmar. "Dismantling Islam: Orientalism and the Women's Perspective in Barbara Frischmuth's Novel *Das Verschwinden des Schattens in der Sonne.* Posthofen, 263-286.
Michaels, Jennifer E. "Multiculturalism in Barbara Frischmuth's Works: The Representation and Mediation of Turkish and Other Islamic Cultures in *Das Verschwinden des Schattens in der Sonne* and in Various Short Pieces." Posthofen, 67-86.
Posthofen, Renate S., Ed. *Barbara Frischmuth in Contemporary Context.* Riverside, CA: Ariadne Press, 1999.
Rau, Petra. "Bildungsroman." *The Literary Encyclopedia.* 2002. http://www.litencyc.com.
Saur, Pamela S. "A Feminist Reading of Barbara Frischmuth's Trilogy." *Modern Austrian Literature* 23.3/4. (1990): 167-179.
—. "Real and Imaginary Journeys in Barbara Frischmuth's Writings." *Germanic Notes and Reviews* 28.2 (Fall 1997): 97-109.

Schwarz, Waltraut. "Barbara Frischmuth: Rebellion und Rückkehr." *Amersterdamer Beiträge zur Neueren Germanistik* 14 (1982): 229-253.
Shafi, Monika. "Resident Aliens: Home and Displacement in Barbara Frischmuth's *Das Verschwinden des Schattens in der Sonne* and Waltraud Anna Mitgutsch's *In fremden Städten*." Posthofen, 242-262.
Sharp, Francis Michael. "Barbara Frischmuth: The Theory and Practice of Mediating Cultures through Literature." *TRANS. Internet-Zeitschrift für Kulturwissenschaften* 15 (August 2004): 05.09 "Austrian Writers and the Unifying Aspects of Cultures. Ed. Donald G. Daviau. 11 pp.
Straňáková, Monika. "Heimat und Fremde im Werk Barbara Frischmuths." *Von Aussen Betrachtet: Österreich und die österreichische Literatur im Spiegel der Auslandsrezeption*. Ed. Anthony Bushell and Dagmar Košt'álová. Wechselwirkungen. Österreichische Literatur im internationalen Kontext, Vol. 13. Bern: Peter Lang, 2007. 57-66.

From Habsburg Princess to Queen of Brazil: Gloria Kaiser's Historical Novel *Dona Leopoldina*

Donald G. Daviau

Dona Leopoldina.The Habsburg Empress of Brazil, translated by Lowell A. Bangerter, Ariadne Press, 1998

Gloria Kaiser became a noted author of historical novels involving the interconnections of the Habsburg Monarchy and Brazil, among others, through a circuitous route involving chance happenings and a kind fate. Her inclination for the world of the imagination manifested itself early in her life, while growing up in the relatively small town of Köflach, Styria, where she was born in 1950. To escape at times from the routine everyday reality, she developed the habit of inventing stories for herself. In addition, at the age of eight, her mother taught her how to keep a diary, a practice which made her a keener observer of the people and events around her as well as sharpening her use of precise language to compress entries into fewer words.[1] The impersonal nature of the career that she pursued as an accountant, bookkeeper, and tax consultant couldn't have been more diametrically opposed to the realm of the imagination, which attracted her so strongly, and which she avidly pursued in her free time by writing about the life and conditions of the world around her that she knew from first-hand experience. In addition to many short texts for literary magazines and for broadcasting on the national radio and television station ORF along with radio plays, she produced two noteworthy novels "Monologues of an Unknown Woman" (*Selbstgespräche einer Unbekannten*, 1980) and "A Victim of No Importance" (*Ein Opfer ohne Bedeutung*, 1990), both beautifully written, dark and tragic works, which introduced Kaiser as a serious, talented author as well as a first-rate stylist with a gift for language. The literary quality of her writings gained her recognition and brought her a number of awards and prizes.[2] Nevertheless, as a cautious, conservative individual, it was not until 1984, after fifteen years of living a conflicted life divided between her business profession and her desire to be a creative author, that she finally felt sufficiently encouraged by the success of her writings to devote herself solely to a career as a freelance writer.

Kaiser joined the Graz Authors' Group when it was founded in 1973, and she also belongs to the Vienna PEN Club. For the most part, however, she remains apart from the literary scene and pursues her own goals quietly and at her own pace. Unlike authors such as Jelinek, Turrini, Menasse, and Frischmuth, she does not aspire to keep her name in the public eye by becoming a political activist, writing articles critical of the government for newspapers and taking part in street rallies. She has also never joined cliques or become involved in literary feuds. Demure and modest as she is, Kaiser stands tall as a true individualist, who dedicates herself to her self-determined goal of creating enduring literature. To accomplish her purpose, she has painstakingly developed her own style and technique and pursues her own timeless and universal themes, which do not follow the current trend of Austrian literature to create ephemeral works–often detective novels (*Krimis*) – written solely for commercial success. If she patterned herself on any model, it would be her countryman Stefan Zweig, whose success as an author of historical biographies is unmatched in Austrian literary history and perhaps in world literature. His biographies are known globally and have remained in print since he wrote them. Kaiser, who admires him greatly and shares his fascination for Brazil, has written and lectured frequently and widely about him. She also holds in high regard the prominent critic and author Hans Weigel, who not only gave her early encouragement on the basis of her impressive writings, but also recommended their publication to the Styria Publishing House.

Kaiser's life and literary career proceeded on a calm, even course on the local level of Graz until 1988, when she decided to tour Brazil. She had begun studying Portuguese in the late 1970s just to engage in an activity totally unrelated to her professional life, and now she wanted an opportunity to practice her language skills. The trip, which took her to four cities, concluded in Salvador in the province of Bahia, a large, northern coastal city of some three million people, heavily populated by descendents of the three to four million African slaves the Portuguese imported into Brazil over three centuries to work on the sugar, coffee, and rubber plantations as well as in the mines. While on the beach one day in Salvador, Kaiser by chance met Celeste Aida Galeao, who not only turned out to be a professor of German at the University of Salvador, but also an enthusiast of Austrian literature, which she wanted to teach in her classes but had difficulty obtaining German texts for the students. This meeting proved highly beneficial to both parties, resulting in a lasting friendship and a productive working relationship that still continues today.

Back in Vienna Kaiser reported this interest in Austrian literature and culture to the Ministry for Education and Art, which not only arranged to send books, but also gave her an appointment to create an official organization for cultural exchange. With the ready assistance of Professor Galeao and Professor Ewald Hackler, an internationally known theater director, Kaiser formally established the Austrian/Brazilian Cultural Initiative in 1989. Later the Hispanic Division of the U.S. Library of Congress, where Kaiser has become a familiar, highly regarded figure through her research stays there and her almost annual lectures and readings, also became a partner in the undertaking. From the founding of the Cultural Initiative up to the present Kaiser spends months each year in Brazil, organizing and hosting literary conferences, arranging musical programs, preparing exhibits and planning future activities. On the basis of the variety and importance of her ambitious projects she merits recognition as the leading cultural liaison between Austria and

Brazil at the present time. In a sense she, as a daughter of Austria, is continuing the cultural mission for which Emperor Franz I originally sent Dona Leopoldina to Brazil. The current Austrian interest recently broadened beyond culture, as Chancellor Gusenbauer and a large coterie of officials and businessmen visited the country in order to open negotiations on trade agreements and business opportunities. To some extent Kaiser has paved the way, for she is well known and well liked in Brazil for her cultural activities and books, all of which are available in Portuguese. She is often invited to read from her works and present lectures in Brazil, Austria, and the USA on such topics as "Stefan Zweig," "Rainer Maria Rilke and Rodin," "Antonio Vieira," "Thomas Ender," "Women's Role in the Historical Novel," and "Mozart. Perspectives from his Correspondence," which has now been published as a book.[3] For Thomas Ender, the artist who accompanied Dona Leopoldina to Brazil and created some seven hundred drawings and aquarelle paintings of the exotic Brazilian fauna and flora as well as landscapes, Kaiser also prepared an exhibit of his drawings and aquarelle paintings in 2007 along with a catalogue entitled *Thomas Ender in Brasilia and Rio de Janeiro*. The exhibit was displayed in Salvador, Rio de Janeiro, Vienna, Graz, and the Library of Congress. In recognition of her cultural contributions, Brazil has rewarded Kaiser with a number of honors over the years, the latest being two awards in December 2005 and being named a Corresponding Member of the Bahian Academy of Letters in 2006.

Kaiser loves Brazil with its natural beauty and vibrant life to the extent of regarding it as her second homeland, and the country has assumed great importance in her life. During her sojourns there she not only actively promotes Austrian culture, but she also researches the earlier Austrian-Brazilian connections, specifically the important role that the Habsburgs played in the development of Brazil in the 19th century. This exploration of Brazil and Brazilian history not only resulted in her role as the most important Austrian cultural mediator in Brazil, but it also expanded the horizons of her life and radically transformed the direction and nature of her literary career. She launched this completely new literary phase in 1991 with the novel "October Spring" (*Oktoberfrühling*), a title which not only reflects the fact that when it is fall in Europe, it is spring in Brazil, but also indicates metaphorically Kaiser's view at that time of a weary and declining postwar Europe juxtaposed with an emerging Brazil burgeoning with opportunity. Kaiser believes that Austrians harbor many misconceptions about Brazil,[4] and her subsequent books all reinforce the aim of her cultural initiative to establish better understanding and closer rapprochement between the two countries: *Dona Leopoldina. The Habsburg Empress of Brazil* (*Dona Leopoldina. Die Habsburgerin auf Brasiliens Thron* [1994])[5], *Pedro II of Brazil* (*Pedro II. von Brasilien. Der Sohn der Habsburgerin* [1997])[6], *Saudade. The Life and Death of Queen Maria Gloria of Lusitania* (*Saudade. Leben und Sterben der Königin Maria Gloria von Lusitanien. 1819-1853* [2003])[7], and *Anita Garibaldi* (2000).

These works include four youth novels, which were written to give young Austrian and German readers accurate information about the lives of children their age in Brazil: *Julchen und Kasimira* (1991), *Violetta* (1993), *Maurice und Violetta* (1995) and *Arnoldo. Ein Strassenkind in Brasilien* (1996, "Arnoldo, A Street Child in Brazil"). She concentrates on the children of the lower classes, depicting with her usual realism the difficulties they face, particularly in obtaining the education that would enable them to break out of the vicious cycle of poverty in which they are trapped.[8] Like Zweig, who glorified the country in his book *Brazil, Land of the Future* (2000)[9] (*Brasilien. Land der Zukunft*, 1941), Kaiser is clearly smitten with her second homeland, and the potential and promise she sees in this fertile land of abundance enables her to look beyond the squalor, the poverty, and the oppression and exploitation of the poor by the wealthy. However, because of her honesty as an author, her books, unlike Zweig's account, describe in detail all of the negative circumstances of life for the uneducated, unskilled, impoverished people. The children must work from an early age on to help support the family. Thus they do not have the time or the tuition necessary to attend school, the only path out of the grinding poverty. In addition to the normal difficulties of finding work, they also have to cope with street gangs, who beat them up and steal their property and money. Also the police regularly raid their shantytowns and destroy their dwellings. Despite all these hazards, Kaiser also depicts moments when the families find happiness together and share warmth and simple pleasures. These books, which are suitable and informative for adults as well as teenagers, have been well received both in Europe and in Brazil.

To further her efforts to develop an Austrian-Brazilian connection in terms of her Cultural Initiative, Kaiser could not have found a better topic than the life of the young Habsburg princess Dona Leopoldina, who in 1817 was given in marriage to Dom Pedro de Bragança, the young king of Brazil, for the express purpose of forging an alliance between the two countries. Actually Austria under the rule of Emperor Franz I and his loyal Chancellor Metternich had little interest in Brazil per se but a great deal in the importance of the Bragança family in Portugal, ruled by Pedro's father King Joao VI. Kaiser did not first learn about Dona Leopoldina through her travels in Brazil, nor had she ever heard about her in school, which, she says, paid no attention to the Habsburgs. Her fortuitous discovery came about in a curious, indirect way. At the age of fourteen, her class visited Schönbrunn Palace, where she found herself attracted to the death mask of the Duke von Reichstadt, the son of Napoleon and Dona Leopoldina's older sister Louise, who died in 1832 at age of twenty-one. Kaiser was so impressed with the face of this handsome young man that she read everything she could find about his family and relatives, one of which was his aunt Leopoldina. Once alerted to this name, she began to notice it frequently in Brazil on streets, schools, and train stations. The author recalls: "And step by step I began to do research systematically about Leopoldina. I did this for years because I always said to myself – what I know is not enough." During this lengthy gestation period

Kaiser located Leopoldina's letters and diaries at the Haus- Hof- und Staatsarchiv in Vienna, in the National Library in Rio de Janeiro, and in the Oliveira Lima Library of the Catholic University in Washington DC. Not wanting to overlook any possible source of information, she also contacted the Bragança family in Rio de Janeiro and Petropolis and reports that this was a very positive and informative experience, for they allowed her to read all of the family letters. Kaiser regards the handwriting of the letters as very important, because she finds that it reveals Leopoldina's state of mind at the time she wrote a given letter.

Finally, thirty years from the time she had first encountered the name, armed with all of her meticulous research combined with her knowledge of Brazil and Brazilian history through her reading and travels around the country, Kaiser felt prepared to write the historical-biographical novel about Dona Leopoldina. She prefers the novel form, which enables her to give free reign to her imagination in creating fully realized characters as they develop in her mind. A history or philological study can only report on external events and activities that can be documented, while the novel allows the author to render the inner emotional life of her protagonist in all its complexity and allow her a voice to contribute to the narration of her own story. Through her methodology Kaiser bonds so completely with her subject that the separation is painful whenever she finishes a work: "The farewell from my protagonist hurts, because I only begin to write when the figure has become as well known to me as a sister." ("Der Abschied tut weh, denn ich beginne erst zu schreiben, wenn mir die Figur bekannt ist wie eine Schwester.)[10] She readily admits that her portrayal is her personal Dona Leopoldina, the same subjective approach that characterizes all of her novels based on historical figures: "No claim is made to know the exclusive truth about Dona Leopoldina. Even after careful research this life can only be interpreted creatively. Even letters, although their contents may be cited ever so precisely, cannot be humanly dependable – after all, they are being read today."[11] Not many letters and diaries of Leopoldina exist, and the absence of such material actually aids Kaiser's technique, for the less documentation available, the greater her freedom to create her own character. To add a touch of realism to the German version, Kaiser employs the original orthography when quoting from Leopoldina's letters and diaries and also from the official communications of the Ambassador Marschall, who was assigned to accompany Leopoldina in order to report regularly on the daughter's conduct to her father Emperor Franz I, and Chancellor Metternich.

Kaiser employs a realistic technique in this novel that places some demands on the reader: she depicts the last 12 days of Leopoldina's life, first while she is awaiting the difficult birth of her seventh child, which is born dead, followed by her painful days of suffering in the throes of succumbing to the accumulated debilitating effects of her hard life on her health. The seven pregnancies in nine years, the difficult miscarriages and painful births had all taken their toll physically and mentally. Previously she had always proved able to regain her strength, but this time her mind and body could not generate the energy necessary to recover. During these final tormented days she relives her life just as it unfolds in her feverish, sometimes delirious mind, that is, with a jumbled time sequence that forces the reader to stay alert to the sudden jumps from present to past, which occur without any transition, exactly the way a dreaming or hallucinating person's mind can flit seamlessly through different time sequences. Kaiser utilizes this highly effective technique not only to convey a sense of the agonizing death of Leopoldina, as her loyal retinue tries to save her life with the crude medical treatments at their disposal, but also to create a powerful, moving and memorable portrayal of the noble and noble-minded human being that Leopoldina was in all her complexity. History can record her deeds, but they alone do not provide any insights into the inner life of the person, which comprises the essential feature of Kaiser's literary technique. Only the rich imagination of the novelist can delve into the mind and soul of her protagonists to show the simultaneous, oftentimes conflicting, forces and pressures at work at any given time, to reveal the complex inner life, which cannot be verified by existing documents but only captured by a creative, empathetic author. After studying all of the letters, diaries, histories and other background information to the point that she knew her subject personally, the author masterfully produced her version of the Leopoldina who took form and came to life in her mind.

To make clear that she aims to capture not only the outer, historical details, but also the inner rhythm of the various phases of Leopoldina's life, Kaiser employs musical terminology in the chapter headings: "Largo," "Tranquillo," "Allegretto," "Animato," "Forte" and "Andante con moto." Accordingly, the narrative does not proceed chronologically but rather Leopoldina's feverish hallucinations, dreams, and recollections group events from the various years of the decade that she lived in Brazil in terms of these various modulations of tempo. Kaiser's absorbing portrayal of this fascinating woman makes reading this novel a richly rewarding experience. It was only possible to employ such a creative approach because of the illness of Leopoldina, who drifted in and out of consciousness. She could employ the same effective technique in *Anita Garibaldi*, who also lived much of her life in her imagination and about whom little information exists. It did not work in *Pedro II of Brazil*, however, but Kaiser came as close as she could by having him review his life in flashback while on the ship carrying him to a new life in Europe. He had resigned as Emperor in 1889 to avoid a civil war and enable the establishment of Brazil as a republic. In the third Brazilian novel, *Saudade. The Life and Death of Queen Maria Gloria of Lusitania*, the oldest daughter, who at age fifteen accompanied her father Pedro de Bragança into exile in Portugal, where she became queen in 1834, Kaiser employs a straight chronological approach.

Leopoldina's marriage to Pedro I for political purposes followed the Austrian adage: *Bella gerant alii, tu felix Austria nube* ("While others wage war, Austria marries"). The wedding of her favorite older sister Louise to Napoleon in 1810 illustrates the practice. The daughters had no choice or say in the matter, they simply accepted the life their father decreed for them and endured their fate as best they could. In the patriarchal society of the time they were so thoroughly inculcated with a strict sense of duty that they could never overcome it, no matter how miserable their lives became. This inability to free herself from this curse of duty eventually caused Leopoldina's premature death. In the beginning, however, optimism reigned. Louise, who also believed strongly in her sense of duty, claimed to be happily married to Napoleon, and on the basis of his pictures the young, innocent unworldly Leopoldina happily looked forward to her marriage to King Pedro. Once the arrangements were settled she devoted herself to preparing for her life in a new country with a new language. Leopoldina possessed great natural intelligence and readily absorbed the education that her teachers could provide. But none of the learning that they could give her could even remotely prepare her for the life that awaited her in this totally different world with a philandering, quixotic husband.

On May 13, 1817, at the age of twenty, the princess Dona Leopoldina, daughter of Emperor Franz I and grand-niece of Empress Maria Theresa, was married by proxy to Prince Pedro de Bragança, heir to the throne of the united kingdom of Portugal, Brazil, and Algarve. Not until six months later on November 5, 1817, did she meet her husband for the first time in Brazil. Her initial impressions of him were all positive and enthusiastic. With his good looks and dynamic personality, Pedro more than fulfilled what she had seen in his pictures, and she was elated at the thought of their future life together. So, too, was she, outdoors person that she was, immediately fascinated by the colorful abundance and exotic landscapes of her new country. The friendliness and openness of the people she met, in contrast to the strict formality of the Austrian court, also made her feel welcome. Her attraction to the natural phenomena of Brazil never changed, but it did not take long before the reality of her new life transformed all her other favorable impressions into their opposite.

After the promising beginning upon her arrival in Brazil, Leopoldina's life became much more complex and difficult than she could have ever dreamed possible. Initially she could bask in the natural splendor of the landscape, and she also found herself comfortable in her new social surroundings. However, although she had been advised against doing so, she began to explore the city independently and was horrified at discovering the reality of existence for the lower classes: the slavery, the exploitation and cruel treatment as well as the sickness and misery of the poor, the slum areas and shanty towns of vermin infested shacks lacking any semblance of proper sanitation, the child labor, making it impossible for the children to attend school, all of which aroused her compassion and desire to improve these conditions. Personally, she soon found herself treated as an outsider, a foreigner, subject to constant political intrigues. Finally, she had to endure the boorish treatment of her profligate husband, who made her life miserable with his inattention to his duties and his flagrant philandering. During the nine years of her life in Brazil Leopoldina lived through a calvary of mental and physical suffering, as Kaiser's deeply felt portrayal illustrates.

Leopoldina possessed great intellectual curiosity and many interests, but none ranked higher than her love for the outdoors. She loved to ride horses and employed this outlet to regain her equanimity whenever she felt unhappy or overwhelmed by the demands on her. Nature in all its forms fascinated her, and the opulence and manifold colors of the landscapes and forests in Brazil overwhelmed her. In Vienna she had already made plans to collect specimens of the flora and fauna, and she had insisted that her retinue include botanists as well as an artist to record the variety of species to be found there. The chosen painter, Thomas Ender, described in one of his diary entries his enthrallment over the colorful splendor that dazzled him upon first viewing Brazil, the same wonderment and appreciation that captivated and thrilled Donna Leopoldina:

> And then, after three months, the ship stood still. We saw bays, out of which a city

grew, the green of the forests, the white of the houses, and the blue of the ocean and sky had melted together into a play of colors, into a wake, by which we let ourselves be drawn to land.
We immediately set to work.
We sketched, painted, wrote, we were often in doubt – could a brush stroke, a pen line, a word express what we saw and felt. We had arrived at that spot of ground, where Mother Earth juxtaposed sun and moon and for this gift is rewarded with the gleaming in the green, blue and yellow tones that it cast over the landscape every morning.[12]

In fact, Ender became so intoxicated by all the luxuriant colorful plants and trees that he obsessively drove himself to create more than seven hundred aquarelle paintings in an attempt to capture the spectacular forms and colors of nature for the people in Vienna. He became indispensable to Leopoldina not only for helping her to fill chests with specimens of plants, flowers, insects, and minerals for shipment to Vienna to dazzle the court and show her father a sample of the abundant richness of Brazil, but also for his companionship during those early months and years of her new life in Brazil as her main link with Austria. Being able to reminisce with him about her homeland in German helped her overcome some of her severe homesickness. Thus it came as a severe blow to her when he announced that he could not continue his work in Brazil because of ill health and had to return to Vienna for treatment. His departure meant that she was now alone in this new land, where she felt totally abandoned by her family. Her only remaining contact with Austria was Ambassador Marschall, who, despite her suffering severely from homesickness, refused to support her wish to return home for a short visit. She had to accept that she was on her own and adjust her thinking to the cold fact and harsh reality that she would never see Austria again. As her sole link to her homeland, Marschall could have greatly aided Leopoldina and alleviated some of her homesickness and other problems. However, the unimaginative, plodding and unfeeling Austrian bureaucrat, who was empowered to serve as the sole liaison between Leopoldina and Vienna, reserved his loyalty solely for the Emperor and displayed no sympathy for the daughter. A great deal of her suffering resulted from his unwillingness to take her side in his reports, his refusal at times even to send her pleading letters and his failure to deliver messages from home to her promptly, even though he was well aware of her severe homesickness and general unhappiness at not receiving any word from her father.

Although Leopoldina received no sympathy, encouragement, or support from her family in Vienna, she could take solace in her correspondence with her sister, Maria Louise, who became her main confidante and for the most part sympathetic listener. Maria Louise claimed to have found greater satisfaction in her marriage to Napoleon than her sister did with Pedro, but, despite her empathy for her sister's unfortunate situation, she remained a pragmatist, who believed that they must accept life as it is and carry out their duty as Habsburg daughters without complaint, regardless of the problems and difficulties this might entail. As Kaiser shows with compassionate empathy, it was that sense of duty that kept Leopoldina in her bad marriage, caused her to suffer through nine years of hardships and humiliations, and finally killed her.

Leopoldina found one bright ray of sunshine in her life in her acquaintance and friendship with the radical priest and possibly most important statesman, José Bonifácio de Andrade e Silva, one of the most enlightened and influential political figures in Brazil at that time. He had been hired to expand Leopoldina's education about Brazil to equip her for serving the people and the country. This farseeing figure in Brazilian politics, who was ahead of his time with many of his social and political ideas, not only served as her mentor and advisor, but also sustained her through the humiliating circumstances caused by Pedro's mistress Domitila and imbued her with strength to overcome her weakened condition resulting from her frequent pregnancies, difficult births and miscarriages. Bonifacio's friendship built up Leopoldina's courage, and his education provided her with practical ideas about how she could bring about such basic social improvements as the cleaner water and better sanitation that the country desperately needed to cut down on disease. She herself recognized that in order to improve the lives of the poor, she needed to educate them to better methods of farming and craftsmanship. On her own initiative she wrote to Vienna requesting that farmers and skilled artisans be recruited and sent to Brazil to serve as models to teach the people more efficient and productive techniques.

Bonifacio admired Leopoldina's desire to improve the lives of her new countrymen and advised her that in order to accomplish her social programs she first had to gain the confidence of the people, who regarded her with suspicion as a foreigner. She had to sever the link to Vienna and devote herself exclusively to thinking and being Brazilian in order to convince her subjects that she was one of them in heart and soul. She made the transition and persuaded Pedro to do the same. He had been begging his father to be allowed to return to Portugal, and now he had received permission to do so – the ship was awaiting them in the harbor. However, on January 9, 1822, he and Leopoldina vowed together to remain in Brazil in order to maintain the unity of the country. Two days later the Portuguese Legislative Assembly staged a revolt which was intended to drive Leopoldina and Pedro out of Brazil or even to eliminate them. She was at home alone with the children and had to flee quickly with them, escaping the danger by – frantically driving a horse-drawn wagon herself through a severe rainstorm. The mad dash and the cold rainy weather caused the death of her oldest son Joao Carlos, named after his grandfather as the future heir to the throne.

Leopoldina had proved her total commitment to Brazil at great personal cost. In August 1822 she had an unparalleled opportunity to demonstrate her loyalty still further by boldly severing all ties to Portugal, thus ending Brazil's status as a colony and establishing it as an autonomous nation. A stroke of good luck had enabled Leopoldina to implement this radical break with the past and launch Brazil on an entirely new course. An important meeting in Sao Paulo required Pablo's attendance, and while he was away Leopoldina was designated to serve in his place as regent. Once empowered, she utilized her authority to declare Brazil's independence, a resolution enthusiastically endorsed by the Legislative Assembly. In one of her last recollections, as she is approaching death, Leopoldina recalls the first time she heard the word constitution at the age of thirteen during a conversation of her stepmother with Goethe. When she asked the Countess Lazansky what a constitution was and what was so terrible about it that made everyone so afraid, the latter made the sign of a cross and said it would bring disorder and anarchy: "We need no constitution, we have the Ten Commandments." ("Wir brauchen keine Constitution, wir haben die zehn Gebote." [364]). She warned that Metternich would be furious if he knew about that conversation with Goethe. For her part Leopoldina wrote the word in her notebook and never forgot it. (*Dona Leopoldina*, 337.)

The backlash from her precipitate action was swift and severe. Pedro's father, King Joao, who was already having problems maintaining his authority as King of Portugal, reacted furiously, as did Pedro and even Bonifacio, a dedicated Monarchist, who, however, came to appreciate her bold move. She also had to suffer a stiff reprimand from her father and Metternich, who thought only about what was best for their relations in Europe rather than what best served Brazil's interests. Moreover, Franz I was a reactionary bent on keeping his own citizens ignorant and the country backward. All his life he lived in fear of an uprising like the French Revolution, and consequently he refused to allow universities to engage in research or teachers to educate students. Their role was solely to make them loyal and malleable subjects of the state.

Leopoldina's audacious act demonstrates how thoroughly she had fulfilled her pledge to disavow Austria and become Brazilian. It also shows her strength and courage as well as her informed understanding of the nation's economy: by controlling the country as a colony, Portugal reaped all the gains from Brazilian exports, because regardless of the final destination all exported goods had first to be shipped to Portugal, which then collected the payments from the purchasers. Portugal blustered and even threatened to send troops to conquer the country again, but it was in no position to carry out such a military campaign. Another deterrent to any Portuguese move was the quick recognition of Brazil as an independent state and the establishment of diplomatic ties by leading nations such as the United States. Leopoldina would have gone even further in transforming Brazil, but the country was not ready to move ahead that fast. She hated slavery but was unable to abolish it during her lifetime because the intractable block of farmers and miners proved to be too strong. Neither could her son Pedro II, who became Emperor at age five when his father was forced into exile, end the practice. It remained for Isabella, the daughter of Pedro II, to pass the law that freed all the slaves in 1888, an act that earned her the name Isabella the Redeemer.

Bonifacio became not only Leopoldina's advisor, but also her soul mate. She invited him to her home at Boa Vista, and they often went horseback riding through the Tijuca Mountains and the Turano Forest or took walks during which he would read to her in German. Leopoldina wrote to Louise about the inexplicably strong impression that this earnest, learned man made on her but did not mail the letter. On one occasion in 1821 Leopoldina, desperate for companionship, for one human being in this new country with whom she could feel comfortable, traveled with the blessings of her Lady in Waiting, the Marquise Aguiar, to visit Bonifacio at his home and spent the night with him.

On one occasion Leopoldina invited Bonifacio to dinner with her and Pedro, a move that proved to be a big and costly mistake on her part. She believed that Pedro would benefit from associating with this intelligent man who served as his Minister and perhaps begin to take his responsibilities seriously. Pedro did listen to his tales of study and travel in Europe, to his explanations of modern mining techniques and his vision of erecting a city in the shape of a cross in the interior of the country. He recognized that this man, who was conversant in six languages, possessed many books and gave his wife the scores of piano sonatas, could be useful to him in his position as Minister, to which he had appointed him in 1822. However, as an uneducated man and anti-intellectual, Pedro's overall reaction mixed admiration with contempt. The main thing he learned on that evening concerned Bonifacio's beneficial influence on Leopoldina. With this strong support it was no wonder that his campaign to break his wife's will was not succeeding. Therefore Pedro put an end to the relationship by banishing Bonifacio, his most important minister in the government, in 1823. Leopoldina was devastated but could do nothing. She saw him off on the ship, their final farewell.

Pedro grew up as a thoroughly spoiled child, who was allowed to do whatever he wished, including whipping and tormenting the children of slaves. He gained little formal education but learned to control horses and everyone around him. He wanted a full life and could indulge himself, but he had no interest in his responsibilities as king and, thanks to Leopoldina, as Emperor of Brazil. He remained a playboy throughout his life in Brazil, and only when he was forced to abdicate in favor of his son Pedro II in 1831 did he change his ways in Portugal. He kept Dona Leopoldina occupied with seven pregnancies in nine years and lived an independent life. His trip to Sao Paulo proved fateful for him. There he met a prostitute named Domitila, who came to dominate his life.

The affair, which was flaunted before the court and the public, caused a great deal of gossip and even street rallies denouncing it, and to end this outcry Pedro demanded that Leopoldina appoint his mistress as her Head Lady in Waiting, indicating that she sanctioned the affair. When she refused to comply, he punished her by cutting off all funds to her, even money to which she was legally entitled. To maintain the household, she was forced to borrow whatever money she could from sympathetic friends. While he kept his wife so destitute that she could not even buy decent clothes for herself, Pedro not only lavished money and jewels on Domitilia, who bore him two children, but he also provided for her entire family, buying them houses and establishing them in good paying positions. No request of his mistress, no matter how outlandish, went unfulfilled. He removed loyal advisors at her demand and appointed others she recommended. At her behest he disbanded the powerful Andrade party in government when he banished Bonifacio and his brother to Europe in November 1823. Her control over Pedro grew ever stronger and caused him to give titles of nobility to her minions, as Bonafacio reported in a letter to Leopoldina: "Who would have thought it possible, nineteen viscounts and more than twenty new barons? The street whore Domitila a Viscountess, a fruit dealer a baron, a lumber merchant a marquis. I have to experience that, to see my homeland so debased." (*Dona Leopoldina*, 311).[13] On one occasion Pedro even struck Leopoldina in Domitila's presence, when she refused to agree to be seen with the mistress in public. After that he ordered that she could no longer even ride a horse without his express permission. Eventually the financial hardship and the toll on her health from the constant pregnancies weakened Leopoldina to such an extent that she had to capitulate and accept the mistress as her Head Lady in Waiting.

    Why did Leopoldina put up with this treatment? Certainly not out of love for Pedro. She had been in love with him in the beginning, despite his philandering, but his debasement of her after he moved in with Domitila in 1822 killed all her feelings for him. She would have had to be a masochist to continue to love him, and she was no psychotic. No, it was only that sense of duty, with which she had been inculcated since childhood, that impelled her to endure such a miserable life:

> *Boa Vista* was now the dungeon for her and the children, the dungeon from which he [Pedro] brought her when he needed Leopoldina for a gala reception, for a theater visit, for a conversation with an ambassador. Leopoldina had gotten into the habit of talking aloud to herself: "The duty to endure, to stay." According to what law? According to the laws of nature, as a mother animal she has to stay with her young. According to the law of the household in which she had grown up, she had to stay because fulfillment of duty was the highest goal." (*Dona Leopoldina*, 312).[14]

Early in life Leopoldina had received further reinforcement of the concept of duty from her beloved sister Louise, who in 1916, upon learning of her decision to marry Pedro, wrote her a letter, which she memorized:

> It is the greatest reassurance to know that you have done what can be useful to your father and the welfare of the nation. But I beg you in the name of our sisterly love, not to imagine the future as being so beautiful. Those of us who cannot choose must look neither at the merits of stature or intellect. If we encounter them, it is fortunate. If we do not encounter them, we can still be happy. The personal awareness that we have done our duty, many and different things to occupy our time, and the education of our children give us a certain peace of mind, a cheerful disposition, which is the only true happiness on earth. (*Dona Leopoldina*, 353).[15]

Louise spoke from her own experience which, however, at no time was ever as difficult as the future life awaiting her sister.

Pedro, more concerned about his private pleasures than about the country, sadly lacking in education and without any knowledge of politics, was no more prepared to rule Brazil than Emperor Franz I's handicapped son Ferdinand was capable of ruling Austria. This idea of royal succession regardless of ability has always been a weakness of the monarchical system. Adalbert Stifter made this point forcefully in his monumental novel *Witiko*, which demonstrates that the person chosen to lead the country should be the one with the intelligence and capacity to do so, not the one whose only credential to rule is being born into the royal family. Since Pedro neglected his responsibilities, the legislative body ruled the country according to its own entrenched interests. The ministers, the members of the Legislative Assembly and particularly the European Portuguese held him in low esteem and increasingly humiliated him by passing changes to the constitution, which they pressured him to accept. In 1822, hating his political responsibilities, which he did not understand, and unable to cope with all the difficulties confronting him because of his lack of experience and education, Pedro begged his father, Dom Joao, in Portugal to relieve him of his position and allow him to return to Europe. A ship actually stood ready in the harbor to carry him and Leopoldina back to Portugal, but the necessary parental permission to travel was not forthcoming. Dom Joao was undergoing his own tribulations in Portugal, where he was regarded with contempt and being held virtually as a prisoner to prevent his return to Brazil. On that occasion, which occurred before Pedro had met Domitila, Leopoldina, who had a better grasp of the politics and more feeling for the people than her husband, was still able to influence him to stay in order to keep the country unified.

The people tolerated Pedro for Leopoldina's sake, but after her death the hostility toward him mounted until he was forced to leave the country and return to Portugal. He was not able to bring Domitila with him because he needed to take a Portuguese wife to establish himself there, so he could have his daughter Maria Gloria named Queen. Her coronation took place after her father's death in 1834, as Kaiser details in *Saudade* (cf. note 7). Domitila had no complaints, however, for Pedro's many gifts had made her so wealthy that she could live in luxury for the rest of her life.

Pedro lacked any discipline, manners, or social refinement. Leopoldina had tried to educate him, but since he did not love her any attempt to change his behavior proved hopeless. She tried to bring him to eat with a knife and fork, but he always preferred to eat with his fingers, even after he became emperor. When he visited people, he felt he was entitled to take away any object that he fancied. Leopoldina would then try to return these items later. After 1822 Pedro's only interest in Leopoldina was in keeping her pregnant. Otherwise he lived with his mistress and even had his mail delivered to her house, visiting his home only occasionally to play with the children.

Although he was not attracted to her, Pedro kept Leopoldina pregnant with seven children in nine years, only five of whom survived. She suffered continuously from her weakened physical state. Leopoldina's last pregnancy, which resulted in a stillborn child, killed her. She was so worn down mentally and physically from the years of her hard life, which she accepted as her duty and her fate, despite the fact that she received neither support nor sympathy from her father in Austria and only hostility from her husband and his ministers. Drained mentally and exhausted physically, she died a drawn out painful death on December 11, 1826, at the age of twenty-nine. On December 8, 1826, when it had become clear to her that she would not recover from her illness this time, she wrote a beautiful letter to Bonifacio, the one person in her life she loved and could always rely on for help. This moving, intelligent letter documents that she experienced completely lucid periods amidst the feverish periods of derangement during the final days. She tells him that she is ready to die since "the powers of my soul are used up and in the same measure my body has been consumed." She has carried out everything that needed to be done in accordance with the strictest fulfillment of her duty and now can address her most pressing concern, "the education of our children, of our son Pedro, who must become a noble, upright Monarch. Dom Jose, in the name of our friendship I beseech you, return in timely fashion and look after our son's education, so that he will receive strictness in the same measure as love."[16] Leopoldina then lists all the values she wants young Pedro to learn, and in fact he turned out to most closely resemble his mother in intelligence, intellectual curiosity, balanced personality, and concern for the welfare of his people and his country. Leopoldina concludes this insightful letter by commenting on her husband: "I have forgiven my husband. His inexperience, his lack of education and the influence of that person [Domitila] have caused him to do so many things that are not understandable."[17]

The people had come to admire and appreciate Leopoldina during her lifetime for all her efforts on their behalf, but, despite all of her contributions, implemented under the most difficult circumstances, they could never openly accord her the gratitude they felt out of fear of retaliation by Pedro and Domitila. Only after he was forced to abdicate in 1831 and go into exile could the populace finally publicly honor Dona Leopoldina, who had accomplished more for the social improvement and betterment of the country than her husband and all of the politicians combined, designating her "The Mother of Nation."

Pedro II, the subject of Kaiser's second biographical novel *Pedro II von Brasilien. Der Sohn der Habsburgerin* (1997) (*Pedro II of Brazil. Son of the Habsburg Empress*[7]) forms a logical sequel to *Dona Leopoldina*, carrying the history of the country forward and recounting how he continued the programs that his mother had initiated. Of her five surviving children Pedro II most resembled Leopoldina in character and intelligence, and, as fate would have it, he shared a similar destiny. He, too, had no choice about becoming Emperor of Brazil at the age of five, when his father, Pedro I, because of his negligent and profligate life, was forced to abdicate in 1831 and go into exile in Portugal, where he died in 1834. Like his mother, Pedro II's childhood was devoted to study to prepare him to rule, and at her wish the man chosen to provide his rigorous education was José Bonifácio, who had played such an important role in his mother's life. She could not have picked a better mentor, for Bonifácio was an enlightened thinker, whose ideas helped shape Brazil through his strong influence on the Royal Family as well as his service as minister during the crucial period of the revolution. Because he was ahead of his time and his thinking ran counter to that of the ruling class, his intelligent ideas were not always appreciated and neither was his liberal education of Leopoldina and Pedro II. Pedro had banished him to end his support for Leopoldina, and the ministers exiled him a second time in 1833 to isolate and weaken Pedro II. However, the young Emperor continued on the progressive course set by Bonifácio, stabilizing the country and enacting humane legislation. He willingly abdicated as Emperor in 1888 and moved to Europe, so that the country could peacefully become a republic. As a result of his innovative and peaceful policies, Pedro II, known as Pedro the Wise, gained during his lifetime the adoration of the people that his mother achieved only posthumously.

What makes *Dona Leopoldina* such a remarkable and compelling novel is the gripping, intensely personal way that Kaiser portrays her protagonist. At the same time this creative biographical work can be viewed as an educational and historical novel, for the author provides a rich tapestry of the background as well as describing the lifelong education of the protagonists and the growth of the nation. The same can be said of all her biographical novels. Each of the historical biographies presents an imposing historical personage, whose contributions to society and courageous approach to life serve as a universal model.

Endnotes

[1] Much of the information in this article about the background of the author and her works came from interviews and email correspondence with the author. Rarely does one encounter a

writer so open to questions and ready to provide materials, and I wish to express my gratitude to her here for her generous assistance.

[2] For a list of her early prizes, see *Gloria Kaiser* at http://www.literaturhaus.at/autoren/K/G-Kaiser/bio.html.

[3] Gloria Kaiser, *Wolfgang Amadeus Mozart. January 27–December 5, 1791. Perspectives from His Correspondence.* Riverside, CA: Ariadne Press, 2007.

[4] Cf. "Gloria Kaiser, vorgestellt von Renate Welsh," in *Autorenporträts.* at http://www.plautz.atautoren/13kaiser.htm.

[5] Gloria Kaiser, *Dona Leopoldina. The Habsburg Empress of Brazil*, Riverside, CA: Ariadne Press, 1998. Translated by Lowell A. Bangerter with "Afterwords" by the author and by Ernestine Schlant.

[6] Gloria Kaiser, *Pedro II of Brazil*, Riverside, CA: Ariadne Press, 2000. Translated by Lowell A. Bangerter with "Afterwords" by the author and the translator.

[7] Gloria Kaiser, *Saudade. The Life and Death of Queen Maria Gloria of Lusitania*, Riverside, CA: Ariadne Press, 2005. Translated by Lowell A. Bangerter with "Afterwords" by the author and the translator.

[8] Cf. Gloria Kaiser, "*Hauptberuf Schüler*," in: hpt Magazine (Vienna), no. 2 (1995), 14.

[9] Stefan Zweig, *Brazil, Land of the Future*, Riverside CA: Ariadne Press, 2000.Translated by Lowell A. Bangerter, with an "Afterword" by the author.

[10] Karin Feldbacher, "*Ein Leben in zwei Welten*," in: *Kleine Zeitung* (Graz), 16 February 2006, 67.

[11] Gloria Kaiser, "Author's Afterword," in *Dona Leopoldina*, 368.(Kein Anspruch wird darauf erhoben, über Dona Leopoldina die ausschließliche Wahrheit zu wissen. Auch nach sorgfältiger Erforschung kann dieses Leben nur schöpferisch gedeutet werden; selbst Briefe, und sind sie inhaltlich noch so exact zitiert, müssen menschlich nicht verläßlich sein, werden sie doch

heute gelesen. G. K., Dona Leopoldina. Die Habsburgerin auf Brasiliens Thron, 397.

[12] "Und dann, nach drei Monaten, stand das Schiff still. Wir sahen Buchten, aus denen eine Stadt wuchs, das Grün der Wälder, das Weiss der Häuser und das Blau von Meer und Himmel waren zu einem Farbenspiel verschmolzen, zu einem Sog, von dem wir uns an Land ziehen ließen.
Wir gingen sofort an die Arbeit.
Wir zeichneten, malten, schrieben, wir waren oft im Zweifel – konnte ein Pinselstrich, ein Federstrich, ein Wort ausdrücken, was wir sahen und fühlten. Wir waren an jenem Flecken Erde angelangt, wo Mutter Erde sich Sonne und Mond entgegenwirft und für diese Hingabe mit dem Leuchten in den Grün-, Blau- und Gelbtönen belohnt wird, das sie jeden Morgen über die Landschaft wirft." Gloria Kaiser, "Thomas Ender, Partida rumo ao desconhecido – Aufbruch zum Neuen," in: *Abre Alas: Öffnen dich für Neues. Thomas Ender: Encontro com Uma Nova Luz. Begegnung mit einem neuen Licht. Austria – Brazil*. October 2007. (My English translation. DGD)

[13] "Wer hätte es für möglich gehalten, neunzehn Vicomtes und über zwanzig neue Barone; die Gassendirne Domitila Vicomtesse, ein Fruchthändler Baron, ein Holzhändler Marquis. Das muß ich erleben, mein Vaterland so erniedrigt zu sehen." Gloria Kaiser, Dona Leopoldina. *Die Habsburgerin auf Brasiliens Thron*. Graz: Verlag Styria, 1994, 336.

[14] "Boa Vista nun das Verlies für sie und die Kinder, das Verlies, aus dem er sie holte, wenn er Leopoldine für einen Galaempfang, für einen Theaterbesuch, das Gespräch mit einem Botschafter brauchte. Leopoldine hatte sich angewöhnt, laut mit sich zu reden, die Verpflichtung, auszuharren, zu bleiben. Nach welchem Gesetz? Nach den Naturgesetzen hatte sie als Muttertier bei den Jungen zu bleiben; nach dem Gesetz des Hauses, in dem sie aufgewachsen war, hatte sie zu bleiben, weil Pflichterfüllung das höchste Ziel war." Gloria Kaiser, *Dona Leopoldina. Die Habsburgerin auf Brasiliens Thron*, 336.

[15]"Die größte Beruhigung ist das gethan zu haben was für seinen Vater und das Wohl des Staates nützlich seyn kann. Aber ich bitte dich im Namen unserer schwesterlichen Liebe, stelle dir die Zukunft nicht zu schön vor. Wir anderen, die nicht wählen können müssen weder auf die Vorzüge der Figur noch des Geistes sehen. Trifft man sie so ist es glücklich. Trifft man sie nicht so kann man auch glücklich seyn. Das Selbstbewusstseyn seine Pflicht gethan zu haben, viele und verschiedene Beschäftigungen, die Erziehung unserer Kinder, gibt einem gewisse Seelenruhe, ein heiteres Gemüth, was das einzige wahre Glück auf Erden ist" (381).

[16]"Nun da alles geordnet ist, kann ich über meine grösste Sorge sprechen, die Erziehung unserer Kinder, unseres Sohnes Pedro, der ein edler, rechtschaffener Monarch werden muss. Dom Jose, im Namen unserer Freundschaft flehe ich Sie an, kommen Sie zuzeiten zurück und nehmen Sie unseren Sohn Pedro in Ihre Erziehungsobhut, auf dass er Strenge im selben Mass wie Liebe bekomme... In: *200 Anniversario Dona Leopoldina Princesa da Austria-Premeira Imperatrix do Brazil*. Brochure published by Initiativa Cultural Austro-Brasiliera, December 1996, 87. (My English translation, DGD.)

[17]"Meinem Gemahl habe ich vergeben. Seine Unerfahrenheit, die mangelnde Erziehung und der Einfluss jener Person haben ihn so viele unverständliche Dinge tun lassen." Ibid.

For Whom the Turtle Weeps:
Paulus Hochgatterer's *Caretta Caretta*

Todd C. Hanlin

Caretta Caretta, translated by Todd C. Hanlin, Ariadne Press, 2010

Adolescence is an apprenticeship, a period of growth – perhaps both physically and emotionally painful – when the innocence and naiveté of childhood is lost, much like a fall from an earthly paradise, and the young must gradually assume the individuality, independence, and responsibility of adulthood. Numerous literary depictions of adolescence bear witness that this process is both significant and unavoidable, from the Hardy Boys and Nancy Drew to current authors like JD Salinger with his *Catcher in the Rye* (1951), William Golding with *Lord of the Flies* (1954), and even JK Rowling with her *Harry Potter* series. As the reception history of these representative works reveals, adolescent fiction appeals to both juvenile and adult readers. And even writers of strictly adult fiction feel compelled to present the trials and tribulations of youth (or, more specifically, of *their* youth), frequently symbolized by unfeeling institutions of socialization, as John Le Carré has done in his early mystery *A Murder of Quality* (1962), where he depicts a satirical boys' school, "Carne," a "carnivorous" institution that figuratively eats its own.
    In German literature, portrayals of adolescent struggles by well-known authors range back a century and more, from Hermann Hesse's *Beneath the Wheel* (*Unterm Rad,* 1906) to more recent works from West Germany, such as Günter Grass's *Cat and Mouse* (*Katz und Maus,* 1961), Hubert Fichte's "Essay on Puberty" (*Versuch über die Pubertät,* 1974), and Verena Stefan's *Shedding* (*Häutungen,* 1975) and to those from the social-

ist East, as exemplified by contributions from Peter Weiss in "Leavetaking" (*Abschied von den Eltern*, 1961) and Ulrich Plenzdorf with his *The New Sufferings of Young W* (*Die neuen Leiden des jungen W*, 1973), to name but a few. Austria has made equally important contributions to the long tradition of adolescent novels, with works by such notable authors as Robert Musil and his *The Confusions of Young Torless* (*Die Verwirrungen des Zöglings Törleß*, 1906), Stefan Zweig and *Burning Secret* (*Brennendes Geheimnis*, 1911), Franz Werfel with his *Class Reunion* (*Der Abituriententag*, 1928), Friedrich Torberg and "Schoolboy Gerber's Graduation" (*Der Schüler Gerber hat absolviert*, 1930), Ödön von Horváth with "Youth Without God" (*Jugend ohne Gott*, 1937), Barbara Frischmuth's *The Convent School* (*Die Klosterschule*, 1968), Christine Nöstlinger's "Class Schedule" (*Stundenplan*, 1975), and Renate Welsh's "Sixteen Once and Never Again' (*Einmal sechzehn und nie wieder*, 1975).

Unlike their predecessors, however, today's youth are plagued by more contemporary challenges – not simply having to deal with puberty, the demands of society, and their own attempts at individuation through rebellion or withdrawal, but, more significantly, with fractured families and ensuing psychoanalysis, with drugs, and with the accompanying distractions of a materialistic society: as children of the so-called *Generation Golf*, youth from Germany, Austria, and Switzerland are thus profoundly defined by the consumer goods with which they surround themselves.[1] The participants in this "generation" are typically from affluent families and thus, already by their teens, are consummate apolitical consumers whose allegiance is not to party politics, but only to brand loyalty.

Paulus Hochgatterer (1961-) was born in Amstetten, Lower Austria, studied medicine and psychology in Vienna, completed his degree and residency in psychiatry and neurology in 1985, and today is a practicing child and adolescent psychiatrist. He lives with his family in Vienna. Hochgatterer began writing short stories in the late 1970s and is now a successful writer, drawing on his extensive experience, both theoretical and practical, to bring a unique perspective to the tradition of adolescent literature.

Hochgatterer's first short stories *Rückblickpunkte/Unbereitete Wege* ("Retrospective Points of View/Unpaved Roads") appeared in 1983. But it wasn't until the 1990s that he began to hit his stride: he published the story *Der Aufenthalt* ("The Stopover," 1990) and then his first novel *Über die Chirurgie* ("About Surgery," 1993), followed in brisk succession by a collection of short stories entitled *Die Nystensche Regel* ("Nysten's Law," 1995), *Wildwasser* ("Whitewater," 1997), *Caretta Caretta* in 1999, and in the new millennium the novel *Über Raben* ("About Ravens," 2002), *Eine kurze Geschichte vom Fliegenfischen* ("A Short Story About Fly-fishing," 2003), *Die Süße des Lebens* ("The Joy of Life," 2006), and his latest novel *Das Matratzenhaus* ("The Flophouse") in 2010. He has received several prestigious prizes over the years to encourage his writing career, primarily from provincial and federal funding agencies, for example, stipends from Lower Austria as well as from the office of the Federal Chancellor. Especially noteworthy are an award from the Jury of Young Readers for his adolescent book *Wildwasser* in 1998, an Austrian National Award in 2000 for Children's and Adolescent Literature for *Caretta Caretta*, and in the following year the Elias Canetti Stipend from the city of Vienna, named for the winner of the Nobel Prize for Literature. He won the German Murder Mystery Prize in 2007 for *Die Süße des Lebens* and in 2009 was awarded the first European Union Prize for Literature for that same work.

Hochgatterer's unique perspective on adolescents and their world affects both the form and content of his works. His preferred style, especially in those works dealing with troubled youth, is predominantly first-person narration, at times employing interior monologue that reveals the psychological basis behind the plot. Moreover, with the adolescent telling his or her own story, and in his or her own words, speech betrays a great deal about the social status and education, experiences and relationships, as well as hopes and fears of the narrator.

Hochgatterer typically uses a *Plauderton*, a chatty, casual conversational tone, not confessional, not feigned, but realistically intimate – with the reader serving as a trusted friend. Some slang is employed to add credibility, but not to the degree that the communication is incomeprehensible, as it might be to adults if one teenager were talking exclusively to another. If an adult (or a therapist) were telling the same story, it would, of course, be from an adult point-of-view and thus not as immediate, not as authentic and "true," and therefore could not adequately reflect the youths' conflicts.[2]

A second feature of Hochgatterer's adolescent novels is his eye for realistic details. In this regard, he is keenly aware of today's adolescents, their preoccupation with brand-name goods and the attendant status among their peers: clothing, sports articles, entertainment, and individual experiences all signify uniqueness and value in their personhood. This innovative literary approach captures youths' identification, indeed their obsession with consumer fads and fashions. As he was once quoted in regard to youth and its labels, Hochgatterer remarked:

> That is not just some gimmick to create atmosphere. First of all, I am constantly confronted with these stories in the hospital, it's also important for the adolescents; granted, more for some than for others. And in the meantime my own son, too, has grown into a boy for whom it is somehow important that his shoes be Timberlands.[3]

Naturally, clothing becomes a crucial visual feature – the immediate impression created by distinct apparel contributes to a unique personality and elevates the individual above the crowd, conveying the bearer's affluence and fashion *savoir-faire*, his social status and thus his "cool"– even if everyone else is wearing a similar brand, thus creating a uniform…as long as it is the "right" uniform. Hochgatterer's main character tends to wear a T-shirt, at times a "Nike shirt" or a "Nike sweater," dons "white Converse basketball shoes" (or "Timberlands" for a boat trip).

Meanwhile, as an observant youth, the protagonist notices other males who wear, for example, "boxer shorts," "Levis," and "Doc Martens." Other accoutrements worn by passers-by include "Calvin Klein eyeglasses," "Nike Air-Jordans," and, for headgear, a "University of Michigan baseball cap," while a classmate can be seen wearing an "L.A. Lakers cap." Females are also outfitted with conspicuous clothing; for example, one girl wears "Boss stretch jeans," and her girlfriend is dressed in a "Minnie Mouse T-shirt."

Hip expressions and slang phrases become prevalent: some in German are the equivalent of "bummed out" or "out to lunch," while one of the boys had a chance "to get in some girl's pants." At other times the international "in"-language of English may be preferred, as in "welcome to the club." In the role of observer of (and commentator on) the contemporary scene, our youthful narrator notices a woman smoking a "Marlboro Medium," one who smells like "Polo Ralph Lauren," and an overweight girl who needs "WeightWatchers." For distraction our teenage narrator himself listens to a "Walkman," plays "Donkey Kong Land III" on a "Game-Boy," throws a "Frisbee," and rides a moped, a "KTM-Pony." His favorite book is a "Calvin & Hobbes" edition, and he also reads "Fun and Vision" by Nintendo, eats pizza, and has (either for protection or as a totem) an aluminum baseball bat. Significantly, today's youth are infinitely more familiar with medications and drugs than their predecessors; the variety of pharmaceutical products is mindboggling, as dispensed here by the local drug-counseling social worker or "Streetworker." Among the drugs of choice are Parkemed 500, Microbamat, Somnubene, Paracodin, heroin, morphine, Heptadon, and Vendal. Whether addicted himself or "only" pushing drugs to others, our adolescent protagonist's familiarity with such a pharmaceutical panorama is revealing.

Hochgatterer had first attempted to capture the environment and character of today's adolescents in his earlier novel *Wildwasser* (1997). Here he presents a seventeen-year-old first-person narrator, Jakob Schmalfuss, whose father, a professional kayaker, has died in a "whitewater" accident; as a result, the boy's immediate family now consists of a mother, who teaches kindergarten, and a thirteen-year-old sister, with predictable results: the main character relates his lack of success in school to the loss of his father. He is also disturbed by contemporary events related to school and some of his classmates; for example, a teacher commits suicide by driving his car into the median pillar of an Autobahn bridge. For the most part the teen narrator uses little slang, although he does incorporate some trendy references, such as his sport-hero, the British Formula-1 racecar driver Johnny Herbert. Other prominent personalities (who serve either as exemplar or cachet for peer approval) are internationally-known entertainers or movie stars such as Michael Jackson, Julia Roberts, Richard Gere, Kim Basinger, Sharon Stone, and Bruce Willis; special favorites are movies and cartoons. As can be expected, clothes are a distinguishing feature, and the boy specifically mentions Ray Ban and Killer Loop sunglasses, along with the ever-present jeans. For leisure, he often rides his "Scott Yucatan Mountain Bike," imbibes "Black Spider Energy Drink," "Flying Horse," or "Sprite"; reads Playboy and Penthouse; listens to Jimi Hendrix and The Doors; watches Monty Python films and laughs at Homer and Bart Simpson. Nonetheless, this abundance of material goods (drugs included) cannot compensate for the paucity of emotional support, empathy, and even love. To limit his pains, both physical and emotional, the boy overdoses on Mundidol, Lexotanil and other, stronger medications.[4]

For *Caretta Caretta*, Hochgatterer provides an introductory quote from one of his own literary influences – Dan McCall's short novel *Jack the Bear*: "One thing I'm learning now is that everybody in the whole world has really terrible problems."[5] That Hochgatterer should call our attention to this particular adolescent novel highlights his affinity for this type of literature.

Briefly, the plot is as follows: The father in this family, John "Jack" Leary, is separated, though not divorced from the mother, who has subsequently died in a car accident; their sons are John "Jack" Jr. (the twelve-year-old narrator, "Jack the Bear," still in junior high school) and Dylan, age 3. The mother's death is a challenge for all to overcome. Basically still an adolescent himself, the father presides over two adolescent TV shows, "Thriller" and "Kid Stuff"; meanwhile he tries to survive with alcohol and pot. Cursing the father he loves, purposely frightening his younger brother when he babysits him, and tormenting a retarded neighbor boy, our youthful narrator is having a difficult time coping with his mother's demise. The eponymous nickname Jack the Bear is taken from a legendary jazz recording by Duke Ellington, though, like the boy, Jack the Bear is a "loser" too: "He keeps on truckin', but he stands in place."[6] The twelve-year-old faces typical adolescent issues, for instance, a desire for popularity among his peers. He wants to be considered clever or talented and thus distinctive, to have relations (if not outright sex) with girls, to receive understanding and sympathy, and to have an outlet for his aggressions against the world. In creating a desirable image, clothes are important, as are an impressive family and parents (or parent, in his case). The narrative, in Jack's own words, portrays his usual daily existence...until his three-year-old brother, who was Jack's responsibility, is kidnapped. Though the brother is recovered, the father suffers an emotional breakdown and the family's future is in doubt – Jack Jr. insists he's going to Europe when he turns sixteen – as the novel ends.

Unlike their literary predecessors, McCall's and Hochgatterer's youthful characters are sympathetic figures, though no longer innocents. They often find themselves in dysfunctional families, without positive role models or protective guardians, and thus vulnerable to life's cruelties; moreover, they must contend with a thriving drug culture in an impersonal, hostile environment, so it is not surprising that they would exhibit violent tendencies toward adults or society in general. Nevertheless, the young protagonists are often clever and resourceful, resilient, inventive, self-sufficient to a great degree, and they employ these talents in their struggle to avoid becoming "victims" – of society, of their peers, or of their families. In exceptional circumstances, they are even able to have compassion for other individuals who have earned or are deserving of their consideration.

In *Caretta Caretta*, Hochgatterer fleshes out his original sketch of a troubled teen, revealing in greater detail the protagonist's personal situation, his world, and its hazards. This insightful portrait features a first-person narration by Dominik Bach, a skinny fifteen-year-old juvenile delinquent and member of a dysfunctional family featuring a narcissistic mother and an abusive stepfather. Yet his tale is neither straightforward nor uncomplicated, for juveniles create their own fictions and their own life stories, which are always more interesting and more creative than reality. Typical for a teenager, Dominik's usual "narration" includes clever obfuscations and inventive fabrications. Thus the reader may be unsure how much of his narration is "true," as we discover in the following monologue:

> I tell them [two unfamiliar adults] about my mother who is working at the University of Strasbourg on computer-based computations of perfect numbers, and how I hate her never-ending research residencies, this time in Strasbourg, that time in Dublin, the time before that in Bologna or Madrid. I tell them about Aunt Elly and Uncle Max, Mom's sister and her husband, along with Samantha, their drooling pit bull, and how I always have to stay with them, how I hate the whole family, even more than Mom's research residencies, and that I didn't have the slightest trace of guilt when I ransacked all the wallets and purses I could find in the house, and in Uncle Max's greasy black wallet there was – no kidding! – 4700 Schillings. And I tell them how my father, who was a construction worker on steel buildings, would stroll along the crossbeams eighteen stories up without a safety har-

ness, dangle his welding apparatus over the abyss as if it was his lunch pail, and how, one day, in one of those crazy situations that occur without warning, he was attacked by a pair of kestrel falcons and fell. "I was five-and-a-half at the time," I tell them, and that's the only thing that's the truth. I don't tell them anything at all about my stepfather (17).[7]

Typical for Dominik's public statements, this monologue is meant to impress (while simultaneously deceiving) his listeners. He indirectly boasts of his mother's prominent position in cutting-edge research at distinguished foreign research institutes, and later tells a taxi driver that his mother is a pharmacist... while at one point he seems to confess that she is a veterinarian's assistant or a dental hygienist in Vienna. He claims to have stolen money from his relative-hosts...while it appears that he lives in a juvenile detention center and does unsavory and even illegal acts to "earn" his money. He also claims his father met an almost romantic fate as a high-rise construction worker who fell to his death (a tale that is vaguely reminiscent of another mythical hero, Icarus), though later he relates that his father was a fireman in charge of rescue and salvage of hazardous materials who was crushed by an oil tanker truck, or that his father was captain of a fire-fighting brigade at the airport who died saving four people when a plane caught fire; and on a later occasion he calmly explains that his father is a chemist and businessman who owns a pharmaceutical company. Such bravado, including the eventual contradictions, is typical for adolescents who wish to impress others.

The challenge for the reader is that Dominik's statements are difficult to corroborate without external verification; we are forced to rely on the young narrator and take him at his (undependable) word. For example, Dominik admits breaking the storefront windows of a motorcycle dealer who took advantage of young girls who were hooked on drugs – a vigilante act of almost laudable intent, though certainly not one that is substantiated. On other occasions, Dominik may share his experiences with little embellishment: he tells about breaking fellow pupil Jimmy's left forearm with a blackboard ruler almost two years ago, which became the proverbial "last straw" for the Juvenile Court that put Dominik in the detention center, since he had already had a run-in with his stepfather two months before that. Dominik's frequent daydreams further undermine our protagonist's credibility, often with violent consequences for those who threaten his wellbeing; by the end of the novel the reader must judge whether Dominik has carried out (m)any of his harmful fantasies.

The one figure that links Dominik's confessions to experiences confirmed by others is his stepfather; Dominik's close relationship with Kossitzky, the prison guard, is based on a shared hatred of the stepfather. From the outset, Dominik alludes to his stepfather's cruelty, mentioning several times a steel rod and scars on the backs of his thighs, or other disciplinary attempts to force Dominik to kneel on steel bars while the stepfather calmly took photos every fifteen minutes – but then Dominik denies that some of this is true. Dominik later relates an incident when his stepfather accidentally closed a car door on two of his fingers, then locked the doors and grinned at his young victim. We learn that the stepfather was later arrested and sentenced to twenty-one months imprisonment.

The fundamental truth is that Dominik is alone: his mother has little patience and understanding for him or for his stepsister, who is with a foster family in Salzburg; his father is absent, presumably dead, and his stepfather is a cruel, abusive sadist. He lives in a juvenile detention center with guardians Chuck, Sally, Ronald, Wolfgang, Inge, Kurt, and Helene as house parents (*Betreuer*); his co-op housemates include other delinquents Christoph, Philipp, Jasmin, Anna, Victoria, Benjamin, and Isabella. In this precarious environment, Dominik must protect and support himself as a minor in a hostile world. For protection he acquires various safeguards: his baseball bat is no longer a piece of sports equipment, but a weapon, offensive or defensive as needed, like his jackknife, the stiletto, and the "Anaconda" Colt revolver. To support himself financially, Dominik has cultivated various sources: he receives some welfare funds from a social worker; he engages in heterosexual or homosexual acts for money; and finally we learn about two young women teachers who pay him 1750 Schillings "per appointment, all inclusive"– and must assume that he provides them with drugs.

While much of Dominik's life story is shared in flashback, often either reluctantly or accidentally, the actual novelistic proceedings span roughly one week in the summer of 1998, beginning with France's World Cup victory over Brazil. The soccer celebration, clearly a male fantasy, allows us to assume a male first-person narrator – though only gradually do we learn his name, that he is not an adult, and that he is running away (from his juvenile detention center and from his distant mother) to Paris, because it is the home of the world-championship soccer team. This fifteeen-year-old petty thief has stolen food at the station and is hoping to ride the train to Paris without purchasing a ticket, thanks to his questionable relationship with a young train conductor on this route.

Our "hero," Dominik, is intelligent, clever, not adverse to illegal acts, such as his casual theft of a sandwich, soft drink, and Gummy Bears; when confronted for not having purchased a ticket, he smashes the conductor's nose, then threatens four adults with a revolver he has stolen, pulls the train's emergency brake, and escapes into the night. He then steals a moped from a nearby house, and finally hitches a ride with a trucker from Germany back to Austria.

He wakes up the following morning back in his bed at the co-op, hung-over – after the debacle, he got drunk hitchhiking back to Vienna, took meds, and has thrown up all over the place. He ventures out to visit a fourteen-year-old dealer named Yoko who gives him sleeping pills and painkillers. Dominik returns to the co-op and meets Isabella, a tall redhead with glasses who has "family problems."

Some contemporary Viennese youth have typical Austrian forenames, though such pedestrian identifiers are clearly unfashionable: to garner distinction, one must have a unique, if not unforgettable name or nickname. Several of Dominik's acquaintances are named (by themselves or their friends, certainly not by their parents!) after comic book characters, such as the Peanuts-like "Chuck" and "Sally," and Batman-names such as "Two Face" and "Joker"; one has even acquired the nickname "Homer Simpson." Others are simply foreign and thus exotic, like "Ronald," "Jasmin," "Buddy." Animals are not able to escape this fad either, as there is mention of a pit-bull named "Samantha," while Chuck's dog is named "Roosevelt." However, from the moment of her first, modest introduction, one new arrival has the distinctly regal name of Isabella; already a standout as a tall redhead with glasses, she acts reserved and independent, neither rude nor profane, not an obviously disturbed individual with eating disorders, etc. She is intellectually curious, and her gentle humming is a soothing leitmotiv:

> "This is Isabella," Sally said, and put her hand on the new girl's shoulder. The girl took a step away from Sally. "Isabella has come to us unexpectedly," Sally said, "because something has happened in her family that makes it impossible for her to stay there" (48-49).[8]

That Dominik can identify with her is confirmed by his comment that things are constantly happening in our families which, indeed, make it impossible to stay. ("Ständig passiert in unseren Familien etwas, das es uns in Wahrheit unmöglich macht, dort zu bleiben, dachte ich" [52]). Dominik, too, has problems that originate with his family, so from the outset, these two teenagers are kindred spirits. Later, when he learns that Isabella's mother is dead (possibly from strangulation) and her father is absent, Dominik can sympathize with her.

He then leaves following a commotion in which Christoph hits new arrival Benjamin over the head with

Dominik's baseball bat. Dominik goes to a phone booth to call a "contact" for an appointment. One source of Dominik's income derives from this "contact," Mrs. Roswitha Lombardi; a divorced benefactor, she sometimes photographs him (possibly nude or semi-nude), serves him a meal, and then sleeps with him. Dominik wakes up the next day in Mrs. Lombardi's bed. He has a 10:30 a.m. appoinment with a certain Kossitzky, who inexplicably fails to appear. Dominik recalls first meeting Kossitzky on a Christmas eve: his mother had begged him to visit the prison guard, since Dominik had recently been arrested three times, apparently for stealing. They had previously met in August while visiting his stepfather in jail; at that time Kossitzky had witnessed Dominik being threatened and gave the boy his business card with his personal telephone number. In reaction to the stepfather's cruelty, Dominik has tried to poison him with allergens like strawberries and walnuts, which put the stepfather in the hospital. Later, in November, Kossitzky himself attempts to poison him in prison, and the stepfather succumbs.

Back at the co-op, Dominik discovers that the drugged-up Jasmin has slashed her arms and then cut Christoph when he tried to stop her. Here, at the mid-point of the book, with chaos seemingly all-pervasive, we come to the crucial encounter between Dominik and Isabella, when he notices her looking intently at a large, colorful, coffee-table book. He asks about the subject matter, and she replies "turtles" (*Schildkröten*). He gazes at a photograph of a sandy beach, a picturesque sailboat wreck:

"Where is that?" I asked. "Zakynthos," she answered.
"Zakynthos? Never heard of it."
"A Greek island."
"A Greek island. And what's there, besides shipwrecks?"
"Caretta caretta."
"Caretta…what?"
She turned the page. The following two-page spread showed a gleaming something as it flew

across the blue-green picture, from the lower left-hand side to the upper right-hand corner, wings spread wide, its head wreathed in sunlight, half-bird, half-turtle. Its mouth was slightly open, gently facing downward like a beak. Its right eye was gazing at me in amazement. "Caretta caretta," the new girl was saying, "the loggerhead turtle." It was the most beautiful animal I had ever seen (102).[9]
As he realizes, Isabella has shared with him an example of true beauty, and a bond has begun to form. As the conversation continues, we learn that the titular subject is a rare species with an amazing feature: "What's so special about this Caretta caretta?" I asked. "Sometimes it cries," the new girl replied (108) ("Was ist eigentlich das Besondere an dieser Caretta caretta?" fragte ich. "Sie weint manchmal," sagte die Neue [107]). The signficance of Isabella and Caretta caretta for Dominik is underscored when, shortly thereafter, he suggests to his dying friend Kossitzky that they venture to Zakynthos...and that they invite Isabella to join them.

Kossitzky is presently in the hospital. He is a short, stocky, white-haired sixty-four-year-old. For the past ten days he has been losing weight, has developed a gray-green facial tint, and is currently undergoing intravenous chemotherapy, since he has been diagnosed with inoperable renal cancer that has spread to his lungs, liver, peritoneum, and brain. Faced with an imminent and unpleasant death, Kossitzky wants to escape, immediately, for a week "in the sun"– and invites Dominik to accompany him. Dominik suggests Zakynthos, the Greek island Isabella has mentioned with the turtles, and also that Kossitzky could take them both along, as his nephew and niece. In return, Dominik promises to provide narcotics to ease Kossitzky's pain during the "vacation." Dominik seeks out "Buddy," a chubby drug counselor with the title "Streetworker," buys forty-five empty drug vials of differing sizes and fifty syringes, and subsequently acquires some strong medications and pain killers from a registered pharmacist who works in a pharmaceutical firm. But a hurried phone call from Kossitzky announces a change of plan: all passages to Zakynthos are booked, so he has chartered a boat in Turkey instead, with the understanding that there are turtles almost everywhere (140) ("Irgendwelche Schildkröten gibt es fast überall." [136]). The flight leaves Vienna at 1:30 a.m. Saturday morning.

Having finalized travel plans and concluded his preflight shopping, Dominik gives the night attendant a sleeping pill so that he and Isabella can slip out of the detention center unobserved and catch a taxi to the airport. Their flight and arrival in Turkey are uneventful – in spite of her smuggling aboard his aluminum baseball bat and him the Colt revolver in a loaf of bread along with Kossitzky's drugs in a life preserver. Safely aboard ship, their journey to Turtle Beach is in vain, since a soldier prevents them from visiting the beach – it is closed for the week, he proclaims. Isabella realizes that they would not have seen any turtles, even if the soldier had allowed them on the beach, and she resolves to continue the vacation and make the most of their time, even in the absence of Caretta caretta. So they swim and visit archeological Roman ruins instead.

Meanwhile, Kossitzky's condition worsens. The old man is dying. He has been one of the few, whether adolescent or adult, who could appreciate the adolescents' plight; he has selected them to accompany him for their benefit as well as his. In his own way, he appreciates and loves them both, and, remarkably, Kossitzky and his death bring the two troubled youths together.

While the Turkish guide Cherim and Isabella venture forth to see the "Eternal Flame," Kossitzky goes to find a miracle curative plant, the *scilla maritima* or sea onion, that rarely blooms and is said to be poisonous to the uninitiated. Meanwhile, Dominik goes snorkeling and finds a huge tortoise shell, drags it onto the beach, only to discover Kossitzky dead – whether resulting from an overdose of the sea onion or from the cancer is unstated. Dominik and Isabella bury him with all the necessary dignity they can provide – their friend and protector is embraced by the turtle shell, a lone salvo is fired in the air in his honor, the two survivors sing Isabella's French Christmas carol, concluding the memorial service with "In the Neighborhood." Then life must go on...though with the novel's conclusion, the reader gains no further insight into the youths' eventual futures.

    Paulus Hochgatterer has provided a sensitive description of the experiences of today's adolescents and thereby affords us a time capsule that captures their contemporary reality, as distinct from that of their literary predecessors. The lives of present-day adolescents consist of a desperate attempt at survival, at best a search for compassion and companionship. In this novel, however, since the reader observes only two adolescents in depth, it is difficult to label them as typical for an entire generation. Yet even at this young age, they do seem representative of many youth today, in that they demonstrate definite likes and dislikes, habits and preferences, though they have not as yet formulated any great career plans; they seem to be trying to survive adolescence as best they can. In life, there are too many immediate obstacles to be overcome, their future is still too distant to be able to predict success or even failure. In the context of Hochgatterer's adolescent novel, we could paraphrase Mark Twain: "Man is the only animal that weeps. Or needs to."[10] That the creature Caretta caretta is capable of shedding tears, implies that it can perhaps communicate its own suffering, or, more significantly, that it has the capacity to empathize with the sufferings of others – an emotion that today's teens sorely crave.

    In desperation, we could even fabricate a false etymology for Caretta caretta, as if the name were derived from *caritas*, as in mercy, charity, and understanding. But then our three "tourists" never encounter an actual turtle, ultimately only the empty shell of one, obviously *sans* eyes, whether weeping or dry. Yet even if they had found the turtle, would it have benefited them? For how could it understand their predicament, relieve their suffering, improve their lives? Sadly, the scientific facts dispel any such hope – this turtle species has glands that allow them to drink seawater and secrete the salt; female loggerheads have been observed apparently "crying" for their offspring, but they were merely secreting excess salt.[11] Therefore even Caretta caretta seems unable to respond to the adolescents' plight.

This odyssey is, once again, a journey of discovering affinities, trust, cooperation, and collaboration – in short, of initiating a new beginning, instigated by an elderly dying man in his humane wisdom; it is not specifically about some romantic notion of seeing rare turtles cry. The two adolescents learn from Kossitzky that there are other things in the world to see. Indeed, Isabella is able to shift her attention to other interests, like Galapagos turtles, Calvin & Hobbes, geophysical wonders such as the "Eternal Flame." As mentioned above, Isabella is not seriously disturbed and has several redeeming qualities, like our protagonist Dominik: both have an inherent quality of decency that could help them, together, to survive. It is Kossitzky's death that puts everything into perspective, because, unlike their parents who disappointed or hurt them, this old man, an adult and fellow human being, turns out to be sympathetic. He is not only able to "cry" for and with them, more importantly he is able to elicit *their* tears through his death, making them once again loving (and thus lovable) human beings, uniting them so that they can move forward together. They do not require the miraculous intervention of some rare natural species, but simply the interaction with another human being, a person in whom they can develop trust, through familiarity, similarity, a growing appreciation and affection, through friendship, and possibly love.

Endnotes

---

[1] A comparable expression in the United States might be "Generation X." The German term derives from a 2001 book by

Florian Illies, *Generation Golf*, that recalls the nostalgia of those born in West Germany between 1965 and 1975 for consumer products of all sorts, such as the VW *Golf* – the VW "Rabbit" in the US – that defined life for that generation, as a replacement for their parents' iconic VW "Beetle." Similar conditions could be identified in Austria at a slightly later date.

[2] In his latest works, *Eine kurze Geschichte vom Fliegenfischen* and *Die Süße des Lebens*, Hochgatterer has adult participants tell the story of a fishing expedition and of a murder, often in third-person; nevertheless, he maintains many of the speech patterns mentioned above to enhance credibility, intimacy, and thus immediacy.

[3] "Das ist nicht nur ein Trick, um Stimmung zu erzeugen. Erstens bin ich permanent mit diesen Geschichten im Spital konfrontiert, das ist für Jugendliche auch wichtig; schon, für die einen mehr, für die anderen weniger. Und der Herr Sohn ist auch einer, dem inzwischen irgendwie wichtig ist, daß die Schuhe von Timberland sind." See the website interview at: < "mich," http://www.wellbuilt.net/literatur/doc/hochgat.html>.

[4] The third book in this series, *Über Raben* (2002), is in many respects the most challenging of Hochgatterer's adolescent novels, depicting a teacher and thirteen-year-old girl as dual main characters in a split narration. The high school teacher (*Gymnasiallehrer*), divorced with a son, absents himself from school to climb in the mountains, carrying a loaded rifle for protection, ostensibly from his colleagues. However, it is the thirteen-year-old girl who is of primary interest, as she relates a typical week in her life, the daily lessons at school, telling about her classmates and about an elderly handicapped neighbor woman whom she nurses with the aid of the woman's debit card. To a certain degree, the plots of the three novels are relatively unimportant; for our purposes they are primarily settings in which Hochgatterer can investigate the lives of today's youth.

[5] Dan McCall, *Jack the Bear* (New York: Fawcett Crest, 1974), 13-14.

⁶*Jack the Bear*, 73.
⁷Ich erzähle von meiner Mutter, die sich an der Universität Straßburg mit der computermäßigen Errechnung vollkommener Zahlen beschäftigt, und davon, wie ich diese ewigen Forschungsaufenthalte hasse, einmal in Straßburg und einmal in Dublin und einmal in Bologna oder Madrid. Ich erzähle von Tante Elly und Onkel Max, Mutters Schwester und ihrem Mann, samt Samantha, dem speichelnden Pitbull, bei denen ich dann immer wohnen muß, wie ich diese Familie hasse, mehr noch als Mamas Forschungsaufenthalte, und wie ich keine Spur von Schuldgefühl hatte, als ich sämtliche Geldbörsen plünderte, die im Haus aufzutreiben waren, und wie in Onkel Max' speckiger schwarzer Börse tatsächlich viertausendsiebenhundert Schilling waren. Und ich erzähle davon, wie mein Vater, der von Beruf Stahlbaumonteur war, sechzig Meter über Grund freihändig die Traversen entlangging, wie er das Schweißgerät über den Abgrund trug, als wäre es ein Proviantbeutel, und wie er eines Tages in einer derartigen Situation ohne Vorwarnung von einem Turmfalkenpärchen angegriffen wurde und abstürzte. "Ich war damals fünfeinhalb," sage ich, und das ist das einzige, das stimmt. Von meinem Stiefvater sage ich gar nichts (23).
⁸"Das ist Isabella," sagte Sally und legte der Neuen die Hand auf die Schulter. Das Mädchen trat einen Schritt zur Seite. "Isabella ist überraschend zu uns gekommen," sagte Sally, "weil in ihrer Familie etwas passiert ist, das es ihr unmöglich macht, dort zu bleiben" (52).
⁹"Wo ist das?" fragte ich. "Zakynthos," sagte sie.
"Zakynthos? Nie gehört."
"Eine griechische Insel."
"Eine griechische Insel. Und was gibt's dort außer Schiffswracks?"
"Caretta caretta."
"Caretta was?"
Sie blätterte um. Auf der folgenden Doppelseite flog ein leuchtendes Wesen durchs blaugrüne Bild, von links unten nach

rechts oben, die Flügel weit ausgebreitet, den Kopf sonnenbeschienen, halb Vogel, halb Schildkröte. Das Maul hatte es vorne sanft nach unten gezogen wie einen Schnabel. Mit dem rechten Auge blickte es mich erstaunt an. "Caretta caretta," sagte die Neue, "die unechte Karettschildkröte. Es war das schönste Tier, das ich jemals gesehen hatte." (101-102).

[10]"Man is the only animal that blushes. Or needs to." From Mark Twain, *Following the Equator* (1897).

[11]According to the University of Michigan Museum of Zoology website (Duermit, L. and J. Harding.) 2007. "Caretta caretta" (Online), Animal Diversity Web, accessed at http://animal diversity.ummz.umich.edu/site/accounts/information/Caretta caretta.html.

The Picaresque in Lilian Faschinger's *Wiener Passion*

Joseph W. Moser

Vienna Passion, Review Books, 2000

Lilian Faschinger's novel *Wiener Passion* (*Vienna Passion*), published in 1999, paints a broad picture of Viennese society at the end of the nineteenth and twentieth centuries. Framed by the story of Magnolia Brown, an African-American woman of Austrian descent who travels to Vienna in the 1990s, the main plot revolves around Magnolia's great-grandmother, Rosa Havelka, who moved to Vienna in the 1880s as a Czech migrant worker and was hanged in 1900 for murdering her husband. Originally Faschinger (1950-) planned to entitle this work *Wiener Stimmen* (*Viennese Voices*), which would have acknowledged the many voices and stories in this text that illustrate Vienna's multi-ethnic heritage, and simultaneously portray the city's perpetual ambivalence towards its rich cultural identity. Several characters from both turns-of-the-century perceive Vienna as monoethnically German, thus drawing eerie connections between Karl von Schönerer's era and that of Jörg Haider. Schönerer was one of the founders of German Nationalism in Austria in the nineteenth century and Haider was the leader of the extreme right-wing Freedom party in Austria from 1986 to 2000. The conflict of a city embracing and rejecting its rich ethnic heritage is thus one of many important themes in this novel. The oppression of women or the class conflicts within Austrian society is another one of many significant themes.

While Austrian and German literatures, with the notable exception of the seventeenth-century novel *Simplicissimus* by Grimmelshausen, are not as famous for the picaresque as, for example, the texts from the Spanish Golden Age, Lilian Faschinger revitalizes the picaresque genre in *Vienna Passion* and thereby stands in stark contrast to the tradition of the German *Bildungsroman* (novel of self-development). Concentrating on the picaresque in the novel and examining the construction of ethnicity in the text, this paper shows how Faschinger links a century of Viennese social history and how she thereby deconstructs the image of a wealthy and glamorous capital of a fading empire.

Before the publication of *Wiener Passion*, Faschinger was best known for her novel *Magdalena Sünderin* (1995; *Magdalena the Sinner* [1997]), which many critics and the author herself have identified as exhibiting the characteristics of a picaresque novel. While Faschinger claims that she did not set out to write explicitly picaresque prose, she admits that she recognizes the picaresque in her texts.[1] The main character Magdalena in *Magdalena the Sinner* and Rosa Havelka in *Vienna Passion* are constantly on the move, but at the times when they are stuck in one place, Faschinger claims that they display an element of fear.[2] This fear is linked to the oppression that these two women experience at the hands of men and to a system of oppression that includes the Catholic Church and the prevalent racism in the Austro-Hungarian Monarchy at the turn of the twentieth century. Faschinger replaces the traditionally male picaresque protagonist or *pícaro* with a female *pícara*, and by crossing this gender boundary she expands this genre, which in German literature is most often associated with the Baroque period.

The story of Rosa Havelka, though quite different from Magdalena's, develops along a picaresque path. Her story is framed by the fact that Magnolia is reading a notebook that contains Rosa's memoir, which was copied by a nun after Rosa was hanged in 1900 for the murder of her husband. From the very beginning the reader knows that Rosa's life story will end tragically. Nonetheless, her memoir still conveys a false sense of hope despite the fact that its author is awaiting her execution. Growing up as the illegitimate daughter of a maid in the house of her father, Herr Gerstner, the Deputy Spa Director (*stellvertre-*

tender Kurdirektor) of Marienbad, Rosa is oblivious to the circumstances surrounding her status and believes that God has predestined her and her mother to be servants. As a member of the large Gerstner household, she is allowed to take lessons from the same tutor as her half-sisters, but she does not fully realize that she will not have the same opportunities as the legitimate daughters of a local dignitary. Throughout the text her situation becomes progressively worse, and Rosa only in retrospect fully appreciates her "expulsion from Paradise" (76) ("Vertreibung aus dem Paradies" [105]). After her mother dies as the consequence of having been overworked by Gerstner's wife, Rosa is sent to a convent boarding school in Prague, which removes the illegitimate daughter from Gerstner's presence. The Ursuline nuns educate her in Catholic doctrine and Rosa is most eager to learn and submit. Yet her life continues along a downward spiral over which she has no control. Reminiscent of the homosexual abuse of Robert Musil's Törless, she falls victim to sexual abuse by her classmate Olga, and is punished by the nuns for this digression to which she had fallen victim. They castigate her for "indulging in unnatural practices at night" (130) ("Ausübung widernatürlicher nächtlicher Handlungen" [173]) and for ignoring "all the fundamental rules of decency and morality" (130) ("sämtliche Grundregeln von Anstand und Sitte" [173]). Rosa's goal of serving God and the nuns as a pious Catholic is destroyed beyond her control by her classmate and the restrictions set forth by the Church. Whereas Olga commits suicide by jumping from a window, Rosa runs away from the school and seeks her fortune in Vienna. Although it is clear that leaving the school and entering domestic service will not improve her situation, Rosa still remains naively oblivious to the consequences of her actions.

After a difficult journey by carriage and by boat, she arrives in the Empire's capital where she encounters the harsh working conditions of Czech migrants. Faschinger has commented that one of her goals for this book was to uncover the myth of Vienna being a glamorous city.[3] Many workers from all over the Habsburg monarchy moved to the capital to seek employment, and yet Vienna already had more than enough workers living and working under unbearable conditions. Rosa has to pay a horrendous fee to a job agency for domestic servants before finding employment as a maid with the family of Regional Postal Manager (*Oberpostrat*) Lindner, where Frau Lindner works her so hard that she collapses, falls off a ladder, and suffers a concussion. After Rosa regains consciousness, her employer tells her that she is fed up with her and that she is fired. Rosa faints again and awakes in a hospital room of the *AKH* (Vienna's General Hospital) and is forced to leave because she cannot afford the hospital costs. Despite the fact that her situation is becoming progressively worse, she writes in her memoir that she was fortunate to find another job with the family of the Edlen von Schreyvogel, with whom she continues down a picaresque path.

Her new employer seduces and impregnates her while his wife starves her. She finally loses this job on account of letting the Schreyvogels' children play outdoors with those of unemployed members of the working class. Frau Schreyvogel refers to these people as a "gang of vagabonds, ruffians and crooks known to the police" (220) ("herumlungernde Rotte polizeibekannter Vagabunden, Strolche und Ganoven" [288]). The role of social class is crucial to the picaresque construction of the novel. The people to whom Rosa refers as friends are petty criminals in Frau Schreyvogel's eyes. The association with these people – from whom she is socially only removed by her employment in a grand-bourgeois household – progressively furthers and confirms the servant girl's decline.

However, her social decline is not the only picaresque aspect of her life. The fact that she has fallen victim to Frau Schreyvogel's avarice and the seduction by her husband puts an even more tragic spin on her fate. Rosa has to visit a woman performing illegal abortions (*Engelmacherin*) to abort the child and the reference that Frau von Schreyvogel writes for Rosa precludes future employment in domestic service. Praying to the patron saint of domestic servants, Rosa meets Dora Vittoria Galli, a widow who invites her to live with her. While Rosa sees this as a lucky turn of events for herself, her fate continues down a picaresque path. Galli, a highly respected member of the Church who secretly believes in witchcraft, preys on Rosa's innocence and forces her to perform acts of self-castigation. Despite Galli's sadistic treatment of her, Rosa is unable to leave the widow, as this is the only person left in her life who could show her some sort of approval: "Happy to hear any friendly remark from a grown woman to me, a motherless girl, I nodded in agreement and blushed for joy to think that my benefactress looked kindly on me again" (260).[4] Galli continues her abuse and forces Rosa to whip herself after she met with a young man, and this drives Rosa insane as she attempts to commit suicide. She and the young man are both locked up in the mental clinic in Vienna's ninth district, while the authorities believe Galli and not the young Czech laborer. After she is released she has nowhere to go, and so she seeks shelter in the city's sewer system. She steals a zither from a music store and makes money as a street musician until someone recognizes the stolen instrument and she is arrested and sent to prison in Wiener Neustadt. Rosa finds herself unable to escape the downward spiral that her life has taken. By mingling with petty criminals in prison, Rosa learns about prostitution and the places in Vienna, where prostitutes pick up clients. After she is released from forced labor because her habit of speaking to herself had started to annoy both the inmates and the nuns who ran the facility, she goes to Vienna's *Volksgarten*, where the locally established prostitutes chase her away to the *Prater Hauptallee*. There she meets a madam who has been in the business for a while and gives Rosa some money to attend a performance at the *Musikverein*, where as a young woman she would be able to attract a higher class customer.

At a concert in this venerable institution, she sees the Crown Prince Rudolph and makes eye contact with the heir to Austria's throne. She also meets Engelbert Kornhäusel, a failing writer, who rents her a room and insists on writing his poetry on her skin. The ink poisons her and she falls ill, at which point the

Crown Prince's personal cabby (*Leibfiaker*) visits her and tells her that Rudolph wants to meet with her. She then becomes his concubine and is set up in a villa in Döbling. Rudolph even invites her to commit suicide with him, but after she declines, he kills himself and his other mistress, Mary Vetsera. Rosa finds herself back in the sewer. She returns to the *Volksgarten*, which "hastened my [her] decline" (352) ("beschleunigt meinen Niedergang" [452]). She contracts syphilis, which she believes will be cured by sleeping with the executioner Josef Lang. In the *Prater*, she meets Dr. Doblhoff from the mental clinic, who invites her to live with him and take care of his household. His wife is deathly ill in a sanatorium in the South Tyrol, so he starts to make plans to marry Rosa and she becomes pregnant. However, when his wife makes an unexpected recovery, Rosa must leave. Rosa's daughter is taken care of by the Carmelite nuns in the second district, while Doblhoff procures her a job in the Hofburg as a silver polisher. She meets a *Fiaker* driver, Karel Havelka, who decides to marry her because he thinks she resembles the Empress Sissi, however, she cannot tell him about her child, who is subsequently sent with friends emigrating to the United States. The child is Magnolia's grandmother.

Her new husband urges her to get him a job in the *Hofburg*, so that he can be closer to Sissi. She is made to wear a Sissi wig and even catches her husband cross-dressing as the empress in front of a mirror. Despite her disappointment, she sneaks Karel into the *Hofburg*, so that he can catch a glimpse of the Empress, but instead of just ogling Sissi, he jumps into a bath with her. He barely escapes this situation and Rosa is fired for her alleged negligence. After this incident, Rosa's life takes another negative turn. Karel sneaks out at night and rapes and murders women who remind him of Sissi. Rosa follows him and in defense of one of his victims, stabs him to death. The courts, however, do not believe her and she is sentenced to death. In her cell she writes down her story and gives it to a nun, who in turn holds on to the writings until she gives it to Magnolia's aunt in 1950. Because of the nun's introduction to Rosa's narrative,

Magnolia and the reader are aware from the beginning that Rosa will be executed for murder. However, it is not completely clear until the end how Magnolia may be related to Rosa, as her family is ashamed of being descendants of a murderer and withholds this information from her.

Magnolia's story in contrast is by no means picaresque. The historical context in which she lives has changed considerably to the extent that Magnolia is able to defend herself against the prejudice that Rosa could not escape. She is an unemployed Broadway actress working as a waitress in New York, where she meets a producer named John, who wants to stage a musical about Freud and decides to cast Magnolia as Anna Freud. John explains to Magnolia that she could play Freud's daughter, because the Jews in Europe resembled the Blacks in the United States. This is certainly an oversimplification of the issue, but it is an interesting point of departure for Magnolia, as she leaves for Vienna to develop her vocal abilities. Her initial impressions of Vienna are skewed by her aunt Pia's strange apartment and her eerie collection of puppets staring down on Magnolia in the guest bedroom, the same room in which the reader later finds out that Pia's daughter Wilma died of carbon-monoxide poisoning from the tiled stove (*Kachelofen*). Despite the racism that she encounters on the streets of the city and from her aunt, Magnolia falls in love with her music instructor, Josef Horvath, and the city, and she even begins to accept her aunt's peculiar habits. The novel closes with her deciding to remain in Vienna with Josef, with whom she is expecting a baby.

The frame of the novel, however, is not a simple story with a happy ending. Faschinger argues that it does not necessarily have a positive ending. As Magnolia helps to assert Josef's feeble personality, he also becomes stronger and starts to put unreasonable demands on her just as some of the men did with Rosa.[5] He tells her where she will live in his apartment and starts making plans without consulting her. However, despite a vague concern that some readers may have about how Magnolia's future with Josef will continue after the end of the novel, in the novel itself she is depicted as a confident young woman, who helps Josef to gain self-confidence and overcome the legacy of an overbearing mother. Rosa's and Magnolia's stories are linked not only by their descendancy but also by their otherness in Vienna and the fact that they belong to an immigrant ethnic minority that the city does not fully acknowledge. In Rosa's case, the prevalent racism in the Empire's capital serves as a downward slope that she cannot escape. The prejudice that she faces as a Czech migrant and as a young woman seeking employment provides the picaresque framework of oppression that precipitates her decline. Faschinger was conscious of the Habsburg monarchy's diversity and the novel concentrates on their experiences in the Empire's capital. Rosa is conflicted about her identity, as she descends from a Czech mother, but is raised in German, the language of the ruling class in Bohemia. Her mother teaches her Czech national folktales, which give her a multi-ethnic identity that she embraces and makes her a quintessential Old Austrian. She reaches Vienna with the help of a young man who belongs to the Young Czechs and introduces Rosa to the ideas of Czech Nationalism. In Vienna, she is drawn to the statue of Anton Pilgram, the mythologized builder of the *Stephansdom*, who also was a Bohemian migrant to Vienna. She seeks to find acknowledgement of the immigrants' achievements in the city; however, she also encounters racism aimed at the new residents. The Regional Postal Manager, for whom she works, criticizes his wife's origins: "women from Bukowina, women from the steppes of Bessarabia, witches of the steppes as you might say, were sly as the devil and had been known to ruin good-natured men like him in short order" (172).[6] This is not an isolated comment and Rosa starts to look for people, who do not greet her with ethnic prejudice. She meets Ljuba Zupan, an activist for the rights of domestic servants who hails from Maribor (in Lower Styria, today Slovenia) and who is quite aware of the discrimination that she suffers because of her Slovenian heritage. Rosa's positive impression of Ljuba, who also happens to be the woman who finally emigrates to Minneapolis with Rosa's daughter, is contrasted with the Schreyvogel superintendent's (*Hausmeisterin*'s) view of Ljuba, who describes her as an "unruly, sly-looking Slovenian girl" (188) ("renitente Slowenin mit dem hinterhältigen Blick" [247]). Rosa experiences solidarity among immigrants to Vienna. A Slovak seamstress makes her a new dress for little money, because she believes that Slavs in Vienna should help each other. Rosa spends one of her happiest moments in Vienna with her friends, when she visits a tavern (*Wirtshaus*) for the first time and learns that it is owned by Primoz, also from Maribor.

Not all immigrants to Vienna embrace the city's diversity. Dora Galli, who tortures Rosa with her obsession for self-flagellation, is of Italian origin from Triest, and yet she has become a supporter of German Nationalism of the time. Rosa sits on a chair with an embroidered Swastika in Galli's apartment and when Rosa suggests playing Chopin, Galli dismisses him as a "decadent Franco-Polish consumptive" (246) ("einen dekadenten frankopolnischen Schwindsüchtigen" [319]). Rosa enjoys the company of other immigrants. When she plays the zither in the *Böhmischen Prater* (Czech amusement park in Vienna), she writes: "Now and then we were joined by two young men from Galicia, one of whom played the hurdy-gurdy and the other the *sopialka*, a kind of shawm, who taught us songs about the deeds of the Cossacks, and if we were in luck we could sometimes join a gypsy band from Temesvar [in Transylvania], which appeared four times a week at the casino Zögernitz in Döbling and made a little extra by playing in the streets of Vienna" (297-8).[7] Rosa's experiences reinforce the idea of Vienna as a melting pot for the Habsburg monarchy's peoples. Rather than just concentrating on zither music that is often associated with traditional German-language music from Austria, the novel goes into quite some detail to show the variety of musical traditions that had reached Vienna at the turn of the century.

This capital, however, was not only the center of migration for the many peoples of this multicultural Empire, but was also the center of Nationalist hatred, and it harbored racist ideologues who would lay the foundation for even more severe racist hatred in the twentieth century. Ljuba and her friends who embrace their Slavic heritage are merely reacting against the German Nationalist rhetoric. While Georg Ritter von Schönerer does not appear as a character in the novel, many Viennese in the narrative cite his views on race. Frau Navratil, the Schreyvogel's *Hausmeisterin*, whose name suggests a Czech origin, quotes Schönerer claiming that "the Slav race [is] notable for its indolence and stupidity...unlike me [Rosa] the extremely amiable von Schreyvogels were constantly and industriously endeavouring to improve their position in life" (357).[8] The *Hausmeisterin*'s belief in these ideas in light of her Czech last name serves as a classic example of ethnic self-hatred. Yet, the ruling class embodied here in the aristocratic Schreyvogel family benefits from this racist ideology, which manages to oppress the most recent citizens of Vienna by installing a sense of racial superiority even in those Viennese who are only one or two generations removed from arriving in the Empire's capital.

In addition to these strong xenophobic and anti-Slavic sentiments, Rosa also encounters Viennese anti-Semitism. Dr. Doblhoff, who first treats Rosa in the mental clinic and then lives with her and talks to her about her dreams, believes that his colleague and friend Sigmund Freud stole his ideas on dream interpretation. He refers to Freud in anger as a "caftan-wearing Jew" (419) ("Kaftanjude" [535]). However, this not the only example of anti-Semitism in the novel, Rosa's Hungarian neighbor, Frau Bartok, blames the crimes committed by the mysterious murderer and rapist on the migration of Jews from the East and claims that Schönerer was right in arguing that these people had caused a rise in the city's crime rate. Rosa cannot believe this talk because she knows that it is her husband, Karel Havelka, who has been sneaking out at night to prey on his victims. Interestingly, the woman who is saved by Rosa stabbing her husband is a waitress, Slavka from Ljubljana. However, Slavka refuses to acknowledge Rosa's help and claims that it was not necessary for Rosa to assault her husband, and this testimony precipitates the court's decision to condemn Rosa to death. These types of racism and prejudice fostered a system of oppression that sends Rosa on a picaresque path that she cannot escape, whereas a century later, Magnolia is still able to stand up for herself, even though she encounters the remnants of this oppression. Arriving in Vienna almost a hundred years after her great-grandmother, Magnolia discovers a city that has certainly undergone some progress over the last century, but that still harbors some racist ideas. It is important to avoid the positivist stance that Vienna at the turn of the twenty-first century was a comparatively open-minded and welcoming society. However, a hundred years later Magnolia is able to overcome the obstacles thrown in her way and even frees Josef from the legacy of an overbearing mother. Nonetheless, she experiences open racism even from her family. Her aunt Pia welcomes Magnolia as a "pretty child...but blacker" (22) ("hübsches Kind...aber schwärzer" [38]) than she would have imagined. When Magnolia asks to adjust the heat on the *Kachelofen*, Pia responds that the task was much too complicated and that Magnolia "being half black African" (46) ("schwarzafrikanische Herkunft" [65]) could not be entrusted to do so. Pia's prejudices extend to all people with a different ethnic background, thus according to Pia, the Bosnian superintendent (*Hausmeister*) overcharges her for his assistance in heating her apartment. At the *Zentralfriedhof*, Pia displays her anti-Semitic side when she complains about the Jewish section of the cemetery and its desolate state. She completely ignores the fact that the abandonment of the cemetery is part of the legacy of the Holocaust and describes it as: "a disgrace to German-speaking Austrians with patriotic and Catholic feelings" (49) ("eine Schande für national und katholisch empfindende Österreicher deutscher Muttersprache" [69]). Strolling past the graves of artists at the cemetery, she continues to reveal her idea of German Nationalism by describing Mozart's music as "such very German music" (49) ("eine so deutsche Musik" [69]) and concludes her tour of the cemetery praising its memorial church, the

Doktor-Karl-Lueger-Gedächtniskirche, and referring to the church's namesake as a "a remarkable mayor, an upright and patriotic Viennese" (49) ("außerordentlicher Bürgermeister, ein aufrechter und patriotischer Wiener Mensch" [69]). While Pia espouses German Nationalist ideas, she is also aware of her Bohemian or Czech origins as she prepares her tripe soup (*Kuttelsuppe*), which she calls the "national Bohemian dish" (47) ("böhmische Nationalgericht" [66]). She also refers to her niece having old Austrian blood and this old Austria is undoubtedly a reference to the multicultural Habsburg Empire. Pia simultaneously accepts and rejects ethnic diversity, including her own Czech origins. However, the fact that Pia sees herself as Austrian, proves that Vienna is an immigrant city and one that does accept newcomers over the course of several generations. Acknowledging Austria as a country that allows for immigration brings up an important similarity to the U.S., with both countries being melting pots of various peoples.

On the streets of Vienna, Magnolia experiences other forms of prejudice and racial hatred that draw their origins from the racism Rosa encountered. An old lady with a dog near the *Naschmarkt* runs into Magnolia and the old lady orders her spaniel: "go on, get that nigger" (52) ("faß die Negerin" [74]). In the narrative, Faschinger portrays this incident with the old lady full of irony, as she paraphrases her: "What were things coming to if such creatures [Black immigrants] were taking over our attracttive district of Vienna 4 too, she added, populating it with their repulsive black brood, going to stay at Bad Gastein, Bad Hall and Baden bei Wien one after another to take the waters, all paid for by Austrian taxes from the Vienna Regional Health Insurance scheme, whereas she was obliged to relieve her multiple arthritis with medicinal herbs laboriously gathered in Vienna's wildlife preserve, the *Lainzer Tiergarten*. Her father, who had retired as a stipendiary councillor in the civil service, had always thanked God he wouldn't live to see our blessed country overrun square metre by square metre by African negroes" (52-3).[9] In addition to exhibiting hateful prejudice against Africans and people of color, the old lady expresses fear that immigrants and newcomers to the city might take away some of the benefits that she is enjoying. Her short-sightedness mirrors some of the resentment and hatred that Rosa experienced. However, while the reader might be able to dismiss the racism of the nineteenth century as being an issue of the past, Magnolia's experiences in Vienna are contemporary and link resentment against immigrants from the territories of the monarchy to present prejudice against immigrants from all over the world.

Roman Catholicism and its role as a politically authoritarian and oppressive force in Austria is a central theme to Faschinger's oeuvre, much resembling Thomas Bernhard's criticism of Austria.[10] In addition to the racism and ethnic prejudice that inhibit Rosa's development, the rigid and authoritarian structure of Catholicism is an important component of the picaresque novel. Whereas Faschinger portrays a woman rebelling against the Church with the female protagonist kidnapping a priest in *Magdalena the Sinner*, Rosa is unable to rebel and suffers from clergy who reinforce the idea that it is God's will that servants serve their masters unquestioningly. This strict doctrine lays the foundation for the abuse Rosa suffers. Dora Galli then introduces Rosa to an exaggerated version of Catholic self-flagellation, and the nuns in the women's prison in Wiener Neudorf are the executers of an authoritarian regime rather than caring religious officials. Through Josef Horvath's homosexual experiences with the prefect who seduced him in the dormitory of the Viennese Boys' Choir, Magnolia soon becomes acquainted with some of the abuses of Catholic officials and fervent believers. Magnolia also experiences racism from supposedly religious Catholics in Vienna who misinterpret church doctrine to espouse xenophobic rhetoric. Outside of the *Peterskirche* a lady stops her and urges her "to be content with the sphere of life assigned to us by God, rather than crossing the frontiers set by race and nationality in an overweening urge to expand" (303).[11] Later on, Fräulein Haslinger, Josef Horvath's neighbor, in reference to the racist attack on the young woman from the Dominican Republic claims that non-Christians could not expect God's help as much as real Christians, and further she claimed that while the victim may have been a Catholic, "in her opinion the true faith decreased in proportion to its geographical distance from the Vatican" (384).[12] This statement mixes Catholic doctrine with Nationalist ideas and bears a striking resemblance to Thomas Bernhard's criticism of Austrians as both Catholics and National Socialists.

The novel also incorporates contemporary issues of the 1990s. A masked neo-Nazi is assaulting female immigrants in Vienna, which causes concern for Magnolia's friends, while she tries not to think too much about these incidents. Pia tells her about this event: "an extreme right-winger had attacked and raped a young Vietnamese nurse in the *Stadtpark* last night, and he didn't even shrink from calling the *Wipplingerstrasse* police station after committing this crime and explaining his reasons, saying that slowly but steadily the number of persons of racially inferior blood in the country was rising above the count of pure-bred Austrians" (273).[13] With this incident, Faschinger brings up the surge in extreme right-wing violence against foreigners in Austria in the 1990s. Magnolia remains unharmed, but the attack on a Vietnamese woman and other foreigners keeps her apprehensive about her surroundings. Of course the reader immediately recognizes a connection between Karel Havelka's assault on women who reminded him of Sissi and the neo-Nazi attacking non-White women. Violence against women is an important theme of the novel, but ethnicity also figures into these attacks in the 1990s. While much has changed over the course of a century, the reader realizes that Vienna is still far from embracing the fact that immigration is an important aspect of the city's social makeup.

Vienna's history in the first half of the twentieth century has been remarkably violent and violence against minorities, culminating most notably in the Holocaust, is hard to ignore. Contrasting Vienna at the end of the nineteenth and twentieth centuries, the novel shows that despite the tragic events of the twentieth century, xenophobia remains high. The world around Vienna has shrunk over the last century. While there is still resentment towards newcomers from countries nearby, such as the prejudice against the Bosnian immigrants, Magnolia as an African-American has come from much further. Her (re-)immigration to Austria and her grandmother's emigration to the United States, link the two countries as immigrant nations, or melting pots of ethnic difference. The picaresque construction of Rosa's fate contrasts well with Magnolia's ability to assert and defend herself. While this is certainly due to different character traits between these two women, there is no doubt that the historical contexts to the two time periods are significant. Vienna at the end of the nineteenth century was a hopeless place for a young migrant, whereas the city in the 1990s despite lingering problems with racism and prejudice has become a more accepting place, and the novel reflects the historical realities.

Endnotes

[1] Ellie Kennedy, "Identity through Imagination: An Interview with Lilian Faschinger," in: *Women in German Yearbook*, vol. 18 (2002): 23.
[2] bid.
[3] Gisela Roethke, "Lilian Faschinger im Gespräch," in: *Modern Austrian Literature*, vol 33.1 (2000): 98.
[4] "Und ich, glücklich über jedes freundliche Wort, das eine erwachsene Frau an mich mutterloses Mädchen richtete, nickte zustimmend und errötete vor Freude darüber, daß meine Wohltäterin mir wieder gewogen war" (336).
[5] Kennedy, 26.
[6] "Frauen aus der Bukowina, aus der bessarabischen Steppe sozusagen, Steppenhexen sozusagen, seien durchtrieben bis in die Haarspitzen und hätten gutmütige Männer wie ihn binnen kürzester Zeit ruiniert" (225).

[7]"Gelegentlich gesellten sich zwei junge Männer aus Galizien zu uns, von denen einer die Leier und der andere die Sopialka, eine Art Schalmei, spielte und die uns Lieder über die Taten der Kosaken beibrachten, und wenn wir Glück hatten, durften wir uns manchmal einer aus Temesvar stammenden Zigeunerkapelle anschließen, die viermal pro Woche im Casino Zögernitz in Döbling auftrat und sich durch musikalische Darbietungen in den Straßen Wiens etwas hinzuverdiente" (384).

[8]"die slawische Rasse...zeichne sich durch Faulheit und Stumpfheit aus, im Gegensatz dazu trachte das außerordentlich sympathische Ehepaar Schreyvogel unentwegt danach, seine Lebensstellung mit Fleiß und Ausdauer zu verbessern" (459-460).

[9]"Wo wir hinkämen, wenn diese Kreaturen auch noch unseren schönen vierten Bezirk überschwemmten, meinte sie dann, ihn bevölkerten mit ihrer abstoßenden schwarzen Brut, sich auf Kosten österreichischer Steuergelder von der Wiener Gebietskrankenkasse einen Kuraufenthalt nach dem anderen in Bad Gastein, in Bad Hall, in Baden bei Wien bezahlen ließen, wogegen sie ihre Polyarthritis mit mühevoll im Lainzer Tiergarten gesammelten Heilkräutern zu lindern gezwungen wäre, ihr Vater, der als Wirklicher Hofrat in den Ruhestand getreten sei, habe immer gesagt, er werde es gottlob nicht mehr erleben, daß unser gesegnetes Land von den Negern aus Afrika erobert würde" (74).

[10]Ibid, 22.

[11] "sich mit dem uns von Gott zugewiesenen Lebensort zu bescheiden und nicht in übertriebenem Expansionsdrang die einem durch Volks- und Rassenzugehörigkeit gesetzten Grenzen zu überschreiten" (390).

[12] "ihrer Meinung nach nehme die wahre Rechtsgläubigkeit allerdings mit zunehmender geographischer Entfernung vom Vatikan ab" (491).

[13]"ein extremer Rechter habe in der vergangenen Nacht im Stadtpark eine als Krankenpflegerin tätige junge Vietnamesin überfallen und vergewaltigt und sich nicht gescheut, nach vollbrach-

ter Tat auf der Polizeiwachstube Wipplingerstraße anzurufen und sich mit der Begründung zu dieser zu bekennen, langsam, aber sicher übertreffe die Zahl der Elemente minderwertigen Geblüts jene der reinrassigen Österreicher" (353).

Kathrin Röggla's *wir schlafen nicht*: Reality Fiction and the New Economy

Rebecca S. Thomas

we never sleep, translated by Rebecca S. Thomas, Ariadne Press, 2009

Kathrin Röggla (1971-) was born in Salzburg where she studied literature and philosophy before moving to Berlin, where she has lived and worked since 1992. She made her literary debut in 1995 with the novel *niemand lacht rückwärts* ("no one laughs backwards"). Her literary career continued in 1997 with the publication of *Abrauschen* ("Rushing Away"), a collection of experimental short prose. In 2000, *Irres Wetter* ("Crazy Weather"), her collection of Berlin sketches appeared, followed in 2004 by the docu-novel *wir schlafen nicht* (*we never sleep*).[1] She is also the author of numerous radio dramas and sound installations, as well as pieces for theater and critical essays. Her style is experimental and ironic and is part of the grand Austrian tradition of skepticism about language that found its most profound modern articulation in Hugo von Hofmannsthal's *Letter to Lord Chandos*. Röggla's work frequently integrates documentary and quoted materials, making her one of the foremost practitioners of documentary realism in contemporary fiction. Röggla is the recipient of numerous prizes including the Alexander-Sacher-Masoch prize and the Italo Svevo prize.

Since the late 1950s, *Vergangenheitsbewältigung*, or coming to terms with World War II and the Holocaust, has been the dominant theme in German literature and literary criticism. Austria's confrontation with its complicity in these events was delayed until the late 1980s after the Waldheim Affair forced the issue into the public eye. Since that time the majority of Austrian literature and film has been devoted to dealing with the historical and political realities of Austria's role in Nazism and the repression of these facts in public discourse and private memory. Authors of the post-war generation, children of victims and perpetrators alike, form a literary generation that remains deeply involved in exposing Austria's past and its repercussions in contemporary Austrian life and politics.

Born in 1971, Kathrin Röggla belongs chronologically and thematically to a new era of Austrian authors, which I refer to as the post-post-Waldheim generation. This generation is not principally concerned with Austrian involvement in events related to World War II as a literary theme. Instead, these authors have turned their artistic gaze to the reorganization of society in the age of globalization, digital media, and neoliberalism. Their fictional worlds represent the postmodern shift away from rootedness in national historical meta-narratives and towards the fragmentation and rootlessness of a post-historical, post-national, global present. Figures in *we never sleep* refer explicitly to their alienation from Germany/Austria as a referent for their identity. The place of national origin is interesting as a commercial venue but does not evoke feelings of guilt, *Heimat,* or belonging. The trade fair which is the novel's venue is as if plucked from any random geographical coordinates. We are told only that it is located at a far remove from "normal life," and that the points of the compass have no relevance here. It is a self-contained universe seemingly beyond the range of national history, culture and geography. It is at once global and acultural in its sterility and reproducibility.

Röggla's novel *we never sleep* places the reader directly into the current of this eternal present. For several years beginning in the late 1990s when the bubble in the tech industry was already beginning to burst, Röggla conducted taped interviews with twenty-four people working at various levels for consulting firms in the communications sector. From the hours of tape, she crafted the text of *wir schlafen nicht,* a narrative montage which, like a photograph, combines elements of naturalistic reproduction (the quotation) with artistic representation (the subjective lens of selection and arrangement). From the myriad voices captured during her interviews, she distilled six representative, fictional figures: the key account manager, the intern, the online editor, the tech assistant, the senior associate, and the partner. The narrative is a dialog that imitates real-time speech. It is distinguished from drama only in that the dialog is often reproduced in indirect speech, which functions as both an editorial filter and as old-fashioned alienation effect through which the author registers her skepticism regarding the recorded utterances. Indeed, the text has been performed and recorded as a radio drama (*Hörspiel*) and premiered as a stage production in Düsseldorf in 2004, and has enjoyed many other stage performances since.

The voice that is conspicuously absent from the narrative is the voice of the questioner, of Röggla herself. Only the responses to unheard, unknown questions are rendered in indirect speech. Questions are hinted at or implied by the answers, but other interjections, observations, and reactions of the interviewing, controlling authorial voice are suppressed. But it is precisely in this absence that the author's critical voice can be perceived most sharply as she lets the dramatic irony between what the figures are saying and what they are unconsciously communicating about themselves and their industry speak for itself. Irony is the key structural tactic of the text, both in the discrepancy between what is said and what is unintentionally revealed, and in the linguistic disjunctions that characterize the communications of the top experts in the field of global communications consulting.

The only direct references to the interviewer herself come at the beginning and end of the text as the figures attempt to place and categorize the woman with the microphone: "what? not a journalist? then what?" (5) ("ach, keine journalistin? Was denn?" [7]) and register their awareness that they are being recorded: " – has it started? – is it running?" (8) ("geht's los? läuft das ding?" [11]). This awareness tips off the reader or listener that the responses are, at least initially, not naive, authentic or honest, but are instead on some level self-consciously constructed for an implied future audience. Part of the text's compelling trajectory is the subjects' fall back into a state of less censored communication, a sort of unconscious confessional mode, in which the psychological and physical realities of their lives and industry are unwittingly revealed to both the interviewer and themselves. The defense mechanism of forgetfulness that usually obscures awareness of their empty lives is temporarily disabled, and the text ends with an abrupt retreat from the uncomfortable self-awareness and consciousness that has been foisted upon the interviewees: "– he didn't think he wanted to continue with this – and she wasn't going to take part in this anymore either – "(194) ("er glaubt nicht, daß er das weiter möchte – auch sie macht das nicht weiter mit" [218]).

Röggla's use of quotation and montage as linguistic foundation for her text is reminiscent of Elfriede Jelinek, whose masterful use of intertextuality and quotation embodies the postmodern observation that nothing evades discourse. Unlike Jelinek, however, whose fictional characters quote and paraphrase from a wide array of sources from pop as well as high culture, Röggla, whose novel is comprised largely of words spoken to her during interviews, defies the boundary between documentary and fiction. This blurring of genres across the board is a by-product of the digital media age. The method and content of documentary and historical film seem to be converging, news and entertainment formats merge as cable news becomes more dependent on entertainment, while late-night comedy mimics and parodies the news. In reality television, real people in contrived situations become characters and caricatures while remaining essentially nonfictional. Each of these conflations erases the solid boundary between fact and fiction and replaces it with a hybrid form.

This ambiguity is not new in literature. Truman Capote experimented with what he referred to as the "nonfiction novel" in his pathbreaking work *In Cold Blood* (1965). In Capote, although the tale remains "true" in each detail to the facts of a particular story, the words through which the events are conveyed are entirely the author's own. Although he did not embellish or alter the facts of the case, his artistic representation of that reality required a poetic register of language beyond mere reportage or quotation. By contrast, Röggla's text meshes documentary reproduction and direct quotation with a highly poeticized form in which neologisms, allusion, and metaphor dominate. It is clearly a hybrid form, not a documentary, not a nonfiction novel, but a docu-novel in which the author's control of the instrument of poetic language and form creates a compelling aesthetic experience out of what would otherwise be a tedious and uninspired collection of data. But the arrangement of the language and events along with the internal repetitions and intensifications Röggla devises give the novel a structure and effect that is unmistakably literary.

This form is not unique to Röggla. Contemporary documentary theater movements in Germany and Austria, in which authentic people and artifacts are not substantially changed by an artistic hand but are instead deployed into an artistic frame or reproduced on stage are increasingly common. As theater, these productions have more the feel of public political "happenings," such as the "*Bitte liebt Österreich*" ("Please Do Love Austria") installation mounted by Christoph Schlingensief in June of 2000, in which asylum seekers from different national origins were displayed in containers in front of the Vienna State Opera with placards hung above them stating "*Ausländer raus!*" ("Foreigners Out!"). Even more similar to Röggla's method is the docudrama *Illegal* by Paula Wilbert, which treats the plight of politically oppressed peoples around the world and is composed exclusively of quotes from interviewees. The play is regarded as "post-dramatic" in that it contains no plot, just characters' voices. In this same sense, Röggla's novel might also be categorized as "post-narrative" fiction.

So Röggla's text shares generic features that partake of documentary in which the facts are, to some extent, allowed to speak for themselves, but it is structured formally and linguistically in ways that rely on the traditions of the drama, the novella, the novel, and poetry. While the participants in the industries of the New Economy speak for themselves in Röggla's text, it is the masterful conflation, repetition, intensification, and juxtaposition of these voices that creates a world at once fictional and real. In addition, Röggla's liberal use of neologisms and abstract, metaphorical language in the non-quoted sections is almost hyperbolic in its intentional distancing from common usage so that the effect is close to that engendered by confrontation with expressionist poetry: it is at once challenging and abundantly rich in possible allusions and associations. The reader will note that as the text proceeds, the use of business jargon to express increasingly intimate, personal, and psychological states also increases with frequency. The use of business language as a language of metaphor and poetic provocation is a hallmark of the text, perhaps its most successful and disturbing technique for revealing the dehumanization of the neoliberal mind.

Adding to the atmospherics of the text is the fact that Röggla suppresses her own voice throughout until the final chapter in which she, the interviewer, provides a coda to the thoughts and experiences she has recorded. In the main body of the text, the reader's only access to the author or interviewer comes through gauging responses and reactions to questions which remain only implied. The most direct allusions to the interview process itself come at the beginning and end of the text when the interviewees are at the apex of their caution and distrust of her motives. Here, the interviewees question Röggla directly about her real role and intentions. The opening and closing references to an external interviewer function as a narrative frame for the intervening dialogs, in which the interviewees seem only intermittently aware that there is a judging ear evaluating their confessions. In spite of overtly dramatic tendencies, therefore, there are facets of the text that function more like a novella. Röggla has created an isolated world connected to a larger context by the frame in which the role of the interviewer and her implied audience is made explicit.

It should be counted as one of the remarkable successes of Röggla's method that she was able to maintain the critical stance necessary for probing beyond the surface of the subjects' consciousness while appearing sufficiently benign to avoid something like the Heisenberg effect, by which observation alone is thought to influence events, in this case responses, and make objective data collection impossible. In this novel, there is a noticeable shift in tone and content during the moments in which the interviewees feel threatened, become guarded, and mold their responses for public consumption. By contrast, there are moments of candid self-revelation and confession that astound and disarm in their guilelessness and honesty.

In spite of the experimental and disjointed nature of Röggla's prose technique, the novel is unified by a specific temporal and spatial context. While the immediate fictional space of Röggla's novel is the trade fair, a dysfunctional, self-contained and self-destructive universe unto itself, this setting is really metonymic for the New Economy and the economic theory of neoliberalism that underlie it. These are the central targets of Röggla's cultural critique. The New Economy of the 1990s refers to the meteoric rise of internet startup companies, along with the proliferation of wildly successful firms in the fields of communication and technology. The New Economy of this boom time was accompanied by euphoria on some fronts, occasioned by the belief that an era of unstoppable economic growth and prosperity had dawned, that permanent employment was guaranteed, and that a constant, geometric expansion of personal wealth was a rational expectation for those involved or invested in the tech sector. This exhilaration was quashed as suddenly as it had been born when, in April of 2000, the stock markets plummeted, and firms and individuals who had accumulated vast wealth almost overnight were abruptly forced into bankruptcy. The ensuing scandals in which leading accounting firms such as Arthur Anderson raced to manipulate their books in order to protect themselves and their wealthiest clients, for example, Enron, from the coming catastrophe, led to the bankruptcy, collapse, or reorganization of many of these formerly prestigious firms. Röggla's novel is set in the period after the bubble had begun to burst and reflects the professional, personal, and existential uncertainties that arose from the collapse of the New Economy. For Röggla and many other European intellectuals, the trajectory of the New Economy and its implications for culture are inseparable from the rise of neoliberalism, an ideology many theorists deem to be the driving force within global markets in the postindustrial age. Classical liberalism on the model of Adam Smith holds that the free market is governed by a set of economic rules and principles that hold it in equilibrium as if by an "invisible hand." On this model, the functions and results of market activity are not assailable on moral or pragmatic grounds. The market is reified to represent a force beyond human agency, a natural process rather than a product of human creation and manipulation. Proponents of neoliberalism embrace the merits of an unfettered, unregulated marketplace as pursued by proponents of classical liberalism but with the added postulate that market principles should define and guide every aspect of social life. There is nothing beyond the reach and determination of the global market and its precepts.

The neoliberal ethos embraces the boundless expansion of time and space in the global market. As a result of neoliberal ideology, stock exchanges are open longer, commodities can be bought ceaselessly from around the world on the internet, and, in some countries, businesses establishments remain open around the clock, resulting in a twenty-four-hour business cycle. The market is continually expanding in time and space, and expanding ever further into what was formerly the personal time and space of employee and consumer alike.

Richard Sennet, one of the theorists who influenced Kathrin Röggla, has done extensive research and published widely on the ways in which "turbocapitalism" affects the identity formation and lifestyle of employees.[2] Sennett concludes that the New Economy demands a total identification of employee with work. The definition of the self is reduced to those values stipulated by the internal logic of economic growth and upward mobility. The Yuppie of the '70s and '80s has been replaced by the Yettie, a term coined by Peter York in *Talk Magazine*, to characterize the lifestyle of those who have bought into the New Economy and have become its "winners."[3] The Yettie is a "young, entrepreneurial, tech-based twenty-something," whose principle attribute is flexibility. Flexibility and mobility are juxtaposed against the stability and security that characterized the "gold-watch-at-retirement" era of the pre-digital age. The novel *we never sleep* is, in many ways, an aesthetic representtation of these theories and observations. Röggla stages the process by which values inimical to personal wellbeing and happiness are internalized and ultimately come to replace any and all other values or desires. The text lays bare the abyss between "rhetoric and consciousness"[4] and makes visible the discursive space in which the internalization and subsequent enslavement to alien values and desires occur. Indeed, the use of indirect speech creates a discursive distance and space in which the ironic detachment between thought and reality, between commercially produced desire and self-interest, are revealed with increasing intensity and bite as the text proceeds.

The demands of the neoliberal marketplace have tremendous consequences for the employees, whose time has no value outside the market economy. Self-worth in the New Economy emanates from the employee's efficiency, productivity, and flexibility, his or her ability and willingness to sacrifice every aspect of personal life for the good of the firm and for the ultimate values of economic and professional advancement. The novel's title refers to the employees' conscious decision to live with as little sleep as possible in order to maximize their competitive edge.

The internalized logic of the marketplace ultimately erodes or deforms every facet of life for participants in the New Economy, and this is what their own narrative unequivocally reveals. For the characters in *we never sleep*, social life is not only impossible but indeed undesirable because its demands would be inimical to advancing the business model. In addition to being victims of the culture of overwork, workers are also driven to long hours because they have no social connections that could fill and fulfill their potential free time. They have no social connections because they must remain flexible, at the mercy of the job which will require them to relocate in a few months anyway, thus making the prospect of interpersonal commitments seem impossible. A normal family life is not possible. The key account manager's dry observation captures the experiences of the group: "she didn't have any private life. not that she was aware of (63) ("sie habe kein privatleben. nicht daß sie davon wüßte" [72]). By choice and necessity, this is a generation of singles. Röggla has even been featured on a Website called *single-dasein* ("single existence") for her representation of this shift away from traditional expectations regarding family, home life, free time, and recreation in *we never sleep*.[5] "Connections," whether political or professional, are the only relationships that have value. Thus all interpersonal relationships are commodified according to market value. The intern's parents are not tax-consultants but only "petit-bourgeois parents" who can't use their connections to advance her career. Hence, by her own assessment, she is an orphan.

The destruction of interpersonal relationships is amplified by the emphasis on competition within the neoliberal marketplace. Competition exists not only among global companies competing for market share but increasingly among employees within firms who undercut each other in the constant struggle for economic advancement and survival. As markets decline, opportunities become limited, and competition becomes more cutthroat. Employees are increasingly pitted against one another to compete for dwindling jobs and opportunities, and the logic of economic Darwinism adds to the alienation of people from one another and undermines trust. For the producers within the digital, global economy, the world as a stage for the unfolding of human potential and experience has contracted to the size and shape of economic relations, and the personal consequences are predictably disastrous.

Now, this all sounds very reminiscent of texts from Germany's economic miracle (*Wirtschaftswunder*), such as Heinrich Böll's "Es wird etwas geschehen" ("Action will be taken," 1954) or the film *Die Ehe der Maria Braun* (*The Marriage of Maria Braun*, 1979) in which work becomes an all-consuming obsession and a value in itself.[6] Röggla's text, however, reflects a shift to a postindustrial model of the work ethic, in which the discourse and activity of work define a closed system outside of which no perceptible life or desire can exist. There are no afterhours. There are no weekends. Fourteen-to-sixteen-hour workdays are the norm. Röggla's figures represent a radicalized identification with work in which the exploitation is no longer perceived as exploitation but rather as desire and a point of honor. Self-willed enslavement to the destructive structures and norms of the market place is the precondition and signifier of success. Thus, ironically, the New Economy's biggest economic winners are also personally its biggest losers. And when the business sector contracts, they are left in a double crisis because loss of employment is not only a financial disaster but an existential impossibility. Hence, when work stops, identity ends. Downtime or lay-offs translate into existential crises, a confrontation with the abyss. Alcoholism, loss of memory, distorted perception, nervous breakdowns, and ultimately suicide are frequent symptoms of employees exceeding human limitations in the pursuit of professional survival. The stale air of the convention center represents the airless personal and professional landscapes in which the characters are trapped.

The degree to which the novel's characters have internalized the values of neoliberalism and to which they unwittingly identify with and affirm these values occurs at the preconscious level of language. America is viewed as the dystopian site of the origin and full blooming of the New Economy, and the shards of English business jargon such as "top down," "downsizing," "integrated systems," "programming structures" and "workflows" that pepper the characters' speech reflect the extent to which American models have infiltrated the global mindset.

The structure and ethics of turbocapitalism inhere in its vocabulary. The language of business administration in both English and German inhabits the characters' consciousness so fully that all other possible discourses that imply different options or ethics have been repressed or forgotten.

Internalized business jargon also reflects an intensified degree of specialization that impedes communication across the branches. The senior associate apologizes:

> she should feel free to warn him if he started throwing around too many english expressions. This had actually become automatic with him by now. Sometimes he didn't even notice what trade jargon he was actually using and what kinds of vocabulary he was letting slip all the time. Very quickly you simply became incomprehensible to outsiders. Especially at a place like this where you were talking with colleagues so much. But this mutual incomprehensibility was one of the exact reasons why consulting existed anyway because the different sectors of a business often couldn't communicate properly with each other, and because the nature of the problems had become so complex, an outside perspective was often needed (7-8).[7]

The comedic notion that the various branches require consultants to facilitate their intra-industry communication underscores the profound breakdown of interpersonal communication and connection that accompanies industry's fragmentation into areas of increasing specialization resulting in increasing isolation and alienation of employees.

The world in which human value and potential are reduced to models of efficiency and productivity has predictably disastrous consequences for identity construction: when works stops, the "I" disappears. Over-identification with work has driven out all other possibilities of self-actualization. The novel reflects a mentality in which the worst thing one can experience is the condition of "non-work," whether in the form of free time, time off, or unemployment. In any of these forms, the separation from work leads to existential crisis as the "I" confronts the absolute void beyond the workplace. It is not just the yawning abyss of time that confronts the protagonists with the empty self. The stress to which these workers have become accustomed produces a constant, addictive adrenaline rush that gives them a false sense of vitality. The stress junkies of Röggla's text can't survive without the adrenaline high from which they don't want to and can't "come down" (107) ("runterkommen" [123]).

In true postmodern form, there is nothing outside the discourse of the marketplace. The market is God: omniscient, omnipotent, omnipresent, beyond question or comprehension. It exists prior to and beyond the control of human agency, obeying infallible laws of supply, demand, and maximization. It is a character on the stage: the market rises, the market falls, what will the market do? Sales figures are fundamental and unassailable truths. The reference to the "invisible hand" of free markets parallels the invisible, omnipotent hand of God. The market is creator, lawgiver, judge, and moral authority. Lost in translation is the religious allusion in the text's fictional location itself, *die Messe*, which is the German term for both "trade fair" and "holy mass." The characters of the novel make their pilgrimage to worship and sacrifice at the altar of the market.

If the market is God, then consultants are the priests of its dogma. Charged with enforcing the laws of efficiency and productivity at the microeconomic level of the company, consulting firms like the mega-group McKinsey are "a religion." The consultants are the link between market and faith. They are the earthly embodiment of market logic, they enforce its commandments, and no one is beyond the reach of omnipresent natural economic law. Even consulting firms hire consultants to ensure that their operations run efficiently. The super-consultants of McKinsey lurk at the trade fair and in the consciousness of the workers. Consultants haunt and menace the characters with the knowledge that the very system in which they believe annuls any argument they could make against their own professional extinction in times of economic crisis. They will all eventually become victims of "the eternal logic of endless growth that you would eventually have to apply to yourself" (34) ("aber auch diese ewige wachstumslogik, die man irgendwann gegen sich selbst anwende" [38]). As the markets begin to collapse, some workers, fearing for their own professional souls, begin to lose faith in the divine law of McKinsey and the infallibility of the economic system. When the bubble collapses and even accounting firms begin to go bankrupt, angst in the face of the virtual death of unemployment rises as well. But those who have faith can hope for professional "resurrection" (182) ("wiederauferstehung" [204]). Those who don't sleep, who are constantly recreating and replicating themselves will come through the crisis alive or at least undead. For them, economic death is just a chance to start over, to remake themselves: "insolvency as opportunity" (182) ("insolvenz als chance" [204]). For those who are flexible, the invisible hand of the market, mediated by entrepreneurial saviors and the high-priests of consulting, will lead to everlasting professsional life. Only those who can't keep up will lose their jobs. Only those not baptized in the faith of the flexible individual are mortal. Instead of resurrection, they can only look forward to "end-of-the-world scenarios" (37) ("weltuntergangsszenarien" [42]), apocalyptic visions of total collapse.

The metaphysical dimension of the novel oscillates between religious metaphor and ghost story. The trade fair itself is increasingly perceived as "uncanny" (100) ("unheimlich" [116]). The novel's characters have forfeited their substance and authenticity to the chimera of success and professional advancement. Hence, by the end of the novel when the interview turns to intimate self-reflections, the characters are led to speak of themselves and their colleagues as ghosts, zombies, undead inhabitants of a professional netherworld in which human beings exist only in relationship to productivity and success, devoid of human life, memory, and experience. The key account manager can only say "how the ghost in her grew and grew, and how the ghostly existence one had been sentenced to became increasingly real" (175) ("wie das gespenst immer mehr stimmt, zu dem man verdonnert wurde, ja, wie das gespenst in einem immer mehr zunimmt" [197]). The fate of the "undead" who have survived but do not live is but a short remove from the fate of those who do not survive. The pace and intensity of the novel accelerate as it moves towards its conclusion in which the professional and literal death of colleagues and associates presses itself upon the resistant consciousness and memory of the interviewees. People disappear from the team and are never heard from again. Rumors circulate that they have suffered a nervous breakdown, a mental and physical collapse. One doesn't talk of such things, however. People simply disappear, leaving only the ghost of rumor, and the pall of anxiety, a half-realized truth that one might likewise be brought to the brink of the abyss, despite one's assertions that one is handling the stress. The key to the novel's conclusion is found in the chapter entitled "exit strategies" (179) ("exit-szenarium" [201]), in which a desperate worker commits suicide. It remains unknown and essentially unimportant whether the proximate cause was the stress associated with continuing the job or the crisis associated with being fired. All alternatives within this system eventually lead to self-destruction, aided and abetted by those whose job it is to ensure the efficiency and ultimate survival of the corporation by maintaining the threat of job extinction over or against the demand for top performance. Confronted with this causality, and the rumors of his ruthlessly efficient administrative style, the senior associate becomes very defensive: "'i mean, they hadn't killed anyone.' at least he hadn't killed anyone, as far as he could remember (laughs)" (173) ("'ich meine, man hat ja niemanden umgebracht.' Er habe zumindest niemanden umgebracht, soweit er sich erinnern könne" [195]). His nervous laughter reveals his represssed awareness that the business model he represents is literally killing people.

In the end, the interviewee's responses begin to circle around the theme of death, both figurative and real. Unwittingly, they have been brought to a consciousness of what their survival demands that they repress. Dead colleagues are the logical extension and physical representation of the zombie-like existence of the living dead which has become their collective fate. The senior associate finds himself admitting "he thought he had already been dead for quite some time" (181) ("er glaube, er sei schon länger verstorben" [203]). The bankruptcy of the self is brought glaringly into focus. The discomfiting questions that are implicitly encoded in the final answers of the text lead the reader/viewer/listener back to awareness of the interviewer, from whose probing questions the subjects of the interview recoil in search of their own exit strategies that will sink them once again into forgetfulness of what they have been brought to acknowledge. Confronted with the conscious awareness of all they must repress in order to continue in their habitual modes, the characters retreat and declare the interview over. They won't be participating any more.

The ghostly absent narrator of the majority of the text first gains substance and presence in the final chapter when Kathrin Röggla reclaims her life and voice in a revival and return from the island of the dead. In the final scenes, Röggla brings the text full circle as she recounts that, in spite of the moment of anagnoresis or tragic recognition achieved by the interviewees in the final interviews, nothing at the convention center has changed in any way from the opening descriptions at the beginning of the book. The endless stream of commerce and unconscious, reflexive self-destruction that the text has unmasked continue unabated: "it was all there again, the business admin jargon" (195) ("wieder da, das bwler-deutsch" [219]). This lack of change may be another nod to the Austrian literary tradition, namely Kafka's short story "The Judgment" (1912). Here too a narrator survives the death of another figure. Here too, instead of the ultimate existential event leaving even a ripple on the pond of human events, the narrator's final description is dedicated to the endless bridge traffic which continues, oblivious to the tragedy of human events. The incessant noise of trivial daily events drowns out the unwanted awareness of the calamity.

Endnotes

[1] Kathrin Röggla, *wir schlafen nicht*. Frankfurt am Main: Fischer, 2004.
[2] "Single-Gerneration, Die New Economy, ihre Folgen und das neue Menschenbild vom flexiblen Yettie," October 10, 2007, http://www.single-generation.de/kritik/rez-yettie.htm.
[3] Single-Generation, Kathrin Röggla, Die Heterogenität der Lebensformen. January 5, 2009, http://www.single-generation.de/österreich/Kathrin_Röggla.htm.
[4] *Die Welt* Online, "Menschen mit Tunnelblick." January 5, 2009, http://www.welt.de/print-wams/article108761/menschen_mit tunnelblick/htm. 2004.
[5] Kathrin Röggla: Die Heterogenität der Lebensformen, January 5, 2009, http://www.single-dasein.de/oesterreich/kathrin_röggla.htm.
[6] Katrin Hillgruber, "Immerhin der Konjunktiv lebt," Review, *Frankfurter Rundschau*, March 24, 2004.
[7] man solle ihn ruhig warnen, wenn er mit zu vielen anglizismen um sich schmeiße, das gehe bei ihm nämlich schon automatisch. Manchmal merke er gar nicht mehr, in welchem fachjargon er wieder einmal rede und was für vokabular er wieder rauslasse. Das passiere schnell, daß man für außenstehende einfach nicht mehr verständlich sei. Gerade an einem ort wie diesem, wo man doch sehr viel mit kollegen spreche. Aber die unverständlichkeit sei ja genau einer der gründe, warum es überhaupt beratungen gebe – weil die unterschiedlichen bereiche eines unternehmens oftmals nicht richtig kommunizierten, und weil die problemlagen so komplex geworden seien, da bedürfe es immer öfter eines blickes von aussen – (9-10).

Strange Bedfellows: Daniel Kehlmann's *Die Vermessung der Welt*

Ronald Horwege

Measuring the World, translated by Carol Brown Janeway, Pantheon Books, 2006.

In the last few years the name Daniel Kehlmann (1975-) has joined the list of best-selling authors in Europe. At the top of the best-seller list for many months was *Die Vermessung der Welt*,[1] by the young Austrian, who has not only acquired academic laurels but has also been producing books already for over a decade. Born in Munich, the son of theatre director Michael Kehlmann and the German actress Dagmar Mettler, moved to Vienna with his family at age six, where he grew up, studied German literature and philosophy, and still resides today. At the age of twenty-two he published his first novel, *Beerholms Vorstellung*, and subsequently three other novels, *Mahlers Zeit* (2001), *Ich und Kaminski* (2003) and *Die Vermessung der Welt* (2005), a novelle, *Der fernste Ort* (2001), a collection of short stories, *Unter der Sonne* (1999), and a collection of essays, *Wo ist Carlos Montufar?* (2005).[2]

When reading Kehlmann's works one notes, among other things, the various strange personalities he chooses to portray. One could perhaps categorize all of them as societal outsiders striving for a way out of everyday existence. They are driven to go in new directions, whether to seek new discoveries, fame, and recognition, or merely to just escape. In the end they either fail or are surpassed by others. For example, Arthur Beerholm wants to become a magician. As his talents develop and he achieves fame, he begins to confuse reality and fantasy, and, when he can no longer recognize the limitations of his own magical abilities, he flees from the public eye.

Physicist David Mahler in *Mahlers Zeit* makes an important discovery in a dream, and spends four years seeking a way to reverse the direction of time. With the solution in hand, he sets out to find an audience for his discovery but ultimately dies of a heart attack and thus leaves the question of the validity of his discovery unsolved.

In *Der fernste Ort* Julian, an insurance representative, stages a fake drowning in order to flee from an unpleasant situation and an unhappy life. In the end he loses all contact to his earlier life, and after losing his passport and having his money stolen, he is left sitting in the snow waiting for the train to come. Certain signs let the reader wonder whether he is indeed heading for a new life on earth or into the great beyond.

In *Ich und Kaminski*. the narrator, a former art history student named Sebastian Zöllner, is assigned the task of writing a biography of the painter Manuel Kaminski, once a protégé of Matisse but now blind and forgotten and living in a small alpine village carefully sheltered from uninvited visitors. Zöllner "kidnaps" the old man with the goal of finally receiving answers to his questions. The two embark on a journey to northern Germany where Therese, Kaminski's first love, whom he had thought to be dead, lives. But the roles are soon reversed, and Zöllner realizes that throughout their encounter he has been the subject of Kaminski's manipulations.

With the publication of *Die Vermessung der Welt*, Kehlmann reached new heights by establishing his reputation outside of the German-speaking world. As a result of rave reviews the book has been translated into over twenty languages after sitting atop the bestseller list in Germany for many months. A review in *The Guardian* noted that it was even outselling *Harry Potter* and that it is the most successful German novel since Patrick Süsskinds *Perfume* two decades ago.[3] Similar comments appeared in *Deutschland Magazine* as sales had surpassed the half million mark.[4] Within several years figures approached one million.

Kehlmann's novel presents the lives of two of the giants of the early nineteenth century, Alexander von Humboldt, the noted explorer of South America, and Carl Friedrich Gauss, the great mathematician and astronomer. While recognizing the many accomplishments of each and retelling noteworthy parts of their lives, the author adds a fictitious and quite humorous and entertaining recounting of their personal lives and their human weaknesses. Humboldt strove to travel to all corners of the known world but hardly knew or cared what a woman was and was quite insensitive to other people, while Gauss developed great ideas in his head but hardly ventured from Göttingen and could not live without women.

The plot is based around a Berlin meeting of the two men at the German Scientific Congress (*Naturforscherkongress*) of 1828 and flashbacks to their earlier exploits. Several recurring themes become evident: the questioning of what it means to be a German, issues of aging and of human striving and accomplishment, and predictions of the future.

As the plot opens, the reader gets a humorous personal look at Gauss during his travel preparations and the trip itself. Gauss had serious conflicts with his son Eugen, who was a German nationalist and follower of Friedrich Ludwig Jahn (Turnvater Jahn) and frustration at his homely daughter's inability to get married. When father and son arrived in Berlin and saw their swampy surroundings alongside the construction of many splendid buildings, Eugen comments that Berlin would someday be a metropolis like Rome, Paris, or St. Petersburg but is rebuked by his father, who considers the city a horrible place. On several occasions humor is derived from predictions about the future. These characters from the early nineteenth century thus seem to have knowledge about the future that would in reality be impossible for them to possess.

At the moment of the first meeting of the two old men, the group assembled is interrupted, first by the photography pioneer Monsieur Daguerre as he tries to take a picture, and then by a policeman, who while trying to break up the gathering, hinders the attempt to take the photo. Despite repeated attempts,

Daguerre fails as Gauss slowly loses patience with the photographer.
   After the initial introduction of the two men, alternating chapters flash back to the exploits of each in their youth. One learns about the background of the Humboldt brothers and about how their expedition to the Americas originated with some basic information one can find in any encyclopedia:
   "Alexander von Humboldt was famous in all of Europe for an expedition to the tropics he had led twenty-five years earlier. He had been in New Spain, New Granada, New Barcelona, New Andalusia, and the United States; he had discovered the natural canal that connects the Orinoco and the Amazon; he had climbed the highest mountain in the known world; he had collected thousands of plants and hundreds of animals, some living, the majority dead; he had talked to parrots, disinterred corpses, measured every river, every mountain, and every lake in his path, had crawled into burrows and had tasted more berries and climbed more trees than anyone could begin to imagine" (13).[5]
   From that point the delineation between fact and fiction dims. After their wealthy father died early, their mother sought Goethe's advice on how to educate her sons and was given a response about how the "whole panoply of human aspirations" (14) ("so recht die Vielfalt menschlicher Bestrebungen" [19]) manifested itself in them. Because no one could fully grasp Goethe's meaning, the two brothers were separated, with the elder one meant to become a man of culture and the younger one a man of science. The decision of which one would be which had been left to the toss of a coin.
   In their childhood the elder brother was looked on as an angel who could do no wrong; he received the best education, learned many languages, and was able to endear himself to everyone, even though he nonetheless tormented his younger brother. The inference is made, that when the younger one was almost poisoned, the rat poison had been set by the elder brother.
   Both boys were encouraged to read stories about ghosts and magic, since "anyone innocent of metaphysical anxiety

would never achieve German manhood" (15) ("wer metaphysische Angst nicht kenne, werde nie ein deutscher Mann" [21]). The younger brother's desire to travel was awakened through reading about Aguirre the Crazy, who on exploring South America tried to make himself emperor. However, his desire to learn was also influenced by a near drowning incident, through which he learned about determination and after which he began to take his studies more seriously. He decided to investigate the mystery of life and became a serious student of science in Frankfurt on the Oder, while his brother went to Göttingen for the better party atmosphere: "While the older brother was finding his first friends there, trying his first alcohol, and touching his first woman, the younger boy was writing his first scientific paper" (20).[6]

While studying in Freiberg, he first came into contact with Neptunism, the theory that the core of the earth was solid rock and one championed both by churches and by Goethe. When Abraham Werner, the proponent of Neptunism, asked Humboldt if he was a Neptunist, Humboldt said he was, but when Werner suggested that he should then get married, Humboldt answered: "One got married only when one had nothing to do in life" (22) ("Man heirate, wenn man nichts Wesentliches im Leben vorhabe" [31]). Werner replied: "No unmarried man had ever made a good Neptunist" (22) ("Ein verheirateter Mann, sagte Werner, sei noch nie ein guter Neptunist gewesen" [31]). Do we dare check the logic here?

In Freiberg Humboldt learned to crawl through caves and began to dissect and examine plants. He noted that instead of getting colder in the depths of caves the temperature actually rose, which contradicted the Neptune theory. He was awarded the title of Assessor in the Department of Mines and donned the uniform he was to wear during all of his travels in South America. The image of a rather stiff, formal little Prussian traveling around Latin America in a blue uniform and looking at the world through his monocle contrasts to contemporary portraits of him. In an interview in the *Frankfurter Allgemeine Zeitung* Kehlmann explains the connection between the uniform and what it means to be German.[7]

As inspector of mines Humboldt achieved great success in spite of scaring workers with his swift note-taking and having no idea of the purpose of his work. At one point he tested Galvani's theory of electric current, but instead of using frog legs he laid zinc and silver on open wounds and let electric shocks go through his own body. He established his reputation as a scientist through a treatise on living muscle fiber as a conductor of electricity. The lesson from this, however, seemed to be his insight that real knowledge can only be gained by enduring pain. He then developed a miner's lamp that used a gas. When using it he developed hallucinations of plants turning into women's bodies and ultimately almost died. This experience led to his development of a breathing machine for use when climbing into mines.

Upon his mother's death Humboldt resigned his post and arranged to voyage to South America. In a lecture Kehlmann pointed out that the main reason for Humboldt's trip to South America was to get away from his family, and especially from his brother. The tropics were for him the place where his brother was not.[8] But first he visited Weimar and met Wieland, Herder and Goethe, who instructed him to investigate volcanoes to find evidence to support the Neptune theory. He then implored him to never forget where he came from and to be their ambassador across the seas. Thus he was supposed to spread Weimar Classicism across the world.

After a year in Salzburg, where Humboldt collected an array of scientific instruments and learned how to use them and how to endure physical pain, he journeys to Paris, where he holds lectures on the conductivity of human nerves, searches for an expedition and met Bonpland, who becomes his traveling companion and assistant. Although both men experience the hardships of the trip together, the Frenchman is often attracted to women, while Humboldt is not. With Bonpland and guides in the new world Humboldt climbs to the top of a volcano, and comes face to face with the first plants. Upon their return Bonpland disappears and Humboldt finds him with one of the native women. He warns him that if it happens again, their collaboration would be over. But in spite of repeated incidents the collaboration continues.

Unlike Humboldt, Gauss came from a humble background – his father was a gardener. He had a close, life-long relationship with his mother. He came to realize his own intelligence, after first being disturbed at the slowness of the thoughts of others as well as by the black marks in books, until he suddenly realized that these black marks were words and that other people were unwilling to use their minds. When meeting the Duke of Brunswick for an interview for a scholarship, Gauss looks into the future and is already aware that someday there would be no more dukes: "Then absolute rulers would only exist in books, and the idea that one would stand before such a person, bow, and await his all powerful word would seem so strange as to be a fairy tale" (49).[9] In spite of hearing of Gauss's accomplishments, the Duke is at first only interested in hearing Gauss count. However, Gauss receives his scholarship, in spite of the fact that he could not count. The Duke only notes that his godson, the little Alexander von Humboldt, was a scientist and was away counting flowers in South America, and that Gauss should return when he had something more to show.

After a ride in a hot air balloon with Pilatre de Rozier,[10] Gauss is hardly disturbed by a fall into a haystack, but instead comes to a new insight that was to shake the scientific world, namely the premise that all parallel lines meet.

Humboldt's adventures during six months in New Amsterdam and Trinidad naturally include his research: "He had measured the color of the sky, the temperature of lightning flashes, and the weight of the hoarfrost at night, he had tasted bird droppings, investigated earth tremors and had climbed down into the Cavern of the Dead" (56).[11] From his quarters at the edge of a city he enjoys researching a recent earthquake and waits for a reoccurrence. Women often visit and he enjoys counting the lice in their hair. He watches the slave auctions, but when he buys three men and frees them, these men do not know what to do.

By a foray into a deep cave where the dead were said to live he discovers plant life and notes that it gets warmer in the depths. But after seeing a vision of his mother (a sign that he was running short on oxygen) he decides not to proceed further. His big adventure, however, is with a naked woman purportedly sent to him by the governor. Despite his objections that he was an official of the Prussian Crown and his lack of interest, she attempts unsuccessfully to seduce him and ultimately apologizes to him for her lack of success in arousing him. Instead of occupying himself with women he concentrates on his research and the possible discovery of a canal between the Orinoco and the Amazon rivers. He misses a solar eclipse because he was fixing his directions on the sextant and had no time to look up. The episode closes with this question of whether one always had to be so German.

Despite a terrible, haunting toothache, Gauss solves one of the world's oldest problems: how to draw with a compass and ruler a seventeen-sided object (*Siebzehneck*). However, in his haste he forgets he is naked and kicks over the chamber pot. He then rushes off to the barber, who removes his tooth – though the wrong one. At that point his thoughts turn again to the future, when there would be actual doctors, who could deaden nerves when removing teeth instead of tying one up.

Gauss decides at age nineteen to become a mathematician instead of a classical philologist. In five years he planned to solve the question of what a number is, the basis of mathematics. From then on he is always accompanied by numbers, even when visiting prostitutes, among whom is his favorite woman from Siberia named Nina.

While waiting to receive his doctorate, Gauss reads about Humboldt's adventures and the eclipse of the sun. His thoughts on the matter: why must one run away to find the truth when it is right here? He wants to write his own great work and never leave the Electorate of Hannover. While working as a surveyor, Gauss meets Johanna, who becomes his first wife, and her ugly and obnoxious companion Minna, whom he later marries. But before he concerns himself with such trivial things, he finishes his life's work, the *Disquitiones Arithmeticae*, at age twenty.

Gauss travels at one point to Königsberg for an audience with Immanuel Kant, to present a copy of his book and with whom he wants to discuss his theory of parallel lines and triangles. But when he finally has his audience, the great philosopher gives only a short comment to all of these great ideas: "Sausage...Buy sausage. And stars. Buy stars too" (80) ("Wurst sagte Kant. Bitte! Der Lampe soll Wurst kaufen, sagte Kant. Wurst und Sterne. Soll er auch kaufen" (96-97).

This is, of course, a surprising answer coming from such a great mind. One must, however, also take Kant's age into account. Was he protesting Gauss's new ideas, which would contradict his own work, or was his mind too far gone to know what was really taking place?

After deciding because of imminent dangers and discomforts not to proceed further through the jungle Humboldt and Bonpland visit a cave of the dead, from where Humboldt takes some specimen bodies and then has to deal with missionaries and Indians angry about the grave robberies.

In a following scene Humboldt takes some of curare, the poison that Gauss also had almost taken, to prove that it has no effect when there are no open wounds. As a result he is unable to move for many hours and speaks with a mustached German who may or may not have been (but most likely was) a figment of his imagination. He also has an encounter with a naked boy, who slipped into his tent in the early morning hours. In fright he beats the boy off and discovers at the same time that Bonpland has found another woman for his bed.

After a huge rainstorm sweeps away the boat leaving them stranded, Bonpland asks Humboldt whether he has ever thought of what he would have had if he had stayed in Germany.

Humboldt looks at a crocodile and replies that he had never given it a thought.

The Duke offers Gauss the position of astronomer, though Gauss aspires to the title of professor. But he is nonetheless now able to afford to marry Johanna, although only after a last visit to his favorite prostitute Nina. His wedding night is only interrupted by a brief pause he took to write down a new mathematical formula that popped into his head.

As he starts his work he becomes impatient over his final arrangements and demands an audience with the Duke to discuss funding, but he is unaware that the reason the Duke does not see him is because of a war with Napoleon. He is also unaware that Göttingen is now in French hands. He takes the position anyway and is then confronted with dumb students and a surprise at home, the birth of a son. He starts to write a book on astronomy, loses more teeth, and suffers from colic. After a second child and a third pregnancy, Gauss decides to go to Bremen to look over the Jupiter tables. During an ocean trip he meets a Prussian diplomat, who turns out to be the elder Humboldt brother. Gauss then returns home to watch both his wife and his new baby die. His new problem is now to find a new mother for the other children. Nothing is said about any grief over the two deaths.

In one expedition that almost ends tragically Bonpland and Humboldt climb the Chimborazo, considered at that time to be the world's highest mountain, but barely escape with their lives. They are both disturbed by visions brought on by the lack of oxygen at the high altitude. Humboldt sees the dog that he had lost during his canal search and Bonpland split into three people. This is one of the most gripping episodes in the whole book, as it shows a definite contrast to the cold, objective description that according to Kehlmann one finds in Humboldt's own work.[12]

As Gauss proceeds with his surveying, he has some interesting dealings with a certain Count Heinrich von der Ohe zur Ohe. After spending a night on a wooden board in a stinky little hole with no toilet facilities in the palace, he has a rather interesting conversation with the Count, who after some beating around the bush and some interrogation by which he seems to know almost everything about Gauss and his work, makes a present of the trees and the shed that Gauss needs to have cleared out in order to continue his measurements.

After Johanna's death Gauss marries Minna, whom he cannot stand: "That her presence made him nervous and unhappy, that her voice was like a piece of chalk on a chalkboard and that the sight of her face from a distance made him feel lonely and even that the thought of her face in the distance made him feel lonely and the very thought of her was enough to make him wish he were dead" (164).[13] He really wants to marry Nina but is advised against it. He knows that he had become a surveyor in order to get away from home. As far as his son Eugen was concerned, Gauss thinks only of the stupidity the boy had inherited from Minna, of the usefulness of his invention for the future and all the work he still has to do in order to cover all of Germany.

Humboldt visits some silver mines, where his breathing mask and lamp made him look to the miners like a demon. After studying the stealing habits of the miners he makes suggestions for improving mine safety, to which the mine superintendent replies: "They had enough people, said Don Fernando. Anyone who died could be replaced" (169).[14] Humboldt replies by asking whether the superintendent has read Kant. The superintendent prefers Leibniz. He then adds that he came from German stock, which was how he knew all these wonderful mad ideas (169).[15]

While observing the excavation site of the temple destroyed by Cortez, a worker makes the observation that twenty thousand people had been sacrificed at its dedication. Humboldt finds this incredulous: "Twenty thousand, in one place, in one day, was unthinkable. The victims would never tolerate it. The audience wouldn't tolerate it. What's more, the world order would not support it. If such a thing ever happened, the universe would come to an end" (172).[16] Humboldt's classical optimism clashes quite significantly with the reality of later events in Germany and around the world.

At a party with the Viceroy Humboldt actually receives an offer to become minister of mines but refuses because he remains loyally Prussian. At the end of the evening Humboldt talks with the last descendant of the Aztec kings, who has absolutely no memory of the horrors in the temple and considers himself to be a Spanish Grande instead of an Indian. The parallel to the reaction of countless Germans to their Nazi past is clear. Humboldt's further adventures in Mexico include finding Bonpland once again with prostitutes, climbing Popocatepetl and measuring the structures in Teotihuacán. He is depressed, probably because he was thinking of the thousands of people who had been sacrificed in the advanced Inca civilization, and makes another reference to Germany, "So much civilization and so much horror," said Humboldt. "What a combination. The exact opposite of everything Germany stood for" (177).[17] At that moment he and Bonpland decide that instead of seeking out the explorer Baudin and going to the Philippines, it is time to go home.

Before departing, Humboldt visits Jorullo, a volcano that had erupted fifty years before his visit. He lowers himself into the crater and when he is pulled up with scorched clothing and coughing, he declares that the Theory of Neptunism is officially buried.

In a discussion with Thomas Jefferson during a brief stop in the United States he unwittingly speaks against slavery, until a kick from Bonpland makes him change the subject. His opinion of Jefferson: "A backwoods president," said Humboldt. "Who cares what he thought" (180) ("Ein Hinterwäldlerpräsident," sagte Humboldt. "Wen interessiere, was der denke?" [211]). And America was "a small protestant community on the edge of the world. Unimaginably far from everything" (182) ("Man sei eine kleine Protestantengemeinde am Rand der Welt. Unendlich weit von allen" [214]).

It appears that Humboldt did not possess the ability to predict the future, at least in this situation. Instead he allows Jefferson to pump him for information about New Spain, its defenses, the size of its military, the mood of its nobles, etc. In spite of his obligations to Spain, he has no hesitation speaking about such matters because he does not think that this small, weak country would ever be a threat.

At this point the plot shifts back to the two old men sitting at the dinner table discussing the glories of their past. The two commiserate about hopes of their youth that were unfulfilled and about the frustrating political situation: "Europe was now a theater and the play a nightmare from which none of them could wake any longer" (186).[18] The Czar had invited Humboldt to Russia but he declined the invitation both for political reasons and because of his age. In the midst of the changes brought on by the restoration Humboldt had been refused a chance to go to India by the English because of his views on slavery, and in Latin America there were dozens of new states and the life's work of his friend Bolivar lay in ruins. Humboldt pointed out that Bolivar had given him the title of the true discoverer of South America, and refers to the book that Gomez has written about him, and then he asks Gauss about his probability theory, which leads Gauss to hold forth on the futility of life and the inability of an individual to prevent growing old. Humboldt takes up the defense of reason and Gauss counters that reason has shaped absolutely nothing. He adds that space is curved and time malleable. In addition they were a long way from understanding how the world could be calculated.

Gauss makes fun of Humboldt's present position as a chamberlain who was paid for meals and chats, and at this point Eugen points out that the true tyrants were not the laws of nature and that there were real freedom movements in the land, with which neither Gauss nor Humboldt have any sympathy. Finally Eugen is able to get an answer about Bonpland's fate: he is under house arrest in Paraguay because he had gotten onto the wrong side in a civil war.

As the two men talk, Eugen wanders around Berlin and becomes acquainted with two students discussing freedom. The conversation turns to the Humboldts and the students criticize the younger brother for staying in Paris during the war and for advertising the fact that he is in the French Academy. Eugen gathers with a large group in a cellar to hear a speech by a man portraying Friedrich Jahn. In the midst of the patriotic speech the gendarmes appear and drag all of the participants away to prison. At the *Kongress* Humboldt holds a long lecture about stars and currents – he started with the universe and the bodies of light swimming in ethereal light-blocking space, which gave proof to the rational order of Nature, and then proceeds with a depiction of the earth as one of the bodies swimming in the blackness, stresses the earth's fiery center, talks about his own travels and about the various stages of life and the spring to reason. He concludes: "The second greatest insult to man was slavery. But the greatest was the idea that he had descended from apes" (203).[19] He then closes with some sweeping statements about how science would solve human problems, even the problem of death.

Daguerre notes at the end how Humboldt is no longer as he once had been, because he seems to repeat himself. Then he adds remarks, criticizing Humboldt's writings, and how he is now getting on the nerves of the Berlin city council (*Stadtrat*). Gauss adds that he did not know any young scientists in Göttingen who were not asses. Humboldt's highest mountain has been surpassed by the Himalayas, and his India expedition has failed. Gauss could not keep quiet any longer and screams out that Daguerre needs a salt solution for his silver iodide in order to get images. This tension had been building up with every attempt to take pictures, and Gauss could finally contain himself no longer.

The evening is capped by the appearance of the other Humboldt brother as well as by the young scientist Weber,[20] who has studied the *Disquitiones* and who also has a beautiful young wife. This awakened Gauss's interest once again and he grants Weber a short audience for the next day.

When both men are again at Humboldt's residence, a messenger comes with a message that Eugen has smuggled out of the jail. Gauss wishes to do nothing about it, but Humboldt takes the matter in hand. The two men visit the commander of the gendarmerie and find him attending a séance. Humboldt is able to make the most of the embarrassing situation and convinces the commander that he would be serving Prussia by sending the son of such a famous scientist out of the country. Gauss is skeptical, almost ruins the deal by complaining about bribery, is almost forced into a duel and in the end laments the fact that his life is now behind him: his home means nothing, no one wants to marry his daughter, his son is in trouble, his mother would not live much longer and he has spent the last fifteen years measuring hills. But, nonetheless, both men feel quite chipper, for Gauss has found Weber and his pretty wife, and Humboldt is reconsidering his invitation to Russia. In addition Gauss is thinking about experimental physics.

Humboldt's trip through Russia is not what he had hoped for. He is carefully watched, does not get to see everything he wished to see nor go where he wished to go to conduct meaningful research. In a letter from Bonpland that he receives in St. Petersburg, he finds that the world of his old companion has shrunk to the size of his compound and that he has given up all hope. In the end two old men are left wondering which of the two has traveled more and which one has stayed home.

The final chapter describes Eugen's exit from Europe and indicates how he as part of the younger generation might also make his mark and how he is perhaps beginning to become more like his father. After being told that he is to be forced out of the country he meets briefly with his father for a final farewell and then sails off. Three days later in England, he wins so much money in a card game that his fellow players are convinced he is a swindler, while he has only used a method learned from his father. After drinking too much, he is robbed of his winnings by his first prostitute. Eventually he makes his way to America. The son arises to take his father's place and to embrace new ideas while exhibiting the same human weaknesses.

Kehlmann chose these two interesting men as his main characters and brought them to life with their great attributes and their accomplishments but also with their human weaknesses. As great scientists and thinkers they had much in common, but they were also in many ways opposites. Humboldt had his goal of measuring the world through his many travels, whereas Gauss sat at home, hated travel and conducted his measurements in his head and, of course, in his minor expeditions around his home State. Humboldt was a child of privilege, who in spite of abuse at the hands of his brother and the loss of his mother enjoyed the best education and privileges of his social class. Gauss came from the lower classes and was able to pull himself up by his bootstraps with the help of colleagues and teachers. He also did not separate himself from his aging mother. Humboldt was seemingly homosexual or perhaps asexual and incapable of much human feeling and compassion, whereas Gauss did not turn away from sexual adventures and even had his favorite prostitute. It should, however, be noted, that Gauss was also devoid of real human compassion, as seen in his dislike of both his ugly daughter and his son and his disdain for his second wife, whom he only married because of the children. It is also interesting to see that he could hop out of bed, even on his wedding night, to write down new ideas.

Both men were oblivious to political events around them. Gauss was happy to land a position as astronomer in his small state, got angry when the position did not materialize and was surprised to find that Napoleon in the meantime had occupied Germany. However, he continued to work under the French authorities. Humboldt also returned to Europe and in spite of his Prussian pride published his works in France. Both men were left behind by the new democratic ideas that emerged during the suppression under Metternich. And, as mentioned above, Humboldt did not foresee the growing importance of America just as Gauss was unable to comprehend that Berlin could ever be anything but a dirty little place.

Neither of the men had any feeling for or any love of the arts. In fact, in their discussion during their meeting this is one thing on which they agreed. Gauss was bothered because Eugen composed poetry, Humboldt was unable to even recite a poem correctly as he demonstrated in one point by messing up one by Goethe. They both hated books without numbers and were bored by the theater, and Humboldt concluded with an attack against novels "that wandered off into lying fables because the author tied his fake inventions to the names of real historical personages" (189).[21] Is that not a clever little jab at the author of this "historical" novel?

Although Gauss and Humboldt were alike in many ways, one of their biggest differences was their differing outlooks on the world. Humboldt still embraced the ideals of classicism and was optimistic about the future of the world and his ability to fathom this "rational" world. Gauss, on the other hand, already upset this rational order at age 20 with his first mathematical masterwork. One then sees that he was in conflict with Humboldt when he contradicted him during his speech before the *Kongress*. Nonetheless, it is also to be noted that Humboldt moved away from the Weimar group, most notably in his research disproving the Neptune theory. He also had innovations, such as the special suit for descending into mines.

Gauss and Humboldt both achieved great fame through their ideas and discoveries but as all great men, they aged and were surpassed by new ideas, new discoveries, the next generation of great thinkers, and the political and social developments around them. Other great men also appear in the book during their later years. Rather than defend his own ideas or embrace Gauss's new ideas, Kant could only think of sausage, and Goethe and his associates were stuck on the idea of Neptunism, which Humboldt eventually proved false. In fact, in an interview Kehlmann notes that the theme of aging should be one of the important themes of the book.[22]

The first main theme, according to Kehlmann, is what it means to be German. In many places in the novel there are references to the Germans, and these two are examples of Germans turned loose in the world.[23] Several references to the "German" behavior of these two men have been pointed out, but a more detailed and more systematic discussion of this theme is left to readers who wish to ponder the details and speculate about the intricacies of being German.

With both humor and sensitivity Kehlmann has been able to combine the great exploits of both men with their human qualities In spite of his nervousness about how critics would receive his novel, especially those experts in the camps of both of these men it has passed muster with both camps, including Hans Magnus Enzensberger, who wrote a definitive work about Humboldt.[24] Both men have also earned a place in Kehlmann's collection of social misfits. However, unlike the other characters in his collection, these two men also succeeded in achieving the greatness they strove for, just as Kehlmann has succeeded in advancing his international reputation as a writer.

Endnotes

[1] Daniel Kehlmann, *Die Vermessung der Welt,* Reinbek bei Hamburg: Rowohlt Verlag, 2005.
[2] *Beerholms Vorstellung.* Deuticke Verlagsgesellschaft m.b.H., Vienna Munich, 1997.
Mahlers Zeit. Suhrkamp Verlag, Frankfurt am Main, 2001.
Ich und Kaminski. Suhrkamp Verlag, Frankfurt am Main, 2003.
Die Vermessung der Welt (2005).
Der fernste Ort. Suhrkamp Verlag, Frankfurt am Main, 2001.
Unter der Sonne. Franz Deuticke Verlagsgesellschaft, Vienna and Munich, 1998.
Wo ist Carlos Montufar? Rowohlt Verlag, Reinbek bei Hamburg, 2005.
[3] Luke Harding, *The Guardian,* Wednesday July 19, 2006. An excerpt from the article:
"Gripped? You will be. In fact, *Measuring the World* has proved

nothing less than a literary sensation. Since it was published last September, the novel has sold more than 600,000 copies in Germany, knocking JK Rowling and Dan Brown off the top of the best-seller list. Last week it was still at number two, 10 months after publication. The book, which also features a senile Immanuel Kant, is the most successful German novel since Patrick Susskind's *Perfume* two decades ago. It hasn't just delighted the readers. It has also enthralled Germany's famously grudging critics, who have swooningly praised the novel and hailed its author – 31-year-old Daniel Kehlmann – as a literary wunderkind."
[4]*Deutschland Magazi*ne 19.05.2006. An excerpt from the article: "Hundreds of thousands of Germans are buying and reading Daniel Kehlmann's novel *Measuring the World*, which has been topping the bestseller lists almost since it first appeared in late September 2005 and, right after the pre-Christmas sales, even toppled Harry Potter to take up pole position, which it has since held week in, week out, unchallenged even by the most popular new spring publications. Meantime, sales have clearly passed the half a million mark and the rights have been purchased for more than twenty countries."
[5]"Alexander von Humboldt war in ganz Europa berühmt wegen einer Expedition in die Tropen, die er fünfundzwanzig Jahre zuvor unternommen hatte. Er war in Neuspanien, Neugranada, Neubarcelona, Neuandalusien und den Vereinigten Staaten gewesen, hatte den natürlichen Kanal zwischen Orinoko und Amazonas entdeckt, den höchsten Berg der bekannten Welt bestiegen, Tausende Pflanzen und Hunderte Tiere, manche lebend, die meisten tot, gesammelt, hatte mit Papageien gesprochen, Leichen ausgegraben, jeden Fluss, Berg und See auf seinem Weg vermessen, war in jedes Erdloch gekrochen und hatte mehr Beeren gekostet und Bäume erklettert, als sich irgend jemand vorstellen mochte" (19).

[6]"Während er dort seine ersten Freunde fand, zum erstenmal Alkohol trank und eine Frau berührte, schrieb der jüngere seine erste wissenschaftliche Arbeit" (27).
[7]"Allein die Uniform, die er immer wieder anlegt, oder wenn er bei der Überfahrt neben dem spanischen Kapitän steht und diesen beim Navigieren korrigiert, oder wenn er Indianerleichen ausgräbt und überhaupt nicht versteht, warum er es von da an schwer hat, einen Führer zu finden. Diese ungewollte Komik ist aber keineswegs die Komik eines Kauzes. Es geht darum, dass solche Begebenheiten sehr viel darüber aussagen, was es heißt, deutsch zu sein. Wir haben es hier zu tun mit einem Weimarer Klassiker, der das ganz andere der Weimarer Klassik vertreten hat, der einzige Weimarer Klassiker, der wirklich ausgesandt wurde, die Weimarer Klassik hinauszutragen, und der mit diesem Weltbild Macondo bereist hat." Interview with Felicitas von Lovenberg, *Frankfurter Allgemeine Zeitung*, 09.02.2006, Nr. 34 / p. 41.
[8] Daniel Kehlmann, *Diese sehr ernsten Scherze, Poetikvorlesungen, (Göttinger Sudelblätter)*, Wallstein Verlag, Göttingen 2007, p. 38.
[9]"Er wusste, dass es bald keine Herzöge mehr geben würde. Dann würde man von absoluten Herrschern nur mehr in Büchern lesen, und der Gedanke, vor einem zu stehen, sich zu verneigen und auf sein Machtwort zu warten, käme jedem Menschen fremd und märchenhaft vor" (61).
[10] Jean-François Pilâtre de Rozier (30 March 1754 – 15 June 1785) was one of the first pioneers of aviation.
[11]"Er hatte die Farbe des Himmels, die Temperatur der Blitze, und die Schwere des nächtlichen Rauhreifs gemessen, er hatte Vogelkot gekostet, die Erschütterungen der Erde erforscht und war in die Höhle der Toten gestiegen" (69).
[12]*The Guardian*, Saturday, April 21, 2007.
"Humboldt's account of his attempt to climb Mount Chimborazo in 1802 is a prosaic recounting of facts couched in the omniscient tone typical of reports of expeditions in the 18th century.

However, anyone reading the writings of contemporary alpinists gets a very clear picture of what actually happens to a mountain climber. Even people who are in excellent physical shape vomit continuously and experience hallucinations. If they try to speak at high altitude, they slur their words like drunks, they cannot think straight, and their mucous membranes and even their eyes start to bleed. Things would not have been any different for Humboldt. The sovereign and detached tone of his description of the climb is not necessarily any less fictional, then, than the scene of utter confusion and lurching aimlessness that I turned it into."

[13] "Das Problem war, dass er sie nicht ausstehen konnte. Dass ihre Nähe ihn nervös und unglücklich machte, dass ihre Stimme ihm vorkam, als kratze Kreide auf einer Schiefertafel, dass er sich schon einsam fühlte, wenn er ihr Gesicht nur von weitem sah, und allein der Gedanke an sie ausreichte, ihn wünschen zu lassen, er wäre tot" (193).

[14] "Man habe genug Leute, sagte Don Fernando. Wer sterbe, könne ersetzt werden" (199).

[15] "Er habe deutsche Vorfahren, deshalb kenne er all diese schönen Phantastereien" (199).

[16] "Zwanzigtausend an einem Ort und Tag, das sei undenkbar. Die Opfer würden es nicht dulden. Die Zuschauer würden es nicht dulden. Ja mehr noch: Die Ordnung der Welt vertrüge derlei nicht. Wenn so etwas wirklich geschähe, würde das Universum enden" (202).

[17] "Soviel Zivilisation und soviel Grausamkeit, sagte Humboldt. Was für eine Paarung! Gleichsam das Gegenteil zu allem, wofür Deutschland stehe" (208).

[18] "Europa sei zum Schauplatz eines Alptraums geworden, aus dem keiner mehr erwachen könne" (219).

[19] "Die zweitgrößte Beleidigung des Menschen sei die Sklaverei. Die größte jedoch die Idee, er stamme vom Affen ab" (238).

[20]Wilhelm Eduard Weber (24 October 1804 – 23 June 1891) was a German physicist and, together with Gauss inventor of the first electromagnetic telegraph.
[21]"Romane, die sich in Lügenmärchen verlören, weil die Verfasser seine Flausen an die Namen geschichtlichter Personen binde" (221).
[22]"Ja, das ist er auch. Das ist die andere Sache, bei der ich mich gewundert habe, dass sie so wenig beachtet wurde – Mich hat das Thema des Alterns immer fasziniert. Schon mein letzter Roman, 'Ich und Kaminski', beschreibt ein Duell zwischen Alter und Jugend, das das Alter gewinnt. Ein Thema, das sich beim Schreiben der 'Vermessung' sehr klar hergestellt hat, ist die Tatsache, dass alle Menschen über die Jahre hinweg ihren Eltern immer ähnlicher werden, ob sie wollen oder nicht – und normalerweise wollen sie ja überhaupt nicht. In diese Richtung spielt übrigens auch das letzte Kapitel mit Gauß' Sohn Eugen. In dem Moment, wo er selbständig wird, beginnt er plötzlich, sich zu entfalten wie sein Vater, ohne es zu bemerken. Das Altern ist insofern tatsächlich das zweite Hauptthema des Buches, und damit verbunden der traurige Umstand, dass man, wenn man lange genug da ist, sich selbst überlebt, sich selbst historisch wird." Interview with Felicitas von Lovenberg, *Frankfurter Allgemeine Zeitung*, 09.02.2006, Nr. 34 / p. 41.
[23] Interview with Felicitas von Lovenberg, *Frankfurter Allgemeine Zeitung*, 09.02.2006, Nr. 34 / Seite 41.
"Eine satirische, spielerische Auseinandersetzung mit dem, was es heißt, deutsch zu sein – auch natürlich mit dem, was man, ganz unironisch, die große deutsche Kultur nennen kann. Für mich ist das eines der Hauptthemen des Romans, wie Andreas Maier so schön im Booklet des Hörbuchs geschrieben hat, 'die große deutsche Geistesgeschichte, eine einzige Lebensuntauglichkeit.'"
[24]Volker Weidermann, "*Der Weltvermesser,*" *Frankfurter Allgemeine Sonntagszeitung*, 18.09.2005, Nr. 37, p. 28. In einem Essay, der parallel zum Roman erscheint, hat er wortreich den

Wert des historischen Romans beschworen, sich gegen dessen Verächter im Vorfeld abgesichert. Er hat das Manuskript des Romans an den Gauß-Experten und Mathematikprofessor Taschner, "der war im letzten Jahr Naturwissenschaftler des Jahres," geschickt und auf sein Urteil so zitternd gewartet wie noch nie auf ein Prüfungsergebnis. Doch Taschner fand alles tadellos. An den Humboldt-Experten Enzensberger schickte er es. Auch der war sehr einverstanden. Und die größte Angst, sagt Kehlmann, habe er jetzt vor seiner bevorstehenden Lesung in Göttingen. Oh, nein, hat er der Lesungsorganisatorin vom Verlag gesagt: "Göttingen – muss das sein?" Ja, warum denn nicht? Weil dort die Gauß-Gesellschaft sitze, und die Herren verstünden keinen Spaß.

Communism, Immigration and the Necessity of Faith: Dimitré Dinev's *Engelszungen*

Helga Schreckenberger

Born in Plovdiv, Bulgaria, Dimitré Dinev (1968-) has been living in Austria since arriving as an asylum seeker in 1990. After being detained at the refugee camp of Traiskirchen for a short time, he was permitted to study philosophy and Russian philology at the University of Vienna. Only two years after his arrival in Austria, the young Bulgarian started publishing plays, film scripts, and short stories in German.[1] Dinev's work quickly attracted critical acclaim for both its literary quality and the fact that the author was not a native speaker of German. In 2000 his short story "Boshidar" was awarded first prize in the annual literature competition "schreiben zwischen den kulturen" ("Writing between Cultures").[2] In 2005 he received the prestigious Adelbert-von-Chamisso-Prize for his first novel, *Engelszungen* ("Angels' Tongues")*.*[3] This work cemented the author's reputation as a master storyteller who skillfully alternates between irony and pathos, the comic and the tragic, the fantastic and the realistic, thereby delighting his readers with his funny, tragic, and absurd stories.

Like many writers who choose to write in the language of their new country, Dinev's work challenges the concept of national literature by transcending literary and cultural boundaries. *Engelszungen* delves deeper into the themes of migration and alienation that Dinev had tackled in his collection of short stories *Die Inschrift* ("The Inscription") published in 2001. In addition, the work takes a critical and subversive look at the socio-political structure of Bulgaria of the last century and its toll on the country's average citizens. By exploring "the present of Europe from two sides"[4] Dinev demonstrates the great potential

of a writer who has transcended the borders between two languages and cultures.[5]
Spanning the beginning of the twentieth century to the end of 2001, *Engelszungen* relates the story of three generations of two Bulgarian families whose destiny is closely connected to that of their country. For the youngest generation, migration represents the last hope for a better life in face of the desperate political and economic situation that followed the collapse of the communist regime. However, the migrant experience brings its own sets of problems for the protagonists: loss of identity, illegality, exploitation, and economic hardship. Thus the novel's criticism is not limited to communist Bulgaria but also offers a critical view of immigration policies, the plight of migrant workers and the indifference of the host countries towards struggling immigrants. *Engelszungen* explores the damaging impact of two extreme political situations – dictatorship and migration – on individual identity, on language and communication, on family, and on relationships. However, the novel also celebrates the survival of the human spirit and its ability to keep faith in a world that is neither predictable nor just and leaves individuals at the mercy of forces they cannot influence or even understand.

Politics, language and identity

Engelszungen consists of two narrative strands, the stories of Svetljo Apostolov and Iskren Mladen, who at the beginning of the novel meet at Vienna's Central Cemetery in front of the grave of Miro, a Serbian criminal turned "angel of the immigrants." Through flashbacks, the narrator relates in alternating chapters Svetljo's and Iskren's family backgrounds, their growing up in communist Bulgaria, and their adventures in exile which ultimately lead to their meeting at Miro's grave. Dinev juxtaposes their stories to illustrate two representative ways of life under the communist regime, the privileged life of the family of a powerful party official (Iskren's family) and the average existence of that of a member of the citizen's militia (Svetljo's family). Moreover, telling the often overlapping and intersecting story of the families allows the narrator to draw attention to its complexity. The first part of the novel focuses on Svetljo's and Iskren's fathers as representatives of the communist regime. Iskren's father, Mladen Mladenov, has emerged as the most powerful man in Plovdiv due to his intelligence, careful strategy, and rhetorical abilities. Svetljo's father, Jordan Apostolov, who works for the people's militia is of rather limited intelligence. However, he is famous for his unfailing ability to obtain full confessions from politically suspect individuals.[6]

The novel demonstrates how both men are shaped (even deformed) by the communist regime through the way they use language. Jordan, whom the narrator characterizes as empty-headed, stubborn, and violent, derives his purpose in life from his blue militia uniform.[7] He has no language of his own but has internalized that of the party together with its ideologies and values as his reaction to party leader Shivkov's praise of the militia demonstrates:

> "A sword of steel for the proletarian dictatorship he called us," Jordan thought proudly. "A sword of steel that's what I want to be." He was still enthralled by the speech, by the power of the words. They were in his flesh (152).[8]

Because Jordan has no thoughts of his own, he is an easy prey for the propaganda of the communist regime. The regime also provides him the job as interrogator of politically suspect citizens at which he appears to be very gifted. Jordan uses the words of others to fill his intellectual and emotional emptiness. Unable to articulate his feelings when his pride suffers a severe blow over his wife's lack of virginity, Jordan appropriates the language of those he interrogates for the secret police:

> He was able to make anybody talk. Since he himself lacked the words, he easily got them out of others. He was concentrated, patient, stubborn, and took his work seriously, because he needed every word, because he secretly hoped

one day to also bring out those words that he could say to his wife (52).[9] Since forced police confessions prove useless for expressing true emotions, Jordan's efforts are in vain. He suppresses the love for his wife that could have helped him overcome the silence. However, as his pride is more important to him, Jordan is unable to find the appropriate words. He turns into the sword of steel that the regime wants him to be: "Only seldom, very seldom, did he say anything at home. His words there sounded like iron. They were cold, they were cutting, and they hurt" (53).[10] Jordan's lack of language marks him as a product of the communist regime which has given him a false sense of pride and an empty purpose in life, at least until its collapse.

As a major spokesperson of the regime, Mladen initially seems to be in control of language. His rhetorical ability is a considerable factor in his rise to the upper ranks of the communist regime as well as in his continued popularity He receives the highest praise even from the party leader Shivkov: "This man has an angel's tongue, I'm told by everyone who has heard you" (333).[11] Years later, after the fall of the regime, his son Iskren still hears his father's speeches praised: "A very gifted speaker he was. Even angels could become jealous. If we had had more people like him, communism would never have failed" (473).[12] However, his speeches owe their success mostly to his lover, the prostitute Isabella. Mladen practices his political speeches in front of Isabella, who edits them and substitutes meaningful phrases for the empty ones:

> Sometimes he even practiced his speeches at her place and seriously listened to her criticism. He acknowledged that words like Marxism and Leninism sounded very non-erotic and unemotional, however they were the very ones he could not completely eliminate or replace as was the case with some of the other words (113).[13]

Isabella's influence can be seen in the ideological content of Mladen's speeches. She renders them less dogmatic and thus more meaningful. When Mladen finds happiness and erotic fulfillment with Isabella, his speeches are "not only good, they are brilliant" (333).[14] They are seductive and thus effective, because their political messages are tempered by real emotions and true feelings. Moreover, Mladen's love for Isabella is subversive since prostitution is illegal under the communist regime. Consequently, her influence on the speeches, her attempt to make them more genuine and real for the audience, can also be seen as subversive. When the party officials require Mladen to give up Isabella, he and his speeches deteriorate: "From now on Mladen no longer visited Isabella, and his days turned grey, his speeches banal, his eyes cloudy, his organs sickly, and nobody claimed any longer that he possessed an angel's tongue" (337).[15] The regime's controlling interference deprives both Mladen's speeches and existence of vitality and meaning.

While Jordan and Mladen assume the language of the communist regime partly from conviction, partly from opportunism, Jordan's son, Svetljo, reacts with silence when confronted with the power of the regime. His first loss of language occurs when his father takes the toddler to listen to a speech by the party leader Todor Shivkov, who emphasizes the importance of the secret police in establishing an ideologically homogeneous, socialist society. Svetljo swallows his tongue, almost chokes and as a result falls silent for more than a year. This loss of voice can be read as reaction to the language of political propaganda.[16] Appropriately, he breaks his silence with an utterly subversive sentence that frightens every adult who hears it: "Comrade Shivkov poops from above and below" (160).[17] "Pooping from above" can be read as a reference to the quality of Shivkov's speech. The fear this child's sentence arouses in every adult who hears it underscores the potential danger of speech in a dictatorship.

The traumatic experiences during Svetljo's military service, the physical hardship, the cruelty of his commanders who attempt to shape him according to the regime's ideals also bring about a loss of language: "All the words, which he had once upon a time so easily had control over, had like his sock become interwoven with his flesh during those twenty-seven months. It hurt to tear them out, some more, some less" (511f.).[18] The experience in the army, the senseless and empty routines, render Svetljo unable and unwilling to talk.

Language fails to truly communicate the pain and humiliation Svetljo has experienced. This is underscored when he finds himself again unable to articulate his experience as an illegal immigrant in Austria:

> He had the feeling that he was lugging stones instead of words…They were hard, they were grey, and if he opened his mouth, they came rolling out and only strike one dead and crush and hurt. He was afraid to show her the poverty of his apartment and of his life. He did not even have a dream that he could tell her about (555).[19]

Exile and its humiliating hardship prove so alienating that there are no adequate words to describe it. Svetljo's life is reduced to survival and work. There is little else to talk about as Svetljo explains:

> If I didn't talk about my friends or simply about others, the last eleven years of my life would be reduced to these words. I would have had nothing to tell…Other than that I haven't experienced anything (598).[20]

In addition to inadequacy, the novel points to the unreliability of language. It can be co-opted and manipulated by political powers and used to seduce, manipulate and betray. It completely fails to communicate experiences of extreme distress as well as happiness.

"Engelszungen" (Angels' Tongues), the title of the novel, reflects a connection between language and politics but also points to the non-verbal language of love. In the novel, the tongue is essential for both. Mladen uses his "angel's tongue" for political persuasion as well as for sexual pleasure. Jordan's wife Marina finds greatest gratification through her lover's tongue. In view of Jordan's inability to speak to his wife, this is also a sign of her longing for communication. For Svetljo especially, meeting of his lover's tongue elicits pure happiness:

> A tongue entered his mouth, playing with his own. Now he had two tongues, and suddenly he felt that everything that was good in his life had doubled. Joy, love, luck (412).[21]

The tongue – so essential for speech – is equally important to communicate love and passion. Moreover, the tongue facilitates meaningful non-verbal communication. This is illustrated through Svetljo's relationship with the Austrian Nathalie to whom he cannot explain the alienating and undignified experience of exile. Their tongues, however, are able to create understanding and closeness where words fail. *Engelszungen* ends with the following sentences:

> Soon thereafter the tongues in his mouth became two, and that was good because no one had ever been able to speak with two tongues. Every word suffers, one's own and that of the other, each, that comes in between and tries to spoil the game of two souls which had become very close (598).[22]

Love is able to bridge the gap between Svetljo and the Viennese Nathalie despite the differences of nationality, background, and experience. Non-verbal communication substitutes for language that often proves inadequate and misleading.

How language can be corrupted and can come between people is demonstrated by Mladen and Jordan. Their identification with the communist regime and its language and ideologies shape their communication with their familes, especially their young sons. Mladen provides his son with all the privileges that come with his elevated status in the communist party: a big house where an entire floor is at his disposal, goods that are not available to the average citizen of Bulgaria, an education at elite schools, and money to buy anything his heart desires. Preoccupied with his career and party demands, Mladen fails to see

Iskren's need for his parents' genuine love and attention. Moreover, it is Mladen's inability to escape his political persona that causes a rift between him and his son. Instead of having real conversations with Iskren, Mladen remains the party official even in his own home and regales his son with the messianic visions of the communist party. However, Iskren's intelligence quickly seizes on the contradictions of his father's indoctrination:

> His grandmother loved most to talk about the past, his father about the future. She, who had personally experienced most of the things that she spoke of, admitted sometimes that she could be wrong; he, who hadn't even seen that which was supposed to come, was always sure of himself. This made Iskren very suspicious of his father (329f.).[23]

Comparing his father's unwaveringly self-assured assertion of the communist future with his grandmother's ability to admit to her fallibility brings to light the inflexibility and weakness of the communist regime's message. Iskren learns to mistrust authority, both his father's and the political regime's.

Jordan's inability to speak a language of his own also influences his relationship with his son Svetljo. Unable to articulate his love for his son, Jordan only communicates his expectations for Svetljo to live up to his and the communist regime's ideal of masculinity. Expecting a "kind word" ("ein gutes Wort") from his father, Svetljo learns is equal to expecting a "letter from a dead man" ("Brief von einem Toten").[24] This pronouncement underscores the hopelessness of a meaningful communication between father and son. Jordan's constant criticism and severe punishments of youthful transgressions cause Svetljo to abandon any desire to win his father's approval. As in the case of Mladen and Iskren, Jordan's inability to initiate a genuine line of communication with his son that goes beyond party doctrine is at the root of the estrangement between the generations.

However, it is not just the relationship between parents and children that breaks down in *Engelszungen* but traditional family structures in general. Both Svetljo and Iskren come from dysfunctional families. Their parents' marriages fail due to a lack of love and communication. As most of their friends also come from broken families, their experience represents the norm rather than the exception. In addition, both Jordan Apostolov and Mladen Mladenov have strained relationships with their extended families, who do not share their devotion to the communist party. Mladen's mother refuses to talk to him because of his compliance with the party ruling to avoid contact with his sister Rosa, who has emigrated to the United States. Mladen's and Jordan's identification with the communist regime isolates them from their families and leaves them with an empty, loveless existence as the narrator's summary of Mladen's situation indicates:

> [H]e was the moral advertisement for the party.
> And this "moral advertisement" had a wife in an insane asylum, a son who grew more and more distant, a brother to whom he had nothing to say, a sister whom he had renounced, a father-in-law who was involved in illegal trade and threatened to kill him, and he had not laughed since the day he was no longer allowed to knock on the door with Isabella's nameplate (366f.).[25]

As Mladen is portrayed as the ideal representative of the communist regime who lives his life according to party rule, the dysfunction of his family and by extension of Bulgaria's family structure in general is linked to the communist regime. Dinev draws a parallel between Mladen's private failure and the political failure of the communist regime.

> Thus spoke comrade Mladenov, a man who had wanted to build communism but who instead had built a three-story house. And what he told himself frightened him, for wasn't communism like a house and who would guarantee that when it was completed one day it wouldn't be just as empty and a person as lonely as Mladen felt in his house (366).[26]

Mladen's three-story house is a symbol of his success, which is the result of his careful planning to achieve power and his willingness to compromise to stay in power. However, his house and his success turn out to be an empty shell that has nothing to offer to its owner. Equating Mladen's house with communism, Dinev suggests a similar failure of the communist regime.

Exile, Memory, and Identity

While their fathers derive their identity from the communist regime, Svetljo's and Iskren's existence is shaped by exile. At first, this has a positive meaning for both as they attempt to escape the legacy of that regime and thus, that of their fathers. Emigration means a break with the past and a beginning of a new life.[27]

Iskren, who has led a restless, driven life before leaving Bulgaria, seems to be made for life in exile, which Edward Said describes as follows: "Exile is never the state of being satisfied, placid or secure…Exile is life led outside habitual order. It is nomadic, decentered, contrapuntal; but no sooner does one get accustomed to it than its unsettling force erupts anew."[28] Financially secure and in possession of the necessary, if forged papers, Iskren flies from one country to another, starting one new life after another: "He loved them, these clouds, because nowhere in the world, except above them was it so easy to start a new life" (484).[29] Iskren's frequent changes of identity serve to cover up his illegal business transactions. Because he is able to purchase the right papers, he does not suffer the anxiety and insecurity of other illegal immigrants. As Iskren knows, it is not the individual but the papers that count in the eye of the law:

> But who in the world was interested in the hearts of the people. Before the law, papers are much more important. It is not what kind of heart you have that matters but what kind of passport. Iskren had the right one and his heart was beating as securely as only hearts of people could beat

who do not need a visa for most of the places in the world (488).[30]

Dinev points to the misplaced priorities of immigration laws that value papers and documents over the individual. Papers can be falsified and tell nothing about the merit or circumstances of the person carrying them. The criminal Iskren is safe, while Svetljo, who tries to make an honest living, is persecuted by the law because he does not possess the correct documents.

However, Iskren's multiple identities catch up with him. When one of his illegal schemes blows up in Vienna and he finds himself without money on the run from the police, he collapses under the burden of his fragmented, nomadic existence:

> His life had splintered into little pieces; he did not have the strength to collect them. He was tired. All of a sudden he felt the entire fatigue of three lives inside him. He was not able to walk anymore. He went into a public toilet, locked himself into a stall and began to cry over one after the other (506).[31]

Iskren, whose restlessness made him so adept for life in exile, can no longer bear its instability. His situation thus echoes Said's characterization of life in exile as described above.

Svetljo's experiences as immigrant are similarly unsettling. His immigration to Austria happens illegally via Czechoslovakia. From the refugee camp Traiskirchen, he fights for the right to stay and work in the country legally. Unable to do so, he enters the insecure, nerve-wracking existence of an illegal alien. Svetljo's experiences demonstrate the marginalization of the immigrants by a legal system indifferent to their plight. The greater the need of the immigrants, the stricter the legal system becomes to keep them from integrating in their host countries. Every time Svetljo believes he has secured a way of making a living, another legal obstacle arises. The narrator comments ironically:

> Unfortunately it was a fact that you could not rely on the laws of this world very long. Year after year they got harder for all those who had be-

lieved that they could move like birds from one
country to the next to save themselves from hunger and danger. Work that was supposed to be
an obligation and a right for all...suddenly had
become a crime...The officials had strained their
heads and had added an eleventh commandment especially for immigrants: "Thou shall not
work without papers," it stated (551f.).[32]

The real need of the immigrants to save themselves from hunger
or danger is thwarted by an arbitrary law that denies them the
only means for survival, their ability to work. In the end, Svetljo
finds his life reduced to the single purpose of finding work:

But his only goal for the past eleven years had
always been the same: to find work. And what
would come after that went beyond his imagination...Hardly had he moved forward a bit, he
was sent back to the beginning. Thus work had
become life's meaning and the search for it a
way of being (573f.).[33]

Work as his sole purpose in life and the constant insecurity of his
illegality diminish Svetljo's sense of self.

Dinev demonstrates the instability of identity in exile by
Svetjo's agreement to being adopted by his employer, the shoemaker Mosche Abramitsch Unreich from Usbekistan, who was
able to gain asylum in Austria in the late seventies (before the
fall of communism). The adoption is Svetljo's last hope to obtain
legal status in Austria, however, it means severing his ties with
his family in Bulgaria. But Mosche's untimely death removes
this option. More importantly, it leaves him without work and
thus, without hope for survival. Said's reference to the constantly
erupting unsettling forces of exile also applies to Svetljo's situation. He is at the mercy of arbitrary and unpredictable powers, be
it the ever changing immigration laws or fate. Both interfere with
his attempts to establish himself, to gain a new identity.

For both Iskren and Svetljo, reconnecting with the past is
a way to regain their sense of self. The memory of his grand-

mother and a lullaby she sang for him allows Iskren to reconstruct his fragmented self:
> Like bats, his thoughts constantly changed direction, and it was difficult for him to follow any one of them. Only after they flew by his grandmother Sdravka a few times, did they calm down a little and submit to Iskren's will. He now thought about Sdravka and remembered that when he was little and could or would not fall asleep, she had always sung a lullaby that never failed to work. No, he had not forgotten the words of the song. One after the other they came to him, they came slowly like fish in the winter and it took him awhile until he had caught them and arranged them in the right order (590).[34]

Remembering his grandmother, whom he associates with love and security, allows Iskren to calm down and reassemble his life. The last image the reader has of him is of him peacefully asleep on a boat bound for Hungary and thus for a new life.

Similarly, Svetlo finds a way into the future by reconnecting with the past:
> Svetljo spent the next day by alternately thinking about his past and about Nathalie. And just as he saw the past not as a whole but distributed over different images and stories, so it happened that he could only recall certain body parts of Nathalie or only certain ones of her words (597).[35]

Like Iskren, the memories of the past come in bits and pieces and need to be reassembled. However, the disjointed images and stories of the past enable Svetljo to face a future that is similarly dissembled.

By remembering their grandparents, Iskren and Mladen connect to a pre-communist generation and, consequently, a pre-communist past. This is where the novel locates tradition and memories that will endure even the destructive forces of the communist regime. Not the parents but the grandparents' generation is able to connect with the children who grew up under Bulgaria's communism. Both Iskren and Svetljo continuously turned to their grandparents for support and guidance. As Martin Hielscher points out in his article, "Andere Stimmen – andere Räume," ("Different Voices – Different Spaces"), the political marginalization of the members of the older generation allows them to impart values that the communist regime does not deem important any longer but which provide them with the means to survive in a hostile, disorienting world: love, hope, words and songs.[36] Moreover, the influence of the pre-communist generation on their grandchildren underscores the transient nature of political movements and the lasting power of love and hope.

Another protagonist whose identity is shaped by exile and migration is Miro, the Serbian criminal turned "angel of the immigrants." He is, in fact, the quintessential exile. Born to a single mother in prison, he grows up in orphanages. Not knowing a home or family leaves Miro vulnerable and unprotected. From early on, he leads the nomadic life of one who never belongs: "Wherever I go, I am at home. Wherever I arrive, I am a guest" (10).[37] Like Iskren and Svetljo, Miro has come to Vienna as a migrant worker. He soon achieves financial success establishing an empire that stretches beyond the borders of Austria into Eastern Europe. A ruthless business man whose criminal activities include sex-trafficking of women from the former communist countries, Miro remains restless even after establishing himself in Vienna. Asked about Vienna, he replies: "Just a city for grandfathers. I have to visit the Balkans continuously in order not to fall asleep" (469).[38] Even after his death, Miro remains an exile "You could not ask Angels for their papers or examine their passport photos suspiciously and compare it with their appearance" (584).[39] Only death has put Miro beyond the power of the law that treats immigrants with distrust and suspicion.

Like Iskren and Svetljo, Miro is not immune to the destabilizing forces of exile. His life is uprooted after he believes himself cursed.[40] As a result, Miro takes on a new identity. He becomes the angel of the immigrants, using his money and influence to help illegal immigrants and refugees by obtaining the necessary working and residency permits for them. The eternal exile Miro is a utopian figure even before his death turns him into a mythical figure. Miro's conversion from a hardened criminal to a selfless promoter of immigrants is as believable as a change in immigration laws. Yet either one would be needed to relieve the plight and hardship of the many illegal migrants who come to the West in search of a better, safer, and more dignified life. Miro's significance is underscored by his burial in "one of the most prominent alleys" of the Viennese Central Cemetery, "surrounded by artists, officers and high officials, by people who silently but more reliable than any textbook reflected the Austrian history" (8).[41] By ranking Miro among these prominent witnesses to Austrian history, the novel bestows honors on the Serbian exile. His place recalls the history and plight of immigrants and refugees who are not aided by the state of Austria but by a fellow immigrant. Thus, Miro's statue commemorates compasssion, hope, and faith.

Communicating with the Dead
    Superstition constitutes a dominant theme of *Engelszungen*. The people of Bulgaria, especially the older generation and the women are characterized by their continued belief in an afterlife, in old superstitions, and in miracle healers. They keep in constant contact with the dead. Iskren's grandmother regularly visits the cemetery where she shares her joy and disappointment with her deceased husband and daughters. Iskren's mother consults a miracle healer to be cured from her mental illness. Svetljo's mother has him secretly baptized to "assure him a place in heaven." His grandfather puts Svetljo's umbilical cord in a medical book to assure his grandson's choice of the right profession. When Svetljo loses his voice at Todor Shivkov's rally, his mother takes him to a miracle healer who promises his complete recovery. When the wife of Mladen's brother Ivan fails to get pregnant, she consults a miracle healer, who correctly predicts

the birth of a child. Another miracle healer frees the house of Svetljo's great-grandfather of his ghost.[42]

This belief in the supernatural or in a transcendent power that can be appealed to for assistance allows citizens to circumvent the prohibition of the country's religious institutions. Mladen's sister Rosa notices the disappearance of synagogues, mosques and churches from the city during her visit of her former hometown:

> They wanted to build communism for which they only needed their hands and their mind but no God. In order that the strength of their hands and their mind would not weaken, they needed bread and that they got. The manna which once had fallen from heaven was now planned and produced in a socialist manner. Everything that God had once taken care of, the party was now taking care of, and for all the bad things that happened in the world not he was held responsible any longer but imperialism and monopoly (265).[43]

The communist regime has set itself up in God's place. But the cold rationality of social realism is not able to take care of the emotional or spiritual needs of the population. The population's continued belief in miracles and miracle healers is thus an expression of its subversive disregard of the regime's will. Moreover, it is a sign of their disillusionment with political ideologies and institutions:

> Was there something in this world in which they could trust? A law, a system, a promise, an ideology, a power, a word?...Where logic fails and no longer offers any support, there was no other choice but to believe in miracles (521).[44]

The belief in miracles offers more hope than the promises and assurances of an unreliable, unpredictable, and arbitrary political power. However, the novel does not attempt, as Hielscher rightly maintains, to argue for the superiority of religion over commun-

ist doctrine. The "miracles" can never truly be attributed to the divine or the supernatural. Rather, the protagonists' belief in a higher power assists them in their fight against the trials and disappointments of their life. According to Hielscher:
> The Christian, Jewish or occult faith stands for a collective, traditional system of values, a system of rituals, rules, tales, but also for the comfort, that you are protected, that someone stands guard over you.[45]

The comfort provided by the belief in a higher power is demonstrated by the story of Miro, who after his death is rumored to have turned into an angel still helping those who come to him in need. Miro's wish to be buried with his cell phone which constantly rang with pleas for help by immigrants seems to have anticipated this communication beyond death. Even his gravestone depicts him as an angel holding a cell phone: "Miro stood before them with his cell phone and his two wings and waited. His cell phone did not ring any longer, but he heard them" (11).[46] Communicating with Miro, telling him of their problems has real benefits for the immigrants and refugees who make the pilgrimage to his grave:
> It could be observed how again and again people from different nations came to his grave, remained there for a while and put their uncertain shadows on top of his grave stone. Then they gathered them up again, put flowers there instead and left. Their shadows appeared much stronger and more compact, their faces much brighter (11).[47]

Believing in Miro's ability to listen to their problems and to help them even after his death provides the visitors with hope and more confidence to master their difficulties. This appears the only way to cope with the uncertainties of life as an immigrant:
> Believing and laughing, that is all that a person has in the end...Believing and laughing, what else can a person do against the engulfing de-

spair than to use these two old, often proven weapons, one after the other or both together" (584).[48]

Believing in help from beyond the grave might be laughable but both laughter and hope against all odds remain the only options for immigrants and refugees who have nothing left to lose. In this way the novel attempts to solicit just this response from its readers. It asks them to believe in the possibility of the redemptive power of compassion that will turn a criminal into an angel. At the same time, the irony and humorous depiction of the novel's protagonists and their tribulations also provokes laughter. Irony and humor are the literary means of criticism and subversion. Dinev uses them against a world whose rules seem unpredictable and arbitrary especially for those without power. Yet humans created the world and they hold the power to change as the narrator's apparent assertion of the unchangeableness of both the world and its human inhabitants actually ironically implies:

> That's how it has always been in this world, and in order to change this, a new world or at least a new human being should be created. But who could do that? You can create new documents, new money, new laws and duties und regulations, new borders and immigrations laws, new machines and new activities, new countries, new ideals, new nations, even new needs, but no new humans (583).[49]

On the one hand, the narrator points to the uniqueness of the human spirit and its ability to keep faith in a hostile and merciless world. On the other hand, the quotation makes clear that this world and its abominations are the creation of mankind. The novel challenges the reader to change the world in a way that renders the belief in miracles obsolete.

Endnotes

---

[1]Dimitré Dinev received his secondary schooling in the German

speaking *Bertolt-Brecht-Gymnasium* Pasardshik. He started writing at an early age and had published works already in both Russian and Bulgarian in 1986.

[2] The competition "schreiben zwischen den kulturen" is sponsored by the "verein exil," which, under the direction of Christa Stippinger, explicitly promotes literature by immigrant writers. Dinev also received awards for his short stories *Ein Licht über dem Kopf* ("A Light Above the Head").

[3] Like "schreiben zwischen den kulturen," the Germany-based Adelbert-von-Chamisso-Prize also honors the work of writers who grew up in a different culture with a different language but choose to write in German. Other (well-known) recipients include Rafik Schami (1985), Emine Sevgi Özdamar (1999), Terézia Mora, Ilija Trojanow and Feridun Zaimoğlu.

[4] See Peter Stuiber, West-östlicher Dinev," in *Die Presse* (Schaufenster), Septermber 19, 2003.

[5] See Hannes Schweiger, "Entgrenzungen. Der bulgarisch-österreichische Autor Dimitré Dinev im Kontext der MigrantInnenliteratur" in: *Trans Intenet-Zeitschrift für Kulturwissenschaften* 15/3 (2004) (http://www.inst.at/trans/15Nr/03_1/schweiger15.htm)

[6] Unbeknownst to Svetljo and Iskren, their family stories intertwine because of a chance meeting of their fathers at the entrance to the hospital where their wives are about to give birth. Mladen's daughter is born dead, and he blames the brash militiaman who delayed him from entering the hospital. Mladen demands Jordan's dismissal from the militia. Although saved by his superior who does not want to lose his able interrogator, Jordan can no longer wear his uniform, his main source of identity and pride. Destroying Mladen then becomes Jordan's new purpose in life.

[7] See Dimetré Dinev, *Engelszungen*. München: btb, 2006. All quotations from the novel refer to this edition and will be cited in the text.

[8] "'Ein Stahlschwert der proletarischen Dikatur hat er uns genannt,' dachte Jordan stolz. 'Ein Stahlschwert, das will ich

sein.'" Er war immer noch von der Rede, von der Macht der Worte gefangen. Sie waren in seinem Fleisch." All translations into English are mine. My sincere thanks to Jacqueline Vansant, not only for proofing the manuscript and the translations, but also for her valuable feedback.

[9]"Er konnte jeden zum Reden bringen. Da ihm selber die Worte fehlten, holte er sie leicht aus den anderen heraus. Er war konzentriert, geduldig, hartnäckig und nahm die Arbeit sehr ernst, weil er jedes Wort brauchte, weil er insgeheim hoffte, eines Tages auch jene Worte herauszubekommen, die er seiner Frau sagen konnte."

[10]"Nur selten, sehr selten, sagte er etwas zu Hause. Eisern klangen dort seine Worte. Kalt waren sie, schneidend waren sie, sie taten weh."

[11]"Dieser Mann hat eine Engelszunge, erzählt mir jeder, der sie gehört hat."

[12]"Ein sehr begabter Redner war er. Sogar Engel könnten neidisch werden. Hätten wir mehr solche Leute wie ihn gehabt, wäre der Kommunismus nie gescheitert."

[13]"Er übte sogar manchmal seine Reden bei ihr und hörte sich ernst ihre Kritikpunkte an. Er nahm zur Kenntnis, daß Worte wie Marxismus und Leninismus sehr unerotisch und emotionslos klangen, aber gerade die konnte er nicht ganz wegstreichen oder einen Ersatz dafür finden, wie es bei manch anderen der Fall war."

[14]"nicht nur gut, sie waren glänzend."

[15]"Ab nun besuchte Mladen Isabella nicht mehr, und seine Tage wurden grau, seine Reden banal, seine Augen trüb, seine Organe kränklich, und niemand behauptete mehr, daß er eine Engelszunge hätte."

[16]See also Hannes Schweiger, "Entgrenzungen. Der bulgarisch-österreichische Autor Dimitré Dinev im Kontext der MigrantInnenliteratur" (note 5).

[17]"Der Genosse Shivkov kackt von oben und von unten."

[18]"Alle Worte über die er einst so locker verfügt hatte, hatten sich in diesen 27 Monaten ähnlich der Socken mit seinem Fleisch verwebt. Es tat weh, sie herauszureißen, bei manchen weniger, bei manchen mehr..."
[19]"Er hatte das Gefühl, daß er statt Worte Steine mit sich schleppte...Hart waren sie, grau waren sie, und würde er seinen Mund aufmachen, würden sie hinausrollen und nur erschlagen und drücken und wehtun. Er hatte Angst, ihr die Armut seiner Wohnung und seines Lebens zu zeigen. Nicht einmal einen Traum hatte er, von dem er ihr erzählen hätte können."
[20]"Würde ich nicht von meinen Freunden oder einfach von den anderen erzählen, würden sich die letzten elf Jahre meines Lebens nur auf diese Worte beschränken. Ich hätte nichts zu berichten gehabt... Ich hab sonst nichts erlebt."
[21]"Eine Zunge drang in seinen Mund, spielte mit seiner. Zwei Zungen hatte er jetzt, und plötzlich hatte er das Gefühl, daß sich das Gute in seinem Leben verdoppelt hatte. Die Freude, die Liebe, das Glück."
[22]"Gleich darauf wurden die Zungen in seinem Mund zwei, und es war gut so, denn mit zwei Zungen hatte noch nie ein Mensch sprechen können. Jedes Wort leidet darunter, das eigene wie das fremde, jedes, das dazwischen gerät und das Spiel zu verderben sucht, zweier einander sehr nahe gekommmener Seelen."
[23]"Seine Großmutter sprach am liebsten von der Vergangenheit, sein Vater von der Zukunft. Sie, die die Sachen, worüber sie erzählte, meist selbst erlebt hatte, gab manchmal zu, daß sie sich täuschen könnte, er, der das, was kommen sollte, nicht einmal gesehen hatte, war sich immer sicher. Das machte Iskren sehr mißtrauisch seinem Vater gegenüber."
[24]Dinev, *Engelszungen*, p. 286.
[25]"er war das moralische Aushängeschild der Partei. Und dieses moralische Aushängeschild hatte eine Frau, die im Irrenhaus saß, einen Sohn, der ihm immer fremder wurde, einen Bruder, dem er nichts zu sagen hatte, eine Schwester, von der er sich losgesagt hatte, einen Schwiegervater, der illegalen Handel betrieb und der

ihn mit dem Tode bedrohte, und hatte seit dem Tag, an dem er nicht mehr an die Tür mit Isabellas Namenschild klopfen durfte, nicht mehr gelacht."
[26]"So sprach der Genosse Mladenov, ein Mensch, der den Kommunismus bauen wollte und stattdessen ein dreistöckiges Haus gebaut hatte.und was er sich sagte, machte ihm angst, denn war der Kommuismus nicht ähnlich einem Hause, und wer gab einem die Garantie, daβ er, wenn er eines Tages fertig sein würde, nicht auch so leer stehen und der Mensch sich darin genauso einsamvorkommen würed wie Mladen in seinem Haus."
[27] Dinev explores this meaning of exile in his short story "Lazarus." An illegal immigrant crosses the border as a dead man in a coffin. He is "reborn" in exile.
[28] Edward W. Said, "Reflections on Exile," in: *Reflections on Exile and Other Literary and Cultural Essays*. Cambridge, Mass.: Harvard University Press, 2000, pp. 173-186, here: 186
[29]"Er liebte sie, diese Wolken, denn nirgendwo auf der Welt, außer über ihnen,war es leichter, ein neues Leben anzufangen."
[30]"Aber wen in der Welt interessierten schon die Herzen der Menschen. Vor dem Gesetz sind die Papiere viel wichtiger. Es ist egal, was für ein Herz du hast, aber nicht, was für einen Paβ. Iskren hatte den richtigen, und sein Herz pochte so ruhig, wie nur Herzen von Menschen, die kein Visum für die meisten Orte der Welt brauchten, pochen konnten."
[31]"Sein Leben war in kleine Stücke zersplittert, er hatte keine Kraft, sie zu sammeln. Müde war er. Die ganze Müdigkeit dreier Existenzen spürte er plötzlich in sich. Er konnte nicht mehr gehen. Er ging in eine öffentliche Toilette, sperrte sich in eine Kabine ein und begann, sie eine nach der anderen zu beweinen."
[32]"Leider war es aber so, daβ man sich auf die Gesetze dieser Welt nicht sehr lange verlassen konnte. Sie wurden von Jahr zu Jahr strenger zu allen, die angenommen hatten, sie könnten wie die Vögel von einem Land ins nächste ziehen, um sich von Hunger und Gefahren zu retten. Die Arbeit, die eine Pflicht und ein Recht für jeden sein sollte…war plötzlich ein Verbrechen

geworden…Die Köpfe der Beamten hatten sich angestrengt und extra für alle Zuwanderer ein elftes Gebot hinzugefügt: 'Du sollst nicht ohne Papiere arbeiten,' lautete dieses."
[33]"Aber sein einziges Ziel war seit elf Jahren immer das gleiche, eine Arbeit finden. Und was danach kommen sollte, überstieg seine Vorstellungskraft…Kaum schritt er ein bißchen vorwärts, wurde er an den Anfang geschickt. So war die Arbeit zu Sinn und aus der Suche nach ihr eine Seinsweise geworden."
[34] "Seine Gedanken änderten wie Fledermäuse ständig ihren Weg, und ihm war es schwierig, einem von ihnen zu folgen. Erst als sie einige Male an seiner Großmutter Sdravka vorbeiflatterten, beruhigten sie sich ein wenig und unterwarfen sich Iskrens Willen. Nun dachte er an Sdravka und erinnerte sich, daß sie ihm, als er noch klein war und nicht einschlafen konnte oder wollte, immer ein Wiegenlied gesungen hatte, das seine Wirkung nie verfehlte. Nein, er hatte die Worte des Liedes nicht vergessen. Eins nach dem anderen kamen sie jetzt, langsam kamen sie wie Fische im Winter, und er brauchte eine Weile bis er sie alle geangelt und richtig nebeneinander gereiht hatte."
[35]"Den nächsten Tag verbrachte Svetljo, in dem er abwechselnd an seine Vergangenheit und an Nathalie dachte. Und so wie er die Vergangenheit nicht als Ganzes, sondern in verschiedenen Bildern und Geschichten verteilt betrachtete, so geschah auch, daß er nur bestimmte Körperteile von Nathalie oder einzelne ihrer Worte in seinem Gedächtnis hervorrufen konnte."
[36]See Martin Hielscher, "Andere Stimmen – andere Räume. Die Funktion der Migrantenliteratur in deutschen Verlagen und Dimitré Dinevs Roman 'Engelszungen'" in Heinz Ludwig Arnold, ed.: *Literatur und Migration*. Text+Kritik Sonderband IX/06. München: text + kritik, 2006, pp. 196-208, here: p. 202.
[37]"Egal, wo ich hingehe, bin ich zuhaus. Egal, wo ich ankomme, bin ich ein Gast."
[38]"Eine Stadt für Großväter eben. Ich muß immer wieder den Balkan besuchen, um nicht einzuschlafen."

[39] "Engel konnte man nicht nach ihren Papieren fragen oder ihre Paßfotos und Visa mißtrauisch ausmustern und mit ihren Erscheinungen vergleichen."

[40] Miro's redemption is brought about by the many coincidences that characterize *Engelszungen*. He believes himself cursed by Radost, Svetljo's and Iskren's former lover. The miracle healer from whom he seeks help turns out to be Jordan who himself changed his life after witnessing the incredible poverty of Ishmail's family. Jordan tells Miro that is not he who helps the people but that it is their own kindness.

[41] "Umgeben von Künstlern, Offizieren und hohen Beamten, von Leuten, die die österreichische Geschichte stumm, doch verläßlicher als jedes Lehrbuch widerspiegelten, [ruhte Miro]."

[42] The various scenes with miracle healers led some reviewers to rank Dinev's novel in the tradition of the literary magic realism. However, there is no evidence of the fantastic occurring in the novel. Neither Svetljo's recovery nor Isken's aunt's pregnancy which happen years after the consultation can be called miracles. The help that immigrants receive from their visits to Miro's grave can also not be termed a miracle as they just find renewed hope and strength there.

[43] "Sie wollten den Kommunismus bauen, dafür brauchten sie nur ihre Hände und ihren Verstand, aber keinen Gott. Damit die Kraft ihrer Hände und ihres Verstandes nicht nachgab, brauchten sie Brot, und das bekamen sie. Das Manna, das einmal vom Himmel gefallen war, wurde jetzt sozialistisch geplant und produziert. Um alles, worum sich früher Gott gekümmert hatte, kümmerte sich jetzt die Partei., und für alles Schlimme, was in der Welt geschah, machte man nicht mehr ihn, sondern den Imperialismus und Monopolismus verantwortlich."

[44] "Gab es denn noch etwas in dieser Welt, worauf sie vertrauen konnten? Ein Gesetz, ein System, ein Versprechen, eine Ideologie, eine Macht, ein Wort?...Dort, wo die Logik versagt und keinen Halt mehr gibt, bleibt einem sowieso nichts anderes übrig, als auf ein Wunder zu hoffen."

[45]Hielscher, "Andere Stimmen," 202. ("Der christliche, jüdische oder okkulte Glaube steht hier für ein kollektives, tradiertes Wertesystem, ein System von Ritualen, Regeln, Geschichten, aber auch für den Trost, dass man behütet wird, dass jemand über einem wacht.")
[46]"Miro stand vor ihnen mit seinem Handy und seinen zwei Flügeln und wartete. Sein Handy läutete nicht mehr, aber er erhörte sie."
[47]"Man konnte beobachten, wie Menschen verschiedener Völker immer wieder an sein Grab kamen, eine Weile vor ihm stehenblieben und ihre unsicheren Schatten auf den Grabstein legten. Dannach nahmen sie sie wieder mit, legten statt dessen Blumen darauf und gingen. Ihre Schatten schienen viel fester und dichter geworden zu sein, ihre Gesichter viel heller."
[48]"Glauben und lachen, das bleibt letztendlich dem Menschen... Glauben und lachen, was vermag sonst der Mensch gegen die auf ihn zuströmende Verzweiflung tun, außer diese zwei alten oft bewährten Waffen anzuwenden, eine nach der anderen oder beide zusammen."
[49]"Neue Papiere konnte man erschaffen, neues Geld, neue Gesetze und Pflichten und Regelungen, neue Grenzen und Einreisebestimmungen, neue Machinen, neue Tätigkeiten, neue Waffen, neue Länder, neue Ideale, neue Nationen, sogar neue Bedürfnisse, aber keine neuen Menschen."

The Feminist Anti-Quest
in Marlene Streeruwitz's *Entfernung*.

Raymond L. Burt

In the late 1990s Marlene Streeruwitz (1950-), the highly successful Austrian dramatist, ceased writing plays and turned to novels as a new form for her artistic expression. From the outset Streeruwitz's approach in narrative and prose was highly experimental and rejected a focus on plot and action. Indeed her theoretical poetics dogmatically call for the rejection of a patriarchal narrative form and for the development of a radically different writing style – one which can express the experiences and perspectives of women. To this end, her novels are often a transformation of traditional genre styles, placing in their middle a female character who is engulfed in a quagmire of day-to-day experiences, while struggling internally and externally with self-actualization.

In 1996 she published her first novel, *Verführungen*. (*Seductions*.),[1] followed in rapid succession over the next decade by Lisa's Liebe ("Lisa's Love."), *Nachwelt*. ("Posterity."), *Majakowskiring*. ("Majakowski Ring."), *Partygirl*., *Norma Desmond*., *Jessica, 30.*, and *Entfernung*. ("Distance.").[2] All her titles are generally one word followed by a period. Streeruwitz's theoretical writings indicate that the 'period' is a marker for silence, and indeed, she refers to the period as a "strangulation mark" (*Würgemal*) which can serve as an artistic means of expressing the inexpressable.[3] Thus the period is a pointer to that which is suppressed. That which is suppressed, according to Streeruwitz, is the feminine narrative voice.

Streeruwitz's poetics are strongly based in feminist theories in which dominant social forces and institutions are identified as the patriarchy – a system which throughout history has suppressed, devalued, exploited, and subjugated women. In this view, the economic system, the political system, the church, the educational system, and popular culture, are all manifestations of the patriarchy. What is unusual in her feminist perspective is the psychological basis upon which the patriarchy is founded. In an almost Freudian discourse, Streeruwitz states that the foundation lies in the relationship of the mother and her child – a relationship characterized by hatred. The child hates the mother since she restricts its freedom, and the mother's hatred is based on the lack of freedom that pregnancy and early motherhood forces upon her. Both parties suppress these feelings. The strong feelings against one's children cannot be put into words and have to remain unexpressed. "There is no language which makes the realm of motherhood expressible."[4] The patriarchy needs this speechless mother, who is left to her fate to be an obedient reproductive organ.

In the realm of literature, Streeruwitz identifies the dominant literary forms and genres as distinctively masculine, and as designed to uphold the patriarchy. She distills the essence of the narrative strategies in the nature of its perspective (*Blick*). In contrast to the two dominant perspectives: the "View towards God" (*Blick zu Gott*) and "God's View" (*Gottes Blick.*),[5] Streeruwitz posits the feminine perspective as the "View Within" (*Blick auf sich*) – the inward-focused, individual-oriented perspective. What is interesting is that Streeruwitz does not follow the strands of feminist thought that move toward the individualistic and relativistic thinking of the post-modern. Instead she implies the existence of a hidden 'truth' – a truth unable to be uttered. Language and literary forms – constructions serving the patriarchy – do not have access to this truth. Instead silence, broken sentences, pauses, and periods point to the unspoken reality beneath the surface.

Katharine Döbler, drawing from Streeruwitz's Tübingen lectures, stated that the apparent simplicity in novels like *Verführungen*. was a narrative strategy aimed at demonstrating the "lack of a feminine voice" (*weibliche Sprachlosigkeit*). Women are devalued and have accepted the devalued image of society.

The writer's task is thus to counteract this society-driven image and to construct a positive feminine self-image and self-appreciation. Taking the lead from Streeruwitz herself, Döbler likens this process to a form of enlightenment. She even reformulates the famous Kantian definition[6] to reflect this mission: "Emergence of woman from the immaturity imposed upon her by the patriarchy and herself as accomplice."[7] Images of the Enlightenment can be found in her Frankfurt lectures on poetics: "I always support the complete illumination of all aspects of life, in contrast to the obfuscation which the patriarchal power always disseminates."[8] This statement evokes one of the symbols of the Enlightenment: the sun breaking through the clouds, but here it is driving out the darkness, not of superstition, but of the patriarchal power.

However, it is not Kant but another reformer that comes to mind in looking at the author's view of society and the role of literature in changing that society, namely Bertolt Brecht.[9] In fact, her view of the pervasive and dominant patriarchy, and the belief that every cultural manifestation serves to maintain the control of those in power, parallels Brecht's view of capitalism. The patriarchy, while decidedly a form of male dominance, has an economic basis. "The question, who is allowed to take part in the feast, was throughout the ages the reason for all conflicts."[10] She states that the basis of the patriarchy rests on money. Women throughout the ages were the subjects, not only of economic exploitation, but also physical and psychological exploitation. Like Brecht, Streeruwitz has aspirations of changing the world through literature. Unlike Brecht, however, she has moved away from theater, with its many communal voices and inputs, to gain more direct contact with her readers. No artistic directors and stage interpretations should come between the author and the reader. She postulates the possibility of an almost psychic connection between author and reader: "The question is about how the text can communicate the mindset of the writers and nevertheless be understood."[11]

Even though Streeruwitz is attempting to express that for which there is no language, she is relying on bridging the gap between reader and author by means of a common set of experiences. This she does through a type of alienation effect (*Verfremdungseffekt*). One method promoted by Brecht to achieve this effect was to have the actors break the illusion by not letting the audience forget that they are seeing actors. The Brechtian actor should show his opinion of the character he is playing in the recitation of the lines. Like Brecht, Streeruwitz wants her work to manifest the views of the author, but to do so by having the reader come to the same conclusions, not by argument or lecture, but by making evident the inherent, but generally invisible, injustices of the capitalist/patriarchal system.

All of her novels are attempts to explore the possibilities of that voice by using narrative styles to awaken self-reflection. In *Verführungen.*, *Nachwelt.*, and *Entfernung.*, the period is the favored form of punctuation, replacing question marks and foregoing quotation marks in dialogue. As she states in her poetics:

> The complete sentence is a lie. To those alienated only fragmentation can be the attempt at expression…With a period the complete sentence can be prevented. The period ends the attempt. Sentences should not be formed.[12]

This theoretical basis explains the fact that many of her novels are written in short sentences, often fragments or mere words. This use of sentence fragments has evolved and become more highly sophisticated in her novels. In her first novel *Verführungen.* this "staccato style," as Streeruwitz herself labeled it, reflected the "hectic pace of the protagonist's life"[13] as well as demonstrating the monotony of her daily life in almost checklist fashion. Perhaps in accord with her "poetics of banality" (*Poetik des Banalen*), Streeruwitz adds word lists in the form of laundry lists, book titles, and contents of a purse. Streeruwitz describes her fragmented narrative style as a conscious attempt to show the fragmented nature of experience – a form of mimesis: As she stated in an interview: "Language must not flaunt a unity, a comprehensive interconnection which doesn't exist."[14]

There is a different sense altogether in *Nachwelt*. No longer does the Streeruwitzian staccato prose focus on the familiar, the everyday, and the mundane. The sentence fragments document both her internal monologue and the moment-by-moment perception of her movement, not through familiar Vienna, but through the alien environment of Los Angeles. The narrative emulates the visual effect of a film. The sentence fragments simulate the single frames of a filmstrip. Viewed in quick succession, these fragments form a narrative. In this regard the dates dividing the chapters function as intertitles of a documentary film.

In *Entfernung*. Streeruwitz continues the familiar use of sentence fragments, stream-of-consciousness, and the neo-naturalism of a strict chronological plot. The strict chronology of the narrative is carried by the fragmented documentary style in all its mundane detail, whereas the stream-of-consciousness emulates the associative structure of memory and reveals the heroine's past in a revelatory fashion. Her future is a total unknown and anticipated with anxiety. Thus the novel's narrative mixture recreates how a person experiences the present, past, and future in reality.

Whereas in *Nachwelt*. the sentence fragments function as individual frames of a film, recording individual visual sensations – ones that appear meaningless in isolation, but when strung together and read quickly, form a flow of images imitating the effect of the eye of the camera in a documentary film, in *Entfernung*. the use of fragments has become even more refined. There are still the laundry lists of inventories which so infuriated critics in her early works. For example, she empties her pocketbook:

> The folder with her papers. A pack of tissues. The money purse with her Euros. The money purse with English money. The case for her credit and debit cards. The case for her driver's license and the car registration. The case for

business cards. The pouch with lipstick and powder case. The pouch for eye drops and a small tube of hand lotion. For her dry hands. Her appointment calendar. Her address book. The cell phone. A small packet of moist Tempos. Eyeglass case. Chewing gum.[15]

What should strike the reader of her novels in this case is that the sentence fragments are less objective and naturalistic than those in *Verführungen.*, but are used to great effect to mimic thought fragments and patterns. One thought loosely connects to another by association:

> And she didn't even have a photo. Of him. Of them. Of anything. The trips. Venice. South America. The USA. And the small expeditions in Austria. Finally. One's trips of discovery. All that shut away in those photos. Anton had taken and arranged the photos. He had stayed with photos. Hadn't been able to decide to give up photography.[16]

Another pattern these fragments employ in the emulation of thought uses a strategy of continuation. The fragments are actually components of a disjointed sentence: for example as she continues thinking about the photos as the artifacts of a failed relationship, we read the following:

> These albums herself she perhaps had. Burned. In the kitchen stove. In the old wood stove, which her father had kept. Because you can never really know.[17]

Another pattern involves repetition – the use of one word in two adjacent fragments. A string of repeated words links the fragments into a larger framework:

> That was the result. All that was the result. And she couldn't now say that she had done everything wrong. She just did it that way. Everything. While doing it. While she had done it.[18]

The final pattern to mention is the elaboration. Each succeeding fragment expands and elaborates the meaning: "That had been. Elegant. That had been elegant. That had been an elegant life."[19] It appears that Streeruwitz is making good on her attempt to create a new way of writing. She is breaking the chronology and logic of sentences and indeed, the dependence on sentences to be the carriers of meaning. Her fragments are like mosaic stones, individually meaningless, but together, with skillful placement, they form meaning.

This mosaic style is also employed at the level of the plot or story line. Her divorce from Anton, her loss of her career, her childhood and relationship with her parents, are only revealed piecemeal. Even her name is revealed in fragments. She is a "she" (*sie*), a pronoun at the beginning of the novel. The third page reveals her father's name when she looks at the nameplate on the door of the apartment, Dr. Karl Brechthold. She has been referring to a Sydler since the second page, and we learn that this is Dr. Evelyn Sydler when she sees the door nameplate four pages later. It is only when she is greeted by this woman that we hear the name of our protagonist, Selma. Her full name doesn't appear until pages later when she hears her answering machine play her recorded message prompt. Her name and other facts about her life are revealed as a result of the sensory perceptions recorded not by the omniscient narrator (*Der Blick Gottes*), though the novel is totally in the third person, but by the documentary film perspective of the narrator. The narrative perspective is like that of a cameraman following Selma throughout her trip. The narrator seems not to be discriminating in selecting a story to reveal. Everything Selma sees and hears, the reader sees and hears. The artistic unwinding of the mosaic storyline is realized through the author's adherence to a "reality-show" technique. In the style of television's Big Brother and The Real World reality shows, the narrative camera does not fade out or jump to high points in the story. It is Aristotle's "unity of time" taken to its logical extreme. The perspective remains unsparingly focused on each moment. We see and hear everything Selma experiences in her trip from her apartment in Vienna to her destinations in London. We are with her every step of the way – in cars, planes, taxis and on foot. We join her in her hotel room, the restaurant, and the bars. The reader is like a viewer of a reality show; we follow Selma unrelentingly, even to the toilet stalls and bathrooms. The effect is not one of sensationalism, but one of realism – almost a neo-naturalism reviving Arno Holz's *Sekundenstil*: the discourse time (*Erzählzeit*) attempts to match the story time (*erzählte Zeit*). For example, in one of the most bizarre scenes in the novel, Selma unexpectedly spends twenty minutes posing nude as a model for a life-drawing class, and a reasonably paced reading aloud of that section requires approximately the same amount of time – twenty minutes.

As an example of how all this comes together in this novel, let's look a little more closely at one of the thirty-one chapters (*Abschnitte*), Chapter Six. On the plot level, Selma awakens after napping in the plane to London. She is seated at the window seat, uncomfortable in this seat as it was not her normal choice – she had to give up her aisle seat to another. Beside her is seated a married couple, and she feels crowded by the man. She looks out the window. As we have come to expect, the reader observes all the routines of a flight: the captain's announcement, the stewardesses serving drinks, making change, the people ordering food, small talk about a baby passenger, the copilot announces in English and German that they will land in twenty minutes. The stewardesses collect the empty cups and trash. We also experience Selma's view of her surroundings: the tightly packed rows of passengers seem to her akin to the transportation of animals (perhaps to the slaughterhouse?). She notes the contrast between herself as a woman traveling alone and the couple. She experiences a panic attack, feeling rising in her stomach which threatens to drive her to jump from her seat and to run down the aisle and to open the side door and a swift – if not spectacular – death. She becomes minutely aware of her body and physical sensations, and this is communicated by one of the narrative "lists" (92-93). This chapter, contributing its mosaic stones to the overall story, tells us of her earlier life with Anton. She spent fifteen years with him. They had taken many trips together and experienced a great deal. She began the relationship illicitly, as the "other woman" and lost him many years later as he cheated on her too, but he blamed himself – not being able to accept growing older – and now Anton lives with his Hungarian girlfriend and their child, Moritz. She doesn't even have a photograph of Anton – he kept all the photo albums. She hired a lawyer and they battled over money in the courts. The feeling in her stomach is identified as a chaotic rage (*Wut*), and in a later chapter, this rage is connected to the rage she inherited from her father when he used to beat her out of his rage at his own impotencies in his career. The mosaic ultimately connects her failed relationship, her problematic relationship to her father, and her own career loss. Selma thinks about the immediate future and her quest. She will go to the hotel first and rest after calling Gilchrist, her business contact, and confirming her appointment. Thus, in the short chapter utilizing a strict linear plot, we travel to the past and the future. The sentence fragments (all examples above come from this chapter) create this neo-naturalism of the present as well as mimic thought patterns which bring the past and the future. They flow uninterrupted by paragraphs into one another: in and out of her consciousness and her awareness of her surroundings. There are some other nice touches in narrative flow. Selma, upon waking in the plane, begins to remember her relationship with Anton and the reason for its failure: his inability to accept aging. Later she follows the thought about the loss of civility in the world with the regret that it overlaps her own aging. Another thematic parallel is the loss of the photos, and the lack of a photo of Anton, and the couple looking at their passport photos in preparation of landing in England. They noted how now new photos are not permitted to show them smiling – another sign of the decline of civility.

    Streeruwitz's penchant for writing in fragments and the mosaic style in building a narrative are not her only trademarks.

If her use of sentence fragments and lists of words operate at the micro level in order to effect syntactic transformation of the novel, and her use of a mosaic strategy brings about narrative change, then her experimentation at the macro level of the literary genre should come as no surprise. Alexandra Kedveš expressed the dynamics of this narrative strategy by noting that "'Feminine' contents are poured into 'masculine' molds."[20] With this she means that the traditional genre forms: travel journal, biography, trivial literature, etc., awaken traditional expectations in the readers, who are then shocked into awareness when, instead of pleasurable expectation fulfillment, the reader is confronted with subjective feminine experience, and the extremes of the non-poetic, non-romantic reality.

This was evident in the author's first novel, *Verführungen*. The novel's subtitle is "3rd Series, Womanhood" (*3. Folge, Frauenjahre*). Döbler points to this as a reference to the genre of teen romance novels (*Mädchenromane*) which trace the life of a girl from her youth to adulthood, presumably to her attaining her life's dream.[21] In this sense, Streeruwitz's novel shows what happens after "happily ever after." Her heroine, Helene, is a divorced, single mother struggling with her career and a love interest who ultimately sleeps with her best friend. Her life is a disappointment.

It is a common strategy of Streeruwitz to reference a genre form and summarily squash all expectations associated with that genre. This is even more so the case with her second novel, *Lisa's Liebe*. Here all three episodes are subtitled "Serial Novel" (*Romansammelband*) with the implied promise of a sequel in pseudo-advertisements for the nonexistent sequel *Lisa's Glück*. ("Lisa's Happiness"). This 'fake' advertisement has the effect of Brecht's *deus ex machina* at the end of the *Three Penny Opera*, where MacHeath is suddenly rescued from the gallows by a mounted messenger with a pardon from the Queen. It is such an obvious impossibility which prompts the reader to reflect on the sharp contract between necessity and ideal.

Her recent works are an ingenious manipulation of literary genres with occasional mythic reverberations. For example, *Nachwelt.: Ein Reisebericht,*. subtitled "A Travel Report," was written in the format of a journal of a woman who was attempting to write a biography of Anna Mahler by recording interviews with those surviving friends, lovers, and compatriots living in Los Angeles. As mentioned above, the basic narrative form mimicked film and provided a documentary feel for the work. Nevertheless, the almost subconscious and sub-narrative story harkens back to Orpheus in the underworld. Los Angeles is depicted as dark, rainy, threatening, and inhabited by those in exile from the horrors of the Holocaust. The word *Nachwelt* literally "Afterworld" is reminiscent of the *Unterwelt*, or Underworld. The main character's struggle to bring her Eurydice back through the art of biography and prose fails. Looking back to the past is paradoxically both a recovery and a loss. The past is lost. One can never recover the true story of the past. The recovery involves the cathartic effect on the main character and her personal history. The protagonist, Margarethe, is a divorced mother and unemployed actor. She has separated herself from her family and, though not by design, from her lover. She is conducting biographical research on Anna Mahler, the daughter of Gustav and Alma Mahler. Anna, an artist of some modest renown, lived in Los Angeles, and Margarethe spends ten days there in March 1990 interviewing Anna's surviving friends and companions. Like her sister characters, Margarethe is enmeshed in a web of emotional torment, and constantly ponders the men in her life, and her struggle to define herself in relationship to them or from them. *Nachwelt.* takes that protagonist and adds to her search for self, the search for the self of others who have fallen victim to the excesses of the system. The novel's plot provides the example of the observer, this time the main character – looking inward when faced with an incomplete historical Anna. The reader, too, is drawn away from the illusory and back toward oneself. *Nachwelt.* presents us, the readers, with the components for our self-actualization – a path to follow – or, if you will, a travel journal. What is interesting is that we have this "realistic" fictional character in pursuit of the illusive facts of an actual, historical person. We can know a fictional person fully, but we cannot truly comprehend a real person. An interesting paradox. One might even view this as the victory of the journal over the biography. Biography has aspirations of capturing a life lived in all its complexity, a lofty but futile goal, whereas the journals is able to record the moment, the fragment, the sensation – and the fragmentary points to the possibility of truth.

In *Entfernung.*, Streeruwitz introduces one of the primal and primary literary genres: the quest. The book's opening sentence poses the question: "What should she do?" (*Was sollte sie tun?*) At this moment, Selma, the familiar protagonist, is standing on the threshold of her apartment door. She is a woman on the threshold between youth and aging, on the threshold between career and collapse. Her career as a successful agent with the Vienna Festival came to an abrupt halt and left her stunned, as her work was her life. Her lover, Anton, has abandoned her for a Hungarian woman. Now she is living with her aging father, with the only prospect a last chance at a theatrical project which she hopes to pitch to a distant business acquaintance in London. It is a long shot. Nevertheless, Selma decides to travel to London, spending her scarce resources on the slight chance that she will revitalize her career.

While its plot is firmly grounded in the realistic world of modern life, *Entfernung.* displays many of the elements of the mythic Quest identified by Joseph Campbell.[22] Selma sets out on the impossible mission to restore her career by traveling to a distant and strange land and undergoes various adventures and dangers. Indeed the characterization on the book sleeve and on her official website announcing the novel called it a modern-day Odyssey. Given the fact that Streeruwitz is consciously seeking a non-masculine literary expression – something she claims has never existed before – the novel cannot be a variant of what she would view as a quintessentially masculine literary expression, the quest. Something else must be happening here. In the quest to restore her career, the question arises: Is she a victim or is she responsible for her own dilemma? As Streeruwitz described in her Frankfurt lectures, the social role of females is predetermined. Women are socialized to relive the roles of their mothers:

> The recognition. A recognition. She did the same as her mother. As her grandmother. Her mother had been forced to marry a man whose family name was the same as the first name of her father. Of the father who had deserted her and had pulled her mother from her. And she was offering herself. As a model. For this grandfather.[23]

Streeruwitz has injected the reality of life as experienced by women into this saga. Selma is representative of the fate of women of a certain age in our society: no longer young, soon to lose her physical beauty, no longer able to advance in her career, she no longer finds herself valued. Streeruwitz sees her destiny as one shared by all of her gender: "All women fight for their positions. All of them have not had it easy. But those who lapse back. Who cozy back to their fathers' care. Back again to their care. She couldn't stand that."[24] Selma's quest is her attempt to regain that which was taken from her, however, this quest brought some ugly facts to light. During her panic attack in her hotel room upon her arrival in London, Selma realizes that her dismissal had nothing to do with her professional abilities:

> She had still believed she only had simply to begin again anew. She had taken the world into consideration. That it wanted simply to be rid of you. That wastefulness was the order of the day. That it didn't matter what she could accomplish, but rather if she would be allowed to accomplish anything. What mattered was the desire for something new. To have something new from someone new. And nobody found anything wrong with that. Nobody would say about this

person: But she is fully capable of achievements and highly successful. She can't simply be placed in the holding tank. That would be a waste. She had still thought that it was a cost factor...It wasn't cost-related. Nothing was really cost-related. That had only been their excuse.[25]

Ultimately Selma has a revelation. Her seemingly powerful job with the Viennese Festival was one in which she merely served the interests of those men in charge. She was a stooge. Her attempt to gain such a real position of authority was futile and was unworthy of her efforts. She had been a pawn in the patriarchal system:

> Suddenly she was relieved. About her alleviation. But what does that mean. She could close this chapter. This chapter of her life. Selma Brechthold. Manager of Cultural Affairs. Dispenser of Brouhaha and Titillation. Satisfier of a post-bourgeois capacity for agitation. Igniter of the masculine atavistic search for God. This woman no longer exists.[26]

One of the characteristics of the quest has the hero leaving the known world and entering a realm of the magical or mystical. Here something radical happens to everyday London in the course of the novel. At what should have been the high point in Selma's quest to restore her career – her dinner with Gilchrest to pitch a new theater project – she meets with utter and instant failure. Upon sitting down to eat, she is told that he cannot help her. It is at this point that everything in the narrative changes. She is swept out of the restaurant by a woman in a red dress, who leads her to an unknown destination for an unknown purpose. It is an escape from her unpleasant reality – but perhaps she is falling down the rabbit hole, as Selma, assuming the name, Thelma, is pulled at a running pace into an adventure. This woman seems to be a colleague from Vienna whom she calls by name, but then Selma later doubts that this is that woman. Things are not as they seem. She has a narrow escape from an unknown danger. She ends up in a taxi cab late at night in which she has no control over her destination. This moment in the restaurant represents the "Crossing of the First Threshold" of Campbell's monomyth. For the rest of the night (and the novel), she can no longer determine where she is and is guided by whim, chance, and the scent of flowers. She stumbles into a basement bar, a realm ruled by Sebastian, the chubby Jesus figure who takes her into a screening room to view with others an avant-garde local production. The film, a dreamlike feminist allegory with Sebastian starring as the Good King, who is trying to make women happy by relieving them of their "I," keeping them masturbating, and giving them all the same name: Vera. The elaborate film is described in detail for two chapters and contains dreamlike primal images of sexual exploitation, androgyny, and sexual identity. Following the film, Selma/Thelma, finds herself mistaken for the expected model for the life-drawing class held in this bar in the late evenings. Trapped by her own indecision and passive attitude, she finds herself posing nude and feeling simultaneously objectified, manipulated, admired, humiliated, ignored, empowered and alienated. Her final pose, curled naked on the floor, represents a Rebirth in the pattern of the Quest. From there she is swept along by younger women to the Minnie Bar, a hidden establishment for lesbians. She dances through the night to brutally rebellious and homicidal songs and becomes so caught up in the Dionysian emotional release that she inadvertently tramples on her remaining possession, her purse, whose mundane contents are connected in her memory with the past. Somehow in early morning she manages to return to the hotel. The next morning Selma seems to have returned to the normal world, however, once again she is derailed – literally. Return to the Father, another element of the Quest, though always viewed by Selma as a failure, becomes impossible, as her cousin, Tommi, reveals to her that she is the illegitimate child of her mother and his father. Her understanding of her past is undermined. In fleeing this reality, she fatefully boards one of the subway trains which were the targets of terrorist bombs during the infamous terror attack of July 7, 2005. Selma survives the blast but is caught in the dark and the chaotic aftermath underground. She is crawling over corpses and facing her own death. After the rescue, she avoids medical care and, in a daze resumes her wanderings through London. While it seems that she has escaped with minor injuries, we must realize that we are dealing with an unreliable narrator – her internal dialogue reveals a serious disorientation and an inability to follow a plan of action rationally.

It is at this point we look anew at the nature of Selma's quest, and the key may reside in the title of the novel. The word *Entfernung*, which serves as the title of the novel, has a range of meanings. In a straightforward manner, the title seems to indicate the distance traveled in Selma's quest. The word appears often in the novel both as a verb and a noun. In general it denotes the distance she feels from others, both significant people in her life and strangers, and the distance she feels from herself. Of particular note, it appears at significant points in her personal history. Once, when she removes (*Entfernung* = removal) the package of condoms from Anton's luggage in the hope of preventing his liaison with the Hungarian woman (56), and once to indicate her attitude (*Entfernung* = distance) at seeing a woman who was the age her own child would have been had she not opted for an abortion (418). The former resulted in her rival becoming pregnant and thus the ultimate loss of her lover; the latter demonstrated her isolation from feelings of motherhood. In her confused post-terror-attack wanderings, she is seeking to unite with Sebastian, imagining that the physical and sexual union of their bodies would overcome her state of *Entfernung* from others and her inner self (446). *Entfernung* is thus, simultaneously, the state of mind that created the need for the quest, the physical destination of the quest, and the ultimate problem to be overcome in the quest.

The final scene is both magical and illusory, as the reader knows that she has not found the help she needs and has slipped into madness. Freed from the fetters of social convention at this point, she wanders the neighborhoods and suburbs of London and is open to the mystical and magical realm. She finds a mute African man who holds a smooth stone in offering to passersby. This unconventional behavior evokes anger from people, and Selma rescues the man. She abandons everything she is doing, perceiving this stone to be the key, or in Quest symbolism, the "Ultimate Boon," an item of great power. She offers all of her possessions in trade, and when rejected, they are placed in a circle on the ground surrounding the two. Her solution, pouring water on the stone, produced the image of a star. The African held the stone high in the air: "The star lines glittered in the sunlight. 'Wow,' said a young woman watching the scene. 'Like a star in the sky.' They all stared at the stone and smiled. Selma had to laugh. The starry heaven. It had all been about the starry heaven. Of course."[27]

Of course? – The stone of power, the magic circle, the offering to the starry heavens, all of this is very appealing and hopeful, and yet, such a mystical ending is unconvincing. It is akin again to Brecht's *deus ex machina*. With Streeruwitz, the technique is more subtle, and her ending is enticing. Does Selma achieve her quest? We as readers still have our foot in reality. Selma is both freed from herself and society, but her epiphany is an illusion, a product of a damaged mind in an uncaring world. There is no Return of the Hero in this quest.

Endnotes

[1]This first novel is the only one translated into English at this time. Streeruwitz, Marlene. *Seductions*. Trans. Katharina Rout. Lantzville, BC: Oolichan Books, 1998.
[2]*Entfernung*. Frankfurt a. M.: S. Fischer Verlag, 2006.
[3]Marlene Streeruwitz, *Sein. Und Schein. Und Erscheinen. Tübinger Poetikvorlesungen*. Frankfurt a. M.: Suhrkamp, (1997) 48.
[4]*Tübinger Poetikvorlesungen,* 26: "es gibt keine Sprache, die den Bereich der Mutterschaft sprechbar machte."

[5] Ibid. 20.
[6] "AUFKLÄRUNG ist der Ausgang des Menschen aus seiner selbstverschuldeten Unmündigkeit. Unmündigkeit ist das Unvermögen, sich seines Verstandes ohne Leitung eines anderen zu bedienen." *Berlinische Monatsschrift.* Dezember-Heft 1784. S. 481-494. "Enlightenment is man's emergence from his self-imposed immaturity. Immaturity is the inability to use one's understanding without guidance from another."
[7] Katharina Döbler, "Schlussfolgerungen aus einem Selbstversuch," *Text und Kritik* 164, (2004) 12. "Aufbruch der Frau aus der von Patriarchat und ihr selbst als Komplizin verschuldeten Unmündigkeit."
[8] Marlene Streeruwitz, *Können. Mögen. Dürfen. Sollen. Wollen. Müssen. Lassen. Frankfurter Poetikvorlesungen.* Frankfurt a. M.: Suhrkamp, 1998, 39. "Ich bin für vollständige Erhellung aller Lebensbereiche im Gegensatz zur Verdunkelung, die patriarchale Macht immer ausbreitete..."
[9] This is not the first time her techniques have been compared to Brecht's. See "In Brecht's Footsteps or Way beyond Brecht? Brechtian Techniques in Feminist Plays by Elfriede Jelinek and Marlene Streeruwitz," by Britta Kallin in *Communications from the International Brecht Society*, 2000 June; 29 (1-2): 62-66.
[10] *Tübinger Poetikvorlesungen,* 17. "Die Frage, wer am Mahl teilnehmen darf, war in allen Zeiten der Grund aller Auseinandersetzungen."
[11] *Frankfurter Poetikvorlesungen*, 54. "Es ging um die Frage, wie kann der Text die Haltung der Schreibenden tragen und dennoch zu verstehen sein."
[12] *Tübinger Poetikvorlesungen*, 76. "Der vollständige Satz ist eine Lüge. Im Entfremdeten kann nur Zerbrochenes der Versuch eines Ausdrucks sein... Mit dem Punkt kann der vollständige Satz verhindert werden. Der Punkt beendet den Versuch. Sätze sollen sich nicht formen."

[13] Helga Schreckenberger, "Die 'Poetik des Banalen' in Marlene Streeruwitz' Romanen *Verführungen* and *Lisa's Liebe*," *Modern Austrian Literature*, Vol. 31 3/4 (1998) 141.
[14] "Die Sprache darf keine Einheit, keinen umfassenden Zusammenhang vorgaukeln, den es nicht gibt." Interview with Günther Kaindlstorfer in *Der Standard* 25th-26th September 1999 as found on the Internet site: http://www.kaindlstorfer.at/interviews/streeruwitz.html
[15] "Die Mappe mit den Unterlagen. Eine Packung Taschentücher. Die Geldbörse mit den Euros. Die Geldbörse mit dem englischen Geld. Das Etui für die Kreditkaren und die Bankomatkarte. Das Etui für den Führerschein und die Autopapiere. Das Etui für die Visitenkarten. Das Necessaire mit Lippenstift und Puderdose. Das Necessaire mit den Augentropfen und der kleinen Tube Handcreme. Gegen die trockenen Hände. Der Terminkalender. Das Adressbuch. Das Handy. Eine kleine Packung feuchte Tempos. Brillenetui. Kaugummi" (48).
[16] "Und sie hatte nicht einmal ein Foto. Von ihm. Von ihnen. Von irgendetwas. Die Reisen. Venedig. Südamerika. Die USA. Und die kleinen Expeditionen in Österreich. Letzthin. Entdeckungsreisen des Eigenen gewesen. Das alles in diese Fotos weggeschlossen. Anton die Fotos gemacht und geordnet. Er war bei den Fotos geblieben. Hatte sich nicht entschließen können, die Fotografie aufzugeben" (89).
[17] "Sie hätte diese Alben ja vielleicht selber. Verbrennen. In den Küchenherd. In den alten Holzküchenherd, den der Vater behalten hatte. Weil man ja nicht wissen konnte"(90).
[18] "Das war die Rechnung. Das war alles die Rechnung. Und sie konnte jetzt nicht sagen, dass sie alles falsch gemacht hatte. Sie hatte es eben so gemacht. Alles. Während des Machens. Während sie es gemacht hatte"(91).
[19] "Das war. Elegant. Das war elegant gewesen. Das war ein elegantes Leben gewesen"(91).

[20] Alexandra Kedveš, "Geheimnisvoll. Vorwurfsvoll. Aber zusammenhängend." *Text + Kritik* 164, (2004) 25. "'Weibliche' Inhalte werden in 'männliche' Formen gegossen."
[21] Katharina Döbler, "Schlussfolgerungen aus einem Selbstversuch," *Text und Kritik* 164, (2004) 12.
[22] See the monomyth and its characteristics in Joseph Campbell's *Hero with a Thousand Faces*. New World Library; Second Edition (July 28, 2008).
[23] "Die Erkenntnis. Eine Erkenntnis. Sie machte dasselbe wie ihre Mutter. Wie ihre Großmutter. Ihre Mutter hatte einen Mann heiraten müssen, dessen Familienname der Vorname des Vaters gewesen war. Des Vaters, der sie verlassen hatte und ihr die Mutter entzogen. Und sie bot sich dar. Als Modell. Für diesen Großvater" (289).
[24] "Alle Frauen kämpfen um ihre Postitionen. Alle hatten es nicht leicht. Aber die, die zurückfielen. Die sich an die Väter anschmiegten. Wieder anschmiegten. Das konnte sie nicht aushalten" (26).
[25] "Sie hatte noch geglaubt, sie müsste nur einfach neu anfangen. Sie hatte nicht mit der Welt gerechnet. Dass die einen wirklich los werden wollte. Dass Verschwendung selbstverständlich war. Dass es nicht darum ging, was sie leisten konnte, sondern was man sie leisten lassen wollte. Dass es darum ging, etwas Neues zu wollen. Etwas Neues haben zu wollen, das von jemandem Neuen kam. Und dass alle das richtig fanden. Dass niemand sagen würde, diese Person. Die ist doch voll leistungsfähig und erfolgreich. Die kann man doch nicht einfach aufs Abstellgleis. Das wäre doch eine Verschwendung. Da hatte sich noch gedacht, dass es um den Kostenfaktor ginge...Das war nicht kostenorientiert. Nichts war wirklich kostenorientiert. Das waren immer nur so Argumente gewesen" (168-69).
[26] "Im Augenblick war sie erleichtert. Über ihre Erleichterung. Aber was bedeutet das. Sie konnte diesen Teil abschließen. Diesen Teil ihres Lebens. Selma Brechthold. Kulturmanagerin. Spenderin von Aufruhr und Kitzel. Befriederin postbürgerlichen

Unruhepotenzials. Sprengmeisterin der männlich atavistischen Gottsuche. Die gab es nicht mehr" (347).
[27]"Die Sternlinien glitzerten im Sonnenlicht. 'Wow,' sagte die junge Frau. 'Like a star in the sky.' Alle starrten auf den Stein und lächelten. Selma musste lachen. Der Sternenhimmel. Es war um den Sternenhimmel gegangen. Was sonst" (475).

Contributors

RAYMOND L. BURT is the Chair of the Department of Foreign Languages and Literatures and a professor of German at the University of North Carolina Wilmington. He was a recipient of two Fulbright Grants to Austria (1983, 1991) where he did biographical research on the folklorist in the Freudian circle, Friedrich S. Krauss. He recently published folklore material from Krauss's posthumous papers, and has published in the areas of folklore, Freud, and contemporary Austrian Literature.

DONALD G. DAVIAU, Professor of Austrian and German Literature at the University of California, Riverside (emeritus), literary critic and historian, translator and editor. President of the International Arthur Schnitzler Research Association and editor of the literary journal *Modern Austrian Literature* from 1974-2000, President of the American Council for the Study of Austrian Literature, organizer of the Annual Austrian Symposium at the University of California, Riverside from 1981-2000, co-founder and editor of Ariadne Press from 1987 to 2000. Member of the Vienna P.E.N. Club and other international literary organizations. Awarded the Austrian Ehrenkreuz für Wissenschaft und Kunst in 1977. Author of numerous books and articles on Austrian authors and cultural and historical topics.

PAUL F. DVORAK is Professor Emeritus at Virginia Commonwealth University in Richmond, where he continues as program coordinator for the Virginia Governor's and STARTALK Foreign Language Academies. A frequent visitor to Austria, he has participated in seminars sponsored by the National Endowment for the Humanities and the Austrian Ministry of Education. His work as a translator and scholar has dealt with Arthur Schnitzler, Hugo von Hofmannsthal, Franz Kafka, Alfred Kolleritsch, Robert Schneider, Peter Henisch, and Alois Brandstetter, among others.

CONTRIBUTORS

ANGELA GULIELMETTI received her undergraduate degree in German Language and Literature from Wesleyan University and her M.A. and Ph.D. in German Languages and Literatures from Washington University in St. Louis. She is currently a Visiting Assistant Professor in German Studies at Wesleyan University and has previously taught at Hendrix College and the University of Southern Maine. Her fields of study include 19th-century German-Jewish literature, modern Austrian literature, and Nazi Propaganda in Children's Literature. She has presented papers and published on topics as varied as Elfriede Jelinek and Johann Nestroy and the Nazi exploitation of animal imagery in children's books.

TODD C. HANLIN is Emeritus Professor of German at the University of Arkansas, has authored a book on Franz Kafka, edited Charles Sealsfield's *Austria as It Is* (Ariadne, 2004), and a collection of essays entitled *Beyond Vienna: Contemporary Literature from the Austrian Provinces* (Ariadne, 2008). He has also written on Peter Henisch, Paulus Hochgatterer, Fritz Hochwälder, Hugo von Hofmannsthal, Felix Mitterer, Arthur Schnitzler, Peter Turrini, and Franz Werfel, translated novels by Gustav Ernst, Anton Fuchs, Hochgatterer, Georg Potyka, Gerhard Roth, Peter Steiner, and Gerald Szyszkowitz, several plays by Hochwälder, Mitterer, and Szyszkowitz, as well as a volume on *The Best of Austrian Science Fiction* (Ariadne, 2001).

RONALD HORWEGE earned his B.A. (1966) from the University of Kansas and both his M.A. (1968) and his Ph.D. (1971) from Indiana University. Since 1971 he has taught at Sweet Briar College in Virginia, where he presently holds the rank of Professor of German and Cameron Fellow. He has served in numerous positions with the AATG, including President of the Virginia Chapter and AATG-PAD Chair. He is also presently serving as First Vice President of Delta Phi Alpha German Honor Society. During the last several years he has organized an annual immersion weekend for Virginia German teachers, a Spring German teachers workshop at the University of Virginia and a Summer TPRS workshop under the sponsorship of the AATG. He also has the position of Assistant Director of a summer program in Münster. He has conducted research in the areas of Early New High German, history of the German language, German literature and nationalism and, most recently, in Austrian Literature.

GEOFFREY C. HOWES (Ph.D., University of Michigan 1985) is Professor of German at Bowling Green State University in Ohio. From 2000 to 2005 he was co-editor with Jacqueline Vansant of the journal *Modern Austrian Literature*. He has published on a variety of topics in Austrian studies, including madness in literature, Robert Musil, Joseph Roth, Peter Rosei, Michael Scharang, Ingeborg Bachmann, Thomas Bernhard, Christine Lavant, Lilian Faschinger, and Peter Turrini. He has translated texts by Peter Rosei, Lilian Faschinger, Doron Rabinovici, Dieter Sperl, Gerhard Kofler, Susanne Ayoub, and Margret Kreidl into English.

MARIA-REGINA KECHT, a Germanist formerly at Hamilton College, the University of Connecticut, and Rice University, is Academic Director at Webster University Vienna since 2010. An expert on contemporary Austrian literature, she served as editor of *Modern Austrian Literature* from 2005-2008 and organized and administered two NEH-Institutes on the topic "Vienna" in 2001 (together with D. James) and 2006 (together with H. Schreckenberger). Her most recent publications are: "Mit der Sprache zum Schweigen hin: Elfriede Jelineks literarische Annäherungen an ihren Vater" (Jelinek Jahrbuch 2011), "Multikulturelles Wien: Entweder-und-Oder-Existenzen in der neuen österreichischen Literatur" (Böhlau, 2011), "Elfriede Jelineks Botenbericht(e) aus, über und rund um Rechnitz" (Praesens, 2010), and "Weltgeschichte in Erinnerung: Kriegsgeschehen in den Texten von Bettina Baláka und Helene Flöss" (Böhlau, 2009)

CONTRIBUTORS

CYNTHIA A. KLIMA received her doctorate in German at the University of Wisconsin-Madison in 1995. She is the author of articles on Czech and Jewish culture and translated Paul Leppin's work *Blaugast* into English. Her BA and MA are from the University of Oklahoma in German and Russian. She is a summer Fulbright recipient and has received DAAD and ACTR/ACCELS grants for German and Czech, respectively. She teaches German, Russian and Humanities at SUNY-Geneseo and is the Director of the Prague/Vienna/Budapest Summer Study Abroad program each year. Her interests lie in Czech/Jewish studies, Austrian literature and in International Studies.

VINCENT KLING teaches English, German, and comparative literature at La Salle University in Philadelphia. His main interest is in Austrian literature. His dissertation was on Hugo von Hofmannsthal, and he has published on Hugo von Hofmannsthal, Heimito von Doderer, Ödön von Horváth, Gert Jonke, Isabel Allende, W. G. Sebald, and the craft of literary translation. He has also written a comparative cultural study around the figure of Johann Breitwieser, the "Viennese Robin Hood." His translations include works by Doderer, Jonke, Gerhard Fritsch, Heimrad Bäcker, and Aglaja Veteranyi.

JOSEPH MOSER is a Visiting Assistant Professor of German at Randolph-Macon College in Ashland, VA. He has been serving as Book Review Editor for *Modern Austrian Literature*/the *Journal of Austrian Studies* since 2006. His dissertation was on "Thomas Bernhard's Dialogue with the Public Sphere," which he defended at the University of Pennsylvania in 2004. His recent publications have focused on Thomas Bernhard, Lilian Faschinger, Franz Antel's *Bockerer* films, and the city of Czernowitz, as well as German and Austrian Film and Television.

PAMELA S. SAUR has taught English and German since 1988 at Lamar University, which named her University Professor and University Scholar in 2007. Saur served as Editor of *Schatzkammer* from 1988-2001, and the *Texas Foreign Language Association Bulletin* from 1995-2004. In 2004 she co-edited *Visions and Visionaries in Contemporary Austrian Literature and Film,* published by Peter Lang with Margarete Lamb-Faffelberger. Her publications include numerous articles and book chapters on modern Austrian literature and other literary and pedagogical topics. Her previous translations with Ariadne Press include *Legacy of Ashes* by Herbert Zand (2001), *Escaping Expectation: Stories by Austrian Women Writers*, edited by Barbara Neuwirth (2001), Graziella Hlawaty, *Broken Songs: An Adolescent in War-Torn Vienna* (2005), and Rosa Mayreder, *Gender and Culture* (2009).

HELGA SCHRECKENBERGER is Professor of German at the University of Vermont. Her research focuses on twentieth century German and Austrian literature and Exile Studies. She has published on such authors as Gerhard Roth, Joseph Roth, Peter Handke, Felix Mitterer, Peter Henisch, Elisabeth Reichart, Lilian Faschinger, Marlene Streeruwitz, Marie-Thérèse Kerschbaumer, Wolf Haas, Vladimir Vertlib, Erika Mann, Adrienne Thomas, Franzi Ascher-Nash, and Erich Maria Remarque. Her most recent publications include the co-edited volume *Erste Briefe/First Letters aus dem Exil 1945-1950 (2011)*.

FRANCIS MICHAEL SHARP is Professor emeritus of German at the University of the Pacific in Stockton, California. His interest in Austrian poets and writers began with a dissertation, a book and several articles on Georg Trakl. In the past few years he has published essays on Expressionist poetry, Max Frisch, Peter Handke, Thomas Bernhard, Martin Walser, Doron Rabinovici and Barbara Frischmuth in various journals and collections. His translations include the Israeli-Austrian Doron Rabinovici's first novel *Suche nach M: Roman in zwölf Episoden*

(*The Search for M*, Ariadne, 1997). Two comparative essays on Bernhard, his most recent research, have appeared in: *Trans: Internet-Zeitschrift für Kulturwissenschaften*. A translation of a book of memoirs by the Viennese Jew Maximilian Reich about his incarceration by the Nazis in Dachau and Buchenwald after the *Anschluß* will soon appear in Ariadne Press.

REBECCA THOMAS is Professor of German at Wake Forest University in Winston-Salem, North Carolina. Her research focuses on modern Austrian literature and culture, and she has published on numerous contemporary Austrian authors such as Elfriede Jelinek, Gerhard Roth, and Doron Rabinovici. She has also published the English translation of Kathrin Röggla's novel *wir schlafen nicht* (*we never* sleep) with Ariadne Press. Thomas currently holds the position of Associate Dean for Faculty Development at Wake Forest University.

FELIX W. TWERASER is Professor of German and Chair of Foreign Languages and Literatures at the University of West Georgia in Carrollton. He works on the literary and cultural legacy of turn-of-the-century Vienna, film theory and criticism, and the instrumentalization of arts and letters during the Cold War. Recent articles include: "Leo Golowski as Minor Key in Schnitzler's *Der Weg ins Freie*: Musical Theory, Political Behaviour and Ethical Action." (2009) and "Elisabeth Reichart's *Komm über den See*: Upper Austria and the Excavation of its Past" (2008). He is the author of the book *Political Dimensions of Arthur Schnitzler's Late Fiction* (1998) and is currently working on a monograph, titled in draft "Vienna and Hollywood: Dream Factories and Cultural Transfer," which traces the contributions of Austrian émigrés to the U.S. film industry and Hollywood's Golden Age.